HIGH-PERFORMANCE GOVERNMENT

Structure, Leadership, Incentives

EDITED BY

Robert Klitgaard & Paul C. Light

PARDEE RAND GRADUATE SCHOOL

This book was made possible by the generosity of donors to the Pardee RAND Graduate School, particularly Paul Volcker and Eugene and Maxine Rosenfeld.

Library of Congress Cataloging-in-Publication Data

Klitgaard, Robert E.
 High-performance government : structure, leadership, incentives / Robert Klitgaard, Paul C. Light.
  p. cm.
 This volume comprises thirteen essays that address the primary problem areas identified by the Volcker Commission, along with the text of the Commission report itself.
 Includes bibliographical references.
 ISBN 0-8330-3740-4 (pbk. : alk. paper) -- ISBN 0-8330-3662-9 (hardcover : alk. paper)
 1. Government productivity--United States. 2. Political planning--United States. 3. Organizational change--United States. 4. Administrative agencies--United States--Reorganization. 5. Executive departments--United States--Reorganization. I. United States. National Commission on the Public Service. II. Title.

JK468.P75K585 2004
352.3'67'0973--dc22

                  2004029557

The RAND Corporation is a nonprofit research organization providing objective analysis and effective solutions that address the challenges facing the public and private sectors around the world. RAND's publications do not necessarily reflect the opinions of its research clients and sponsors.

Cover design by Pete Soriano

Published 2005 by the RAND Corporation
1776 Main Street, P.O. Box 2138, Santa Monica, CA 90407-2138
1200 South Hayes Street, Arlington, VA 22202-5050
201 North Craig Street, Suite 202, Pittsburgh, PA 15213-1516
RAND URL: http://www.rand.org/
To order RAND documents or to obtain additional information, contact
Distribution Services: Telephone: (310) 451-7002;
Fax: (310) 451-6915; Email: order@rand.org

Preface

Early versions of most of the chapters in this book were presented in August 2003 at the Pardee RAND Graduate School in a two-week course convened by Paul C. Light. Then, at a PRGS conference in March 2004, the authors presented their revised papers to each other and to five distinguished experts: Mark Abramson, Eugene Bardach, Steven Kelman, Barbara Nelson, and Hannah Sistare. These experts made presentations at the conference and contributed written commentaries afterwards, which assisted the editors and authors in generating the final versions assembled here. Jim Dewar, Lynn Karoly, and Jane Ryan later provided helpful comments, and Janet DeLand was the book's speedy and efficient editor.

The course, the conference, and this book were made possible by the generosity of donors to the Pardee RAND Graduate School, particularly Paul Volcker and Eugene and Maxine Rosenfeld.

Contents

CHAPTER ONE

Introduction

Robert Klitgaard

When we think about the performance of our government, we tend to focus on four questions:

1. Who should our political leaders be?
2. What policies should be chosen?
3. How big should the government be?
4. How can public managers do better, given the organizations they inhabit, the personnel rules they face, and their incentives for performance (or lack thereof)?

Each of these questions is vital. But focusing only on them can lead us to ignore some deep causes of underperformance, those "givens" in the fourth question: organizations poorly aligned to their missions, malfunctioning systems for selecting leaders, and ineffective or perverse incentive systems.

This book incites us and invites us to address these deep causes of underperformance. Chapter 2 is the report of the Volcker Commission, a devastating nonpartisan indictment of public service in America. Low-performance government provides too little service for too much money. Breakdowns and failures are a serious risk, if not already widespread. The Volcker Commission is a call to action, the most important critique of the federal government since at least the 1980s.

The rest of the chapters ask us to consider new approaches to structure, leadership, and incentives. The authors are researchers at the RAND Corporation—most of them are also professors at the Pardee RAND Graduate School. In the past 15 years, they and other RAND researchers have produced more than a thousand studies of public management across an array of government agencies. In this book, the authors step back from specific research findings to address the Volcker Commission's deep questions. How might structural reforms be successfully undertaken? What practical steps would result in better leaders? How can we create performance-driven, flexible public agencies?

Chapters 3 and 4 show how the challenges facing government are compounded by a changing role of the state and by increasing uncertainty. Gregory Treverton argues that ten years from now, the lines between state and market will be even more blurred than they are today. In areas from health care to anti-poverty programs, from homeland security to military procurement, government must work in tandem with the private sector and civil society. In these partnerships, government faces new challenges of structure, leadership, and incentives that transcend the borders of the public sector.

In Chapter 4, Robert Lempert and Steven Popper speak of the "deep uncertainty" in issues ranging from counterterrorism to global warming. Our government organizations and our analytical tools are ill equipped to deal with such problems. Fortunately, the information revolution may offer relief. Lempert and Popper describe new computer-based tools for handling complex problems that involve deep uncertainty and many interested parties. These tools enable more-effective collaboration across offices and agencies. In the future, they may allow a kind of "virtual restructuring"—reorganization without the need to shuffle organizational boxes.

Better Structures

Government structures should follow missions, as form follows function—at least, so both the Volcker Commission and common sense would suggest. But existing organizational structures have grown roots of interests. Powerful forces in Congress, in business, and in the civil service constrain change. These facts have led to a kind of paralysis. On one side are rationalists who note that things don't work as they should and who promote reforms. On the other side are sophisticates who chant, "Don't forget the politics." The two sides seldom connect, and the results are frustration and gridlock.

The RAND approach, exemplified in this book, is different. It looks at examples of successful reforms to see what we can learn from them. It imagines different organizational forms, almost as scenarios, and analyzes their benefits and costs. And it takes seriously the new organizational forms that are emerging as the boundaries between state, market, and civil society erode.

In Chapter 5, Susan Gates takes as given both the Volcker Commission's rationalist critique and the sophisticate's appreciation of the "structural politics" that constrain reorganization. She asks, "How might we imagine overcoming these constraints?" She invites us to consider an example of successful restructuring. If one proposes closing a few among many military bases in the United States, one can anticipate that every state's representatives will fight to keep their state's bases open. The result could be paralysis—unless a process can be devised that includes an independent panel, criteria that are objective and transparent, and an overall up-or-down congressional vote on the proposal. This is what the Department of Defense Base Realignment and Closure (BRAC) process did, and it worked. Gates stimulates us to think creatively: What might we take from this example to help us with the recommendations of the Volcker Commission?

Lynn Davis takes a broad look at national security in Chapter 6. Given today's changing security missions, how might the U.S. government reorganize? She presents four quite different scenarios and considers their pros and cons, including political controversies and ease of implementation. Her method—and what might be called her spirit, the calm examination of rather wild alternatives—is also in the

RAND style, and it should be transferable to other areas of government as well.

In Chapter 7, Frank Camm reviews public-private partnerships, a rapidly growing way to reorganize what government does. We are beyond the time when the choice is between privatization and nationalization. Hybrids and collaborations are the rule now, and Camm (and RAND) have been at the forefront of both analysis and implementation. His chapter provides new evidence and new guidelines. Indirectly, he demonstrates how valuable research will be in tailoring public-private partnerships to particular problems, technologies, and partners.

Better Leaders

Leadership is addressed in three chapters. In Chapter 8, John Dumond and Rick Eden reexamine the broken system of presidential appointments. The current process is too slow, too expensive, and too erratic. The authors suggest an unexpected analogy: systems for providing spare parts. Dumond and Eden have led several RAND projects that created new, effective systems for speeding delivery of spare parts, reducing costs, and making supply systems more reliable. Their secret was building an interagency team that diagnosed problems, created measures of success, and devised and implemented new solutions. Dumond and Eden invite us to consider how a similar process might work for presidential appointments. As long as we don't tell an aspiring assistant secretary that we are modeling his appointment after a replacement part for a tank, the suggestion just might work. At the very least, those who now are responsible for presidential appointments, as well as critics of the process, will find in this chapter something quite different (and quite a bit more useful) than the customary every-other-year critique and call to action.

Al Robbert looks at leadership in the civil service in Chapter 9. He wonders what we might learn from the military's methods for creating senior leaders. In the military—but not in the civil service, except in a few specialized agencies—career paths are designed to create leaders through carefully conceived combinations of training and experience. Without trying to make office managers into lieutenant colonels, are there programmatic lessons that the civil service might take from studying the military? Once again, the logic of Robbert's contribution is not "this worked there, so do the same thing over here." Rather, it is "look at how this system works compared with that system; note the key factors involved; is there any way we can take advantage of what we've learned in experimenting with the future?"

Speaking of the future, Gregory Treverton's chapter on leadership (Chapter 10) looks at the challenges over the next several decades in government, corporations, and nonprofits. He and others at RAND have been studying trends and, also in the RAND style, talking with practitioners and leaders. The data on trends speak to the story, but they are not the whole story; one also needs to listen to the opinions of those inhabiting the institutions involved. The result is a richer appreciation of the challenges of selecting and developing leaders.

Better Incentives

The final four chapters are devoted to performance-based incentives. These chapters together convey a couple of big messages: Better incentives can result in much better performance. But even if the politics of change are favorable, incentive reforms are complicated. They require careful measurement. They require a detailed understanding of institutional economics. Beth Asch, in Chapter 11, shows that many complicated economic considerations should shape a system of personnel incentives. One implication is that no one system will fit all circumstances. Another is that reforms will require both political will and analytical acumen. In Chapter 12, Jacob Klerman focuses on statistical issues at the heart of determining performance. In social programs, the performance of an office or a program or even an agency may depend not only on the office or program's value added, but also on factors such as which clients or students or recipients receive service. How can one take these many factors into account so that stronger incentives reward and induce socially productive behavior—and discourage creaming, obfuscation, or deceit? Again, beyond the rationalist's promise that incentives work and the sophisticate's reminder that politics matter, we encounter a host of complications. Addressing them correctly may enhance the effectiveness of incentives while mitigating at least some of the political resistance.

Education is a prime example where incentives have apparently gone awry. Laura Hamilton's masterful analysis (Chapter 13) takes stock of what we have learned from performance measurement in public schools, and her findings have relevance for most other social services. In the final chapter (Chapter 14), Johannes Fedderke, Kamil Akramov, and I note that performance-based incentive systems have effects on (1) the allocation of resources, (2) the distribution of allocations across groups of interest, (3) the incentives created for recipients as they react in the future to the performance system, and (4) what we call the "fundraising effect." The last effect pertains to those providing an agency's budget—Congress, voters, funders. They, too, may react to the performance measures chosen and how they are used. We argue that all of these effects should be taken into account—and we then show how quantitative analysis can help in doing so.

I would like to close this introduction with an observation about the value of essays such as these. They are designed to kindle the reader's creativity. This is policy analysis that helps us rethink the problems. The job of the researcher is to help government, business, and citizens together expand the alternatives and broaden the appreciation of objectives and consequences. This is not analysis that dictates, but analysis that invites. Its goal is not to determine a decision by a limited elite, but to enhance participation and understanding by all those involved in and affected by government.

In other words, these chapters are not the stereotypical policy analysis in which an expert whispers in the ear of a policymaker and says, "Do B, boss." They are not what the anthropologist Clifford Geertz once spurned as "size-up-and-solve social science." They are instead what RAND and the Pardee RAND Graduate School try to do in all their work—expand the reach of reason with a combination of rigor and imagination, theory and case study, the visionary and the practical.

CHAPTER TWO

Urgent Business for America: Revitalizing the Federal Government for the 21st Century[1]

National Commission on the Public Service

Preface

Fifty years have passed since the last comprehensive reorganization of the federal government. The changes proposed by The Hoover Commission served the nation well as it adapted to the mid-20th century world. It was a world transformed by World War II and the new responsibilities of the United States government at home and abroad.

It was also a world in which television was still a curiosity, transportation without jets was slow and expensive, typewriters were still manual, and Xerox machines, personal computers, microchips, and the Internet were unknown and beyond imagination.

Medicare and Medicaid did not exist. There were no nuclear power plants and no national highway system. The government organization table contained no EPA, OSHA, NIH, or dozens of other now familiar institutions.

The relationship of the federal government to the citizens it serves became vastly broader and deeper with each passing decade. Social programs are by far the largest component of a federal budget that now amounts to over one-fifth of the gross national product. National security and foreign policy issues, the environment, protection of human rights, health care, the economy, and questions of financial regulation dominate most of the national agenda.

---

[1] This chapter was adapted from *Urgent Business for America: Revitalizing the Federal Government for the 21st Century*, Report of the National Commission on the Public Service, Washington, DC: Brookings Institution, January 2003. The preface was written by Paul A. Volcker, Chairman of the National Commission on the Public Service.

Something less tangible, but alarming, has also happened over the last 50 years. Trust in government—strong after World War II, with the United States assuming international leadership and meeting domestic challenges—has eroded. Government's responsiveness, its efficiency, and too often its honesty are broadly challenged as we enter a new century. The bonds between our citizens and our public servants, essential to democratic government, are frayed even as the responsibilities of government at home and abroad have increased. Government work ought to be a respected source of pride. All too frequently it is not.

The members of this commission—Republicans, Democrats, and independents—have joined in a common conviction. The time has come to bring government into the 21st century. We take as a given the Constitutional division of authority among the legislature, the judiciary, and the executive. Our proposals mainly concern the organization of the administrative side, but there are implications for the Congress and for the effectiveness of our courts.

We are a small group, with limited resources. But beyond our own combined experience in government, we have been able to draw upon an enormous amount of research and professional analysis in conducting our work. That evidence points unambiguously toward certain conclusions:

- Organization: A clear sense of policy direction and clarity of mission is too often lacking, undercutting efficiency and public confidence. As a result, there is real danger of healthy public skepticism giving way to corrosive cynicism.
- Leadership: Too many of our most competent career executives and judges are retiring or leaving early. Too few of our most talented citizens are seeking careers in government or accepting political or judicial appointments.
- Operations: The federal government is not performing nearly as well as it can or should. The difficulties federal workers encounter in just getting their jobs done has led to discouragement and low morale.

Disciplined policy direction, operational flexibility, and clear and high performance standards are the guiding objectives of our proposals. Our report calls for sweeping changes in organizational structure and personnel incentives and practices. Clarification and consolidation of responsibility for policymaking executives, combined with greater delegation of operational functions to agency managers, should be the hallmark of progress. Implementation and effective oversight will require clear-sighted action by the President, the cabinet, and the Congress.

I have great appreciation for the men and women who agreed to give their attention and knowledge to the mission of this commission. They are people of all political persuasions who have time and again demonstrated their commitment to excellence in government. They came together in the wake of 9/11/01 with a common desire to help our government meet the critical challenges of this new century.

Most of all, the support of a concerned public for bold change is critical. Only then will we be able to rebuild trust in government.

It is our belief that these are matters of consequence to all who are interested in government and its performance.

The members of the commission commend the report to the attention of the American public and our elected and appointed leaders.

Paul A. Volcker

The Case for Change

In the 21st century, government touches every American's life. It affects, often profoundly, the way we live and work. So we have a deep and growing concern that our public service and the organization of our government are in such disarray.

The notion of public service, once a noble calling proudly pursued by the most talented Americans of every generation, draws an indifferent response from today's young people and repels many of the country's leading private citizens. Those with policy responsibility find their decisionmaking frustrated by overlapping jurisdictions, competing special interests, and sluggish administrative response.

Those who enter the civil service often find themselves trapped in a maze of rules and regulations that thwart their personal development and stifle their creativity. The best are underpaid; the worst, overpaid. Too many of the most talented leave the public service too early; too many of the least talented stay too long.

Those who enter public service often find themselves at sea in an archipelago of agencies and departments that have grown without logical structure, deterring intelligent policymaking. The organization and operations of the federal government are a mixture of the outdated, the outmoded and the outworn. Related responsibilities are parceled out among several agencies, independent of each other or spread across different departments.

In this technological age, the government's widening span of interests inevitably leads to complications as organizations need to coordinate policy implementation. But as things stand, it takes too long to get even the clearest policies implemented. There are too many decisionmakers, too much central clearance, too many bases to touch, and too many overseers with conflicting agendas. Leadership responsibilities often fall into the awkward gap between inexperienced political appointees and unsupported career managers. Accountability is hard to discern and harder still to enforce. Policy change has become so difficult that federal employees themselves often come to share the cynicism about government that afflicts many of our citizens.

> "A strong workforce comes from having the right people with the right skills in the right place at the right time. Only then will government operate in an effective, efficient, and economic manner."
>
> *U.S. Senator Daniel K. Akaka*

The system has evolved not by plan or considered analysis but by accretion over time, politically inspired tinkering, and neglect. Over time the "civil service system" was perceived as a barrier to effective government performance. Few leaders in Washington, even those who understood the importance of revitalizing the public service, were willing to expend the political capital deemed necessary to do so.

And government reorganization has come to be viewed as a task so daunting, requiring such extensive and excruciating political negotiations, that it takes a national emergency to bring it about.

Without government reorganization, it will be very difficult to revitalize the public service. The fact of the matter is that we need both government reorganization and revitalization of the public service. Without structure and organization, no political leaders or body of public servants will be able to do the kind of job the citizens want and demand.

Recognition that there is much wrong with the current organization and management of the public service is widespread today. It stimulated the creation of this National Commission on the Public Service, and it has inspired our determined effort to call upon expert testimony and analysis to address what lies at the core of the current problems. We believe that the proposals in this report, when implemented, will make a significant difference in the quality of government performance.

The need to improve performance is urgent and compelling. The peace dividend many Americans expected from the end of the Cold War has quickly vanished in the face of new and sinister threats to our national security. The economic boom of the 1990s has ended, and Americans look to their government for fiscal and regulatory policies to cope with harsh new economic realities. The looming baby boomer retirement bulge will put greater pressure than ever before on government human services programs. Across the full range of government activities, new demands are accelerating, and the pace of change is quickening. At the same time, the federal government has had difficulty in adapting to the knowledge-based economy and taking advantage of the significant advances in technology.

The federal government is neither organized nor staffed nor adequately prepared to meet the demands of the 21st century. It was in recognition of that fact that the President found it necessary last year to propose the most sweeping change in the organization of the federal government in decades by creating the new Department of Homeland Security. But that imperfect reorganization covers only part of the government. With every passing day, the gap between expectations and responsive capacity is growing. If we do not make the necessary changes now, when our needs are clear, we will be forced to cope with the consequences later in crisis after crisis.

In this report, we have not shied away from proposing radical change. Our analysis and recommendations may discomfort parts of our audience. We accept that inevitability for a simple but important reason: the current organization of the federal government and the operation of public programs are not good enough. They are not good enough for the American people, not good enough to meet the extraordinary challenges of the century just beginning, and not good enough for the hundreds of thousands of talented federal workers who hate the constraints that keep them from serving their country with the full measure of their talents and energy. We must do better, much better, and soon.

> "We've got to get the public engaged and we've got to get the media to understand the importance and the linkage between getting good public servants and having a nation that works."
>
> *Constance Berry Newman,*
> *Assistant Administrator for Africa,*
> *U.S. Agency for International Development*

The Task We Face

American citizens and their national government face a variety of new and demanding challenges in the 21st century. People live longer and the average age of the population will continue to increase. We are experiencing ever greater racial and religious diversity. By mid-century there may be no majority race in the United States for the first time in our history. New technologies are bringing far-reaching changes in the way we work, produce our food, obtain and communicate information, and care for ourselves. Globalization, the extraordinary needs of developing nations, and the availability of weapons of mass destruction to nonstate actors are redefining national security and international relations.

In the United States, there are accelerating demands on limited resources like fuel and water. And there is ever-increasing demand for expensive services, especially medical services and especially for the elderly. We will need to find ways and means of keeping our financial markets both free and honest. We will be forced to confront hard and deeply contentious questions about the proper role of government and the extent to which government can aid its citizens with services and burden them with taxes. And overlaying all this are the now constant challenges to our national security and to our role and responsibilities in shaping a peaceful and prosperous world.

Americans expect more of their government than ever before, not necessarily in size but in responsiveness, and, inevitably, good government will demand more of the American people than ever before. For the relationship to work well, the American people must trust and respect their government, but that will only occur if the quality of government performance improves.

No one should expect a 21st century population confronting 21st century problems to be satisfied with a government hamstrung by organizations and personnel systems developed decades ago. The organizational structure of the federal government was last reviewed in a comprehensive way in the mid-20th century, first with a significant modernization of the defense establishment after World War II and then in response to the two national commissions created during the administrations of Presidents Truman and Eisenhower and chaired by former President Herbert Hoover. Since then, new entities have been created to cope with new technologies, greatly expanded social programs, and commitments to enhance the health, safety, and environment of the nation. This ad hoc layering of agencies, departments, and programs greatly complicated management, expanded the influence of powerful interests, and diminished coherent policy direction. The federal government today is a layered jumble of organizations with muddled public missions.

A government that has not evolved to meet the demands of the early 21st century risks being overwhelmed by the even greater demands that lie ahead. Capacity and performance in government do

HOW THE WORK OF GOVERNMENT HAS CHANGED

As the current director of the U.S. Office of Personnel Management has noted, the government of 1950 was largely a government of clerks. The newly created General Schedule, covering 96 percent of the nonpostal, white-collar federal workforce, provided specific job descriptions and salary ranges for 15 grades, each of which contained ten distinct steps. Most federal employees worked in the lower levels of the administrative hierarchy—GS-3 was the most populous grade and more than half of the General Schedule employees occupied grades at or below GS-4.

For most federal employees, the work was process oriented and routinized. It required few specialized skills. Because the character of work was consistent across agencies, public service policies could demand consistency as well. The federal workers in one agency were paid and treated just like federal workers with the same classification in all others. The bedrock principle of the government's employee classification system was—and is—that job description and time in service determine one's compensation, not skill nor training nor education nor performance.

But as these consistent and rigid policies of equal treatment and protection of employee tenure took deep root, the character of federal responsibilities and the nature of work began to change in ways that would dramatically alter government functions and revolutionize the workplace in the second half of the 20th century. Nearly every aspect of government became more technically complex. A space program emerged and quickly became a significant federal activity. Foreign aid and foreign trade became important components of foreign relations. Ensuring the safety of food and drugs, of travel, and of the workplace loomed larger in importance. Science and technology research, complex litigation, rigorous analysis, and innovation in service delivery became critical responsibilities in agency after agency. Financial regulators became hard pressed by the competitiveness of modern capital markets. Increasingly, government operations were contracted to the private sector. A simple comparison of the grade distributions between 1950 and 2000 reveals one dimension of the change. In 1950, 62 percent of the basic federal workforce was in GS grades 1–5, with only 11 percent in the top five grades; by 2000 those relationships were reversed: 15 percent of the federal workforce was in the bottom five grades, compared to 56 percent in the top.

Rigid federal personnel policies, designed to enhance consistency and employee tenure, have become an ever tighter straitjacket for a government that needs to place a higher value on creativity and flexibility to meet rapidly changing and increasingly complicated demands. As the country, the world, and the federal government have evolved into entities very different from their 1950 forms, the principal structural elements of the federal public service have remained largely the same.

Occasional legislative initiatives, including the much-trumpeted Civil Service Reform Act of 1978, brought some measure of flexibility to a few agencies with critical needs and created the promise—too often unfulfilled—of performance-based compensation for some federal workers. But central principles and core structures changed little.

SOURCE: Office of Personnel Management, *A Fresh Start for Federal Pay: The Case for Modernization*, April 2002.

The Changing Federal Workforce, 1950–2000

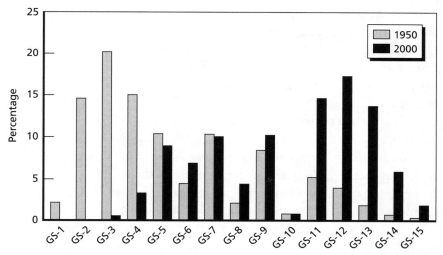

SOURCE: Office of Personnel Management, *A Fresh Start for Federal Pay: The Case for Modernization*, April 2002, p. 5.

RAND *MG256-V-1*

not now equal public demands and expectations. Public trust steadily declines as a result. The gap will only grow larger in the years ahead, and the consequences and costs of that gap will grow as well.

> "And it was 12 years ago when Paul Volcker chaired the first commission that dealt with a quiet crisis. Well, it's no longer quiet and it is a crisis of even more remarkable dimensions."
>
> *Connie Morella, U.S. Representative*

Problems—and Opportunities

Our collective experience matches the central theme of most research and expert opinion on the functioning of the federal government: problems of organization and of human capital have combined to produce results far short of what is needed.

Our recommendations deal with seven key areas of concern, beginning with the overriding importance of the relationship between the American people and their government.

Citizen Disaffection and Distrust of Government. Too many American citizens do not respect and trust their government—often for the very good reason that government has not earned their trust or respect.

Survey after survey confirms that the past 40 years have been marked by a steep decline in levels of public trust in government.

This is not a simple phenomenon and has no single cause. But recent opinion polling finds strong relationships between negative perceptions of the performance of government and distrust of government.

The public policies needed to meet the challenges of the 21st century will require sacrifices and strong support from the American people.

Trust in Federal Government, 1964–2000

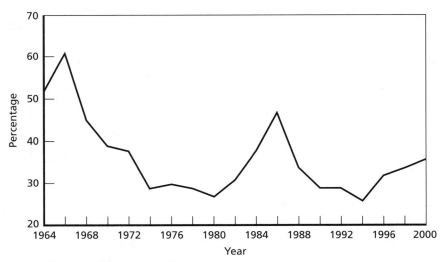

SOURCE: Based on data from National Election Studies "Trust in Government Index 1958–2000," http://www.umich.edu/~nes/nesguide/toptable/tab5a_5.htm.
RAND *MG256-V-2*

OPPORTUNITY LOST: SEPTEMBER 11 AND PUBLIC TRUST IN GOVERNMENT

In the aftermath of the tragedy of September 11, public trust in the federal government spiked dramatically upward. In July 2001, only 29 percent of participants in a national survey said they trusted the government in Washington to do the right thing "just about always" or "most of the time," the standard measure of trust in government. That finding was consistent with the low levels of public trust that have been normal for many years. But in October 2001, a few weeks after the tragedy, trust in government exploded upward to 57 percent. One had to return to the 1960s to find such high levels of public trust.

The September 11 impact on trust in government was short lived, however. As stories of intelligence failures, confusion over the collection and distribution of victims' relief funds, and the issuance of visas to terrorists emerged, public trust quickly began to fall back to earlier levels. By May 2002, it had dropped to 40 percent.

Favorability ratings for some visible leaders like the President, Vice President, Secretary of State and Secretary of Defense shot up after September 11 and remained unusually high in the months that followed. But individual favorability did not translate into positive ratings of government performance.

SOURCE: G. Calvin Mackenzie and Judith M. Labiner, *Opportunity Lost: The Rise and Fall of Trust and Confidence in Government After September 11*, Center for Public Service, Brookings Institution, May 30, 2002.

Those will be hard to achieve if citizens distrust the government. But such distrust will continue to be the norm until government performance improves sufficiently to earn greater respect than it does now from the American people.

Organizational Chaos. The seemingly coherent mid-20th century organizational structure of the federal government has been overtaken by events. Today, we have inherited an accumulation of particular organizations that follow no logical pattern. As a consequence, public servants often find themselves in doubt about the relevance and importance of their agency's mission while spending inordinate amounts of time coordinating or battling with their counterparts in other agencies. In energy policy, health care, environmental protection, resource management, and scores of other important public matters, decisions are made and remade from different perspectives, while the need for coordination and for complementary policy approaches is neglected.

A dramatic reflection of the problem was made evident in the President's call and Congress's endorsement for massive reorganization of the disparate agencies with responsibility for homeland security. That proposed reorganization involves at least 22 agencies drawn from across government, affects at least 170,000 federal employees, and acknowledges the need for flexibility not possible under the old organizational structure and personnel system.

One-Size-Fits-All Management. The major public service reform commissions of the 20th century sought to find single, consistent, overarching solutions to broad and complex organizational and management challenges. The first and second Hoover Commissions, most notably, sought to develop common departmental and agency structures and uniform management practices.

If that was ever a viable or relevant approach, it is no longer. One size does not fit all in a government performing tasks as complex and varied as ours. Agencies have broadly different missions. One delivers monthly pension checks, another regulates the securities industry, a third conducts research on the frontiers of science, and so on. Because missions differ so widely, no single administrative structure or management approach can work effectively in all cases. Excellent performance requires organization, leadership, and culture that fit the mission, not just a single theory of administration.

> "Our federal civil service today stands at the intersection of opportunity and peril."
> *U.S. Representative Steny Hoyer*

Vanishing Talent. The middle decades of the 20th century were in some ways a golden age for public service recruiting and retention. First, public response to the Great Depression, then to the war against the Axis powers, drew committed and talented Americans to government to manage those enormous enterprises. In the 1960s, as the federal government took the lead in efforts to define and broaden the civil rights of citizens and to protect consumer and environmental rights, government again became a powerful magnet for the passion and commitment of talented citizens. Those generations of young

Americans were drawn to public service by a powerful sense of mission.

But those highly motivated public servants are now gone or soon will be. Within the next five years, more than half the senior managers of the federal government will be eligible to retire. Not all will, but the best estimates are that by the end of this decade, the federal government will have suffered one of the greatest drains of experienced personnel in its history.

That would be less worrisome if there were evidence that the middle ranks of government contained ready replacements and the entry levels were filling with people full of promise for the future. But the evidence, in fact, points in the opposite direction. Far too many talented public servants are abandoning the middle levels of government, and too many of the best recruits are rethinking their commitment, either because they are fed up with the constraints of outmoded personnel systems and unmet expectations for advancement or simply lured away by the substantial difference between public and private sector salaries in many areas. Some employees leave federal service because they can no longer tolerate the dismal facilities and working conditions in many agencies. Drab and tiny workspaces, inadequate room for storage and record-keeping, and aging lighting, heating, and air conditioning systems—too common in the federal government—seem to many employees emblematic of the low value in which they as workers are held. The invasions of personal privacy resulting from financial reporting, background investigations, and public scrutiny in general also take a toll on morale. Increasingly, federal workers have real cause to be concerned about their personal safety.

Too often, as well, federal employees depart before their time in frustration over the strangling organizational and procedural complexity of contemporary government decisionmaking. For too many, even their best efforts to be responsive and creative end up in organizational oblivion.

The entry-level situation is equally dismaying. Rarely in recent history has there been a time when public service was so far from the minds of America's young people. The federal government is no longer viewed as the destination of choice for many graduates of the nation's top public policy and administration programs.[2]

Those who do have an interest in public service soon find that it is one of the most difficult professions in America to enter. Complex and contorted entry procedures stop too many potential applicants in their tracks. Those who apply for jobs in the private sector typically find the application process much simpler and more streamlined and they get responses to their applications much more quickly. Faced with a job offer from a private sector employer in one hand and the prospect of many months of tedious review of their government job application in the other, they make the rational choice to take the sure thing.

So we confront a classic "catch-22." As the government's experienced workers depart for retirement or more attractive work, it creates an opening for new energy and talent; yet the replacement streams are drying up. Left unchecked, these trends can lead to only one outcome: a significant drop in the capabilities of our public servants.

Personnel Systems Out of Touch with Market Reality. For more than a century, the central principle of federal personnel management has been equity across agencies in personnel matters. In a personnel system dominated by relatively low-level jobs, "equal pay for equal work" was a reasonable and workable management theory.

But we no longer have a government dominated by people performing low-skilled jobs. The concept of "equal work" is now impossible to apply to many of the tasks undertaken by government agencies. To be sure, there are employees in every agency who perform work similar to that of other employees in other agencies. Every agency has security personnel, human resource staff, accounting specialists, and so on. And efforts to ensure commonality in their treatment and compensation still make sense.

In the broader array of professional and managerial jobs, however, such comparisons are often impossible. There is no basis for

---

[2] Paul C. Light, "To Restore and Renew," *Government Executive Magazine*, November 2001.

comparing a trade analyst to a microbiologist or a space shuttle designer to an airport security manager.

There have been efforts in recent years to inject flexibility and market-relatedness in setting compensation for some agencies with critical missions and recruitment crises. In effect, there has been a reluctant concession to reality. The benefits have been evident but scattered and uneven. The broader issues of how compensation can rationally be determined across the government remain to be adequately addressed.

> "The problem with the pay system is there is no incentive structure, no recognition of hard work . . . it is very hard to maintain my motivation knowing that even if I worked half as hard, I would still receive my scheduled 'step' increase each year."
>
> *Employee, U.S. Department of Health and Human Services*

Personnel Systems Are Immune to Performance. Three factors, far beyond any others, determine the compensation of the overwhelming majority of federal employees. The first is how individual jobs fit into the General Schedule classification system; the second is the geographical location of the job; and the third is the employee's time in service. Quality of performance, which ought to be the central factor in determining compensation, is too often ignored.

With the Civil Service Reform Act of 1978, bonuses, merit pay, and performance awards were instituted for high-performing civil servants, especially top managers. However, those efforts failed to produce the intended results. Congress has rarely provided sufficient appropriations to fund the bonuses, and the performance evaluation system that supports them has too often been rendered ineffective by managers seeking to spread bonuses around as compensation supplements for large numbers of employees instead of incentives or rewards for top performers. "An employee needs to do little, if anything, to earn these increases," according to the Office of Personnel Management. "They are essentially entitlements."[3]

The consequence is a compensation system that makes few distinctions between hard-working high-achievers and indifferent nonachievers. There are too few rewards for those who do their jobs well and too few penalties for those who perform poorly. The Senior Executive Service (SES), created as part of the Civil Service Reform Act of 1978, was an attempt to use pay-for-performance measures to reward senior level managers. Every three years, members of the SES are subject to recertification based on their performance levels. However, a study conducted in 1997 by the Office of Personnel Management found that 99 percent of SES members were routinely recertified in each three-year cycle, indicating that recertification is merely a rubber stamp and not a measure of, nor an incentive to, performance.[4]

This has added to the great discouragement among many federal employees with the performance of some of their colleagues. A recent Center for Public Service survey of federal employees found that the average estimate of the number of poor performers in their midst was about 25 percent, and more than two-thirds had negative views of their agency's system for disciplining those poor performers.[5] Such a system, of course, also discourages potential employees, especially the most talented and promising, who are reluctant to enter a field where there are so few financial rewards for their hard work, where mediocrity and excellence yield the same paycheck.

Labor-Management Conflict. The extended debate over the creation of a Department of Homeland Security through the summer and fall of 2002 makes clear that labor-management relations will pose a challenge to reform. Some of the disagreement was the result

---

[3] Office of Personnel Management, *A Fresh Start for Federal Pay: The Case for Modernization*, OPM White Paper, April 2002, p. 22.

[4] Office of Personnel Management, Senior Executive Service, "Recertification Assessment—1997" (http://opm.gov/ses/recertifyinro.html).

[5] Paul C. Light, *The Troubled State of the Federal Public Service*, Washington, DC: Brookings Institution, June 27, 2002.

of clear substantive differences; some was a reflection of partisan political jockeying; much was the result of inadequate communication. It was only after the November elections presaged a switch from Democrat to Republican control of the Senate that a compromise was reached. What is clear is that a new level of labor-management discourse is necessary if we are to achieve any serious reform in the civil service system.

The commission believes that it is entirely possible to modernize the public service without jeopardizing the traditional and essential rights of public servants. Federal employees should be hired based on their demonstrated skills and talents, not their political affiliations. They should enjoy protection from discrimination and from arbitrary personnel actions. The traditional values of merit hiring, nondiscrimination, protection from arbitrary discipline or dismissal, and freedom from political interference should remain paramount. Engaged and mutually respectful labor relations should be a high federal priority.

> "The fact is we all share the same goals: We want the federal government to be the employer of choice, to create an environment where the employees who are here, who are dedicated and committed, want to stay, and where we are able to hire those who are looking to enter federal service."
>
> *Colleen Kelley, President, National Treasury Employees Union*

The President, department and agency heads, members of Congress, and federal employee representatives can examine earlier public sector labor-management collaborations to find models for a new dialogue. Examples include the Quality Service through Partnership program developed by former Governor George Voinovich and the Ohio American Federation of State, County and Municipal Employees Union. Mayor Stephen Goldsmith of Indianapolis and employee representatives collaborated successfully to address deep differences over contracting for city services. At the federal level, President Clinton established a National Partnership Council to foster better labor-management communications at the agency level. Internal

Revenue Service Commissioner Charles Rossotti used the 1998 IRS reform legislation, and an internal culture that already encouraged open relations, to forge a constructive labor-management relationship at the IRS.

A Time for Action

Our analysis yields one overarching conclusion above all others: The task we face is not small. There is no magic bullet.

But neither are solutions beyond our grasp. Often in our past—in the 1880s, during the two world wars, and in meeting the threat of a great depression—we have faced pressures and demands that required government to alter its structure and operations. In recent years, we have seen some state and local governments successfully confront many of the problems identified here.

In Washington, too, thoughtful people throughout the federal government have experimented, often successfully, with innovative approaches to staffing and managing the public service. There is much cause for optimism. Governments and government agencies can change, even in ways that seem far-reaching, and those changes can produce significant improvements in efficiency and performance. Partly in response to the terrorist threat, there is today greater understanding that government plays an indispensable role in American life. This role cannot be responsibly fulfilled by mediocre performance or mediocre talent.

We also note a confluence of conditions that make this a propitious time for innovation in the public service. The enormous retirement bulge facing the federal government in this decade, though worrisome in many ways, is also an opportunity to rebuild and fortify for the future the senior levels of the public service.

We also detect a strong and growing bipartisan understanding in Washington that the public service must be modernized to meet the demands of an environment very different from the one in which the current rules were shaped. Most obviously, the debate over the creation of a new Department of Homeland Security has raised important issues about the organization of government, the role of the public service, and the ways in which it must be managed to respond to 21st century needs. Plainly, frustrations with the old order are not limited to questions of national security. Across the political spectrum, there are calls for new approaches and new ideas.

Important as well, we note deep disaffection within the public service. Federal employees themselves are unhappy with the conditions they face. They are frustrated and fatigued. They lack the resources they feel they need to do their assigned jobs. They struggle with the constraints of an outmoded personnel system that keeps them from fully developing or utilizing their talents. They resent the protections provided to those poor performers among them who impede their own work and drag down the reputation of all government workers. While understandably wary of reforms that might do little more than introduce new political pressures into their work environments, the vast majority of federal employees know the system is not working and is in need of repair.

Moreover, we sense a substantial meeting of the minds among independent researchers, good-government groups, educators, and experienced public managers about the main items of needed reforms.

For all these reasons—because there is much wrong and a great need for change, because the American people and their elected representatives seem unusually disposed to consider such change, and because the government employees who will be most affected are themselves often advocates of change—we believe the time is right, indeed the time is ripe, for action on a broad front.

We hope the recommendations that follow from our own analysis of the problems will provide focus for public debate and needed decisions.

> "Our members tell us that they desperately want to make a difference in their jobs and provide efficient service to the public, but lately, more than ever, they have less of a say over how the work can best be done and they are frustrated."
>
> *Mark Roth, General Counsel,*
> *American Federation of Government Employees*

Recommendations

The compelling need to address the pressing problems identified in this report cuts across regions, generations, and political affiliations. We must have a government that can respond efficiently and effectively to political direction. When the American people, through their representatives, express a desire for policy change, the operating agencies of the government should be able to deliver that change promptly and efficiently. We believe that the recommendations that follow will greatly enhance their capacity to do so.

Taken together, these recommendations call for far-reaching changes in the structure and operations of the federal government. But it is not enough to call for large-scale organizational changes. These changes will not be effective without able public servants who are equipped and motivated to do their best in implementing public policies. And it is equally true that new approaches to recruiting and managing federal employees cannot be effective without a complementary organizational framework.

Tinkering around the edges is not enough. Decades of disjointed tinkering, in fact, have contributed to many of the problems we must now correct. It is time for deliberate, comprehensive review and reconstruction. This will not be completed soon, perhaps not even in a decade, but it must begin now and must reach deeply into all federal activities. The creation of the Department of Homeland Security was a first step. The effort that led to the development of that reorganization must now be applied governmentwide.

The Organization of Government

Fundamental reorganization of the federal government is urgently needed to improve its capacity for coherent design and efficient implementation of public policy.

The structure of the federal government is outmoded. Some programs no longer have viable missions. More often, too many agencies share responsibilities that could profitably be combined.

Decisionmaking is too often entangled in knots of conflict, clearance, coordination, and delay. The necessity for coordination and consultation cannot be permitted to overwhelm and needlessly delay decisionmaking.

The simple reality is that federal public servants are constrained by their organizational environment. Changes in federal personnel systems will have limited impact if they are not accompanied by significant change in the operating structure of the executive branch. This is why we begin our recommendations with an emphasis on issues of organization.

Every agency has—or should have—a clear mission with structures and processes that follow from their particular responsibilities. With rare exception, agencies with related mandates should fit together in a broad organizational scheme that permits and encourages constructive interaction rather than battles over turf. Federal departments should be reorganized to bring together agencies that contribute to a broad mission in a manner responsible to direction from elected leaders and their appointees, and subject to careful oversight by Congress but sufficiently independent in administration to achieve their missions.

Recommendation 1. The federal government should be reorganized into a limited number of mission-related executive departments.
As the debate about homeland security illustrated, large-scale reorganization of the federal government is no easy task. In some ways, the barriers to success are compounded by a piecemeal approach. Consequently, we urge a broader, more comprehensive vision, recognizing that implementation will take considerable determination and time. The basic point is that a significant change in structure is essential for the responsive and efficient implementation of public policy that the new century demands.

Our goal is enhanced mission coherence and role clarification. Federal agencies that share closely related missions should be administered by the same organizational entity. A few large departments in which those agencies are grouped together should enhance their employees' sense of purpose and loyalty, provide opportunities for advancement and job mobility, and encourage interagency cooperation. It is a much more sensible approach to government organization than the current pattern in which agencies with similar responsibilities have been scattered throughout the government.

The reorganization that we recommend here will require significant improvements in the quality of top executives, in the management of operating units, and in the ability of agencies to meet their unique staffing needs. There must also be clearer definition of the distinct roles of federal employees. Those charged with policy decisions should be political appointees, most of whom would work in the central offices of the large departments. Under the secretary would be deputy, under, and assistant secretaries to manage the budget and policy development. Although we contemplate that these appointees would oversee the individual operating agencies within their departments, operational responsibility would be delegated to the operating agencies. This would promote the dual advantages of mission cohesion and of smaller operating units.

There is extensive evidence now of duplication, overlap, and gaps in many critical government functions. This pattern consistently undermines effective government performance. Examples are plentiful and consequences are deeply damaging to the national interest.

1. **Waste of limited resources.** As many as 12 different agencies are responsible for administering more than 35 food safety laws. Testimony before the Senate Governmental Affairs Subcommittee on Oversight of Government Management, Restructuring and the District of Columbia noted that fragmented responsibility under the current food safety system leaves many gaps, inconsistencies, and inefficiencies in government oversight and results in an unacceptable level of public health protection.[6]

2. **Inability to accomplish national goals.** For example, with 541 clean air, water, and waste programs in 29 agencies, no one in the

---

[6] Senate Governmental Affairs Committee, Subcommittee on Oversight of Government Management, Restructuring and the District of Columbia (S. Hrg. 107-210, October 10, 2001 and S. Hrg. 106-366, August 4, 1999).

federal government can effectively manage the application of federal resources devoted to these goals.

3. **Impediments to effective management.** Some government missions are so widely dispersed among so many agencies that no coherent management is possible. Some examples:
   — Seven different federal agencies administer 40 different programs aimed primarily at job training.
   — Eight different federal agencies operate 50 different programs to aid the homeless.
   — Nine agencies operate 27 teen pregnancy programs.
   — Ninety early childhood programs are scattered among 11 federal agencies.[7]

4. **Danger to our national security and defense.**
   — The Hart-Rudman Commission (U.S. Commission on National Security/21st Century) found that as a result of excessive layering, performance suffered profoundly. The commission highlighted the problem of "gaps and seams" in mission responsibilities:

   Redundancy and overlap between organizations, as well as greatly diffused lines of authority, responsibility and accountability, generally point to "gaps and seams." These generally lead to the creation of "patches" or "workarounds," and the migration of functions and power to different organizations that would seem to lie outside their traditional core competencies.

To better address the nation's homeland security needs, the Hart-Rudman Commission recommended extensive reorganization of the Department of Defense, Department of State, and even the National Laboratories. The commission found that "there is a critical need to reshape the Department of Defense to meet the challenges of the 21st Century security environment." And the commission warned

---

[7] Senator Fred Thompson, Chairman, Committee on Governmental Affairs, United States Senate, "Government at the Brink: Urgent Federal Management Problems Facing the Bush Administration," June 1, 2001.

that the U.S. intelligence capabilities were hindered by "organizational constraints that limit the Intelligence Community's ability to optimally address emerging security threats." All of these recommendations were made prior to the attacks on the United States on 9/11/01.[8]

- Those participating in the Joint Congressional Committee inquiry into the intelligence failures of 9/11 repeatedly raised questions about the organization of U.S. intelligence agencies, the overlap and gaps in responsibilities, and the failure to share information within and between agencies.[9]
- There are 123 federal offices and agencies located in 16 federal departments with responsibility for counterterrorism.[10]

We believe that essential reorganization must begin with commitment to a few basic principles. First, programs that are designed to achieve similar outcomes should be combined within one agency unless there is a compelling case for competition. Second, agencies with similar or related missions should be combined in large departments that encourage cooperation, achieve economies of scale in management, and facilitate responsiveness to political leadership. Third, these new agencies and departments should be organized so that there are as few layers as possible between the top leadership and the operating units. Fourth, agencies should have maximum flexibility to design organizational structures and operating procedures that closely fit their missions.

Such reorganization takes time and patience. We believe a program on the scale we recommend here may take a decade or more to

---

[8] Report of the U.S. Commission on National Security/21st Century, February 2001.

[9] Transcript of final hearing of Joint Congressional Committee, October 8, 2002.

[10] Senate Governmental Affairs Committee, compiled from First Annual Report to the President and the Congress of the Advisory Panel to Assess Domestic Response Capabilities for Terrorism Involving Weapons of Mass Destruction, Assessing the Threat, Appendix 1, December 15, 1999, and Office of Management and Budget, Annual Report to Congress on Combating Terrorism, August 2001.

complete. But it is a task we must begin now and seek to accomplish with dispatch. The federal government will never fully meet the needs of the American people until this work is done.

Recommendation 2. The operating agencies in these new executive departments should be run by managers chosen for their operational skills and given the authority to develop management and personnel systems appropriate to their missions.

Subject to clear objectives and performance criteria, these agencies should be given substantial flexibility in the choice of subordinate organizational structure and personnel systems. Employees governmentwide should continue to have the basic employment guarantees of merit hiring, nondiscrimination, and protection from arbitrary or political personnel actions. These grants of authority would be defined by the President and subject to oversight by the Office of Management and Budget and the Office of Personnel Management, as well as Congress. The Office of Personnel Management, the management side of OMB, and human resources and management specialists governmentwide have been subjected to personnel reductions in recent years. The added responsibilities recommended here will require a strengthening of these capabilities.

Many agencies currently have executives who serve in the role of chief management or operating officer, either by administrative appointment or by statute. The new Department of Homeland Security will have a presidentially appointed, Senate confirmed, Undersecretary for Management. There is considerable support for the view that such an officer can provide important management focus, particularly where the leadership of the agency is focused on policy development and implementation. We recommend that the decision as to whether such a position should exist be considered on an agency-by-agency basis, at smaller as well as larger agencies.

Of particular importance is that managers, whether political or career, have the appropriate experience, training, and skills to manage effectively. This should be a priority for the President in identifying executives for appointment and a matter for congressional inquiry during the confirmation process. Finally, we recommend that Congress pay particular attention to the management implications of any legislation it considers.

Recommendation 3. The President should be given expedited authority to recommend structural reorganization of federal agencies and departments.

We recommend a qualified restoration of the President's authority to reorganize departments and agencies as the most efficient way to ensure that the operations of the federal government keep pace with the demands placed upon it. We suggest as a model the executive reorganization authority that began with the Reorganization Act of 1932 (5 USC 901 et seq.) and continued with its successor statutes through the middle decades of the 20th century.

We would assign the initiating role to the President. He would propose structural reorganizations or new management approaches that would contribute to the accomplishment of agency missions. In general, these proposals would take into account recommendations from the departments and agencies, from the President's policy and management advisers, and from Congress and its committees.

To take effect, these proposals would have to be approved by Congress. But such reorganization proposals would have two characteristics intended to ensure both their coherence and a timely congressional response. Specifically, we suggest that each proposal:

- Not be subject to amendment,
- Be given an up-or-down vote within 45 legislative days of submission.

With these characteristics, Congress could reject a reorganization proposal through a majority vote against approval in either chamber.

Recommendation 4. The House and Senate should realign their committee oversight to match the mission-driven reorganization of the executive branch.

Operating agencies desperately need the support of an active Congress if they are to perform effectively. At the same time, broad grants of administrative flexibility demand effective congressional oversight, transparency, and clear reporting relationships, which in turn require that congressional committees and subcommittees organize themselves around the same central missions as the departments of the executive branch.

A mismatch of missions reduces Congress's ability to provide broad effective oversight and can lead instead to micromanagement of those aspects of agency activities that happen to be most visible.

At critical junctures in its past—in 1911, in 1946, and in 1973—Congress has reorganized its committee jurisdictions to reflect changes in the country and in the executive branch. As the executive branch evolves in the new century, the organization of Congress must evolve as well.

Leadership for Government

Effective government leadership requires immediate changes in the entry process for top leaders and the long-term development of a highly skilled federal management corps.

No organization in this country is more dependent on qualified senior leadership than the federal government. Yet few organizations in our society have paid so little attention to leadership succession and leadership quality.

Senior leadership in federal agencies comes from two sources: political appointments by the President and the career ranks of the Senior Executive Service (SES). Today, both leadership sources are seriously flawed, and the awkward intersections of the two frequently compound these flaws. The challenge is to recruit the most talented individuals for service as presidential appointees and senior career managers and find a better approach to allocating positions and coordinating efforts between them.

Recommendation 5. The President and Congress should develop a cooperative approach to speeding and streamlining the presidential appointments process.

Repairing the presidential appointments process must be a high priority in any effort to strengthen public service leadership. Other commissions have recommended a number of thoughtful reforms of the appointments process, most notably a long-overdue streamlining of the myriad forms that political appointees must complete. And at the time of our work, there is legislation pending in Congress that would implement those changes. We endorse these efforts.

But more is needed to fix the presidential appointments process than legislation alone can provide. An attitude change is essential as well. The appointments process has become a political battleground. Presidents and senators are the principal warriors, but candidates for presidential appointment are the principal victims. We desperately

---

THE PRESIDENTIAL APPOINTEE PROBLEM

Contemporary presidents face two daunting difficulties in filling the top posts in their administrations: the number of appointments is very large, and the appointments process is very slow.

When President Kennedy came to office in 1960, he had 286 positions to fill in the ranks of Secretary, Deputy Secretary, Under Secretary, Assistant Secretary, and Administrator—the principal leadership positions in the executive branch. By the end of the Clinton administration, there were 914 positions with these titles. Overall in 2001, the new administration of President George W. Bush confronted a total of 3,361 offices to be filled by political appointment.

The time required to fill each of these positions has expanded exponentially in recent decades. (See graph.) In part, this results from the more thorough and professional recruitment procedures employed by recent administrations. But most of the elongation of the appointments process is the consequence of a steady accumulation of inquiries, investigations, and reviews aimed at avoiding political embarrassment. These include extensive vetting, lengthy interviews, background checks, examinations of government computer records, completion of questionnaires and forms composed of hundreds of questions, FBI full-field investigations, public financial disclosure, and conflicts of interest analysis. Much of the process is duplicated when a nomination goes to the Senate and is subjected to the confirmation process.

Potential appointees sometimes decline to enter government service when confronted by this process. Others drop out along the way. But the principal impact of the modern appointments process is the delay it imposes on the staffing of new administrations.

Average Time to Complete an Appointment, by Administration

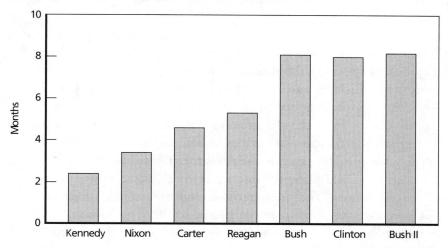

SOURCE: Calculated by The Presidential Appointee Initiative, Brookings Institution. Calculations reflect the average time elapsed between Inauguration day and Senate confirmation for initial appointees in each administration.
RAND *MG256-V-3*

need a mutual recognition on the part of Senate leaders and the President that they must change their approach to the appointments process.

We believe that both branches should work toward a compact that would assure expeditious treatment of appointments, disciplined constraints on attacks on appointees or improper delay of their appointments as ways to gain political leverage, and an enhanced emphasis at both ends of Pennsylvania Avenue on doing what is necessary to attract America's most talented and creative leaders to public service.

Recommendation 6. Congress and the President should work together to significantly reduce the number of executive branch political positions.

The first step in any effort to improve leadership in the public service must be a rationalization of the leadership structure of federal agencies and departments. Over the past half-century, the layers of political appointees and senior career managers have grown steadily, without regard to organizational needs or any sustained effort to tie structure to performance.

When a new administration takes office or a new agency head is appointed, it often seems too politically difficult, or the time horizon too short, to reshape the top ranks or to improve accountability. So more leadership posts are created to help agency heads and presidents work around old leadership posts they cannot control or remove. Compounded over the decades, this pattern has yielded a federal management structure that is top-heavy, cumbersome, and contrary to the goals of effective leadership and meaningful accountability.

Now we find ourselves in a situation that is deeply problematic on several counts. The presidential appointments process simply cannot keep up with the burden of filling all these positions with properly qualified leaders in a timely way. Political appointees may enter their jobs with too little trust in the competence and loyalty of career executives. Newly selected department and agency heads are often unable to keep control of their own subordinate appointments due to pressure from the White House, special interest groups, or determined members of Congress. Thus these department and agency heads are forced to lead disparate teams of strangers, some of whom owe little loyalty to the senior leadership. Talented and experienced senior career managers find themselves forced further and further away from the centers of decisionmaking, even as they create new management layers to compensate for pay freezes and the lack of opportunity for advancement created by an aging workforce.

No one benefits from this situation, and an essential first step toward improvement is a significant cut in the number of political executive positions. We believe that a reduction of at least one-third is an appropriate first target.

The number of political appointees grows with each succeeding administration. We recommend that the executive branch and Congress work together to selectively identify political positions that could be changed to career positions or that could be terminated altogether.

Recommendation 7. The Senior Executive Service should be divided into an Executive Management Corps and a Professional and Technical Corps.

Reducing the layers of executive management in government will require more from the executives who remain in the chain of command.

Unfortunately, the Senior Executive Service (SES), created in 1978, has never developed into the hoped-for corps of experienced managers that would move across agencies, deploying their skills and bringing the benefit of their experience to a broad array of management venues. Because the SES is the main route for senior employee advancement, many members of the SES are not managers at all but scientists, other professionals, and technical specialists. Few SES managers have ever worked, or applied to work, outside of the agency in which they are currently employed.

The original design also included a rewards and incentive system where compensation for senior managers would be closely tied to performance. Those who performed at the highest levels would get bonuses and merit awards equal to a substantial portion of their annual pay. But Congress has often failed to appropriate the funds necessary to fuel that reward system. In addition, by tying senior executive pay to its own pay, Congress has prevented senior executives from receiving the annual increase provided to most government workers. Although there are six levels on their pay scale, 70 percent of all SES members now earn the same compensation. So much for performance incentives.

We believe that dividing the Senior Executive Service into a corps of professional and technical specialists and another of highly talented executives and managers can address these problems, as set forth below:

First, the new Professional and Technical Corps (PTC) and Executive Management Corps (EMC) would draw their talent from government and also from the private and public nonprofit sectors as needed.

Second, agencies should be given maximum flexibility in assigning members of the EMC. Greater flexibility is important at all levels of government but is especially significant at the senior management levels where individual performance is more broadly significant. Mobility across agencies should characterize service in the EMC. We also believe the EMC should be structured around performance-based contracts for specific terms of service and that a significant portion of EMC compensation should be related to performance.

Third, the EMC should be separated from the PTC for purposes of recruiting, compensation, assignment, and effective utilization. In general, we believe that compensation for members of the EMC will be similar across the government, while compensation for technical and scientific specialists would vary much more in response to differences in individual labor markets.

Finally, and most important, greater attention must be paid to the development within the federal government of strong management talent. The quality and motivation of government managers determine whether policy decisions will be successfully implemented and whether government programs will run effectively.

Greater effort must be made to identify potential managerial talent early in employees' careers and to nurture it through adequately and consistently funded training, professional development, and subsidized opportunities for graduate education and work experience outside government. While we noted that there should be greater receptivity to lateral entry into these management ranks, the bulk of government managers in the future will and should come from the lower and middle ranks of government employees today.

The military services have long been more effective in this area, with great benefit to the quality of the senior officer corps. The pending deluge of managerial retirements in the civilian service would be far less ominous if the civilian agencies had been doing a better job of leadership succession, planning, and preparation.

Recommendation 8. Congress should undertake a critical examination of "ethics" regulations imposed on federal employees, modifying those with little demonstrated public benefit.

Over the past 40 years, Congress has enacted laws and presidents have issued executive orders that have produced a deeply layered and extraordinarily cumbersome regulatory scheme designed to ensure the integrity of federal employees. Every isolated scandal seems to produce new laws designed to prevent its recurrence.

We believe that the ethics regulations imposed on public servants have grown out of proportion to public need and to common sense. The system has become dysfunctional and must be reexamined.

It is now the case that more than 250,000 federal employees must make annual disclosure of the full details of their personal finances; for nearly 25,000 of them, the disclosure is public.

As noted above, every presidential appointee must navigate through endless forms and questionnaires probing into every detail of his or her life before entering public service. Thousands of federal employees spend their days investigating the behavior of other federal employees. Requirements that employees divest themselves of financial holdings sometimes go beyond what is rational and can result in unjustified financial loss to the employee.

> "Our study found that in the years from 1995 through 2000, 99.3% of all the public financial disclosure forms filed in those years were never viewed by anybody in the public."
>
> *G. Calvin Mackenzie, Visiting Fellow*
> *The Brookings Institution*

The "ethics" barriers create a climate of distrust that limits lateral entry of talent into government, which in turn creates a gulf of misunderstanding and suspicion that undermines government performance. Mission-related personnel interchanges would benefit those in government who work with the private sector and those in the private sector who work with government. At critical junctures in our past—during the two world wars, for example—such interchanges contributed vitally to the accomplishment of important government missions. But current ethics laws now prohibit virtually all such personnel movement.

We urge Congress to make federal ethics rules cleaner, simpler, and more directly linked to the goals they are intended to achieve. Specifically, we recommend that legislation be enacted to reduce the number of federal employees required annually to disclose their personal finances and that Congress enact legislation recommended by the Office of Government Ethics and currently pending in the U.S. Senate to simplify the personnel disclosure forms and other questionnaires for presidential appointees.

We urge Congress to seek a better balance between the legitimate need of the public for certain limited personal information about public servants, and the inherent rights of all Americans—even public servants—to protection from unjustified invasions of their privacy. Such a restriking of the balance, we firmly believe, will make public service much more attractive to the kinds of talented people government must recruit and retain in the years ahead.

Recommendation 9. Congress should grant an immediate and significant increase in judicial, executive, and legislative salaries to ensure a reasonable relationship to other professional opportunities.

Judicial salaries are the most egregious example of the failure of federal compensation policies. Federal judicial salaries have lost 24 percent of their purchasing power since 1969, which is arguably inconsistent with the Constitutional provision that judicial salaries may not be reduced by Congress. The United States currently pays its judges substantially less than England or Canada. Supreme Court Justice Stephen Breyer pointed out in testimony before the commission that, in 1969, the salaries of district court judges had just been raised to $40,000 while the salary of the dean of Harvard Law School was $33,000 and that of an average senior professor at the school was $28,000.

That relationship has now been erased. A recent study by the Administrative Office of the U.S. Courts of salaries of professors and

> "Inadequate compensation seriously compromises the judicial independence fostered by life tenure. The prospect that low salaries might force judges to return to the private sector rather than stay on the bench risks affecting judicial performance."
>
> *William H. Rehnquist, Chief Justice, U.S. Supreme Court*

deans at the twenty-five law schools ranked highest in the annual *U.S. News and World Report* survey found that the *average* salary for deans of those schools was $301,639. The average base salary for full professors at those law schools was $209,571, with summer research and teaching supplements typically ranging between $33,000 and $80,000. Federal district judges currently earn $150,000.[11]

Also in testimony before the commission, Chief Justice William Rehnquist noted that "according to the Administrative Office of the United States Courts, more than 70 Article III judges left the bench between 1990 and May 2002, either under the retirement statute, if eligible, or simply resigning if not, as did an additional number of bankruptcy and magistrate judges. During the 1960s on the other hand, only a handful of Article III judges retired or resigned."

The lag in judicial salaries has gone on too long, and the potential for diminished quality in American jurisprudence is now too large. Too many of America's best lawyers have declined judicial appointments. Too many senior judges have sought private sector employment—and compensation—rather than making the important contributions we have long received from judges in senior status.

Unless this is revised soon, the American people will pay a high price for the low salaries we impose on the men and women in whom we invest responsibility for the dispensation of justice. We are not suggesting that we should pay judges at levels comparable to those of the partners at our nation's most prestigious law firms. Most judges take special satisfaction in their work and in public service. The more reasonable comparisons are with the leading academic centers and not-for-profit institutions. But even those comparisons now indicate

---

[11] A confidential survey conducted by the Administrative Office of the U.S. Courts, September 2002.

a significant shortfall in real judicial compensation that requires immediate correction.

Executive compensation has reached a similar crisis. Today, in some departments and agencies, senior staff are paid at a higher level than their politically appointed superiors. We recognize that some appointees enter office with enough personal wealth to render salaries irrelevant, while others see great value in the prestige and future earning potential associated with high public office. Increasingly, more are dependent on the salary of an employed spouse. But the good fortune—or tolerance for sacrifice—of a few cannot justify the financial burdens that fall on the many.

Cabinet secretary pay rose 169 percent between 1969 and 2001. But in that same period, according to the Bureau of Labor Statistics, the Consumer Price Index for urban consumers increased 391 percent. Measured in constant 2001 dollars, the salaries of cabinet secretaries have actually declined 44 percent since 1969. During this thirty-two year period, the salaries of cabinet officers have lost more than 50 percent of their value with respect to the median family income.[12]

These declines in real compensation have real effects. Too many talented people shy away from public service because they have large mortgages to pay, children in college, or other financial obligations that cannot be met on current federal salaries. Too many others enter public service but stay too briefly for those same financial reasons.

It is difficult to generate public concern about the salaries of senior federal officials because those salaries are higher than the average compensation of workers nationwide. But the comparison is not apt. The talent and experience needed to run large and complex federal enterprises are not average. Eighty-seven percent of the people appointed by President George W. Bush in his first year in office had advanced degrees. Most had extensive experience in the management

---

[12] Gary Burtless, *How Much Is Enough? Setting Pay for Presidential Appointees*, a report of The Presidential Appointee Initiative, Washington, DC: The Brookings Institution, March 22, 2002.

Executive Pay Comparison

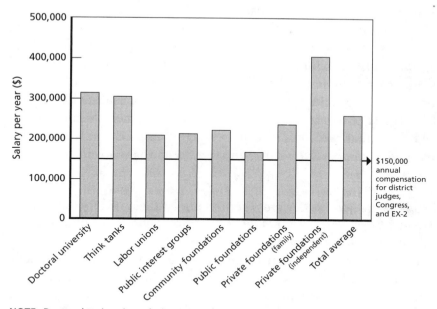

NOTE: Doctoral university salaries taken from "The Chronicle of Higher Education." Think tank salaries represent those with ≥$10M in assets, labor union salaries represent those with ≥$100M in assets, public interest groups represent those with ≥$10M in assets, community foundations represent those with ≥$250M, public foundations represent those with ≥$100M in assets, private foundations (family) represent those with ≥$250M in assets, private foundations (independent) represent those with ≥$1B in assets, and total average equals the average salary of an executive level officer from the above groups.

RAND MG256-V-4

of large organizations. Excellence in government performance requires excellent leadership. We must be willing to pay enough to bring such leaders into public service and to keep them there.

To restore fairness and improve the appeal of public service, we believe appointees' salaries must be raised. They need not equal the salaries of senior corporate executives or even approach those. But they should be on a par with the compensation of leaders in educational and not-for-profit organizations, or even with counterpart positions in state or local government. It is not unreasonable in our view that a secretary of state should be paid a salary that compares with a university president or that a secretary of education should earn what a superintendent of a large urban school district earns.

Legislative salaries have shown the same general decay as executive salaries. Few democracies in the world expect so much from their national legislators for so little in compensation. Indeed, salaries of members of Congress fall well below the compensation of the nation's top college and university presidents and the executive directors of its largest philanthropic foundations and charitable organizations. We believe that members of Congress merit a salary that is commensurate with comparable salaries in the educational and not-for-profit sectors.

Recommendation 10. Congress should break the statutory link between the salaries of members of Congress and those of judges and senior political appointees.

Congress has traditionally tied the salaries of senior executive branch employees and federal judges to its own. In 1989 the linkage was set in statute. Given the reluctance of members of Congress to risk the disapproval of their constituents, a phenomenon first seen in 1816, Congress has regularly permitted salaries to fall substantially behind cost-of-living increases and trends in private, educational, and not-for-profit compensation.

We are aware that recent research suggests that pay disparities at the middle and lower levels of the federal workforce may be less significant than previously believed. However, the "pay gap" at the top of the salary structure is indisputable, as are its consequences in lost morale and uncertain accountability. Its consequences are also clear in the presidential appointments process, which must increasingly focus on the relatively affluent or those for whom an appointment represents a dramatic increase in compensation, neither of which is appropriate in itself for public service.

We believe that members of Congress are entitled to reasonable and regular salary adjustments, but we fully understand the difficulty they face in justifying their own salary increases. They must answer to the voters when they make such choices, and most of the voters have annual incomes significantly lower than members of Congress. Whatever political difficulties they face in setting their own salaries, however, members of Congress must make the quality of the public service their paramount concern when they consider salary adjustments for top officials of the other branches of government. We believe that executive and judicial salaries must be determined by procedures that tie them to the needs of the government, not the career-related political exigencies of members of Congress.

> "Salaries do matter. If you keep cutting and cutting, you will find the institutional strength sapped. You will find it harder to attract and keep people. The reputation of the agency will fall. The public will become disenchanted. It will begin to distrust the organization. It will lose interest. As a result, morale within the organization falls."
>
> *Stephen G. Breyer, Associate Justice, U.S. Supreme Court*

Although members of Congress have the power to adjust their own salaries, judges and senior executives do not have such power. Under current law, they are at the mercy of Congress when it comes to salary adjustments. That mercy should not be strained by the inherent difficulty of congressional salary decisions. Salaries for leaders of the other branches should be based on the compelling need to recruit and retain the best people possible. Unlinking congressional salaries from theirs is an important first step in accomplishing that.

Operational Effectiveness in Government

The federal workforce must be reshaped, and the systems that support it must be rooted in new personnel management principles that ensure much higher levels of government performance.

As noted earlier, much of Title 5, the section of the U.S. Code that regulates the public service, was written at a time when government was composed largely of lower-level employees with relatively routine tasks that required few specialized or advanced skills. The principal purpose of much of the substance of Title 5 is to protect federal workers from political influence, from arbitrary personnel actions, and from unfair and inequitable treatment compared to other federal workers. Those are important protections to preserve. But they must coexist with a much broader recognition of the needs of modern agencies to perform missions that are more complex and much more specialized than those of the government for which much of Title 5 was written.

In recent years, Congress has begun to permit some exceptions to Title 5 constraints for agencies facing critical mission challenges or personnel needs.[13] We believe these experiments have demonstrated beyond a doubt that, in the performance of mission-related functions, agencies often benefit when they are liberated from Title 5 constraints. And we believe the results of those experiments should now be extended much more broadly across the government.

The simple fact is that many agencies would perform better if they had greater freedom to design personnel recruitment strategies and define conditions of service, more latitude to assemble competitive compensation packages and align compensation policies with performance criteria, expanded freedom to reorganize to meet emerging needs, and greater authority to use contracted outsourcing when that is the most efficient way to meet mission objectives.

We clearly recognize the risks in some of these new approaches, especially when they are deployed unevenly. In the development of the new Transportation Security Agency, for example, we have seen how greater management and compensation flexibility in one agency can cannibalize others that lack that flexibility. Federal employees act rationally; the best are drawn to environments where their opportunities to advance in their careers and their compensation are affected by their performance. When one agency follows that principle and another does not, employees will naturally be drawn away from the latter and toward the former. That is one reason why we believe it is time to treat these matters as governmentwide issues, not merely as

---

[13] Examples of new approaches to personnel management are given in Appendix A of this chapter.

stopgaps for agencies in distress, to move from experimentation and testing to broad implementation of ideas whose time has come.

Recommendation 11. More flexible personnel management systems should be developed by operating agencies to meet their special needs.

We recommend that the General Schedule classification system be abolished. As the U.S. Office of Personnel Management recently noted, "The resources and effort needed to maintain the General Schedule system—which include developing precisely defined locality pay areas and adjustments, establishing and administering special rates, developing and applying classification standards and day-to-day pay administration—are substantial. . . ."[14] A system like the General Schedule that emphasizes internal equity in compensation will always demand constant tinkering to define "equal work" so that it can ensure "equal pay."

Under the pressure for better performance, movement away from the General Schedule has already begun. Nearly 20 percent of nonpostal career federal employees now work under other personnel systems, many of which were enacted by Congress in response to the particular needs of high-impact agencies such as the Federal Aviation Administration and Internal Revenue Service. Again, the President's proposal for a new Department of Homeland Security illustrated the desire for a much greater degree of discretion over salaries, hiring, and disciplinary action.

> "Ultimately, an effective performance management system must link pay and incentive programs to individual knowledge, skills and ability, and contributions to achieving organizational results."
>
> *David Walker, Comptroller General, U.S. General Accounting Office*

As a default system, we recommend a "broadband" system under which the 15 pay grades and salary ranges would be consolidated into

---

[14] Office of Personnel Management, *A Fresh Start*, p. 46.

six to eight broad bands with relatively wide salary ranges. Managers would be able to determine individual pay based on competence and performance. Other agencies might adopt systems with an entirely different form. The goal of all agencies must be the same: a commitment to designing a personnel system that best supports its own mission. But that cannot happen until we have seen the last of the General Schedule. "Continued reliance on this antiquated system," notes Kay Coles James, Director of the Office of Personnel Management, "is comparable to insisting that today's offices use carbon paper and manual typewriters."[15]

Consistent with our other recommendations, we envision the development of modern personnel management approaches that afford agencies far more flexibility and responsiveness in packaging attractive job offers at the entry level, while fitting talent to task across the full spectrum of federal activity, permitting lateral movement within the government and between government and the private sector recognizing and rewarding performance.

Recommendation 12. Congress and the Office of Personnel Management should continue their efforts to simplify and accelerate the recruitment of federal employees.

Recruitment to federal jobs is heavily burdened by ancient and illogical procedures that vastly complicate the application process and limit the hiring flexibility of individual managers. A college graduate applying for a federal job confronts a complex and lengthy application form demanding far more information than any employer reasonably needs. The very nature of the application deters applicants.

College campuses should be prime recruiting sites for federal agencies. Recently OPM and individual agencies have initiated programs to compete for talented graduating men and women, but as the personal anecdotes in Appendix A indicate, government must do more and do it better.

---

[15] Kay Coles James, testimony before the National Commission on the Public Service, July 15, 2002.

PROMISING APPROACHES TO PERSONNEL REFORM

Voinovich / Akaka Personnel Policy Reforms

The following personnel reforms were proposed by Senator George V. Voinovich and Senator Daniel K. Akaka and included in the Homeland Security Act.

1. Establishes a Chief Human Capital Office at each major agency to oversee recruitment, retention, and training efforts and raise the profile of human capital needs within agencies.

2. Establishes an interagency council of Chief Human Capital Officers to exchange best practices.

3. Gives agencies the choice of placing job applicants in categories, such as basically qualified, highly qualified, and superior, rather than being limited to considering only the top three applicants.

4. Allows agencies to offer up to $25,000 in buyouts and use early retirement packages in the executive and judicial branches to reshape workforces to correct skills imbalances.

5. Expands the ability of agencies to pay for job-related training, including studies leading to an academic degree.

6. With certain preconditions, allows senior managers to receive their full performance bonus in a single year, rather than having to spread it over two years.

7. Requires that human capital planning activities be included in annual agency performance and management reports mandated by the Government Performance and Results Act.

8. Allows agencies to hire candidates directly and bypass current Title 5 requirements once OPM has determined that there is a severe shortage of candidates for the position.

9. Eases restrictions on the placement of National Security Education Program (NSEP) participants by allowing fellows to meet their service requirement by working in non-national security positions in the federal government, if national security positions are not available.

10. Repeals ineffective recertification requirements for Senior Executives.

11. Provides federal employees compensatory time off for official travel.

SOURCE: These provisions were included in an amendment to H.R. 5005, to establish a Department of Homeland Security, when it was ordered reported to the full Senate by the Senate Governmental Affairs Committee. Senator Daniel K. Akaka (D-Hawaii) was Chairman of the Subcommittee on International Security, Proliferation and Federal Services of the Senate Governmental Affairs Committee. Senator George V. Voinovich (R-Ohio) was Ranking Member of the Senate Governmental Affairs Subcommittee on Oversight of Government Management, Restructuring and the District of Columbia.

PROMISING APPROACHES TO PERSONNEL REFORM

Office of Personnel Management Initiatives to Modernize Federal Personnel Practices

OPM manages governmentwide the Human Capital Initiative of the President's Management Agenda.

1. Held government's first "virtual job fair" in April 2002, which drew more than 20,000 applications for 270 available jobs.

2. Enhanced the USAJOBS website to make the system more user-friendly and helpful for those seeking jobs in the federal government.

3. Instituted a multipronged approach to utilizing e-government technology to assist job seekers and employees governmentwide. Components include the improved USAJOBS website, e-Clearance, e-Training, Enterprise HR Integration, and e-Payroll.

4. Provided agency customers with tools and advice to help recruit, hire, and retain quality employees; train and develop workforces; and manage performance.

5. Initiated a project to assist agencies in identifying and utilizing personnel flexibility provided in current law.

6. Initiated an interagency project to modernize federal job vacancy announcements. Over 350 colleges were enlisted to participate in a national "Call to Serve."

7. Undertook a major review and critique of the federal pay structure, preparatory to formulating recommendations for modernization.

SOURCE: Kay Coles James, Testimony before the National Commission on the Public Service, July 2002.

Agencies have been burdened for decades by the "rule of three," which required agencies to hire only from among the top three candidates, chosen through a rigid scoring system. Only in November 2002, with the enactment of the Homeland Security Act, was this counterproductive process reformed. Now agencies governmentwide will be allowed to establish broader categories of applicants from which to choose the individual who will best fulfill the needs of the job.

We note that the government recruits most effectively when it recruits most specifically. And it appeals most to talented applicants when it recruits for clear and compelling missions. What sells in the employment marketplace is the appeal of a specific job to perform specific tasks for specific rewards. Bright young people will be more interested in microbiological investigation of a particular disease, managing foreign aid for a particular part of the world, or bringing work to unemployed single mothers than to "working for the federal government." We believe that Congress should provide the funds necessary for agencies to compete effectively for the employees they need.

Recommendation 13. Congress should establish policies that permit agencies to set compensation related to current market comparisons.

Proper adjustment of public service compensation is a conundrum as old as the Republic. Broad satisfaction with the way compensation decisions are made has always been elusive. But rarely has the compensation system been as misaligned as it is now. As noted earlier, recent research suggests that the pay gap between federal employees and their private sector peers is not consistent across all pay levels and all occupations. However, the pay gap in hard-to-recruit positions, from engineering to acquisitions, remains a significant barrier to recruitment and retention.

Repairing the system requires a reconsideration of first principles. That will require firm establishment of the notion that markets must play a larger role in setting compensation. Individual agencies need greater freedom to determine the relevant market for their employees, to adjust their compensation to its exigencies, and to connect pay to performance.

> "So we must decide: Are we going to continue to respond to the pay crisis agency by agency, occupation by occupation, running from one fire to another, or are we going to provide an overall structure within which we can provide the compensation necessary to attract and retain the talented experience we need?"
>
> *Carol Bonosaro, President, Senior Executives Association*

In fact, we have already begun to move in that direction. A number of agencies have been granted critical compensation flexibility in recent years to allow them to hire and retain employees in the face of demanding market conditions. In each case where those flexibilities have been granted, the recruitment and retention crises have been brought under control and the long-term personnel management prospects for the agency have brightened considerably.

We believe those have been valuable lessons and should be extended throughout the government. The goal of internal equity, which has dominated federal compensation practices for more than a century, still has a place in some aspects of the personnel process. But it must be balanced more thoughtfully now with the external equity that is increasingly important to many agencies seeking to hire or retain employees with rare or unusually valuable skills in highly competitive markets. As noted earlier, any system adopted must be grounded in long held merit system principles.

What are the relevant markets for most federal employees? The commission does not believe that the federal government needs to match salaries of corporate managers in most instances to ensure a quality workforce. The proper marketplace comparisons will more often be with the independent sector: with universities, think tanks, and nonprofits rather than with business corporations. As one of our witnesses suggested, the federal government should be able to compete with the dot-edus and the dot-orgs, but not with the dot-coms.

> "The public sector should mirror those organizations in the private sector who appreciate that the most valuable organizational asset is the workforce itself and who recognize that you get what you pay for."
>
> *Darryl Perkinson, President, Federal Managers Association,*
> *Mid-Atlantic Region*

Ceilings imposed by Congress for many years have created tight compression of salaries at the top of all three branches of government. Currently, approximately 70 percent of the Senior Executive Service receive exactly the same compensation due to compression. This is deeply discouraging to the government's most talented civil servants, and as Carol Bonosaro, the President of the Senior Executives Association, testified, many of them "plan to retire as soon as they're eligible because they are demoralized by the failure to address pay, and they can't resist attractive offers from private industry."

Recommendation 14. Competitive outsourcing should follow clear preset standards and goals that advance the public interest and do not undermine core competencies of the government.
The issue of who does the work of government has become a leading source of labor-management conflict. Recent years witnessed increased interest in allowing private firms to compete for work currently being done by federal employees. Competitive outsourcing may be needed, for example, to acquire additional skills, to augment capacity on an emergency or temporary basis, and to save money on goods and services that are not inherently governmental.

Whether it is called competitive sourcing, strategic sourcing, outsourcing, contracting out, or privatization, the general hope is that private competition can bring both cost savings and higher performance in certain functions such as information technology services or facilities maintenance. While we see many virtues in the competition that outsourcing can bring, we are also concerned that when competitive sourcing is perceived as unfair or for the purpose of reducing the government workforce, it breeds mistrust and undermines employee morale.

Whether work is performed by government or contracted to the private sector, it should be overseen with high performance and transparency standards.

Interim Steps Toward Implementation

We recognize that these recommendations are sweeping in scope and cannot all be implemented at one time. Some will require planning and study prior to presidential and congressional action. Implementation of the broad reorganization activity in this report will not be the work of months or a single session of Congress; it should be an agenda for years.

There are, however, steps that can and should be taken promptly and which will create the momentum necessary for a longer period of needed reform.

1. The President should be given expedited authority to recommend structural reorganization of federal agencies and departments.
2. The President and Congress should develop a cooperative approach to speeding and streamlining the presidential appointments process.
3. Congress should grant an immediate and significant increase in judicial, executive, and legislative salaries to ensure a reasonable relationship with other professional opportunities. Its first priority in doing so should be an immediate and substantial increase in judicial salaries.
4. Congress, the Office of Personnel Management, and individual agencies should continue their efforts to simplify and modernize the recruitment of federal employees.

Proposals to accomplish these four interim recommendations have been considered by both the Executive branch and Congress during recent legislative sessions. We believe that quick action on these proposals is possible and will demonstrate the value of further progress on our other recommendations.

Lastly, planning and specific decisions with respect to large department and agency reorganizations will logically fall within the competence of OMB and OPM. This development process will take a concerted ongoing effort and involve Congress, affected agencies, and the public. The sense of this commission is that the Administration and the Congress might tap the resources and expertise of nongovernmental public service organizations for assistance and support. Several such organizations assisted the commission and are cited herein. We recommend that a continuing advisory board drawn from these groups be established forthwith to assist in this process and to encourage continuing reform.

Conclusion

America begins the 21st century with a national government that is ill suited to the critically important challenges that confront us. We have already seen how structural and personnel deficiencies have left our intelligence and security operations vulnerable to devastating attack. In many other areas of government responsibility—health care, environmental protection, Social Security—our capacities are similarly threatened. Across the government, in one functional area after another, we find the same persistent problems: organizational structures and personnel policies that are inconsistent with and thwart important public missions.

We must recognize the magnitude of those problems and move boldly to fix them.

We have sought in this report to point the way to a modern, revitalized federal government. The government we envision, the government America so clearly needs, would look like this: Federal operations would be organized within fewer departments with lean, senior management levels, composed of operating agencies sharing similar substantive responsibilities. Government leaders would have the necessary flexibility to shape their organizations and management processes to fit the substantive tasks assigned to them. Federal personnel policies would be designed to attract and retain energetic and creative employees, to permit their talents to flourish, to be free of the drag of poor performers, and to imbue federal employees with pride in their service to the public.

The government we envision would be organized around critical missions, with management keyed to performance. It would be a dynamic government, prepared to meet the multifaceted and evolving needs of a complex modern society. Federal employment would appeal to highly competent people because it would encourage and reward their best efforts. This would not be a bigger government, but it would be a better government.

We do not underestimate the scope and challenge of this task, but neither are we daunted by it. Reorganizing a government as large and old as ours and redesigning personnel polices so deeply ingrained will take time and the steady commitment of our national leaders. It is task for all of us—for the President, for Congress, for members of all political parties, for private citizens everywhere who understand that only a government that is very good is good enough.

The need could not be more urgent. We pay a high price every day we fail to act. That price grows with each passing year, as expectations of government exceed government capacity. Our country grows steadily in population and diversity. Escalating demands are placed on limited resources. The biggest generation in American history approaches retirement with longer life expectancies than ever before in human history.

The world beyond our shores now confronts us with unprecedented opportunities and grave danger. We cannot wait until the price of delay is one we cannot survive.

We recognize that we may not have all the answers, or all the ideal ones, but we are convinced that our nation can wait no longer. Fundamental change must become a high priority for the President and Congress. Encouraging and supporting that change must become a high priority for American citizens.

This is a vital responsibility for all of us. It deserves our most urgent and profound commitment.

APPENDIX A

The Government at Work

Examples of Jurisdictional Chaos

The federal government is a flotilla of many distinct organizational units. Virtually every year new vessels are added to respond to the demands of the time. Occasionally, in response to a broadly perceived national emergency, the vessels are regrouped. The Department of Homeland Security is a case in point, as was the Department of Energy when it was created in the late 1970s. Virtually never are they combined to eliminate program duplication.

Missions are not realigned or even rationalized. Program laps upon program. Responsibilities are not coordinated.

Moreover, while for most of its history our government has grown and evolved on an issue-by-issue and "need to" basis, the Hoover Commission of 1949 stands—fifty-three years later—as the sole serious effort to keep the parts from undermining the mission of the whole.

These phenomena have resulted in a virtually unmanageable tangle of government activities. In those areas where there is a clear and readily definable program goal, such as getting benefit checks out, the work gets done, albeit with varying degrees of efficiency and often with considerable waste of personnel and program funds. In all too many cases, however, one program's goals are intertwined with those of similar programs. Cross-program communication and coordination rarely takes place. Programs that no longer serve a good purpose—or which are inferior in impact to others with similar goals—continue on, never to be merged with those that are doing a viable job.

Examples of this phenomenon and its impact on the government's ability to accomplish its responsibilities are legion. Just a few of them are highlighted below.

OVERLAP AND DUPLICATION IN FEDERAL PROGRAMS

- Prior to the post 9/11 reorganizations, over 40 federal agencies were involved in activities to combat terrorism.

- The Department of Housing and Urban Development operates 23 self-sufficiency and economic opportunity programs that target tenants of public housing and other low-income clients.

- Responsibility for federal drug control strategies and their implementation is fragmented among more than 50 federal agencies.

- There are over 90 early childhood programs scattered among 11 federal agencies and 20 offices. Nine federal agencies administer 69 programs supporting education and care for children under age five.

- There are 342 federal economic development-related programs administered by 13 of the 14 cabinet departments.

- Seven agencies administer 40 different programs that have job training as their main purpose. At least 86 teacher-training programs in nine federal agencies fund similar types of services.

- Four agencies are responsible for federal land management.

- Over 200 different programs operated by 23 agencies have provided assistance to countries formerly part of the Soviet Union.

- There are 50 homeless assistance programs administered by eight agencies.

SOURCE: Senator Fred Thompson, Chairman, Committee on Governmental Affairs, "Government at the Brink," June 2001.

Obviously, this situation has a negative impact on program performance. For example, there are over 90 early childhood programs in 11 federal agencies and 20 offices. The system of multiple early childhood programs with firm cutoffs could lead to disruptions in services from even slight changes in a child's family status. While multiple programs target disadvantaged preschool children, most such children do not participate in any preschool program.[16]

Of even more critical concern is the September 19, 2002, report of the Joint Inquiry Committee of the Congressional Intelligence Committees examining the September 11, 2001, terrorist attacks on the United States. A major conclusion of the investigators was that a failure of communication and coordination within and among our intelligence agencies had greatly hampered their ability to assess the danger posed by al-Qaeda terrorists.

In a recent effort to address the performance problems created by dysfunctional organization, the Inspector General of the Environmental Protection Agency undertook a study to examine the degree to which other agencies share EPA's responsibilities for protecting our environment. In September 2002, the IG issued a report documenting that 29 agencies collectively share responsibility for federal clean air, clean and safe water, and better waste management programs. As the chart on the next page illustrates, these divided responsibilities have produced 541 separate areas of program activity. Given that most federal efforts to protect and improve the environment are regulatory in nature, the opportunity for duplicative or counterproductive regulatory requirements is significant. Finally, the IG's report notes that EPA's budget of over $7 billion is only 18 percent of federal spending on environmental and natural resource programs and that, "therefore, the achievement of EPA's broad goals cannot be accomplished without the coordinated and collaborative efforts of many federal partners."

Case Examples of Entry-Level Hiring in the Civil Service
Three applicants, all with graduate degrees, describe the federal application process.

---

[16] General Accounting Office, *Management Reform: Continuing Attention Is Needed to Improve Government Performance*, May 4, 2000.

General Statements

"In almost all of the cases [of applying for a federal job], I found the process to be frustrating, time-consuming, and, even on some level, bewildering."

Shared Federal Responsibility for Environmental Protection

Federal Departments and Agencies	Participation (No. of Programs/Activities Identified)			
	Air	Water	Waste	Totals
Department of Agriculture	16	73	6	95
Department of Interior	9	68	12	89
Department of Transportation	36	12	14	62
Department of Commerce	13	33	6	52
Department of Defense	7	21	18	46
Department of Energy	22	5	16	43
Department of Health and Human Services	14	14	12	40
Tennessee Valley Authority	19	8	0	27
Department of Justice	0	1	15	16
National Aeronautics and Space Administration	9	2	1	12
National Science Foundation	3	3	1	7
Federal Emergency Management Agency	0	0	6	6
Office of Science and Technology Policy	5	0	0	5
Department of Treasury	0	0	5	5
Housing and Urban Development	1	3	1	5
State Department	1	0	4	5
Postal Service	0	4	0	4
Nuclear Regulatory Commission	0	1	2	3
National Academy of Sciences	2	1	0	3
Small Business Administration	0	2	1	3
General Services Administration	0	2	1	3
Department of Labor	1	0	1	2
Agency for International Development	0	2	0	2
Federal Housing Finance Board	0	0	1	1
Veterans Affairs	0	0	1	1
Joint Subcommittee on Aquaculture	0	1	0	1
North American Research Strategy for Tropospheric Ozone	1	0	0	1
International Boundary and Water Commission	0	1	0	1
Endocrine Disruptor Screening and Testing Advisory Committee	0	1	0	1

SOURCE: President's Council on Integrity and Efficiency, Compendium of Federal Environmental Programs, September 2002.

"It seems to me, the more one tries to get in [to the federal service], the more barriers that are put up to prevent it. It almost seems like a test—how much is a person willing to go through to get this job?"

"With the time it takes to even apply and then play the wait and see game, is it any wonder so many people don't even consider applying to the federal government for work?"

"Just thinking about writing separate essays on every KSA (knowledge, skills, and abilities) question for each application to the federal government, knowing that I probably will never hear back about my application, makes me rethink my desire to serve in the federal service."

Federal Recruiting Efforts

"I understand that it might not always be possible to interview interested applicants on the spot, but what is the point of going to a career fair if all an agency is going to do is refer people to their website?"

"Conversely, the private organizations I met with took my resume, did some quick Q & A, and passed the information along to their HR department, who in turn called me within a week."

"I studied at a state university for a BS and then attended a private university for graduate school to obtain an MPA, and it still amazes me that I never saw recruitment efforts by the federal government other than their presence at career fairs where potential applicants were referred to their website."

Federal Application Process

"Trying to circumvent the lengthy and overwhelming federal application process, I applied and was nominated to be a Presidential Management Intern from the graduate school I attended (only 10 percent of the graduating MPA/MPP class can be nominated). Unfortunately, after going to an all-day test provided by OPM, I was notified that I had not passed, and only 400 postgraduate students from across the country are accepted into the program. With numerous reports stating that our country is facing a looming retirement bulge, shouldn't the number of PMI invitees be a little larger? The PMI program may be a good initiative to bring new and fresh talent into federal service, but a mere 400 people countrywide isn't enough to solve the federal government's problems."

"In almost all of the [federal] jobs I have applied for, it has been necessary to fill out separate lengthy applications, background information, and other materials. This process is very time-consuming and often requires gathering a plethora of information, which by itself can be very frustrating. However, this combined with the general inertia of paperwork moving through the system is enough to make anyone forgo an attempt at working for the government."

Trying to apply for two separate job announcements at the Application to Defense Finance and Accounting Service–Designated Examining Unit (DFAS-DEU): "Now I don't know about the rest of the applicants, but if Monster.com, Hotjobs.com, and USAJOBS. com can allow one to save and edit resumes, I would think it would be possible for the DFAS-DEU to allow the same for its applicants."

"This [having to reinput resume information for each specific job announcement] is just another 'barrier to entry' into the federal civil service that needs to be taken down."

"A very frustrating problem is the fact that most of the professional-level positions listed there [USAJOBS.com] do not have a link where someone can send their electronic resume stored on the website. What is the point of having applicants create the online resume if it is never going to be used?"

"There are jobs, with the U.S. Border Patrol and FEMA [Federal Emergency Management Agency], that I started the application process for over a year ago and have been told to expect to wait even longer. In other cases, I have never heard from some agencies that I applied to or, after contacting someone there to follow up, have never had my phone calls returned."

Written statement after applying for a budget officer position in Anniston, Alabama: "I was told by the human resources person I spoke with that there were in excess of 300 applicants for this one position and some 55 phrases that the selecting official required the automated system to key on. This is ridiculous. Those 55 phrases (requirements, to me) weren't even known to the applicants. . . . If you don't know exactly what they [human resource personnel] are looking for, how can you compete with someone who may already have that information? It does appear pretty ludicrous to me."

Results

"In my case, I have become fed up with the process and have decided to pursue opportunities in the private sector."

"If the process is not streamlined, government agencies will continue to be unable to attract talented individuals to careers in public service."

"I'm seriously considering giving up [applying for a federal job] altogether. There are simply too many barriers to overcome. . . ."

Federal Employee Appeal Process[17]
Appellate Bodies

Merit Systems Protection Board (MSPB). Responsible for appeals from major disciplinary actions and other adverse actions. (Bargaining unit employees may appeal these actions through a negotiated grievance procedure with binding arbitration.)

Office of Special Counsel (OSC). Investigates "prohibited personnel practices," e.g., denying employment for political reasons and nepotism, Hatch Act violations, and whistle-blower complaints.

Federal Labor Relations Authority (FLRA). Broad authority for federal labor-management relations program, including adjudicating disputes between agencies and unions with exclusive bargaining rights, resolving appeals of arbitration awards, investigating and prosecuting unfair labor practice charges, and resolving negotiation impasses.

Office of Personnel Management (OPM). Authority to review position classification decisions.

Equal Employment Opportunity Commission (EEOC). Authority to adjudicate federal employee complaints of discrimination.

---

[17] United States General Accounting Office, *Federal Employee Redress: A System in Need of Reform*, April 1996.

Today, executive branch civil servants are afforded opportunities for redress at three levels: first, within their employing agencies; next, at one or more of the central adjudicatory agencies; and finally, in the federal courts. Although one of the purposes of the Civil Service Reform Act of 1978 was to streamline the previous redress system, the scheme that has emerged is far from simple. Today, four independent agencies hear employee complaints or appeals. The Merit Systems Protection Board (MSPB) hears employee appeals of firings or suspensions of more than 14 days, as well as other significant personnel actions. The Equal Employment Opportunity Commission (EEOC) hears employee discrimination complaints and reviews agencies' final decisions on complaints. The Office of Special Counsel (OSC) investigates employee complaints of prohibited personnel actions—in particular, retaliation for whistle-blowing. For employees who belong to collective bargaining units and have their individual grievances arbitrated, the Federal Labor Relations Authority (FLRA) reviews the arbitrators' decisions.

While the boundaries of the appellate agencies may appear to be neatly drawn, in practice these agencies form a tangled scheme. One reason is that a given case may be brought before more than one of the agencies—a circumstance that adds time-consuming steps to the redress process and may result in the adjudicatory agencies reviewing each other's decisions. Matters are further complicated by the fact that each of the adjudicatory agencies has its own procedures and its own body of case law. All but OSC offer federal employees the opportunity for hearings, but all vary in the degree to which they can require the participation of witnesses or the production of evidence. They also vary in their authority to order corrective actions and enforce their decisions.

What's more, the law provides for further review of these agencies' decisions—or, in the case of discrimination claims, even de novo trials—in the federal courts. Beginning in the employing agency, proceeding through one or more of the adjudicatory bodies, and then carried to conclusion in court, a single case can take years.

New Approaches to Personnel Management

OPM. Numerous demonstration projects, approved by OPM, have succeeded in allowing agencies flexibility in hiring during difficult market conditions. The first personnel demonstration project after completion of the Civil Service Reform Act of 1978 was the Department of the Navy's "China Lake" demonstration project. Here the Navy established performance-based pay systems, increased flexibility in starting salaries, and broad-banded pay structures for 10,000 employees. OPM's review of the China Lake project found significant improvement in recruitment and retention of high performers because of the Navy's ability to meet market challenges for personnel.

NIST. In 1988 the National Institute of Standards and Technology started a demonstration project broadly aimed at recruiting high-quality personnel and retaining good performers. Through greater flexibility in hiring, the NIST gained freedom to adjust starting salaries, encouraging more talented applicants. NIST also found that changing its pay system from narrow classifications to broader pay bands enabled it to retain a higher number of good performers.

Department of Agriculture. The Forest Service and the Agricultural Research Service used a demonstration program to streamline hiring by eliminating the "rule of three" and hiring from broader groups of applicants. After five years, the number of applicants had grown, hiring speed increased, and there was more satisfaction with the hiring process among applicants.

GSA. Stephen A. Perry, Administrator, United States General Services Administration, advocates the use of existing workplace flexibility by posting the authorities on the agency's Intranet. This provides managers with the information they need to determine where and when the use of these authorities is appropriate. A variety of flexible alternative work schedules and workplace arrangements is available in two categories: compressed work schedules and flexible work schedules. An example of compressed work schedule flexibility is the ability of an associate to work 80 hours within nine or eight workdays instead of the traditional 10 days. With flexible work schedules, managers may offer associates various arrival and departure times.

IRS. The IRS Restructuring and Reform Act of 1998 mandated a comprehensive, customer-based reorganization of the IRS. The act allowed for numerous human resource flexibilities, with OPM oversight, to help implement the revised organizational structure and to promote new approaches to compensation and staffing. Provisions were included to allow hiring at "critical pay" levels (i.e., up to the salary of the Vice President) so that the agency could attract key executives from outside government into critical leadership positions. The act also gave the IRS the authority to redesign its hiring mechanisms for technical employees, which they used to create a ranking system based on categories of employees rather than the "rule of three." Using the flexibilities in the act, IRS established new career paths for employees who wanted to move up in rank but not enter management, redesigned its performance management system, created a broad-banded pay system for senior managers, and used its authority to reshape its workforce during the reorganization.

FAA. The FAA introduced a new agency human resource management system in April 1996 after it was authorized by the 1996 Department of Transportation Appropriations Act. The reforms were developed to meet the unique human resource needs of the FAA and provide greater flexibility for hiring, training, compensating, and deploying personnel. The 1996 legislation exempted the agency's personnel system from Title 5 of the United States Code, except those parts which provide preference for veterans, protect whistle-blowers, require employees to be loyal to the government, prohibit strikes, restrict certain political activities, and prohibit discrimination. The FAA chose to follow certain other parts of Title 5, including those that covered merit principles and prohibited personnel practices. All FAA employees were covered by pay-for-performance and pay-band provisions. Air traffic control regulations also allow for collective bargaining for pay for controllers.

GAO. Significant reforms were allowed legislatively for the General Accounting Office. In the mid-1980s, legislation was enacted to allow GAO to institute pay bands, thus allowing more flexible staffing. Later, additional legislative and administrative flexibility allowed improvements in the areas of recruitment, training, promotions, bonuses, and dealing with poor performers. Additional flexibility that Congress granted GAO in 2000 allowed early-outs and buyouts to be used for workforce reshaping. The changes allowed GAO to increase the number of reports and testimonies each year and improved the quality of GAO products.

The National Commission on the Public Service

Chairman

Paul A. Volcker

Paul Volcker served in the federal government for almost thirty years during five presidential administrations. Appointed as Chairman of the Board of Governors of the Federal Reserve System by President Jimmy Carter in 1979, he was re-appointed by President Ronald Reagan in 1983. After leaving the Federal Reserve in 1987, he became Professor of International Economic Policy (now emeritus) at Princeton University and served as Chairman of the firm of James D. Wolfensohn & Co. until his retirement in 1996. He currently works with a number of institutions concerned with both domestic and international affairs. As Chairman of the first National Commission on the Public Service ("The Volcker Commission") in 1988, he established himself as one of the nation's strongest advocates for the revitalization of the public service.

Members

Charles Bowsher

Appointed Comptroller General of the United States by President Ronald Reagan in 1981, Charles Bowsher led the General Accounting Office (GAO) for fifteen years. For the 25 years prior to his appointment, he was associated with Arthur Andersen & Co., except for a four-year period between 1967 and 1971 when he served as Assistant Secretary of the Navy for Financial Management. He currently serves on a number of corporate boards.

Bill Bradley

Bill Bradley represented New Jersey in the United States Senate from 1979 to 1997. Senator Bradley held seats on the Finance Committee and the Energy and Natural Resources Committee and also served on the Special Committee on Aging and the Select Committee on Intelligence. He was a key leader in the development and passage of the 1986 Tax Reform Act. A Democratic candidate for President in 2000, Senator Bradley is a former Chairman of the National Civic League and is currently a managing director of Allen & Co., Inc.

Frank C. Carlucci

Frank C. Carlucci served as Secretary of Defense under President Ronald Reagan from November 1987 to January 1989, during which time he oversaw the Defense Secretary's Commission on Base Realignment and Closure. Secretary Carlucci also served as Assistant to the President for National Security Affairs under President Reagan. Currently Chairman of the Carlyle Group, Secretary Carlucci has amassed more than 25 years of government service within the Departments of Defense and of Health, Education and Welfare; the Central Intelligence Agency; the Office of Management and Budget; and the Foreign Service.

Kenneth M. Duberstein

Kenneth M. Duberstein served as President Reagan's Chief of Staff in 1988 and 1989, following his previous service as Deputy Chief of Staff and in other senior positions in the Reagan Administration. He serves on the boards of several corporate and nonprofit organizations, including the Boeing Company, Fannie Mae, Kennedy Center for the Performing Arts Vice Chairman, the Council on Foreign Relations, the Brookings Institution, and others. He is currently Chairman and Chief Executive Officer of the Duberstein Group.

Constance Horner

Constance Horner served as Assistant to the President and Director of Presidential Personnel for President George H. W. Bush. During the Reagan Administration, she headed the Office of Personnel Management, which oversees the federal civilian workforce. Her government experience also includes service as Deputy Secretary of the Department of Health and Human Services and Associate Director of the Office of Management and Budget. She is currently a Guest Scholar in Governance Studies at the Brookings Institution and serves on several foundation and corporate boards of directors.

Franklin D. Raines

From 1996 to 1998, Franklin D. Raines served as the Director of the Office of Management and Budget for President Bill Clinton. He previously served as Assistant Director of the Domestic Policy staff and Associate Director of OMB in the Carter Administration. Prior to joining Fannie Mae in 1991 he was a general partner with Lazard Freres & Co. He is currently Chairman and Chief Executive Officer of Fannie Mae and serves on several corporate boards.

Richard Ravitch

Richard Ravitch is the Co-Chair of the bipartisan Millennial Housing Commission, a congressionally charted organization examining the status of affordable housing in the United States. He was appointed to the United States Commission on Urban Problems by President Lyndon Johnson in 1966. In 1975 he became Chairman of the nearly bankrupt New York State Urban Development Corporation at the request of Governor Hugh Carey. After restoring the corporation to solvency, Ravitch served as Chair of the New York Metropolitan Transportation Authority for five years. He is currently a principal in Ravitch, Rice & Co.

Robert E. Rubin

Robert E. Rubin served as the 70th Secretary of the United States Treasury from January 1995 to July 1999. Prior to joining the Treasury, Secretary Rubin served as Assistant to the President for Economic Policy in the Clinton Administration and directed the National Economic Council. Before he joined the Clinton Administration, Secretary Rubin served as Co-Chairman of Goldman Sachs & Co. Secretary Rubin is currently Chairman of the Executive Committee and Member of the Office of Chairman of Citigroup.

Donna E. Shalala

Donna E. Shalala served as Secretary of Health and Human Services in the Clinton Administration from 1993 to 2001. Prior to joining the Clinton Administration, Secretary Shalala served as Chancellor of the University of Wisconsin-Madison. She has taught political science at Columbia, the City University of New York, and the University of Wisconsin-Madison. In the Carter Administration, she served as Assistant Secretary for Policy Development and Research, U.S. Department of Housing and Urban Development. She is currently a Professor of Political Science and the President of the University of Miami. Secretary Shalala was a Commissioner on the first National Commission on the Public Service.

Vin Weber

Vin Weber represented Minnesota's Second Congressional District in the United States House of Representatives from 1980 to 1992. During that time, Representative Weber was a member of the Appropriations Committee and an elected member of the House Republican leadership. Representative Weber is a Co-Director of Empower America, Chairman of the National Endowment for Democracy, and a Senior Fellow at the Humphrey Institute of Public Affairs at the University of Minnesota. Representative Weber is also a managing partner of Clark & Weinstock.

Ex-Officio Members

Bruce Laingen

Bruce Laingen served as the Executive Director of the first National Commission on the Public Service. He was a member of the U.S.

Foreign Service from 1949 to 1987. Laingen served as U.S. Ambassador to Malta from 1977 to 1979 and as chargé d'affaires of the American embassy in Iran in 1979. Ambassador Laingen is currently the President of the American Academy of Diplomacy and serves on the boards of the Presidential Classroom for Young Americans and the National Defense University Foundation.

Strobe Talbott

Strobe Talbott assumed the presidency of the Brookings Institution in July 2002 after a career in journalism, government, and academe. His immediate previous post was Founding Director of the Yale School for the Study of Globalization. Talbott served in the State Department from 1993 to 2001, first as Ambassador-at-Large and Special Adviser to the Secretary of State for the new independent states of the former Soviet Union, then as Deputy Secretary of State for seven years. Talbott entered government after twenty-one years with *Time* magazine.

Executive Director

Hannah S. Sistare

Hannah S. Sistare was Staff Director and Counsel to the U.S. Senate Governmental Affairs Committee for U.S. Senator Fred Thompson from 1995 to 2002. She has held positions within the Departments of Health and Human Services and Labor and has taught at George Washington University and American University. She served as Chief of Staff to Senator Charles H. Percy and as Chief Legislative Assistant to former Senate Republican Leader Hugh Scott. She is a Visiting Fellow at the Brookings Institution.

Senior Advisors

James N. Dertouzos

James N. Dertouzos is a Senior Economist at the RAND Corporation in Santa Monica, California. He has taught at UCLA, Stanford, and the RAND Graduate School. His research interests include technological change, in particular its effects on displaced employees and military manpower, with primary focus on the principal-agent problems associated with the management of army recruiting personnel.

Paul C. Light

Paul C. Light served as Senior Advisor to the first National Commission on the Public Service. He is the Founding Director of the Brookings Institution Center for Public Service and also the Paulette Goddard Professor of Public Service at New York University. He was previously Director of the Public Policy Program of the Pew Charitable Trusts.

G. Calvin Mackenzie

G. Calvin Mackenzie is a Visiting Fellow at the Brookings Institution and holds an endowed chair as the Goldfarb Family Distinguished Professor of Government at Colby College. As a senior research analyst for the U.S. House Commission on Administrative Review, he was the principal author of its analyses of administrative operations in the House of Representatives.

Commission Staff

Amber B. Brooks, Research and Editing Consultant
   William C. Fanaras, Research Assistant
   Rosslyn S. Kleeman, Senior Consultant
   Erin Murphy, Production Manager
   Gina Russo, Communications Director
      Laurence A. Benenson, Benjamin T. Brickner, Kathleen M.
        Hitchins, Sherry Orbach, Research Interns

The commission is a project of the Brookings Institution Center for Public Service and is supported by a grant from the Dillon Fund.

Acknowledgment of Sources Utilized by the Commission

Witnesses at Commission Hearings

Monday, July 15, 2002
- Chief Justice William H. Rehnquist
- Associate Justice Stephen G. Breyer
- Kay Coles James, Director of the Office of Personnel Management
- David Walker, Comptroller General

Wednesday, July 17, 2002
- Donna Beecher, former director, Office of Human Resources Management, U.S. Department of Agriculture
- Matt Crouch, President, Presidential Management Alumnae Group
- Constance Berry Newman, Assistant Administrator for Africa, U.S. Agency for International Development. Former Smithsonian Institution Undersecretary; Director Office of Personnel Management; Assistant Secretary, Department of Housing and Urban Development; Commissioner, Consumer Product Safety Commission; and VISTA Director
- Judge Deanell Reece Tacha, Chief Judge, Court of Appeals, 10th Circuit, and Chair, Committee on the Judicial Branch, Judicial Conference of the United States
- American Federation of Government Employees: Mark Roth, General Counsel
- Federal Managers Association: Darryl Perkinson, President, Mid-Atlantic Region
- National Treasury Employees Union: Colleen Kelley, President
- Senior Executives Association: Carol Bonosaro, President
- Brookings Institution, Presidential Appointee Initiative: G. Calvin Mackenzie
- Council for Excellence in Government: Patricia McGinnis, President and CEO

- Kennedy School of Government: Steve Kelman, Albert J. Weatherhead III, and Richard W. Weatherhead, Professor of Public Management
- National Academy of Public Administration: Bob O'Neill, President
- Partnership for Public Service: Max Stier, President and CEO
- RAND Corporation: Susan D. Hosek, Senior Economist

Thursday, July 18, 2002
- U.S. Senator Daniel K. Akaka (D-HI), Chairman, Subcommittee on International Security, Proliferation and Federal Services, Governmental Affairs Committee
- U.S. Senator George V. Voinovich (R-OH), Ranking Member, Subcommittee on Oversight of Government Management, Restructuring and the District of Columbia, Governmental Affairs Committee
- Congressman Steny H. Hoyer (D-MD), Ranking Member, Subcommittee on Treasury, Postal Service and General Government, House Appropriations Committee
- Congresswoman Connie Morella (R-MD), Chair, District of Columbia Subcommittee, House Committee on Government Reform

Institutions Providing Research and Other Information to the Commission

The commission thanks the following organizations for their ongoing assistance.

Brookings Institution Presidential Appointee Initiative
The Presidential Appointee Initiative operates on the premise that effective governance is impossible if the nation's most talented citizens are reluctant to accept the president's call to government service. http://www.appointee.brookings.edu/

Brookings Institution Center for Public Service
The Center for Public Service is dedicated to generating ideas that policymakers can use to encourage America's most talented citizens to choose a career in the public service, wherever those careers might be. The Center looks at both the status of the public service and the challenges government, nonprofits, and the private sector face in adjusting to today's highly diverse, mobile, and less loyal pool of public service talent. http://www.brook.edu/dybdocroot/gs/gs_hp.htm

Congressional Budget Office
The Congressional Budget Office's mission is to provide Congress with the objective, timely, nonpartisan analyses needed for economic and budget decisions and with the information and estimates required for the congressional budget process. http://www.cbo.gov/

Congressional Research Service
The Congressional Research Service is committed to providing Congress, throughout the legislative process, comprehensive and reliable analysis, research, and information services that are timely, objective, nonpartisan, and confidential, thereby contributing to an informed national legislature. http://www.loc.gov/crsinfo/

Council for Excellence in Government
The Council for Excellence in Government works to improve the performance of government and government's place in the lives and esteem of American citizens. The Council helps to create stronger public sector leadership and management, driven by innovation and focused on results, as well as increased citizen confidence and participation in government, through better understanding of government and its role. http://excelgov.xigroup.com/

General Accounting Office
The General Accounting Office exists to support Congress in meeting its constitutional responsibilities and to help improve the performance and ensure the accountability of the federal government for the benefit of the American people. http://www.gao.gov/

Kennedy School of Government at Harvard University
The Kennedy School of Government prepares leaders for service to democratic societies to contribute to the solutions of public problems. http://www.ksg.harvard.edu/

National Academy of Public Administration
The National Academy of Public Administration is dedicated to improving the performance of governance systems—the network of public institutions, nonprofit organizations, and private companies that now share in the implementation of public policy. http://www. napawash.org/

National Association of Schools of Public Affairs and Administration
The National Association of Schools of Public Affairs and Administration is an institutional membership organization that exists to promote excellence in public service education. The membership includes U.S. university programs in public affairs, public policy, public administration, and nonprofit management. http://www.naspaa.org/

Office of Personnel Management
The Office of Personnel Management (OPM) is the federal government's human resource agency. The role of OPM is to help agencies get the right people in the right jobs with the right skills at the right time so they can produce results for the American people. http://www.opm.gov/

Partnership for Public Service
The Partnership for Public Service is a nonpartisan organization dedicated to revitalizing the federal civil service. http://www.ourpublic service.org/

RAND Corporation
The RAND Corporation is a nonprofit institution that helps improve policy and decisionmaking through research and analysis. http:// www.rand.org/

Published Studies and Written Commentary

Akaka, Daniel K., U.S. Senator, "Civil Service Reform and the Rights of Federal Employees," *Congressional Record*, June 19, 2001, at S5767.

American Bar Association and the Federal Bar Association, *Federal Judicial Pay Erosion: A Report on the Need for Reform*, Washington, DC, February 2001.

Bauer, Francis X., et al., "A Call for Competency: Report to the [First] National Commission on the Public Service by the Education, Training and Development Task Force of the Management Development Center." Written testimony submitted to the commission, September 1988.

Bell, Richard W., National President, Classification and Compensation Society, letter submitted to the commission, August 20, 2002.

Birch, Elizabeth, Executive Director, Human Rights Campaign, statement submitted to the commission, June 15, 2002.

Birchman, Bruce, Legislative Chairman, Forum of United States Administrative Law Judges, paper submitted to the commission, June 13, 2002.

Bonosaro, Carol, President, Senior Executives Association, "The Federal Workforce: Legislative Proposals for Change," written testimony submitted to the U.S. Senate Governmental Affairs Subcommittee on International Security, Proliferation, and Federal Services, March 18, 2002.

Castel, P. Kevin, President, Federal Bar Council, statement submitted to the commission, October 28, 2002.

Chronicle of Higher Education, "Facts and Figures" (available at http://chronicle.com/stats/990/ 2001/results.php3?Carnegie_Type=doc).

Culkin, Charles, Executive Director, Association of Government Accountants, letter submitted to the commission, July 15, 2002.

Demaio, Carl D., Adrian Moore, and Vincent Badolato, *Designing a Performance-Based Competitive Sourcing Process for the Federal Government*, Reason Foundation and Performance Institute, October 2002.

Eisner, Neil, Chair, Section of Administrative Law and Regulatory Practice, American Bar Association, letter submitted to the commission, October 9, 2002.

Feinberg, Wilfred, Circuit Judge, U.S. Court of Appeals for the Second Circuit, written testimony submitted to the commission, July 9, 2002.

Guttman, Dan, "Who's Doing Work for Government? Monitoring, Accountability and Competition in the Federal and Service Contract Workforce," written testimony submitted to the U.S. Senate Committee on Governmental Affairs, March 6, 2002.

Hirshon, Robert E., President, American Bar Association, "Statement on the Need for Judicial Pay Reform Submitted to the National Commission on the Public Service," paper submitted to the commission, July 2002.

Hofmeister, Kent S., National President, Federal Bar Association, letter submitted to the commission, October 17, 2002.

Ink, Dwight, President Emeritus, Institute of Public Administration, "Suggestions for Consideration of the National Commission of the Public Service," paper submitted to the commission, July 2002.

Jacobson, Louis, "Soaring Salaries," *National Journal*, Vol. 13, March 30, 2002, pp. 919–930.

Jolly, E. Grady, President, Federal Judges Association, letter submitted to the commission, July 2, 2002.

Jones, Reginald M., President, Council of Former Federal Executives, letter submitted to the commission, July 19, 2002.

Light, Paul C., *The True Size of Government*, Washington, DC: Brookings Institution, 1999.

Mackenzie, G. Calvin, *Scandal Proof*, Washington, DC: Brookings Institution, 2002.

Mecham, Leonidas Ralph, Secretary, Judicial Conference of the United States, letter submitted to the commission, June 14, 2002.

National Academy of Public Administration, Report of the Panel for the National Commission on the Public Service, July 2002.

National Academy of Public Administration, Report on the Senior Executive Service prepared for the Office of Personnel Management, December 2002.

Nickles, Steve, Chairman, Personnel and Organization Committee, IRS Oversight Board, letter submitted to the commission, July 3, 2002.

President's Council on Integrity and Efficiency, "Compendium of Federal Environmental Programs," September 1, 2002 (available at http://www.epa.gov/oigearth/index.htm, last accessed October 15, 2002).

Price, Jeff, President, National Association of Disability Examiners, "Challenges Facing the New Commissioner of Social Security," written testimony submitted to the U.S. House of Representatives Subcommittee on Social Security and Human Resources, May 2, 2002.

Procurement Round Table, "Statement of the Procurement Round Table to the National Commission on the Public Service," paper submitted to the commission, July 12, 2002.

Rosen, Bernard, letter submitted to commission, August 29, 2002.

Shiffert, Sarah, Senior Director of Association Services, International Personnel Management Association, "A Call to Action: A Coalition on the Future of the Federal Human Resource Management Profession," paper submitted to the commission, July 2002.

Thompson, Fred, Chairman, U.S. Senate Governmental Affairs Committee, *Government at the Brink, Vol. I and II: An Agency by Agency Examination of Federal Government Management Problems Facing the Bush Administration,* Washington, DC: Government Printing Office, June 2001.

U.S. Congressional Budget Office, *CBO Memorandum: Comparing the Pay and Benefits of Federal and Nonfederal Executives,* Washington, DC: Government Printing Office, November 1999.

U.S. Office of Personnel Management, *A Fresh Start for Federal Pay: The Case for Modernization,* Washington, DC: Government Printing Office, April 2002 (available at www.opm.gov/strategiccomp/whtpaper.pdf, last accessed October 15, 2002).

U.S. Office of Personnel Management, Center for HR Innovation, *Human Resources Flexibilities and Authorities in the Federal Government,* July 25, 2001.

U.S. Office of Policy and Evaluation, Merit Systems Protection Board, *Making the Public Service Work: Recommendations for Change,* Washington, DC: Government Printing Office, September 3, 2002.

U.S. Office of Policy and Evaluation, Merit Systems Protection Board, *The Federal Merit Promotion Program: Process vs. Outcome*, Washington, DC: Government Printing Office, December 2001.

U.S. Railroad Retirement Board, *Examining the Inefficiencies of the Federal Workplace: Recommendations for Reform*, Washington, DC: Government Printing Office, July 2002.

Voinovich, George V., Chairman, Subcommittee on Oversight of Government Management, Restructuring, and the District of Columbia, Governmental Affairs Committee, *Report to the President: The Crisis in Human Capital*, Washington, DC: Government Printing Office, December 2000.

Walker, David M., Chairman, Commercial Activities Panel, *Improving the Sourcing Decisions of the Government: Final Report*, April 30, 2002.

Organizations and Individuals Contributing to the Commission's Knowledge

The commission wishes to acknowledge the additional following organizations and individuals who have contributed to its knowledge and understanding of the issues impacting the public service:

American Bar Association, Section of Administrative Law and Regulatory Practice

Carolyn Bann, Dean, University of Pittsburgh Graduate School of Public and International Affairs

Carol A. Bonosaro, President, Senior Executives Association

Michael Brintnall, Executive Director, The American Political Science Association

David S.C. Chu, Under Secretary of Defense for Personnel and Readiness

Coalition for Effective Change

Marion F. Connell, Executive Director, Public Employees Roundtable

Council on Foundations

Mortimer L. Downey III, Chairman of the Board, National Academy of Public Administration

Maureen Gilman, Director of Legislation, and Susan L. Shaw, Deputy Director of Legislation, National Treasury Employees Union

Dennis G. Green, President, Federal Magistrate Judges Association

Mary Hamilton, Executive Director, American Society of Public Administration

Judge E. Grady Jolly, President, Federal Judges Association

Judicial Conference of the United States

Corneilius Kerwin, Provost, American University

Jack D. Lockridge, Executive Director, Federal Bar Association

Leonidas Ralph Mecham, Director, and Steven M. Tevlowitz, Assistant General Counsel, Administrative Office of the United States Courts

Robert E. Moffit, Director, Domestic and Economic Policy, Heritage Foundation

Beth Moten, Director, Legislative and Political Affairs Department, American Federation of Government Employees, AFL-CIO

National Conference of Bankruptcy Judges

Kathryn Newcomer, Chair, Department of Public Administration, the George Washington University

Organization of Professional Employees of the U.S. Department of Agriculture

James Pfiffner, School of Public Policy, George Mason University

Procurement Roundtable

Anthony C. E. Quainton, President and CEO, National Policy Association

David H. Rosenbloom, Distinguished Professor of Public Administration, School of Public Affairs, American University

Susan C. Schwab, Dean, School of Public Affairs, University of Maryland

Carl Stenberg, Dean, Yale Gordon College of Liberal Arts, University of Baltimore

Virginia L. Thomas, Director of Executive Branch Relations, Heritage Foundation

Robert Tobias, Director, Institute for the Study of Public Policy Implementation, American University

U.S. House of Representatives Government Reform Committee Staff

U.S. Senate Governmental Affairs Committee Staff

Casimir A. Yost, Director, Georgetown University Institute for the Study of Diplomacy

What Broad Changes Will Transform Government in the Future?

CHAPTER THREE

Governing the Market State

Gregory F. Treverton

Two broad trends—the rise of the market state and the threat of terrorism—will shape the future nature of government and public service.[1] The market state is the product of the global economy; in contrast to the traditional nation-state, it is driven by commerce, not conquest, and it is permeable, not sovereign within its boundaries.[2] As the global economy and the market state erode the boundary between public and private, we should see dramatic new opportunities to advance the Volcker Commission's objectives of better structures, leaders, and incentives, perhaps in ways unforeseen by the commission.

The war on terrorism will also have important effects on government. For at least the last half-century, federal Washington has been more a military headquarters than a national capital, with fighting first hot war then cold as its organizing principle.[3] Now, changes in the nature of the threat, in the international system, and in technology will have far-reaching implications for the way governments work. The threat of terrorism will argue for a strong security

---

[1] The term *market state* is from Bobbitt, 2002. He and I, friends and colleagues, came to the concept simultaneously but by different intellectual routes.

[2] To be sure, the change, if dramatic, is relative, and it is uneven across the globe. I use the term *market state* as much as a metaphor as a precise descriptor. Its implications are spelled out further below.

[3] In May's words, Washington would seem "to those sage, naïve Orientals favored by the philosophers: 'Yes, a city. But, at heart, a military headquarters, like the Rome of the Fabians or the Berlin of the Hohenzollerns'" (May, 1992, p. 270).

state, though one quite different from that during the Cold War. In contrast, the rise of the market state will weaken the state and diminish the role of the federal government. In the process, the role of government will change, and so will the roles of the various private sectors and their interactions with government.

Drivers of Change

The drivers of the two trends are fairly clear. They are interconnected but can be grouped into five clusters: [4]

1. The communications revolution
2. Economic globalization
3. The rising politics of "identity"
4. Changing demographics
5. Environmental concerns

The Communications Revolution

The information revolution is a key enabler of economic globalization. It was the information revolution that undid the Soviet Union, for while planning and brute force could produce roads and dams, they could not induce innovation in computer chips. However, information technology also makes it possible, for instance, for terrorists and drug traffickers to encrypt their communications or for would-be Haitian boat people to learn within a day what fraction of their predecessors have been screened into the United States. When guerrillas of the Zapatista National Liberation Army challenged the Mexican government in Chiapas in the 1990s, they used e-mail and the Internet to organize and plan operations; they set up Web bulletin boards to build support (Arquilla and Ronfeldt, 1996, pp. 72–73).

---

[4] See Treverton, 2001, Chap. 2. Also see UK Ministry of Defence, Joint Doctrine and Concept Centre; National Intelligence Council, 2000; Center for Strategic and International Studies.

The information revolution also segments societies, both within and across states. While the information revolution can sometimes help people in poor countries connect, as is occurring in some parts of Africa, earlier communications technologies—radio, telephone, and television—were easier to use and thus diffused rather rapidly. In contrast, entry cost in skill is higher for computers and their associated technologies, so their diffusion from richer, better-educated users to the rest of society has so far been slower. As telephone, computer, and television converge, using them will become easier. But whether, despite more user-friendliness, there will continue to be a high payoff to those who can employ the still more advanced, less friendly technologies remains a question. At a minimum, it is hard to foresee anything like the long periods of stability in technology that until quite recently characterized radio, telephone, and, to a lesser extent, television.

The information revolution has several more-specific implications. One is that the power of states to control information seems to be waning, for good or ill. Two generations ago, it was feared that computers would abet dictators; Big Brother seemed close at hand. Now, the opposite seems true. Administrations in Washington cannot control the "spin" on a news story. The right image for the future is the Internet, private and driven by the needs of commerce, not Radio Free Europe, with information supplied by government. European governments could not control capital flows if they tried; and China seems less and less able to control what its citizens read and hear. A government can try to cut the country off from international communications, but it is not easy and can only be done at a high price. Isolation may be attainable only at the price of poverty.

The information revolution also powerfully influences expectations all around the globe. The "CNN effect" seems to shorten time horizons; governments find it harder to plead for time to deliberate when correspondents report an unfolding crisis minute-by-minute. Governments are expected to react—and to react to events as shaped by the media. In the autumn of 1998, for instance, President Clinton's national security advisor, Samuel ("Sandy") Berger, alerted the president *one hour short of war* that Iraq was offering a settlement to the crisis, and he did so on the basis of a CNN report from Baghdad.[5]

Those same communications technologies also shape the expectations of citizens. Just as citizens of the former East Germany acquired their images of life beyond communism from West German television—and protested from the one part of East Germany that could not receive West German television—so Bosnians, Rwandans, and Iraqis framed expectations about what other states would or would not do from what they saw on TV or the Web, or what their kinsmen reported from cell phones.

On the negative side of the communications revolution, terrorists take advantage of new communications techniques. When it was revealed that the United States was intercepting Osama bin Laden's cell phone communications, al Qaeda shifted both to old-fashioned communication, such as messengers, and to more advanced ones, such as messages embedded in Web images. With unbreakable encryption available at Radio Shack, new communications technology puts law-enforcement and counterterrorism officials into a continuous game of move and countermove with their adversaries.

Economic Globalization

Economic trends are both integrating and disintegrating. They integrate in that national borders and distances matter less. When I am sitting in California, it doesn't make much difference to me whether a bit of data or a physical product is made in San Diego or Helsinki. Those of us with an interest in the data or product are drawn together to become intellectual collaborators or business partners.

At the same time, in a world where people and skills are really the only factor endowments that matter, the gap between the haves and have-nots is growing, not just between rich nations and poor nations, but also within nations, including the rich ones (Frost, 2001, p. 40). Most projections suggest that the large developing countries—especially China and India, but also Mexico, Brazil, and the

---

[5] As reported in the *Washington Post*, November 16, 1998, p. A1.

countries of eastern Asia—will grow faster than the rich countries, so the share of world output in the developing countries will continue to grow. That, however, means that the poorest countries will become, in relative terms, poorer (Larrabee et al., 2003, Chap. 9).

Plausibly, but not indisputably, globalization and the information revolution are contributing to growing income inequality within countries. In the United States, the top fifth of incomes was ten times that of the lowest fifth in 1977 but more than 15 times greater in 1999 (Bernstein et al., 2000). Internal inequality also seems to be growing in many poorer countries, from India's high-tech enclaves to China's and Russia's new plutocrats, though rigorous evidence is only starting to be available.

Rising Politics of "Identity"—Us vs. Them

Perhaps partly because of alienation from processes of global integration, people seek some form of transcendental association. They increasingly seek to differentiate "us" from "them," in ethnicity, religion, or some other characteristic. One manifestation is the quest of ethnic groups for smaller units, often for states of their own. In only about half of the world's 170 states does one ethnic group make up more than 75 percent of the population.

A related phenomenon is the rise of belief in the nonmaterial. Men and women may lay down their lives for freedom, but not for the free market; if they ever did for Marxism, that commitment ended long ago. The loss of community in modernizing societies may propel the search for something in which to believe; the anomie of being marginalized may sharpen the search. Today, religion most visibly provides such a purpose, but it is not beyond imagining that in the future other motivations will arise. Francis Fukuyama argued that with the end of the Cold War, history's long dialectic of alternating ideologies had come to an end. Liberal democracy had won (Fukuyama, 1992). In fact, history had ended only in the sense that there had proven to be no rival, in principle, to liberal democracy as the way to organize national political life. But radical Islam already is a pretender to the throne, and others will arise, perhaps especially among groups of people that feel dispossessed by states or are left behind as state power wanes.

Communications technology is facilitating connections among those who feel dispossessed; this happened first primarily in the richer countries, but now it is occurring in the poorer ones as well. Yesterday's communications technologies, such as radio and television, were "broadcast," one sender transmitting the same message to many receivers. Americans who watched the network news on television saw the same national news whether they lived in California or South Carolina. By contrast, today's technologies are "narrowcast," one sender to one receiver or many senders to one receiver. Those on the Web can seek out the chat rooms that appeal to them, whether the subject is sports or Bosnia or the UN conspiracy to impose a global government. They can thereby be in touch with kindred spirits.

September 11 put a punctuation point onto, if it did not finally settle, the debate about how much religion is and will be a factor leading to conflict. Samuel P. Huntington evoked the "clash of civilizations" as the shaper of the future world (Huntington, 1993, 1996). Although his clashers are civilizations, not religions, religion is a key definer of them. The civilizations are broad and internally heterogeneous; the variations within them seem as large as those among them, and so their coherence as units of analysis, much less clashers, has been criticized. Still, conflict does seem most likely to arise in or from the areas where civilizations intersect—in central or southwestern Asia, or across the Mediterranean, or in Southeast Asia, where the clashing civilizations exist within states as well as across them. Osama bin Laden condemned the corrupting effect of the West in general, and the United States in particular, on the civilization of Islam and its nations. His grievance was and is largely civilizational. The eminent Arabist, Bernard Lewis, said as much more than a decade ago (Lewis, 1990).

Changing Demographics

Over time, the enormous disparities in north-south growth rates will sharpen emigration pressures. Years ago the distinguished economist Thomas Schelling wondered what the world would look like in a few decades. Chillingly, he said he thought it would resemble South Africa—enclaves of rich people, mostly white, literally fencing themselves off from multitudes of poor people, mostly dark (Schelling, 1992). If his vision has not quite come into being, it is because migrating is difficult for most people, it is often dangerous, and border controls remain pretty effective. And South Africa's own progress since then may mean that Schelling's analogy need not condemn the world to apartheid.

Still, if the most striking development of recent decades has been the slowdown in population growth rates around the globe, the second most striking has been how uneven that slowdown has been. More than 90 percent of population growth is occurring outside the industrial democracies, and some of those democracies will, according to current trends, actually decline in population. A few other key countries, like Russia and South Africa, are also set to shrink. The United States has continued to grow, at slightly under 1 percent annually; almost two-thirds of that growth is due to immigration. By contrast, population growth rates in the Middle East and sub-Saharan Africa remain over 2 percent, despite the AIDS epidemic. Not only will these regions account for most of the world's population growth, they will also be home to very large populations of young males. Currently, 33 percent of the population of the Middle East consists of males under 30 years of age. In sub-Saharan Africa, this ratio runs 36 percent (Larrabee et al., 2003, pp. 171–172).

These high growth rates run the risk of creating "youth bulges"—that is, cohorts, especially of young men, much too large to be integrated into the workforce. Those bulges may be sources of dissatisfaction, and thus of instability, in key developing countries, such as Egypt and Turkey. Even some of the oil-producing countries are so threatened. Iran, Iraq, and Saudi Arabia have been growing rapidly (Wolf, 2002). Thirty-seven percent of Iranians, 42 percent of Iraqis, and 43 percent of Saudis are under 34 years of age. With open and disguised unemployment at about 45 percent in Iran and Iraq and around 40 percent in Saudi Arabia, the risks of volatility are evident.

For the United States, the crucial demographic future is not a youth bulge, but rather, an "elderly bulge," with striking implications for what government does and can do. The basic facts are familiar (U.S. Congressional Budget Office, 2002). The postwar "baby boom" was followed by a "baby trough," then by a modest increase in birth rates that may now have leveled off. Meanwhile, life expectancy continues to increase. The cohort over the age of 65, growing rapidly, constitutes 12 percent of the population today but is expected to grow to 18 percent in 2025, 21 percent in 2050, and 23 percent in 2075. At the same time, growth in the nation's workforce is expected to slow, resulting in a more slowly growing economy. By 2035, the number of elderly will double, while the number of workers contributing to Social Security and Medicare will rise by only 17 percent. The ratio of the population aged 65 or older to the population in its prime working years (ages 20 to 64) will grow from 21 percent today to 32 percent in 2025 and 42 percent in 2075.

For government, the "mountain moving toward us" means that taxes will go up, Social Security and health care entitlement benefits will go down, or the rest of government will shrink, or all three in some combination. Now, though, with prescription drug subsidies, benefits are going up. Today, the cost of Social Security and federal health-insurance programs is about 8 percent of all the economy produces. The Congressional Budget Office estimates that 40 years from now, these programs will take nearly twice that. Over the past decade, federal revenues averaged about 19 percent of gross domestic product, just a little more than what the entitlement programs are projected to require 40 years hence. Something has to give.

Environmental Concerns

From one year to the next, an environmental indicator may simply worsen gradually, almost imperceptibly, then come to a sharp crisis when some tipping point is reached. When the chronic becomes acute, not only does the environment surge to the top of the agenda, but the categories "foreign" and "domestic" cease to have much meaning.

For instance, if China continues to grow as rapidly as it has been growing, it will produce not just terrible local pollution in China, but also dramatic increases in global warming, not to mention upward pressure on prices of fossil fuels. And the chronic environmental processes will be punctuated by acute episodes. Imagine what two nuclear meltdowns, two Chernobyls, within a year would do to the international agenda.

Or consider the outbreak of major regional fires in the late 1990s, from Southeast Asia to Mexico. Long droughts were chronic, but fires breaking out became acute. When land-clearing fires in Indonesia got out of control, the smoke from the fires respected no national borders and eventually closed the airport in neighboring Singapore. The Asian fires also underscored how far institutions lagged behind the need for them, for the countries affected had no forum for beginning to turn Indonesia's crisis into a matter for regional action.

The five drivers of change and their implications are summarized in Table 3.1.

The Rise of the Market State . . . and Its Discontents

The world before us will be the political sum of the drivers that are under way, especially in information and economics. The world of the market state is one in which the United States is the world's largest economy, but also its biggest source of envy, hence the most tempting target. Many regions will become richer, but other regions will, for one reason or another, be left further and further behind. The latter will provide breeding grounds or sanctuaries for terrorists. And urgings to distinguish "them" from "us"—on the basis of region, religion, ethnicity, or something else—will rise, perhaps at home as well as abroad.

The age of information is also the coming of the market state, which will dramatically change the roles of government and of private actors. While governments still are the most important actors in international politics, their power is being challenged from both above, by the constraints of the global economy, and below, by non-state actors. Power is dispersing around and through them, and the

Table 3.1
Drivers of Change and Their Implications for Governance

Driver	Principal Effects	Implication for Government
Communications revolution	Shifts comparative economic advantage Enables civic action and terrorism communication Segments populations	Reduces government control Limits government—changes expectations, limits time to respond
Economic globalization	Quality of skills matters more; resources, distance much less Gap between haves and have-nots grows, at least in the medium run	Reduces government control, constrains policy Makes United States the biggest target of grievance Imposes the need to deal with have-nots
Rising politics of "identity"—us versus them	Divides "them" and "us" in new ways Makes for less loyalty to the state (or the market) Feeds new kinds of terrorism, including global networks Abets clash of civilizations	Requires dealing with new kinds of threats—non-states driven by religion or other passions Produces a more divided American society
Global demographics	Global growth slows Rich countries age, even shrink; some poor continue to grow "Youth bulges" of young males arise in poor countries "Elderly bulge" occurs in the United States	Labor shortages, including for military services, arise in many countries, though not in the United States Pressure to migrate increases Imposes a need to deal with failed or failing societies Taxes rise, entitlements fall, government shrinks, or all three
Environmental concerns	Tipping points and catastrophes can occur Some crises will be global or regional, not national	Rises or falls on government agenda, somewhat unpredictably

role of nation-state governments is changing.[6] The broad shape of the future international system will reflect the interactions of the major nation-states, but by then it will be apparent that critical drivers of that system are elsewhere. The change in the role of the state is inseparable from the economic transformation. The territorial state was

---

[6] For early discussions of other actors on the world stage, see Keohane and Nye, 1973; and Keohane, 1984.

born in the period of agrarian economics, but it was the industrial revolution that gave it iron and steel. It was only then that state power began to be measured by economic output, not territorial size or the wealth of the sovereign's purse. The post-industrial economy, by contrast, cuts across territorial states, devaluing the icons of their power (Toffler, 1980). Lord Keynes was right in 1919 in his fore-boding about the Treaty of Versailles:

> Political considerations cut disastrously across economic. In a regime of Free Trade and free economic intercourse it would be of little consequence that iron lay on one side of a political frontier, and labor, coal, and blast furnaces on the other. But as it is, men have devised ways to impoverish themselves and one another; and proffer collective animosities to individual happiness (Keynes, 1920, p. 99).

At that time, it did matter where the factories were located. But today, in the era of the market state, it matters much less to national well-being or power. From above, international commerce is eroding what used to be thought of as aspects of national sovereignty: States are hard-pressed, for instance, to sustain controls on their currency. Of large states, only China has continued to do so with some success, through a system of dual exchange rates, but the country is still relatively poor.

Critical levers, many of which used to be in the hands of government, are passing to the private sector. Each of the ten largest companies in the world has an annual turnover larger than the GNP of 150 of the 185 members of the United Nations, including countries such as Portugal, Israel, and Malaysia.[7] More subjectively, at least 50 non-governmental organizations (NGOs) have more legitimacy than 50 UN member nations have. Official government aid to developing countries now is trivial by comparison with private capital flows, though governments and their institutions, including the World Bank and the International Monetary Fund (IMF), may continue to have some leverage because of their official status.

---

[7] I am grateful to Nicholas Butler for this statistic.

The market respects neither the borders nor the icons of the traditional territorial state. It does not care whether the worker is Filipino or American, Chinese or German, man or woman, homosexual or military veteran. More speculatively, as the traditional politics of interstate rivalries cedes place to the global market, governments lose unique attributes of their power. Armies and territory count for less. The world has not seen the end of armed conflict; on the contrary, warring seems built into the human species. But for the market state, any threat to go to war with another major state is a threat to cut off the nose to spite the face. The war on terrorism does not change that calculation.

If bankers and international finance are eating away at states from above, terrorists and drug traffickers challenge state power from below (Mathews, 1997). They make use of technology and international networks to act around and through states, pursuing their objectives by trying to compel states to acquiesce or by eluding their control. Again, al Qaeda and its associates make the point graphically. In 1996, the Tupac Amaru guerrillas in Peru set up their own home page on the Web, Rebel Voice. A loose network of sympathizers—including one site at the University of California, San Diego—grew up and began to channel propaganda back into Peru. Peru's government could not stop the inflow without cutting off the country's communications with the outside world.[8]

For all the change, existing habits of thought and institutions, such as the public service, remain powerfully conditioned by the concept of the nation-state that was enshrined in the Treaty of Westphalia: the sovereignty of nations and the principle of nonintervention in their internal affairs. Increasingly, we experience a mismatch between what drives many issues and the way we address them. Emigration is an example. War aside (a large aside), economics is the main force behind migration, as people seek better lives elsewhere. Yet policy approaches to migration derive from the older vision of international politics, one dominated by notions of border controls,

---

[8] See the *Wall Street Journal*, January 6, 1997, p. A8.

citizenship, and sovereignty. Their mismatch is almost complete. Beginning to rectify it would imply recognizing that the market state requires people to move freely across borders to work, perhaps temporarily, but not necessarily to acquire the benefits of citizenship where they live. "Sojourner rights" might permit people to work where they needed to but not to receive health care, social security, or other specific benefits of citizenship (Bennett, forthcoming).

Changing Public and Private Roles

The circumstances of the market state will transform the role of government. The government of the territorial state was a doer; students of public administration and, later, public policy learned that government's choice was "make, buy, or regulate." For tomorrow's public managers, the choice will be "cajole, incentivize, or facilitate"—a very different task (one perhaps rendered in punchier prose as "carrots, sticks, and sermons") (Bemelmans-Videc, Rist, and Vedung, 1998). What the government, and particularly the American federal government, will have is infrastructure and, perhaps, legitimacy. Taxpayers provide the infrastructure of buildings, secretaries, and travel budgets. Government *may* also have the legitimacy conferred by its custodianship of the public interest. It may be that private organizations will talk to it, or through it to other private organizations, in ways those organizations could not or would not talk to each other.

In the 1990s, the National Intelligence Council (NIC) began doing yearly estimates of projected humanitarian needs, and thus of possible relief operations.[9] Its primary customer was the U.S. military's Transportation Command (TRANSCOM), which would end up providing the airlift and so, wisely, thought it might try to plan ahead. In preparation for the estimate, the NIC invited representa-

---

[9] The NIC works for the Director of Central Intelligence in that official's capacity as overseer of the entire community of intelligence agencies, not as CEO of the CIA. It brings together all the intelligence analytic agencies to produce National Intelligence Estimates (NIEs) or other assessments outlining what "the government" thinks about particular issues or threats.

tives of the dozen largest humanitarian NGOs, including CARE, to prepare short papers and attend a conference. Surprisingly, they all agreed, most of them eagerly. For them, the taint of "intelligence" was an obstacle but not an overriding one. Taint aside, they welcomed the fact that *some* part of the U.S. government was paying attention. They gave the impression that in convening them, the NIC did them a favor: They may have found it easier to respond to an invitation from a neutral, official institution than they would have found it to be convened by any one of their number.

More and more, the role of government will be to convene groups of the willing, as was done in Afghanistan and in both Iraq wars. In the future, those groups will bring together public institutions and private entities; like the partners in Operation Iraqi Freedom and even more so in Desert Storm, they will come from more than one nation. What the government will provide is its power to convene, its infrastructure, perhaps its legitimacy, and its information. The shift in mindset this will require of government can hardly be overstated. Many government agencies, especially intelligence agencies, came only slowly to the realization that they work for Congress as well as the executive branch. They will not come easily to the idea that they work with, and sometimes for, CARE and Amnesty International, not to mention Shell and Loral.

The market state implies dramatic changes in "private" responsibilities, a transformation that is the other side of the changing role of government. Traditionally, private actors were objects, not subjects, of international politics. States or groups of states acting through international institutions might try to regulate the behavior of private groups, but the groups had little responsibility for setting norms. To that extent, they were free riders on the international order.[10] The transition to the market state implies a vast increase in the

[10] Of course, private efforts to influence state policies are a familiar feature of democratic politics, and those efforts also include the international policies of states. Such efforts were apparent in the U.S. debate over according most-favored-nation (MFN) trade status to China; major U.S. companies with stakes in China trade became more and more vocal advocates of MFN. Occasionally, private companies have acted more creatively; for example,

responsibility of private actors, from companies and individuals to so-called NGOs—notice that the label itself is a remnant of the old order. They are becoming—in ways hardly realized, let alone charted—not the objects of the international order, but its subjects, its architects. They are becoming the setters of international norms, not free riders on rules set by states. The IMF was discredited during Asia's crises as an after-the-fact fire brigade at best, and at worst as a brigade whose presence might have tempted governments to be careless with fire before the fact. In that event, private international banks negotiated with and through local governments, helping to begin the process of establishing norms of more transparency in Asian finance. One set of private actors, environmental NGOs, now negotiates with another set, major corporations, over a "public" purpose, carbon saving in Latin America.

The logic of the market state also devalues some existing international organizations. For all their efforts to reach out to NGOs and the private sector, they remain creatures of states, rooted in notions of state sovereignty. This observation applies as much to NATO as it does to the United Nations. Even economic institutions, such as the World Bank and the World Trade Organization, are tenuous. On the one hand, they may be less devalued by the market state than are international political or security institutions, for they have value as rule-setters for international commerce, but on the other hand, not only are they swamped by private international transactions—what the IMF or World Bank does is more and more overshadowed by private capital flows—but the status of those institutions is itself ambiguous. They, too, are creatures of governments, not of the forces that are coming to drive international politics.

Thus, the transition to the market state will raise enormous issues of legitimacy and accountability, both within states and across them. As the rise of the market state devalues governments, their citizens will accord them less loyalty, a trend probably abetted by the rise

---

Dupont worked to rally chemical companies to support, not oppose, the 1996 Montreal Protocol's ban on damaging fluorocarbons. But those instances are rare.

of identity politics. At the same time, those citizens may seek to hold their governments accountable for the results of global market forces—witness the curious election-year debate over "outsourcing" in the United States in 2004. If the global economy is a train without a conductor, then who or what is accountable? And if global companies and NGOs are powerful shapers of both national and international society, who selected them for that role? How are they to be held accountable?

The National Security Exception: Re-energizing the State?

All these trends argue for a different and reduced state, but the question remains as to how much the 21st century's terrorist threat will exert a countervailing pressure. Surely, the war on terrorism will give the American state, and its civil service, some renewed writ and vitality. The renationalization of airport security in the Transportation Security Administration (TSA) is testimony to that fact. After all, defending their citizens from foreign threats is at the core of what states are about. The questions are how much and what sort of renewed vitality? The easy answer is that it depends on how serious a threat terrorism turns out to be. From this vantage point, it looks serious but not on a par with the Soviet Union, which was the organizing principle not only for American government, but for American life as well.

Both Iraq and Afghanistan are reminders that if terrorism again drives "national security" to the fore, the definition is likely to be different. During the Cold War, there was neat one-to-one correspondence between the threat and the institutions, mostly government and mostly at the level of the federal government, that were developed to deal with it—that military headquarters again. To be sure, private contractors and private citizens were involved, but for most Americans, fighting the Cold War meant paying their taxes.

Now, by contrast, the threat is more diffuse and so will be the ways of dealing with it. It may be a war, but it will be a war fought with local police as much as federal armies. It will be fought multilaterally, with coalitions of the willing cutting across nations and across the public and private sectors, with the government providing carrots, sticks, and, mostly, sermons. Private citizens will be much more engaged, and, as the intrusive security procedures at airports suggest, they may have to change their behavior much more than was the case during the Cold War.

It is not clear whether these will be propitious circumstances in which to streamline government into a smaller number of more mission-oriented agencies, as the Volcker Commission has recommended. The commission looked with favor on the creation of the Department of Homeland Security (DHS) as one built around a mission. DHS very much reflects the diversity of the new security threat, as its purview ranges from screening baggage to policing borders to following immigrants. Some of the department's teething problems have been understandable results of trying to assemble a very large department from a number of preexisting pieces with different organizational cultures. In the end, though, it is not clear that "homeland security" is much cleaner as a mission than is "defense" or "health and human services."

Not surprisingly, many of the institutions of government that are ranked most highly are those that do have clean missions that point in one direction. They tend to be agencies or smaller, not departments. The Social Security Administration (SSA) gets high marks, for instance, in disbursing a quarter of the federal budget.[11] Its mission is very straightforward: get checks and information to those who are entitled to them. Still, the government may be streamlined, if not quite in the way the Volcker Commission recommends. That seems likely to happen less by conscious choice than by the force of competition, as agencies move toward their core missions, privatizing or otherwise shucking off ancillary activities. After September 11, for instance, the FBI embraced counterterrorism and ceded primacy in the anti-drug mission to the Drug Enforcement Administration. The

---

[11] It was rated at the top in *Government Executive*'s rankings of federal agencies for both 1999 and 2002. See Treverton, 2004.

question will be whether that competition impels agencies to consolidate in ways that serve the public interest, rather than agency convenience.

New Leaders and New Patterns

The logic of the market state points to dramatic changes in patterns
of leadership in government. In the future, it will probably have to be
recognized that talented people will be government officials one year
(or day) and private sector executives the next. Indeed, even those
labels should cease to be meaningful. But that vision runs smack into
American procedures for conflict of interest. Here, too, something
will have to budge (see Chapter 10 on leadership).

In the federal government, there is almost no lateral entry from
other sectors except at the very top, so its organizations deprive themselves of talent with experience outside the government. In the short
run, the answer for government is to seek much more flexibility to
acquire talent laterally and for short periods. While managing the
NIC, I wanted to recruit National Intelligence Officers (NIOs) from
outside government. In many areas, such as the quest for top-flight
economists, the government was and will continue to be hard-pressed
to compete with the private sector. It will have difficulty attracting
and retaining such talent for a career. But at the NIC, that talent
could be recruited for several-year stints; top-flight professionals,
many of whom had no more worlds to conquer in their present positions, were motivated by some combination of patriotism and a desire
to see how the government worked.

Over the longer term, the logic of the market state suggests
"portfolio careers," that is, young professionals acquiring breadth of
vision through working across various jobs and, ideally, sectors. Government officials, in particular, would break out of the "stovepipes"
most of them inhabit, often for entire careers. Not only would such
moves fit with the desires of the best younger professionals, who seek
continual challenges, but the boundaries among the sectors will be
breaking down in any case. As a result, it will not be merely broad-

ening to have had some experience in the business world or the non-profit sector, it will be more and more necessary.

Homeland security and the terrorist threat are impelling new kinds of cooperation across those boundaries. In interviews, government officials report an explosion in the number and kinds of partnerships they found, especially after September 11, necessary to do their job (Treverton and Bikson, 2003). In the intelligence area, not only are U.S. intelligence agencies sharing information with counterparts from foreign countries they would have regarded as targets two years ago, they are also having to find ways to share information with state and local officials and with private groups. Those intelligence agencies can foresee a future in which colleagues from Nike or Amnesty International will be colleagues one day, sources the next, and customers the next.

Intelligence, however, also illustrates the obstacles to realizing that vision, since secrecy and compartmentalization sharply limit sharing, let alone collaboration, beyond the bounds of intelligence or the government. Those constraints may bind other agencies less tightly, but those other agencies still confront the formidable set of restrictions that arise from political clearance procedures in the short run and from conflict-of-interest legislation in the longer term. The logic of the market state suggests that those conflict-of-interest provisions are outmoded, but that logic may not be the logic of politics. The drivers of technology and global economics are likely to continue to push the incomes of Americans apart. Given traditional American attitudes, that is not likely to produce sharp class conflict, but it does seem likely to produce increased suspicion of all large institutions, public and private.[12] It may also produce more than traces of the undertone, one visible in the Enron, Halliburton, and other financial scandals of the early 2000s, that private rascals are in cahoots with public ones, political leaders if not senior civil servants.

---

[12] A December 2002 poll reported that 19 percent of Americans think they are in the richest 1 percent of the nation, and another 20 percent think they will enter that 1 percent in their lifetime. See "A Tale of Two Legacies," *The Economist*, December 21, 2002; and *Financial Times*, January 25–26, 2003.

New Forms of Performance

The Volcker Commission also recommended new ways of enhancing the performance of the government. With respect to enhancing performance, the logic of the market state indicates continuing pressure to judge efficiency by the (sometimes imagined) standards of the for-profit sector. Within existing public agencies, this is reflected in greater pressure to measure results, on the one hand, and greater flexibility in seeking revenues or dealing with employees, on the other. The pressure to devise measurable indicators of results was codified in the Government Performance and Results Act of 1993, and it was reflected in the Clinton administration's Reinventing Government initiative and the Bush administration's President's Management Agenda.

Under pressure to perform, government agencies have sought and used more flexibility. In 1993, the Office of Personnel Management (OPM) abolished the massive Federal Personnel Manual and delegated to departments most human resource responsibilities, then delegated further down. Recent legislation has freed both the DHS and the Department of Defense (DoD) from many of the existing civil service constraints, and now more than half of the civilian employees of the federal government do not work under traditional civil service rules. As a result, their managers now have much more latitude in rewarding performance. For instance, the Federal Aviation Administration (FAA), where labor relations had been embattled since the air traffic controllers' strike of 1981, negotiated a five-year agreement with its union in 1998, and by 2002, three-quarters of FAA employees worked under a pay-for-performance system.

On the revenue side, a number of agencies have sought and received permission to charge fees for their services. The one bright spot in the Immigration and Naturalization Service's (INS's) otherwise dreary management picture—before it was divided and joined the DHS—was on the services side, where offering faster processing of visas for a $1,000 fee enabled the agency to hire more people, do more training, and acquire better technology.

The logic of the market state will also continue to be played out in more cooperative regulatory and other arrangements across the public-private divide. In some cases, such as in protecting information or electricity infrastructures, "regulation" has become the government requiring the private sector to take responsibility for "public" purposes. As other examples, the Food Safety and Inspection Service (FSIS) shifted from traditional "poke and sniff" inspection to working with food producers to develop and monitor inspection processes, and the Occupational Safety and Health Administration (OSHA) developed the Cooperative Compliance Program, giving work sites with poor records the option of working with the agency to note and fix hazards. These more-cooperative approaches will continue, as will pressure to be more flexible in personnel practices. The changes will also continue to erode the traditional security of civil service employment. FSIS's shift to cooperative inspection was seen as a threat by existing inspectors, only a quarter of whom had college degrees.

The unspoken truth at the core of all efforts to make government more efficient is that it was not designed to be efficient. It was designed to be accountable, which often in practice means minimizing "fraud, waste, and abuse." Escaping that trap is a powerful impulse to privatization, which is very much a part of the logic of the market state. There will be more public-private partnerships, and there will also be much more "government by market" (Kamarck, 2002b). As the Volcker Commission emphasizes, government has moved from clerks to specialists. The pressure to make use of market forces—and indeed, to try to create markets—will continue.

Privatization will be constrained in national security functions, but even there, it will grow. The number of private contractors engaged in Iraq after the 2003 war and the range of their activities are testimony to that fact. Already, there are three times as many security officers in the private sector as there are police in the public sector. The military has privatized far beyond logistics, the State Department can now buy much of the political and economic reporting it used to do, and the CIA has developed a private company, In-Q-Tel, not, as in the past, to provide cover for covert operations, but rather to openly troll for innovations in information processing and analysis.

If it is becoming unclear why and who should wear a uniform in the military service, it is hardly a surprise that what is done by government, what is competed, what is outsourced, and what is regulated are all unclear too. It will be more and more necessary to spell out why government does much at all, especially as demographics plus entitlements mean it has less money to do anything. The SSA earns high marks for customer services and getting checks out, but lots of private companies also do that well. The SSA is efficient at serving customers, but then so is Wal Mart, and Wal Mart comes with potential "offices" almost everywhere. If Disney runs theme parks, why not national parks, where much is already outsourced?

In the longer sweep of history, much more than institutional tinkering is occurring, for the depression, hot war, and the Cold War gave Americans more government, and more federal government, than had been the custom. The United States, a strong nation but a weak state, came to acquire many of the trappings of the European territorial state with which America's founders had broken. It acquired that imperial military headquarters. At the same time, immigration was making the American nation more and more heterogeneous.

And so there are in this transition real questions about both "state" and "nation," all of them sharpened by the rise of the market state and the paradox it imposes for governance: The global economy moves rapidly and takes risks, while formal governance is slow and risk-averse. It takes time to build legitimacy and accountability. Absent a crisis, it takes time even to construct a vision and to achieve broad buy-in for it. The nation's—and the government's—evident lack of preparation for the events of September 11 opens an opportunity to move the government in directions the Volcker Commission recommends—toward a tighter focus on mission, more reaching out to the private sectors, and more nimbleness.

The federal civil service of the market state will be smaller in people, if not in budget, and it will be more privatized. The exception to the drive to privatize will be in functions, like those of TSA, where the market's drive for efficiency is regarded as simply too risky in security terms. The lines separating the public sector and the private sector and civil service from private employment will blur, as people move from one sector to another. There, the constraints will continue to be both procedural and legal, and how formidable they are will depend, ultimately, on how distrustful Americans remain—the war on terrorism notwithstanding—of all large institutions, public and private.

CHAPTER FOUR

High-Performance Government in an Uncertain World

Robert J. Lempert and Steven W. Popper

A high-performance government must possess the capability to design, choose, and justify policies that stand a reasonable chance of
achieving their goals. This challenge becomes more difficult when
information to support such policies is ambiguous, a situation that is
increasingly a characteristic of our era of rapid and revolutionary
change. A salient example is the novel, fast-changing, and unpredictable threat of the new terrorism. Echoing the themes of the Volcker
Commission, the September 2002 National Security Strategy argues
that "the major institutions of American national security were designed in a different era to meet different requirements. All of them
must be transformed."[1] Secretary of Defense Donald Rumsfeld made
famous the concept of "unknown unknowns," that is, the need to
prepare for challenges for which we don't even know we are unpre-
pared.[2] President Bush sees his role as a strategic thinker in assessing
U.S. strategies against a wide range of risks.[3] Yet the policy process

---

[1] *The National Security Strategy of the United States of America*, Washington, DC: The White
House, September 2002, p. 29.

[2] "As we know, there are *known* knowns: There are things we know we know. We also know
there are known *unknowns*; that is to say, we know there are some things we do not know.
But there are also *unknown* unknowns—the ones we don't know we don't know" (Department of Defense news briefing, February 12, 2002, punctuation and emphasis added).

[3] "I think my job is to stay ahead of the moment. A president, I guess, can get so bogged
down in the moment that you're unable to be the strategic thinker that you're supposed to
be, or at least provide strategic thought. And I'm the kind of a person that wants to make
sure that all risk is assessed. There is no question what the reward is in this case. But a president is constantly analyzing, making decisions based upon risk . . . risk taken relative to the

shows little sign of escaping the inexorable pull of uncertainty absorption, stovepiped information, and what has been called "over-arguing." Despite best intentions, poorly hedged strategies still rise to the top of organizational structures not designed for the problems at hand, and arguments that are rhetorically compelling rather than ultimately solid can still carry the day.

This chapter suggests that a radically new approach to supporting decisionmaking under such conditions of deep uncertainty must be a key component in building a high-performance government for the 21st century.

The 21st century threatens to challenge government's ability to craft policies that can succeed in the face of unpredictable, often rapid transformations. Numerous forces—globalization, rapid technological advance, diffusion of massive destructive power into private hands, environmental pressures, and the evolution of deadly new diseases—will combine in a dynamic of continuous and accelerated change affecting people's options, the way they think, and how they behave in the world. Our government appears to be entering an era, unprecedented since the development of our modern bureaucratic state, where decisionmakers' personal and historical experience provides imperfect guidance. The best expert forecasts, however scientific, may prove ambiguous at best and contradictory at worst.

Such deep uncertainty presents several key problems for government's ability to design, choose, and justify successful policies. It can become difficult for organizations to provide decisionmakers the information they need. Indeed, in a world of novel and often interconnected problems, it becomes increasingly difficult for decisionmakers to specify *a priori* what information they would find most valuable. Rapid and revolutionary transformations deprive people of relying upon rules of thumb and past experience as guides. Organizations designed to implement a particular set of activities often have trouble addressing contingencies outside the norm.

—what can be achieved. . . . I think it is just instinctive. I'm not a textbook player. I'm a gut player" (George W. Bush as quoted in Woodward, 2002, pp. 136–137).

Uncertainty can also strain the standards of government accountability and contribute to paralysis of decisionmaking. Opposing parties to a decision will often exploit uncertainty to stake out different expectations about the future that support their favored policy choice. Because these positions are often non-falsifiable given the currently available information, the government may have difficulty gathering a consensus for any effective course of action. Even when the government does act, it often lacks any standard of accountability. When risks are novel and uncertain, how does one assess appropriate government actions? Is a policy failure or midcourse correction due to carelessness a mistake or just a natural rough patch for a well-conceived policy response?

These challenges afflict numerous policy areas besides counterterrorism. For instance, government agencies produce regular long-term forecasts suggesting looming financial problems for entitlement programs such as Social Security and Medicare. Even these troubling official scenarios may understate the challenge, since they rarely stray far from extrapolations of current trends and thus ignore potential shocks to the system such as increased longevity or early retirement driven by advances in medicine or changing economic conditions. Corrective actions, however, may involve near-term sacrifice, and all parties recognize that decadal forecasts by necessity are most likely to prove wrong. The uncertainty of the warning helps reduce any pressure for the government to act.

Similarly, the government often uses formal tools such as cost-benefit analysis to adjudicate many types of environmental policy. But in many areas, such as climate change or the protection of biodiversity, decisionmakers lack the necessary information to predict the benefits of alternative policies or the costs of pursuing them. Even the best science can only suggest concern.

Today's new terrorist threat poses an archetypal challenge of crafting high-performance government in the face of unpredictable contingencies. Organizations such as al Qaeda aim to inflict massive casualties on Americans and have few apparent inhibitions on the means they choose to do so (Benjamin and Simon, 2002). They thus present U.S. government bodies with a profoundly difficult dilemma in planning under deep uncertainty. To wait for clear evidence of planned attacks invites disaster, as captured in the oft-quoted aphorism of National Security Advisor Condoleezza Rice when speaking of Saddam Hussein:

> The problem here is that there will always be some uncertainty about how quickly he can acquire nuclear weapons. But we don't want the smoking gun to be a mushroom cloud.[4]

Such threats compel the government to act on ambiguous warning, whether the action is grounding civilian air transport to forestall a presumed attack or toppling adversarial regimes. The range of threats to be countered and the potential unintended consequences of government actions are so vast and numerous that any reasonable assessment of available intelligence may lead to a multitude of plausible interpretations and therefore conflicting implications for policy.

Dispassionately viewed, 21st century terrorism confronts planners with a heightened level of intellectual intimidation. Experts were once confident that they understood the nature of the threat and only needed warning of when and where terrorists would strike. Now, recent experience and information inadequacy give experts serious pause before they categorically discount almost any conceivable threat. Questions of how and why—to say nothing of who[5]—are now as preponderant as when and where. Seemingly compelling arguments may be mustered to support many contradictory claims about the effectiveness of any U.S. response that might be proposed. Yet even the U.S. government is insufficiently powerful and the soci-

---

[4] Widely reported on September 8, 2002 (see http://www.cnn.com/2002/ALLPOLITICS/09/08/iraq.debate/).

[5] At this writing, eight months after the cessation of major combat operations in Iraq, the identity of the prime perpetrators of attacks on foreign personnel and Iraqi civilians remains largely unknown. This may be viewed less as a case of intelligence failure than as another instance illustrating the challenges the 21st century will present to traditional intelligence services.

ety insufficiently resilient to take all possible actions against all plausible threats.

The organizations of 21st century governance will face many such difficult, ambiguous challenges. High-performance government will require new tools for crafting adaptive policies that are reasonably effective under a wide variety of unpredictable and often fast-changing circumstances.

This chapter suggests the need for attention to computer-based tools that make effective management of this ambiguity possible. Supported by such tools, decisionmakers can comprehend a multiplicity of plausible futures. More important, they can engage in systematic consideration and selection of strategies that enhance the chances for achieving their goals despite uncertainty over what the future actually holds.

Organizations and Ambiguity

A fruit-laden tree grows on a prehistoric savanna. A bipedal ape-human comes to the edge of the brush and ponders the risk of crossing the grasslands to gather a meal. Is a lion lurking in the high cover? She notices the swish of a tail: Swishing tail => Active lion => Danger. She withdraws. Later, a second ape long familiar with this patch comes by. No swishing tail, yet she knows that every so often a troop mate has been lost gathering fruit here. How often? She considers the risks, balances her need, and determines whether to cross. Now a third ape approaches this stretch of savanna for the first time. She can draw upon neither concrete information nor familiarity with this patch as a basis for logical deduction. She is, however, quite hungry and her survival hangs in the balance. She searches for familiar patterns and weighs them against her experience. She takes a few steps forward and then looks for changes in the patterns. How far can she proceed and still scramble back to safety? Where might a lion hide in this brush? Is that movement over there solely due to the wind? She ven-

tures forth step-by-step, updating information, planning for contingencies, perhaps tossing a rock or two to probe for any lurking predators. In this manner she proceeds into a potentially terrifying unknown.[6]

Individuals or small groups routinely and successfully manage under the conditions of ambiguity and deep uncertainty.[7] Whether raising their children, bringing new products to market, or commanding a platoon in battle, humans often draw inductively upon their experience, intuition, and narrative ability for *"what if?*-ing" to achieve their goals in an unfamiliar and unpredictable world.

As problems become more complicated and interests become more widely shared, humans rely on more formalized processes and organizations to array, assess, and apply available information to decisionmaking. Bureaucracies support information flows needed to address the challenges they are expected to face. But in novel situations, the flow of information within and across organizational boundaries may easily become suboptimal. More troubling, in a world that admits many plausible interpretations of available data, predetermined information flows may force an organization to settle on a single interpretation that may be more closely tied to the design of the organization and the interests of its members than to the realities of the world. Mistakes result, even from an organization's own perspective.

------

[6] Abstracted from Popper, 2004.

[7] Deep uncertainty is the condition where analysts do not know, or the parties to a decision cannot agree upon, (1) the appropriate models to describe the interactions among a system's variables, (2) the probability distributions to represent uncertainty about key variables and parameters in the models, and/or (3) how to value the desirability of alternative outcomes. This chapter uses the terms *ambiguity* and *deep uncertainty* interchangeably. A number of different terms are used for concepts similar to what we define as deep uncertainty. Knight (1921) contrasted risk and uncertainty, using the latter to denote unknown factors poorly described by quantifiable probabilities. Ellsberg's (1961) paradox addresses conditions of ambiguity where the axioms of standard probabilistic decision theory need not hold. There is an increasing literature on ambiguous and imprecise probabilities (de Cooman, Fine, and Seidenfeld, 2001). Ben-Haim's (2001) Info-Gap approach addresses conditions of what he calls *severe uncertainty*. The precise definition of the term *deep uncertainty* is our own.

Alternatively, an organization may fail to act at all when different groups within it settle on conflicting plausible interpretations that the leadership is unable to reconcile. And within large organizations, the ability to cope with ambiguity can be severely degraded.

March and Simon first used the concept of "uncertainty absorption" to describe how organizations can lose important but ambiguous information:

> In our culture, language is well developed for describing and communicating about concrete objects. . . . On the other hand, it is extremely difficult to communicate about intangible objects and non-standardized objects. Hence, the heaviest burdens are placed on the communications system by the less structured aspects of the organization's tasks, particularly by activity directed toward the explanation of problems that are not yet well defined. . . . Uncertainty absorption takes place when inferences are drawn from a body of evidence and the inferences, instead of the evidence itself, are then communicated. . . . Through uncertainty absorption, the recipient of the communication is severely limited in his ability to judge its correctness (March and Simon, 1958).

Uncertainty absorption aptly describes the flow of information through today's government organizations. In his study of the challenges facing U.S. intelligence agencies and their senior policymaking clients, Treverton (2001) notes that the government's conventions and institutions promote what he calls over-arguing. Senior decisionmakers communicate with one another, their organizations, and the public by using narratives—stories that combine statements of goals, assumptions about the world, and plans for actions. Policymakers craft these narratives knowing that a full acknowledgment of the underlying uncertainty would undercut their authority in policy debates.[8] This practice, however, can cause them to implement poli-

---

[8] Jonathan Baron of the University of Pennsylvania conducted an experiment that vividly illustrates a source of policymakers' concerns. Two groups of students were given the Intergovernmental Panel on Climate Change's (IPCC's) best estimates for future climate change. The control group was given these best estimates without uncertainty. Initially extreme positions about policy responses moderated. That is, the "certain" information created more

cies unnecessarily vulnerable to unexpected contingencies. In addition, Treverton notes that the inability of organizations to embrace multiple views of the future simultaneously may well lead them to miss telltale signs of emerging problems.[9] For instance, no one in the U.S. intelligence community expected India to test a nuclear weapon in 1998 because no American officials could tell themselves a likely story justifying why India would take such a step. Inability to see the world through the eyes of a Hindu nationalist politician made it difficult to place the evidence into the context of the actual story that was unfolding.

The formal analytical tools organizations use to process and summarize data in support of decisionmaking exacerbate these tendencies to concretize descriptions of risk in ways that ignore valuable information. For example, decision analytics combine economic models of rational decisionmaking with methods for treating uncertainty derived from science and engineering. These tools assess alternative decisions by first enumerating all the potential consequences of each decision and then assigning a value (utility) to each consequence. They treat uncertainty by assigning a probabilistic likelihood to each of the range of consequences and recommend the decision that provides, on average, the best value (optimum expected utility). These tools formalize the reasoning of the second ape.

Under conditions of well-characterized risk, these powerful quantitative tools have proved valuable in fields ranging from engineering to finance (Morgan and Henrion, 1990). They help structure extensive information; offer a systematic, objective comparison of alternative solutions; and usefully expose the logical fallacies to which human reasoning is prone (Dawes, 1998). Even when (as is frequently the case) the steps envisioned are not carried out in full detail,

---

consensus. The experimental group was given best estimates with the uncertainty. The extremes hardened in their positions, so that the uncertain information generated less consensus (see http://www.sas.upenn.edu/~baron/green.htm).

[9] Scenario-based planning (Schwartz, 1996) can successfully help organizations consider multiple views of the future. However, it is often difficult for an organization to link such scenarios to particular decisions.

this "predict-then-act" framework of information processing informs planning in a typical bureaucracy.

But the predict-then-act framework faces serious problems under conditions of deep uncertainty. The framework encourages organizations to underestimate the level of ambiguity. Quantifying risks with the consensus probability distributions required by predict-then-act analyses may convey an unjustified level of accuracy. Choices about the structure of such analyses often embody hidden but important value judgments. Organizations quite frequently possess important information that does not fit easily into the consensus models and probabilistic judgments demanded by these formalisms. For instance, debates over the federal budget and financing of long-term entitlement programs such as Social Security are regularly stymied by the tradition of presenting one or a small number of official forecasts. Such forecasts are routinely wrong, depend critically on the assumptions made, and obscure valuable information analysts possess about a wide range of uncertain contingencies facing the system and the impacts of potential responses to these contingencies.

Seasoned human decisionmakers, especially those who rise to lead large organizations, often understand quite well the limitations of predict-then-act analysis under conditions like that faced by the third ape. Organizations that require forecasts and more-sophisticated analyses as inputs to their planning often use them for a variety of roles unrelated to providing an accurate map for the future. Predict-then-act analysis can demonstrate due diligence, suggest potentially important trends, and encourage systematic consideration of many relevant factors. For instance, while no one may believe the literal results, the process of generating a ten-year federal budget forecast does require analysts to construct a self-consistent set of assumptions about all of the government's important future revenues and expenditures.

Senior decisionmakers generally interpret the results of predict-then-act analyses in the context of other crucial, non-quantitative information. They rely heavily on their experience and intuition as a guide to the credibility of any particular analysis and the best means to incorporate the underlying thinking into their decision process. The integration of predict-then-act analyses into planning is most successful when the decisionmakers' past experience provides a reliable context for applying the analytic output to the decision at hand. Rather than having a system in place to support this process, the integration of the decisionmakers' intuition and predict-then-act analyses takes place at the level of the individual. This can and does fail under conditions of deep uncertainty. Decisionmakers may base their estimates of risks on the conceptions formed at the start of discussions and use their most accessible experience as their basis of comparison. But when conditions of deep uncertainty offer multiple competing forecasts and analyses with different policy implications, decisionmakers have much opportunity to confuse what is true with what they wish to be true.

When confronting surprising or ambiguous information, the human reasoning process and computer-generated, predict-then-act analyses are each flawed in their separate ways. How can high-performance governmental processes be constructed to provide the proper information in a usable form to decisionmakers under conditions of deep uncertainty?

New Tools for Reasoning Across Multiple Futures

In the 21st century, government organizations will increasingly face novel and deeply uncertain challenges. In areas ranging from defeating terrorism, to halting new diseases, to spreading democracy and development, to protecting the environment, government will face problems like those of the third ape. New computer-based capabilities offer these organizations the ability to describe ambiguous information concretely, to consider multiple views of the future simultaneously, and to articulate strategies likely to yield favorable outcomes despite deep uncertainty.

In recent years, the fast processing, virtually unlimited memory, and powerful, interactive visualizations of modern computers have spawned new quantitative approaches to the ubiquitous, yet tenaciously problematic, task of decisionmaking under deep uncertainty (Lempert, Popper, and Bankes, 2003). Robust decisionmaking, a class of methods increasingly employed at RAND, uses the computer to support an iterative process in which humans propose strategies as potentially robust across a wide range of futures and the computer then challenges these strategies by suggesting futures where they may perform poorly. The alternatives can then be revised to hedge against these stressing futures, and the process is repeated for the new strategies. This iterative process addresses the challenge of uncertainty absorption, because the computer retains the full range of uncertainties, multiple interpretations, and other ambiguities and can bring key bits of information, consistent or contradictory, to decisionmakers' attention at any point where it might help distinguish among the merits of alternative decision options. This process can help break down institutional barriers to considering multiple futures, because it provides systematic criteria for determining which futures (those most important in distinguishing the choice among strategies) ought to be considered. It can help decisionmakers avoid over-arguing by allowing them to acknowledge multiple plausible futures and to make strong arguments about the best policies for hedging against a wide range of contingencies.

Robust decisionmaking rests on several principles, all familiar to the third ape, if impossible for her to articulate:

1. Reason over *multiple scenarios.* The set of plausible futures expressed in the scenarios should be diverse, in order to provide sufficient challenges against which to test alternative near-term policies. These scenarios can also facilitate group processes designed to elicit information and achieve buy-in to the analysis from stakeholders with very different values and expectations.
2. Seek *robust*, rather than optimal, strategies that do "well enough" across a broad range of plausible futures and of alternative ways of ranking the desirability of alternative scenarios. Robustness provides a useful criterion for organizational decisionmaking under uncertainty because it reflects both the normative choice required, while requiring specificity in characterizing the nature of "good enough," and the approach many decisionmakers actually use under such conditions.

3. Employ *adaptive* strategies to achieve robustness. Adaptive strategies change over time in response to new information; the predict-then-act framework takes little cognizance of this possibility.

4. Use computers to *characterize uncertainties* by their relevance to the selection of robust strategies. Predict-then-act analyses begin with consensus on a model for how actions are related to consequences and on specific probability estimates of risks. In contrast, robust decisionmaking seeks to identify strategies whose acceptable performance is largely insensitive to the wide ranges of uncertainties characteristic of many problems. It then characterizes a small number of key, irreducible tradeoffs inherent in the choice among such robust strategies. Predict-then-act methods use the computer as a calculator to yield "best" strategies contingent upon selected assumptions. Robust decisionmaking uses the computer as a tool for interactive exploration to discover and test hypotheses about robust decisions.

An Example from Business

The forces for change are already at work in the private sector. Business is beginning to utilize robust-decision approaches when faced with problems like that confronting the third ape. As an example, consider the problems inherent in launching a new line of automobiles—products of amazing complexity whose commercial success requires sophisticated engineering inextricably linked with hard-to-quantify judgments about the future course of technology and consumer aesthetics.[10] The product planning group at Volvo Car Company was charged with recommending a radical new product line to the company's senior management and board. The planning group consisted of analysts representing different parts of the firm—finance, marketing, design, engineering, production, and so forth—and was led by a senior vice president. The deep uncertainties surrounding

---

[10] This unpublished work was conducted by Evolving Logic, a firm specializing in the development of robust-decision support software applications.

this recommendation resulted in group gridlock. Some argued that a new product line was vital to maintaining a presence in important emerging niches. Others felt that the new products might compromise one of the firm's most valuable assets, its strong brand identification. The group heard compelling yet contradictory stories supporting a wide range of choices. Which story would ultimately prove correct would depend on consumer tastes, economic conditions, and competitors' innovations a half decade or more after the time for decision had passed.

The planning group attempted to assess the firm's options, using the same types of analyses commonly employed for less-radical new product lines. They constructed a series of spreadsheets capturing facets of the decision relevant to some part of the organization. The spreadsheets remained independent from one another. For instance, marketing focused on price points—that is, relative price—for different vehicles within a line, while finance focused on net revenues. The analysts working each spreadsheet gathered their own data, conducted their own sensitivity analyses over the uncertainties they recognized, and then passed a small number of outputs along to their colleagues who used them as inputs to their own extensive calculations.

This method had worked reasonably well for many of the firm's previous planning exercises where past experience served as a guide. But the process broke down when steps into a more uncertain future for a radically new product were being considered. The need for each group to produce transmissible outputs required making largely implicit and hidden assumptions, sometimes in direct contradiction to those made in other departments. These assumptions defeated any attempt to integrate the models into a unified planning tool. When the team gathered to debate the options, each member understood the weaknesses in his own models and the numbers he had passed along to his colleagues. But there was no way to discuss the interaction among these uncertainties, and thus there was little confidence in the overall results—a classic case of uncertainty absorption. Deep uncertainty overwhelmed the ability to use quantitative results to adjudicate among the fundamentally different stories about the firm's best choice. The manager leading the exercise worried that in the planning process, the best rhetoric, not the best argument, might carry the day.

A robust-decisionmaking system helped this product planning team use its quantitative information more effectively in the emotional, intuition-driven debate over the future direction of the firm. The system built for them had two parts:

- Scenario-generator software that could trace out a wide range of futures in the form of time series of key factors (e.g., revenues, costs) relevant to the firm's decision.
- Exploratory modeling software (Bankes, 1993; Bankes, Lempert, and Popper, 2001) to enable the generation, management, and visualization of the results of many scenarios.

The scenario generator was created by linking together into a single integrated assessment tool all the individual spreadsheets developed independently by members of the group. The product planning team had been unable to link these spreadsheets into a forecasting tool because each spreadsheet contained different estimates, frameworks, and languages. But framed as components of a scenario generator, the individual pieces could be glued together precisely by rendering explicit the wide range of plausible, but uncertain connections among the parts.

The project planning team used this robust-decisionmaking system to create two types of visualizations. These artifacts gave the group a visual language to describe the information it had, the ambiguities in the information, and the potential responses to them.

Figure 4.1 shows the first type of visualization, a landscape of plausible futures.[11] The landscape shows the performance of one of the alternative product strategies across the range of plausible futures defined by the spread of possible values for two key uncertainties, market demand and production costs. The cells display the internal

---

[11] All numbers used in this example have been changed from their original values to preserve confidentiality.

Figure 4.1
Landscape of Plausible Futures

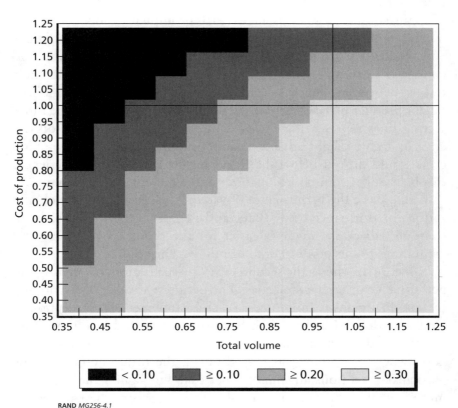

RAND *MG256-4.1*

rate of return (IRR) to be expected for the circumstances characterized by the values of the horizontal and vertical axes. The shading of
each square is keyed to various IRR thresholds. For example, the
lightest-colored cells represent scenarios where contingencies cause
the product line to exceed the 30 percent IRR threshold. In the black
region, where sales volume falls below expectations and product costs

are higher than expected, the product line fails to meet an IRR threshold of 10 percent.[12]

Visualizations such as Figure 4.1 prompted a flood of fundamental inquiries because they made explicit the extent of assumptions and choices embedded in the analyses. Even individuals who had conducted extensive sensitivity analyses were confronted with their results' dependence on basic assumptions. The figure shows one particular product plan whose core assumptions are defined by the intersecting lines representing the base case. This plan is poised on the edge of a cliff. Slight adverse changes in either sales or production costs would drop it below the firm's hurdle rate. In our experience, this behavior is common: Organizations are adept at generating forecasts that place the performance of valued plans just above the organization's performance goals (Park and Lempert, 1998). These landscape visualizations made it easier for the group to recognize and communicate this point to others in the organization.

Figure 4.2 shows the second type of visualization, comparing the performance of several strategies. The net present value of six alternative product plans is computed as each is simulated across a common landscape defined by deviation from the planned sales volume as indicated on the vertical axis. Again, each cell may be viewed as a scenario where one strategy is played out in the future defined by the particular conditions attached to that cell. The lighter the color, the more favorable the simulated result. Plan 1 performs best under the most optimistic forecasts but can fail if demand is less than expected. In contrast, Plan 3 has a good upside but fails more gracefully than Plan 1. This figure provides one compact visual representation of Plan 3 as the firm's robust strategy.

---

[12] The views are static representations generated using Computer Assisted Reasoning® system (CARs™) software. CARs operates dynamically so that those variables not actively represented in any view are present as slider bars in the graphic user interface. These may be moved individually or in groups to see how changes in other variables would affect the landscape views present on the screen. Visualizations such as Figures 4.1 and 4.2 are interactive. Planning teams subject these visual artifacts to extensive "what if" queries, thus testing the robustness of various plans over a very wide range of futures either manually or by launching computer searches.

Figure 4.2
Comparison of Product Plans Across Plausible Futures

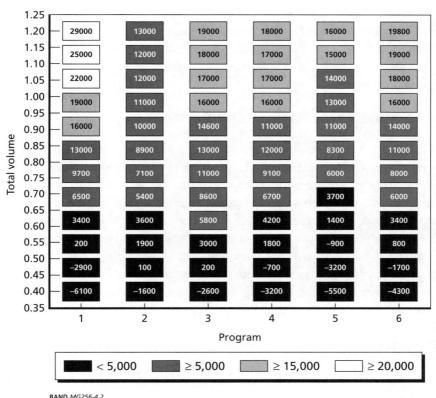

RAND MG256-4.2

The robust-decisionmaking system helped Volvo avoid the pit-falls of uncertainty absorption. The product planning team had be-gun its work with the expectation that it would recommend Plan 1, because that plan performed best under the optimistic assumptions that drove the team's interest in building a new automobile line. While using the robust-decisionmaking tool, the team settled on a recommendation for Plan 3, a version of which has since been pro-duced and marketed successfully. Although consideration of Plan 3 had already begun, visualizations such as Figure 4.2 provided the het-erogeneous team with a common language and common understanding of the uncertainties most important to the success of the product plans. The tools allowed the team to debate proper responses to these uncertainties, to crystallize the reasons for preferring Plan 3, and to communicate those reasons throughout the organization. The analysis helped the team avoid over-arguing by constructing narratives that acknowledged uncertainty but made strong claims about good strategy.

A Possible Application to Counterterrorism

We now present one vision of how such a robust-decisionmaking system might improve senior U.S. national security decisionmakers' ability to craft more-robust strategies in the war against terrorism. Such a tool might operate as a decision-support portal available from the desktop computers of staff members of the National Security Council (NSC) or other relevant agencies. The system would have available vast quantities of data relevant to terrorist operations, including a variety of government reports, as well as briefs and assessments from individual intelligence analysts. It would include the original data used to make the assessments. The data would be protected by the security procedures of different agencies. In principle, the entire body of information available in the U.S. government would be accessible through the system.

The NSC staff might turn to such data when preparing policy options to address some emerging crisis—for instance, a response to warnings of an imminent attack by man-portable air-defense missiles on a U.S. civilian aircraft—or addressing more strategic decisions about funding allocations across different counterterrorism activities. Without the help of analytic tools, NSC staff would find the mass of contradictory and partially developed information nearly impenetrable, often more hindrance than help. A robust-decisionmaking system would help them identify the information most relevant to the government's deliberations. The system would help staff create visualizations that would improve the ability to identify and articulate key risks posed by alternative policy choices, identify the individuals and/or data in the government most important in judging the seriousness and credibility of the alternative risks, and frame and then evaluate alternative policy options for hedging against weaknesses.

Suppose, for example, the NSC faces a decision falling in the broad middle range between extreme short-term tactical response and long-term strategic posture. Ambiguous warnings have been received in the form of increasing signal intelligence concerning a new form of potential terrorist strike on the United States. It is not clear who is involved or what state of terrorist preparations this traffic represents. Several options for countermeasures have been tabled. They each entail certain costs, with the options most likely to be successful in warding off such attacks being the most expensive in terms of dollars and domestic and international politics.

The NSC staff might then present traditional intelligence briefings based on the best available evidence to senior decisionmakers, the President, and the cabinet, who would devise some course of action. At this point, the staff could turn to the robust-decisionmaking system to identify any crucial information that might suggest and help assess unrecognized vulnerabilities in this plan and point to means for hedging against these weaknesses. Using embedded system tools, they might sketch a flow chart of the steps needed to implement the policy successfully. They could identify the evidence that supports the assumptions behind this policy, and the system would launch a search over numerous databases, looking for plausible data and hypotheses that could cause the chosen strategy to fail.

The system would return a number of visualizations similar to those shown in Figures 4.1 and 4.2, each suggesting scenarios and the key assumptions behind them that might cause the plan to fail. The system would identify the most credible information supporting each of these scenarios and help identify the individuals and groups in the government most knowledgeable about this information. Ad hoc interagency groups, working face-to-face and through computer-based collaborative tools, could review the scenarios to determine which should be brought to the attention of the senior decisionmakers.[13]

---

[13] These ad hoc groups would be facilitated by computer-based "center-edge" collaborative tools that enable groups of individuals relevant to some emerging problem to form quickly

Let us speculate on what might happen next. Suppose the system identified a dozen potential "breaking scenarios" showing the failure modes for some proposed policy. The NSC staff might immediately reject four scenarios as clearly impossible, recognizing that the search algorithms that discovered them were not accounting for information known to the human analysts. Three additional scenarios might be similar to ones already examined in detail by existing ad hoc interagency teams. The system would bring these teams to the NSC staff's attention. The remaining five scenarios might fall naturally across the expertise of three separate, ad hoc interagency teams. Rapidly convened through a mix of face-to-face meetings and online workspaces, the three new groups could review the evidence behind each of the potential breaking scenarios. Upon such analysis, three more scenarios might be rejected as implausible. The NSC staff might then convene a new ad hoc group to propose adjustments in the administration's policy to counter the five remaining difficult scenarios. The group might identify easy hedging actions against three of them. Two scenarios might remain as serious risks to the plan, and the individuals most knowledgeable about the evidence behind them could be summoned to brief senior decisionmakers.

In addition, during the course of its work, as it builds deeper insight into the strengths and weaknesses of the proposed strategy, one of the ad hoc groups might identify a potential missed opportunity not included in the computer systems' models and data. The group

---

regardless of their organizational affiliations, work effectively together on a specific challenge as if they all resided within a single organization, and then disband when that challenge has been met. The "center" rubric describes the hierarchical pinnacle within each government organization to which information is designed to flow, where decisions are taken, and which is ultimately accountable for the way government resources are used. The "edge" refers to those lower in or even outside of each organizational hierarchy who are in contact with the external environment and may have the most ready access to the organization's relevant data and expertise. Center-edge concepts aim to provide a full suite of rapidly customizable computer-based applications—tools for data and other resource discovery, role negotiation, policy development and enforcement, planning, execution monitoring, knowledge capture, after-action review—and aim to provide an alternative to the need for creating new or interagency organizations to handle quickly emerging and/or transitory problems. Bardach's work on the enablers and dynamics of interagency collaboration provides a useful framework for considering the effectiveness and design of such systems (Bardach, 1998, 1999).

could add the relevant information to then assess the credibility of such surprises (Lempert, Popper, and Bankes, 2002). Any such credible scenarios and the evidence behind them could be passed along to NSC staff and senior decisionmakers.[14]

The resulting process would contribute to high-performance government in several ways. Uncertainty absorption could be considerably reduced when senior decisionmakers have the capability to test their plans against multiple interpretations of available data. The tendency toward over-arguing could also be relaxed by allowing decisionmakers to make strong claims about the best strategy, based on a systematic consideration of these multiple interpretations. Further, such a system could resolve the principal conundrum surrounding "red-teaming," where a group is tasked to challenge a proposed course of action during or after its gestation. On the one hand, those best placed to effectively red-team are those who are most vested in the emerging strategy or policy. On the other, while outsiders will hold no such allegiance, this very fact makes them both less knowledgeable about the nuances of the plan and potentially dangerous to have engaged. Having in place a system such as the one we have described would permit red-teaming to emerge naturally from the policy formulation process itself.

The greatest potential benefit is also the most crucial. Such a process increases the chances of yielding policies that are implementable, robust, adaptive, and effective in the face of the potentially great challenges with which government will be confronted. The ability to reliably meet such challenges characterizes high-performance governance.

---

[14] Current embodiments of this technology have already shown their value in strategic thinking. One might expect such systems to follow the learning curves typical of new technologies. That is, as the tool is more widely diffused and experience with its use grows, the time horizon of the problems it could address will rapidly shorten. Similarly, the ease and rapidity with which its full capabilities could be used to good effect will also increase over time.

The Opportunities and Challenges of Implementation

Few private or public organizations will escape the need to apply the lessons of the third ape to the challenges of the 21st century. In particular, these lessons have important implications for the Volcker Commission's goal of restructuring government institutions in an era of rapid and revolutionary change.

In addition to their promise for improving the ability of organizations confronted with deep uncertainty to make good decisions, these new decision tools (and the organizational changes that accompany them) may reduce the need for fundamental government reorganizations. The current organizational boundaries can be made more permeable with better integration of the decision process with information flows and analyses. The national security example offered above shows how government bodies might use available information more wisely and with greater purpose. The example also illustrates how robust-decisionmaking tools embedded in the system for information transfer can enable the rapid teaming and information sharing across organizations' boundaries that is often required to deal with unexpected challenges. Reorganization designed to incorporate new mechanisms for handling ambiguous information may offer an escape from the treadmill of perpetually revisiting organizational architectures. That is, the same transformations required to replace the predict-then-act model with an analytic-decision nexus incorporating robust decisionmaking may also relieve the pressure for constantly reformatting the apparatus of governance in the face of recurring novelty and deep uncertainty. *Virtual* government reorganization, assisted by new computer-based tools, could become a more commonplace response to the emergence of new, ambiguous threats.

Finally, some argue that the cynical view of government process is the most realistic: Decisions are based less on analysis than on political exigency. True enough, in many instances. Yet this is possible partly because of the difficulty experienced by those both inside and outside the process in visualizing all relevant elements and their complex interactions. We have seen in the past how access to better conceptual tools has affected not only the quality of government decisions, but also the acceptable space within which the inevitable trade-offs are made. The development of national income accounting, for example, and the diffusion of vocabulary such as "gross national product," "balance of trade," and "unemployment rate" created intellectual tools that enabled wiser economic policies to be adopted and enabled the public to hold the policymakers accountable. The vision portrayed in this chapter should have a similar effect. Advances in instrumentation will permit more-effective government and enhance its credibility among the various communities of interest—a likely hallmark of effective governance in a future of rapid change and voluminous information flows.

Volcker Commission Recommendation 1: Reorganize by Mission

CHAPTER FIVE

Organizing for Reorganizing

Susan M. Gates

The Volcker Commission's argument for a mission-based reorganization is logically compelling, almost unassailable. Indeed, the recommendation is so logical that the following question immediately comes to mind: Why is the government not organized along mission lines already? The answer, in brief, is what has been called "structural politics." Any fundamental reorganization would have to overcome many political obstacles. This essay considers an analogy, the Defense Base Closure and Realignment Act, which created a way to organize for reorganizing that overcame what seemed to be intractable political obstacles. This chapter asks, might a similar process be used to implement the Volcker Commission recommendations?

Background

The progressive model of government reform suggests that the structure of government is a key barrier to effectiveness (Knott and Miller, 1987). High-performing organizations have clear missions and are structured in such a way as to focus energy toward the achievement of those missions. The progressive model or approach suggests that government should be organized like a corporation, with divisions that have clear and focused missions. A government so organized would be more effective and efficient.

The Report of the National Commission on the Public Service (reproduced in Chapter 2 of this volume) presents 14 recommendations. The first recommendation is arguably the linchpin of that package: *The federal government should be reorganized into a limited number of mission-related executive departments.*

> The simple reality is that federal public servants are constrained by their organizational environment. Changes in federal personnel systems will have limited impact if they are not accompanied by significant change in the operating structure of the executive branch. This is why we begin our recommendations with an emphasis on issues of organization (Chapter 2, p. 29).

This is certainly not the first time the issue of bureaucratic restructuring to improve effectiveness has been suggested. Knott and Miller describe a series of failed presidential efforts advocating the centralization of federal government activities dating back to the Johnson era (Knott and Miller, 1987, pp. 158–164), including the Ash Council recommendations and the President's Advisory Council on Executive Organization of the 1970s. These efforts, grounded in the progressive model of administrative reform, advocated that corporate-style organizational structure be applied to government bureaucracy to achieve a bureaucracy that is accountable, neutral, and efficient.

The Volcker report provides some guidance as to what the restructured government should look like. Effective government management requires mission coherence within federal government departments. Thus, the executive branch should be reorganized into mission-based departments and agencies that would be structured in a way that enables each to fulfill its mission. The number of independent departments would be relatively small and organizational subunits (agencies) performing activities that support or are related to a particular mission would fall within the relevant department. This structure would promote coordination and limit redundancy and bureaucratic competition.[1]

---

[1] In this chapter, we focus on how the recommendations of the Volcker report could be implemented, essentially assuming that those recommendations are worthwhile. It should be noted, however, that some view bureaucratic competition as a positive aspect of our federal

With rare exception, agencies with related mandates should fit together in a broad organizational scheme that permits and encourages constructive interaction rather than battles over turf (Chapter 2, p. 29).

Rather than prescribe a structure for federal departments, the Volcker report suggests that the structure of any department be dictated first and foremost by what will help it achieve its mission most effectively. However, the report does suggest that an effective structure would involve a limited number of large departments responsible for high-level policy decisions. Individual operating agencies, reporting to a department, would perform the day-to-day government functions. Flexibility, minimal hierarchical layers, and small, focused operating units overseen by politically appointed department-level managers are presented as key elements of new federal departments.

The concept of a mission-focused structure for the federal government provides the cornerstone for the recommendations that follow in the Volcker report. However, there is little in the report to suggest *how* this would be accomplished, implemented, and maintained beyond a suggestion that the President be given the authority to restructure the executive branch. The report discusses the transition as if it would be a one-time process in which the President, or a group of wise men and women at the President's behest, would look at everything the government is currently doing and group these activities into mission-based organizations. The new federal departments would be subject to congressional oversight but would be given substantial autonomy to achieve their missions.

Federal departments should be reorganized to bring together agencies that contribute to a broad mission in a manner responsible to direction from elected leaders and their appointees, and subject to careful oversight by Congress but sufficiently independent in administration to achieve their missions (Chapter 2, p. 29).

government and suggest that efforts to reduce overlap and redundancy are misguided. For an overview of these alternative views, see Knott and Miller, 1987, p. 267.

The implicit assumption is that these efficient, mission-based organizations would not only be accepted and faithfully implemented, they would also be immune to the bureaucratic accretion process that led us to the situation we have today.

This premise is questionable at best. As dysfunctional as the current structure may be, key players in the system have figured out how to work within that structure, get things done, and ensure that their interests are considered. Change implies uncertainty—in particular, uncertainty over who will have access to political decisionmakers and who will be able to exert influence. As a result, it is unlikely that the restructuring recommendations could be developed in an apolitical context or be readily accepted, implemented, and maintained. This point is not fatal for the Volcker Commission's recommendations, but it does point to the need to develop something beyond the scope of the commission's purview, i.e., an implementation strategy.

The process of reorganizing the government will not be a single action or a directive driven entirely by efficiency objectives. Rather, it will be a long-term and highly political process. What might a successful process look like? Experience and theory can provide some useful guidance. In the next section of this chapter, we explore the implications of the politics of structural choice for the mission-based reforms presented. We then flesh out the key tasks involved in making the transition to and maintaining a mission-based structure for the federal government. Finally, we present a scenario for accomplishing those tasks as a way to stimulate an appreciation of the underlying challenges.

The Role of Structural Politics

During congressional hearings, Paul Volcker emphasized that government reorganization involves "very sensitive political constituency problems that have been turf problems between agencies." These political concerns are echoed in academic work. Behn argues that structural reforms, while attractive, are virtually impossible to achieve. Rather than wasting energy trying to fix the system, we should "get on with the task of helping public managers function effectively within these constraints" (Behn, 2003, p. 193). He goes on to recommend that the government stop wasting time on restructuring initiatives and should focus instead on emphasizing the development of leadership capacity among civil servants as a strategy for improving public service. However, political science theory, as well as historical experience, suggests that changes of the magnitude sought by the Volcker Commission must be grounded in structural reform. If even high-quality, well-trained public managers are seriously constrained by today's bureaucratic structures, rules, policies, and procedures, it is crucial to devote energy to fixing the system.

Restructuring would be simple if all parties had in mind the same goal, i.e., to structure the government so as to maximize its effectiveness. But the objective of maximizing efficiency is neither widely embraced in public administration nor politically benign. Moe asserts that "American public bureaucracy is not designed to be effective. The bureaucracy arises out of politics, and its design reflects the interests, strategies, and compromises of those who exercise political power" (Moe, 1989, p. 267). Although restructuring proposals emphasize administrative issues, political considerations are never far from the surface. Aberbach and Rockman caution those promoting administrative reform not to ignore politics: "Bureaucracy is very much about power; it is thus eminently political" (Aberbach and Rockman, 2000, p. 3). Efforts to restructure the federal bureaucracy will certainly change the balance of power. As Seidman aptly notes, "In the choice of institutional types and structural arrangements we are making decisions with significant political implications" (Seidman, 1980, p. 315).

Moe's theory of structural politics provides insight into the political challenges involved in attempting to restructure the government to promote efficiency. The theory is based on a review of the evolution of several federal agencies. The lesson is that public agencies cannot be expected to behave like private corporations. The contrast is summarized thus: "In the private sector, structures are generally designed by participants who want the organization to succeed. In the public sector, bureaucracies are designed in no small measure by participants who explicitly want them to fail" (Moe, 1989, p. 326).

Although individual citizens don't know or care much about the details of public administration, organized interest groups are extremely aware of the bureaucratic structure and what it can do for them. In Moe's theory,[2] the structure of federal agencies becomes a pawn in the process of political negotiation, and strategizing interest groups think hard about what structures will best serve their needs. Because political negotiation involves groups both for and against specific policies and programs, the structure that results from such negotiation need not be the structure that most effectively achieves the policy aim. The inefficiencies that exist in the federal bureaucratic structure are not always unintended mistakes or historical relics from a time when the government needed a different structure to serve different purposes. Instead, Moe argues, politicians and interest groups intentionally impose inefficiencies in the design of federal agencies to serve short- and long-run political purposes. Winning pressure groups recognize that they may not always be in power, and they create structures to limit change within the agency in the event of changes in political control. As a result, organizational design may intentionally involve convoluted and inefficient procedures designed to limit the influence of the new party in power.

Congress also has an incentive to create structures that allow for political intervention. Because legislators need the support of interest groups in order to win elections, they promote political structures that provide opportunities to "intervene quickly, inexpensively, and in ad hoc ways to . . . advance the interests of particular clients in particular matters" (Moe, 1989, p. 278).

The presidency is another factor in the politics of structural choice. According to Moe, presidents are less susceptible than legislators to the demands of interest groups. The presidency seeks to control bureaucracy in order to make it an effective instrument for achieving the administration's goals and objectives (particularly if

---

[2] There are two basic mechanisms for creating federal agencies: presidential-driven reorganization and the legislative process.

those goals are in opposition to the goals of victorious coalitions of interest groups).

In the end, Moe argues, the objectives of interest groups and of Congress are most closely aligned in the politics of structural choice, and "groups on both sides will find Congress a comfortable place in which to do business" (Moe, 1989, p. 281). In other words, interest groups will work through the legislative process to implement structures that are inefficient but serve their interests. Although some may complain about the inefficiency that results, Moe argues that no strong, coherent constituency for "efficient government" exists to work against these forces.

This perspective of structural politics has important implications for the restructuring proposed in the Volcker report. The implementation and sustainability of Volcker-style reforms will require an explicit commitment on the part of both the legislative and the executive branch of government to change fundamentally the politics of structural choice. Moe was not optimistic that such change would be possible (Moe, 1989); however, his pessimism may reflect a focus on piecemeal rather than revolutionary, governmentwide change. Aberbach and Rockman are equally pessimistic, following their review of broad, governmentwide reform efforts. They emphasize that real reform "will require fundamental political choices that go far beyond management issues" (Aberbach and Rockman, 2000, p. 187), and they doubt that the political will exists to make choices that would support more-effective management.

The recommendations of the Volcker Commission are based on a belief that dramatic structural and organizational change is indeed possible today.[3] The terrorist attacks of September 11, 2001, highlighted the fact that overlapping missions and bureaucratic redundancy can have grave consequences. Organizational issues were highlighted as a prime culprit in the government's failure to anticipate the attacks. By obscuring lines of authority and responsibility and impeding information flows, structural issues pose challenges for our

---

[3] For the contrary view, see Light, 1997.

national security. The creation of the Department of Homeland Security calls into question the pessimistic view that restructuring is simply an impossible task.

In the remainder of this chapter, I assume that the potential exists for large-scale political acceptance of systematic organizational reforms that would limit the extent to which structure is subject to political negotiation. Identifying whether such support actually exists and designing strategies for tapping into it for change are important issues that are beyond the scope of this essay. In the following, the core tasks involved in such a restructuring effort are defined, and suggestions for how these tasks might be accomplished are advanced. These suggestions are made bearing in mind the specific challenges posed by the politics of structural choice.

Four Tasks of Government Redesign

To restructure the government around core missions and to ensure that an effective structure is maintained, four key tasks must be performed:

1. Identify core missions
2. Divide current executive branch activities along mission lines
3. Make midcourse corrections
4. Maintain the mission-based structure over time

The final task, maintenance, includes activities such as dealing with boundary issues, making organizational changes, figuring out where new activities should be housed, and determining when a new core mission should be added. The implications of structural politics must be considered in relation to all four tasks.

What Are the Core Missions of the Executive Branch of the Federal Government?

The first task is to identify the core missions of the federal government. Core missions are different from activities. The Volcker Commission muddles this point by emphasizing the tremendous duplication of effort across the federal government in terms of the number of agencies operating similar programs.

The report seems to suggest a bottom-up approach for identifying core missions, recommending, for example, that programs designed to achieve similar outcomes be combined within one agency. It also suggests that agencies with similar or related missions should be combined into one core department. An important challenge inherent in such an approach is that of determining the basis upon which related programs will be grouped. One program might be related to six other programs, but those six programs may or may not be related directly to one another. Without an overarching sense of core missions, it may be difficult to determine which related programs should be grouped together. Another concern with the bottom-up approach is that the entire set of Volcker Commission recommendations is based on the finding that the current structure of government is inefficient. As a result, it is possible that the restructuring process will involve pruning in addition to reshuffling and reorganization.

Finally, a bottom-up approach might misinterpret the objective of many existing activities. Labels can be misleading. For example, the Volcker report notes that the federal government operates more than 90 early childhood programs. One might be tempted to group all these activities into a Department of Early Childhood or a Department of Education. However, some, even many, of these programs exist primarily to serve objectives unrelated to education or early childhood development. For example, Department of Defense (DoD) early childhood programs may be serving an underlying workforce management objective for DoD (i.e., to better meet the specific child-care needs of military personnel so they can support and fight wars without worrying about whether their children are well cared for). Programs sponsored by the Department of Labor may be intended to facilitate full-time employment for single mothers. And programs sponsored by the Department of Education may be designed to promote school readiness for disadvantaged children. Grouping all three programs together may not yield efficiency gains or economies of scale, because the programs have different aims. Similarly, to prevent an organization with a mission that is not related to early childhood, such as DoD, from running an early childhood program if it determines that such a program is needed to help the department meet its overall mission would seem to go against the Volcker Commission's recommendations that government agencies be given the flexibility to achieve their missions. It is important to keep in mind that any department pursuing its mission may engage in a wide variety of activities in support of that mission.

There is a strong argument for creating an organizational structure that encourages awareness of similar programs across agencies and at least considers whether replication could be reduced. This could be accomplished through cross-cutting task forces on topics or issues that cut across agencies. Awareness, information sharing, and professional development might be encouraged across these programs, but such coordination need not imply reorganization or structural integration.

A more practical approach to defining the core missions of the federal government would begin by articulating those missions and only then grouping existing activities related to them into departments, as is suggested by the strategic planning literature. In his congressional testimony on the Volcker report, Frank Carlucci recalled the proposal of the Ash Commission that all domestic agencies be grouped into four departments: community development, human resources, economic affairs, and natural resources. It would seem that in today's complex world, more specific missions, and hence more departments, may be needed. The blank-slate core missions might include the following:

- Providing for the national defense
- Ensuring the security of the homeland
- Supporting the transportation infrastructure and ensuring its safety
- Representing U.S. interests in foreign countries and supporting Americans abroad

- Gathering and disseminating objective information on the U.S. population, economy, workforce, etc.
- Protecting the environment and managing public land
- Ensuring that a minimum standard of education is available to all children
- Ensuring equal opportunity (in various contexts)
- Managing the social safety net
- Enforcing the tax code, collecting taxes, and managing the federal budget
- Managing the structure of the federal government

Restructuring the Government Along Mission Lines

Once the core missions have been identified, the real work begins. It is unreasonable to expect that the new structure can be redesigned in a one-shot effort. Reorganizing current activities along mission lines will be a large undertaking. If the new department structure is to be truly mission-based, there will be substantial change. Some agencies will be moved wholesale into new departments; some agencies or programs will be restructured before being moved; other agencies or programs will be dissolved, with their responsibilities possibly assumed by other agencies.

In congressional testimony on the Volcker report, Donna Shalala suggested that "each of the new mission-centered departments would be composed of the agencies tasked with contributing to that mission. Programs with similar objectives would be combined in the same agency" (*From Reorganization to Recruitment*, 2003, p. 35). Some activities will relate to several missions. Other activities may relate to no missions. The process of restructuring the federal government must be capable of resolving conflict among departments that may lay claim to a particular agency and of placing those activities that are deemed necessary but don't have an obvious home.

Making Midcourse Corrections

Just as framers of the U.S. Constitution could not account for all potential changes or future needs, those designing the new organizational structure cannot be expected to get everything right the first time. As a result, substantial midcourse corrections will likely be needed to adjust the new structure as departments try to deal with boundary issues or simply discover errors that must be corrected.

Maintaining the Mission-Based Structure

Over the longer term, new activities and even new missions will emerge for the federal government. Determining where new activities should be housed within the structure and when new core missions should be added—ensuring that this is done in a manner that is consistent with the core principles of the reorganization and is not subject to structural politics—will be ongoing tasks.

In sum, the process of reorganizing the federal government according to key missions will be a long and iterative process that will require continuous effort if the new structure is to be sustained. Existing activities must be restructured according to the core missions, adjustments must be made to the new structure in the short run, and there must be active oversight to ensure that the new structure doesn't fracture under the pressures of structural politics. To accomplish these aims, the restructuring process will thus need something akin to the process for constitutional amendments in order to allow for changes and oversight in both the short and the long run. The manner in which this process is approached will influence just how difficult it is. In the next section, we propose a strategy for accomplishing these tasks in a way that might limit the difficulties.

A Strategy for Accomplishing the Tasks

In view of the discussion of structural politics, the challenge is to allow for substantial input from interested parties without creating the same political dynamic that has led to the current ineffective government structure. We propose dividing the four tasks into two phases that are tackled separately by separate structures. The first phase—the design phase—involves the first task, identifying the core missions. The second phase—the implementation and maintenance phase—involves the other three tasks.

At the Congressional Hearing on the Volcker report, Paul Volcker suggested that the President be given expedited authority to recommend structural reorganization of federal departments (Chapter 2, p. 56) and that those proposals should be subject to a yes or no vote within a specified time frame. A comprehensive approach would be more likely to succeed than a sequential one. Weingast and Marshall argue that political exchange and coalition building on issues that are not being considered simultaneously is very difficult because of the high level of uncertainty in the political environment (Weingast and Marshall, 1988). As Frank Carlucci noted in his congressional testimony, "Only a total approach makes sense. Doing it bit by bit stirs up just as many hornets as total overhaul. Moreover, an overarching concept is essential to mustering the necessary political support" (*From Reorganization to Recruitment*, 2003, p. 39). Similar arguments in favor of a comprehensive approach to major reform were advanced in the early 1990s when Eastern European governments were grappling with the question of how to transition from a communist political and economic system to a market economy (Lipton and Sachs, 1990).

These two principles thus shape the recommendations below: (1) the initial reorganization must be simultaneous rather than piecemeal, and (2) structural politics must be considered at each stage.

A BRAC-Style Process Could Be Used to Define Core Federal Missions

During congressional hearings on the Volcker report, Paul Volcker likened government reorganization to base closure decisions and trade negotiations. This is an important insight for the design phase of this strategy. If a comprehensive reorganization of the U.S. government is possible, it may require a bold way to organize for reorganizing. The Defense Base Closure and Realignment Act of 1990 (Public Law 101-510) may provide a useful template.[4] The decision to close a military base has important similarities to administrative restructuring

---

[4] Hix (2001) and Levy et al. (forthcoming) provide useful overviews of the base realignment and closure (BRAC) process.

decisions. The impetus behind both types of decisions is efficiency and/or cost savings. As with the benefits of government restructuring, the benefits of base closure are diffuse, while the costs are concentrated and imposed upon groups with a strong incentive to oppose the reforms or closure. The 1990 act grew out of the perceived failure of alternative approaches over the years. Kirshenberg provides a brief history of base closure leading up to the act (Kirshenberg, 1995). Base closure actions initiated by DoD in the 1970s created tremendous political controversy, leading to congressional legislation providing Congress with the authority to determine which bases would be subject to closure. Not surprisingly, given the concentrated costs and diffuse benefits, Congress recommended no bases for closure between 1977 and 1988.

The act called for the creation of an independent defense base closure and realignment commission, responsible for reviewing and approving or modifying recommendations made by the Secretary of Defense regarding the list of bases to be closed or realigned. The independent commission is to comprise eight members. The President is authorized to make recommendations for appointment to the commission but is required to consult with the Speaker of the House on two of the members, with the majority leaders of the Senate on two members, and with the minority leaders of the Senate and House on one member each. The base closure process begins with the Secretary of Defense, who must articulate a force structure plan and a list of criteria to be used in making recommendations for base closure and realignment. After opportunities for congressional and public comments, the criteria must be applied in developing a list of military installations to be closed or realigned, and those choices must be justified vis-à-vis the force structure plan and the approved closure criteria. The role of the independent defense base closure commission is then to hold public hearings, review the Defense Secretary's list, and report its findings and recommendations to the President. The President must then approve the list in its entirety before the recommendations are forwarded to Congress. The President is not allowed to pick and choose individual bases and exclude them from the list.

Congress must consider the recommendations in total on a specified time schedule.

Two key features of the BRAC process would be essential in any process for identifying the core missions of the government:

1. Broad political input would be required in developing the procedures for identifying the missions and in approving the final list of missions.
2. A single list of core missions would be developed, and there would be no opportunity for individuals or groups to demand the inclusion or exclusion of a particular mission. Congress would be responsible for passing legislation to authorize the mission determination process. An important element of this legislation would be core principles to be followed in identifying the missions. A potentially effective approach would be to appoint a commission of nine or ten individuals and task them with the responsibility of identifying the core missions. Congress could establish a limited set of guidelines regarding the characteristics of this list (e.g., there can be no more than 15 core missions and no fewer than seven) but would not specify that certain things be included as core missions.

Given the importance of this task, it would be wise to require the appointed individuals to be well respected, with high-level management experience in the federal government and/or the private sector. These individuals should be familiar with the federal government, but they must be viewed as independent parties with nothing to gain or lose from the identification of core missions. Therefore, these individuals would be required to resign from any current federal government position. Participation on the committee must be a full-time, short-term appointment. The appointment process must carefully consider conflicts of interest. Importantly, those who are part of this commission would not be eligible to play a role in phase-two efforts involving implementation and maintenance. The President would be responsible for appointing the members of the commission, subject to congressional approval. As with appointments to the

BRAC commission, Congress may require the President to collaborate with party leaders in the selection of members.

This committee would be responsible for submitting a draft list of core missions along with a justification for those choices within a specified time frame (e.g., three months). The draft list would include no commentary related to which programs, agencies, or activities should or should not be attributed to particular missions. The list would be subject to comment from all existing cabinet secretaries, the House, and the Senate, as well as public hearings. After considering comments from various sources, the committee would submit a final list of core missions for congressional approval. In presenting that list, the committee might be required to explicitly respond to comments from Congress and cabinet secretaries. Congress would then consider the list in total for approval or rejection, with no opportunity for modifying it in a conference committee or through other mechanisms. If both houses of Congress approve the list, it would then be sent to the President for approval or rejection.

Implementing and Maintaining Structural Reforms Will Require the Establishment of a New Federal Entity

Upon approval of the list of core missions, phase two would begin. Again, the key challenge is finding a way to allow political input without returning to the political dynamics that led to the current situation through bureaucratic accretion. Even with agreement on the core missions of the federal government, fierce battles will be waged regarding whether certain programs or agencies will continue to exist and, if so, under the auspices of which department. The reorganization process must allow for political input while guarding against the danger of being frozen by political wheeling and dealing. Given the inevitability that mistakes will be made, the plan for phase two must allow for some (but not too much) tinkering.

The starting point for the restructuring effort would be the development of a set of core principles or guidelines according to which the restructuring would take place and federal departments would be managed in the future. These rules might be developed by Congress or by the executive branch (e.g., the Office of Management and

Budget), subject to congressional approval. The rules would specify basic management principles—such as the types of positions to be filled by political appointees as opposed to career civil service employees—or general employment principles but would provide the flexibility and latitude needed to implement the initial reform and ensure that it is maintained over time. The challenge will be to strike a balance between guidance related to core principles and overly prescriptive directives on specific issues. For example, the rules might specify general procedures for disposing of potentially redundant or unnecessary functions, but they should not require that specific programs or agencies be eliminated or retained. The basic principle of these guidelines should be that structural decisions should enhance the ability of federal departments, agencies, and programs to achieve their missions.

To limit the extent to which management and structural decisions are driven by structural politics, the implementation and long-term maintenance of the restructuring initiative would be the responsibility of a newly created "Good Housekeeping Office." The office's first responsibility would be to carve up current federal government activities according to the new department structure defined by the list of core missions. The activities of the office would be guided by the general parameters or restructuring rules provided by Congress. These rules could specify issues or decisions that require congressional approval, establish limits on the number of agencies created, and so forth. Within those rules, this office would have substantial authority and autonomy to determine the precise structure of federal government agencies. It would allocate existing programs or agencies to departments, eliminate unneeded activities, and perhaps suggest the creation of new programs or agencies in cases where the current portfolio of government functions appears insufficient for meeting the mission of a particular department. That initial plan would be subject to input from Congress and current cabinet officials. As in the BRAC process, this input would be provided within a specified time frame as a single response to the initial plan developed by the Good Housekeeping Office. A final design that considers, but need not accept, the input and that covers each department and all current government functions would be developed and presented to Congress for approval as a whole.

Once the new structure has been approved, the role of the Good Housekeeping Office would become more reactive. The initial restructuring effort will not get everything right. Some functions will have been overlooked or placed into the wrong department; the need for links between certain programs will be underestimated; changes that occur between the time the new structure is approved and the time it is implemented will create new demands. The Good Housekeeping Office would be responsible for dealing with these growing pains—resolving disputes or problems related to the current structure, determining how boundary issues should be resolved, and determining how new functions authorized by new legislation should be implemented bureaucratically. A key point is that the Good Housekeeping Office should assume responsibility for implementation, removing these structural decisions from the legislative process. The Good Housekeeping Office's mandate will be to align structures with the articulated objectives of the legislation. In addition to these reactive functions, the office would also assume the active function of monitoring the management practices of existing departments to ensure that they are in fact consistent with the mission and either notify Congress or recommend or mandate changes where needed. Assigning these responsibilities to an independent, objective office would limit political struggles.

Because its role would be so important and potentially powerful (if such an office is indeed given the authority to impose changes when the structure of agencies is found to be in violation of the core principles), the guidelines to be followed by the Good Housekeeping Office and the appointment structure for officials serving in that office must be carefully thought out. One approach would be to follow a model similar to that of the Supreme Court. This is an attractive approach because after the initial structure has been put in place, the role of the agency would be similar to that of a court—adjudicating disputes related to the government structure and ensuring that the structure of the federal government enables the implementation of legislation. The Good Housekeeping Office might then be structured similar to a court, i.e., comprising a limited, odd number (perhaps nine or eleven) of individuals who must achieve agreement by majority rule in addressing any disputes. Each officer might have a support staff to accomplish background research and legwork required in the decisionmaking process, as do the Supreme Court justices. Supplemental staff would be required to support the monitoring activities designed to ensure that the structure of departments remains consistent with legislative aims.

Such a Good Housekeeping Office could have substantial power and authority over the bureaucracy as well as Congress. Such a shift in authority over structural issues might be necessary to implement and maintain real reform. Given the power this office would have, the appointment and approval process for these positions must be carefully constructed and must allow for substantial political input. Because the members of this office would be designing the new federal government, it is likely that individuals who have worked in the federal government or are currently working there would be prime candidates for these positions. However, it is essential to avoid any incentive for favoritism or bias toward particular departments, programs, or activities on the part of office members. As a result, individuals who accept appointments must not be allowed to work in the executive branch after having served in these high-level, important positions. In exchange for agreeing not to serve in other federal positions, they should receive long-term (e.g., ten years) or even lifetime appointments.[5]

It is likely that the workload of the Good Housekeeping Office would be very high initially, would taper off gradually over ten years or so, and would remain stable thereafter. In establishing the office, Congress might want to consider a planned reduction over time in staff support for each officer. Among other things, this would prevent

---

[5] In arguing for permanent appointments for U.S. Supreme Court justices in the *Federalist 78*, Alexander Hamilton argued that lifetime tenure would promote two aims: It would insulate the justices from political influence, increasing the probability that the justices' primary focus would be defending the Constitution; and it would provide the necessary incentive for individuals to give up a lucrative law practice to serve in this government role. Both of these aims would be relevant to the Good Housekeeping Office as well.

the agency from becoming too "activist" or from tinkering excessively with the organizational boundaries.

Conclusion

High-performing organizations have a clear mission, and they direct the activities of the organization toward achievement of that mission. Echoing a theme of the progressive reform movement, which suggests that structure is a key barrier to government effectiveness, the first recommendation of the Volcker report is that the government be reorganized along mission lines. The recommendation appears benign and logical. How could anyone be opposed to an effort to restructure the government so that it is better able to do its job? However, after decades of failed or partially realized attempts to restructure the government in the interests of efficiency, many have given up and concluded that such systematic reform is not possible. Under the assumption that the first recommendation is the key to the success of the entire set of Volcker report recommendations, this chapter questions such cynicism and explores what might be possible. Building on the theory of structural politics and the more general observation that structural decisions are highly political, the chapter presents options for achieving restructuring in a manner that recognizes and deals with political realities.

The suggestions we present are extreme, but they are intended to stimulate discussion of the challenges of designing and implementing federal government restructuring. The politics of structural choice suggest the need to organize in order to reorganize. The strategy proposed here provides for objective third-party cognizance over structural issues with significant political input in terms of the selection of individuals who would make up that "third party" and the guidelines those individuals would follow in fulfilling their mandate. The establishment of a Good Housekeeping Office would remove authority over structural decisions from Congress and the President and would reflect a fundamental change to the way the government is currently managed. Absent such fundamental change, any attempt at restructuring is likely to consist of half-measures that will be undone over time by structural politics.

CHAPTER SIX

Four Ways to Restructure National Security in the U.S. Government

Lynn E. Davis

The global spread of technologies, commerce, and investments has made it more and more difficult to define the mission of national security in traditional ways. Borders are disappearing. The influence of multinational and non-governmental organizations is growing. Economic crises, environmental pollution, and infectious diseases now all have global effects, and successful responses must integrate foreign and domestic activities. The direct security threats to individuals have also changed, with terrorism and the proliferation of dangerous weapons now as serious as the rise of hostile states. As al Qaeda has demonstrated, it has the ability to attack anywhere in the world by exploiting new communications technologies, global financial networks, and the ease of movements of people. Combating security threats increasingly requires governments to integrate their foreign and domestic activities, coordinate closely their overseas foreign and military policies, and be able to act rapidly anywhere in the world.[1]

Do these changes imply a need to reorganize the American national security structure? Since the end of the Cold War, many steps have been taken to make the executive branch of the U.S. government more responsive to the demands of the new security environment. These steps have been evolutionary in character, apart from the creation of the Department of Homeland Security (DHS) in 2003.

---

[1] For a discussion of these trends and their implications, see Davis, 2003.

Yet even in this case, the reorganization did not incorporate the FBI's terrorism responsibilities.

The result, in the view of many both inside and outside the government, is a national security structure with many problems. These have been described most dramatically by the National Commission on the Public Service (also known as the Volcker Commission). According to the commission, "Across the government, in one functional area after another, we find the same persistent problems: organizational structures and personnel policies that are inconsistent with and thwart important public missions."[2] These organizational structures create two types of problems. Decisionmaking is impeded by the duplication and overlap in functions, and "accountability is hard to discern and harder still to enforce."[3] Thus, the commission calls for the reorganization of the federal government "into a limited number of mission-related executive departments" composed of operating agencies sharing similar substantive responsibilities and with lean senior management levels.[4] It then outlines a few basic principles to guide the recommended reorganization: organize the government around critical missions; combine agencies with similar or related missions into larger departments; and eliminate duplication.[5] The commission does not, however, go on to suggest how these recommendations could or should be implemented. This chapter undertakes to fill this gap by sketching out four different approaches to restructuring the executive branch of the U.S. government for the mission of national security.

To set the stage, the chapter describes how the national security structure has evolved historically, focusing on the efforts to improve the coordination of various types of national security activities and then on the steps taken to respond to the new demands of the national security environment. In both cases, the result has been a

---

[2] Chapter 2 of this volume, p. 57.

[3] Ibid., p. 12.

[4] Ibid., pp. 29, 57.

[5] Ibid., p. 32.

duplication of staffs and coordinating processes. The chapter then describes four approaches to reorganizing the executive branch of the U.S. government to implement the commission's goals:

1. Create a limited number of mission-related departments, one being a Department of Security.
2. Establish a new National Security Department by combining and eliminating staffs in the Department of State and the Defense Department.
3. Retain the Department of State and the Defense Department and reform State.
4. Forgo restructuring of the departments and reorganize the White House staff.

The approaches are derived from different views of what the new national security environment now demands and then from different answers to two organizational questions: Should foreign and domestic activities be combined? Should new mission-focused departments be created or existing departments reformed? The approaches are displayed in terms of their answers in Figure 6.1. The chapter concludes by suggesting ways to evaluate these approaches in terms of their potential benefits and costs and then proposing what the way ahead should be.

Figure 6.1
Characteristics of Structural Approaches

Combine foreign and domestic activities	Create new departments	Reform current departments
Yes	1. Department of Security	4. White House Staff
No	2. National Security Department	3. State Department

RAND *MG256-6.1*

Three of these restructuring approaches are my own creation, drawing on my personal experiences in the government. The approach that involves a reform of the State Department is based on the recommendation of the Commission on National Security/21st Century, commonly known as the Hart-Rudman Commission. The genesis of this proposal lies with James Lindsay and Ivo Daalder, with whom I worked on the Hart-Rudman Commission staff.

Evolution of the Current National Security Organization

Today's national security structure dates back to the 1947 National Security Act, which was enacted to remedy military coordination problems that arose during World War II and that were becoming more urgent with the emerging power of the Soviet Union and the potential spread of communism.

Both to ensure civilian control and to encourage cooperation in the operations of the military services, the act created the Department of Defense (DoD) and the three service departments (Army, Navy, and Air Force). The chiefs of the services were formally recognized and, together as the Joint Chiefs of Staff (JCS), were given coordinating responsibilities and provided with staff. (The position of chairman was added to the JCS in 1949.) The act also created the Central Intelligence Agency (CIA) as well as the Director of Central Intelligence (DCI) to provide the President with a coordinated intelligence product that was independent of the perspectives of the departments. Finally, the act created the National Security Council (NSC), giving it the role of advising the President on the integration of domestic, foreign, and military policies relating to national security and facilitating interagency cooperation.

What emerged from the 1947 National Security Act were new but very weak coordinating processes. Presidents and Congress have acted over the years to enhance the responsibilities and authorities of the Secretary of Defense, the Chairman of the JCS, and the DCI, yet the military services have retained considerable power. The most important of these steps for DoD was the 1986 Goldwater-Nichols Act, which strengthened the roles of the Secretary of Defense and the Chairman of the JCS and aimed to promote jointness among the military services. In 1992, Congress codified many of the DCI's specific coordinating and budget authorities into law. Nonetheless, we still see a structure of widely dispersed military and intelligence activities and a variety of overlapping authorities and coordinating processes.

By contrast, the role and responsibilities of the NSC Advisor and staff have steadily grown over the years as a result of many different pressures. The President looks to the NSC staff to ensure that his goals and political agenda are served by the government's policies. The staff plays a critical coordinating role, given the growth in the breadth of activities that today constitute national security and the number of departments and agencies involved. The NSC staff also finds itself stepping in when departments are unable to act quickly enough, which is a criticism often leveled against the State Department. The result is a staff that has offices that cover all the regions of the world and the full range of functional issues (economics, counterterrorism, nonproliferation, and so forth) and an NSC Advisor who not only advises the President and coordinates the interagency process, but also has become both a key spokesperson and a diplomatic negotiator on national security policies.

Beyond these steps to improve coordination among the various national security activities, the evolution of the national security organizational structure can be understood as responses to (1) the changing national security agenda as old security threats waned and new threats emerged, (2) various pressures within departments to duplicate the expertise of others, and (3) periodic congressional interests and direction.

With the end of the Cold War, a number of restructuring efforts were made to respond to the new security environment. New offices were created throughout the government to deal with the threats posed by terrorism, weapons proliferation, drug smuggling, environmental change, the spread of infectious diseases, and the desire to promote economic development, human rights, and democracy. Moreover, responding to the new security threats and opportunities required the involvement of more and more domestic agencies, thereby calling for new and expanded government coordinating processes. In 2003, DHS was created, consolidating activities ranging from border and transportation security to emergency preparedness and protection of the nation's infrastructure.

In the course of their histories, the national security departments and agencies have each developed strong and independent centers of power that to this day continue to exercise considerable influence in the decisionmaking processes. In the case of the State Department, the regional bureaus play a predominant role; and in DoD and the intelligence community, the military services predominate.

One reason, then, for the organizational steps that have produced duplication has been the desire to introduce perspectives other than these dominant ones in the different departments. For example, in the State Department, the regional bureaus tend to give priority to keeping good relations with governments overseas rather than raising issues that create problems, e.g., counterterrorism, human rights, or even trade. This has led to pressures within the executive branch and especially in Congress to create separate functional offices (and advocates) within the State Department. In the cases of trade and arms control, entirely new entities were created outside the State Department: the Office of the U.S. Trade Representative (USTR) and the Arms Control and Disarmament Agency (ACDA).

Within the past few years, countervailing pressures have led to the reintegration of ACDA and the U.S. Information Agency (USIA) into the State Department, and the Director of U.S. Agency for International Development (USAID) now reports through the Secretary of State to the President. But the combination of bureaucratic and congressional pressures meant that in the end, the reintegration involved very little rationalization of responsibilities. Indeed, an entirely separate bureau for arms control verification was established in order to secure the support of Senator Jesse Helms, Chairman of the Senate Foreign Relations Committee.

In DoD, two parallel efforts have produced duplication. One involves the steps on the part of the Secretary of Defense to increase his influence over the military services by expanding his own staff;

creating cross-service processes for program acquisition, programming, and budgeting; and establishing departmentwide agencies. The other involves congressional efforts to introduce "jointness" into the policymaking processes of the military services. The result is the existence of multiple staffs with shared responsibilities for the same policies and programs. Congress has also intervened when the department was viewed as not giving sufficient priority to certain activities, such as the creation of a separate bureau with its own budgetary authority for special-operations/low-intensity conflict.

A lack of trust within the government has also given rise to widespread duplication. Each department, agency, and even office wants to have its own experts. So, for example, Middle East experts reside not only in the regional bureaus of the State Department but also in the functional bureaus, in USAID, in at least three offices in the Office of the Secretary of Defense (OSD), in the Joint Staff, in the staffs of each of the services, in all the intelligence analytical offices, and in the Treasury Department. State and DoD have parallel offices for most policy issues, e.g., NATO, nonproliferation, arms control, and security assistance; and offices for these exist as well in OSD, the Joint Staff, and the military services. State and Treasury have parallel offices on international development. Two separate systems for controlling exports exist, one in State for military items and one in Commerce for dual-use items. Most departments and agencies negotiate directly with their counterparts overseas, leaving the State Department with a diminishing set of responsibilities.

The national structure that has emerged is the result of ad hoc and evolutionary steps. No fundamental restructuring occurred at either the beginning or the end of the Cold War. So it is hard to argue with the Volcker Commission's view that today's system of government "has evolved not by plan or considered analysis but by accretion over time, politically inspired tinkering, and neglect." Nor is it easy to disagree with the assertion that the organization and operations of the federal government are "a mixture of the outdated, the outmoded, and the outworn. Related responsibilities are parceled out among several agencies, independent of each other or spread across different departments."[6]

At the same time, it is important to note that in most cases, good reasons for the organizational steps existed at the time they were taken, even though the consequences were not always the intended ones. Moreover, within the government and the country as a whole, value is seen in policymaking processes with multiple centers of expertise and analysis, and even overlapping responsibilities, since these bring to bear a variety of perspectives and encourage differences in views.

Reorganization Approaches

Much has been written about the new national security environment, both the threats and the opportunities. In such an environment, the nation must be able to, among other things, act quickly, integrate foreign and domestic activities, apply military power at home and abroad, and interact with government and non-governmental organizations. In terms of structuring the government and its decisionmaking processes, two central questions emerge:

- Are there compelling reasons to combine foreign and domestic activities into single departments and decisionmaking processes, or can we live with the historic divisions?
- Do departments need to be created with new missions, or is it enough to reform the existing departments and coordinating processes?

Let us consider four possible approaches to providing answers to these two questions. Each of the approaches adopts a view of what the national security environment calls for in terms of defining the missions of the executive departments and then seeks to advance the

---

[6] Ibid., p. 12.

goals of eliminating duplication, enhancing accountability, and improving the decisionmaking processes.

The first approach fundamentally restructures the executive branch of the U.S. government, integrating into one department all foreign and domestic activities involved in dealing with threats that present serious and direct dangers. The second approach would retain the current organizational division between domestic and foreign security, keeping in place the Department of Homeland Security, but would create a new single Department of National Security by consolidating the activities of the Department of State and DoD. In the third approach, State and DoD would remain responsible for international diplomacy and military operations, respectively, but State would be fundamentally reformed. The fourth approach would forgo any restructuring of the executive departments and instead seek to improve the decisionmaking processes by reorganizing the White House staff.

Create a Limited Number of Mission-Related Departments, One Being a Department of Security

The first approach is based on a view that the new security environment calls for policies, and therefore the operations of the executive departments, that closely integrate foreign and domestic activities. A single department would be responsible for security. Its mission would be defined narrowly as preventing and responding to threats that present serious and direct dangers. Other departments would serve other "national goals"—for example, a Department of Economic Well-Being, a Department for Health and Public Safety, and possibly others.

Each new department would be responsible for policies involving both domestic and foreign activities and for conducting all implementing operations, including negotiations with foreign governments and interactions with state and local governments. Thus, the present main function of the State Department, negotiating with foreign governments, would disappear. Experts on foreign countries would reside in each of the new departments. Ambassadors would report directly to the President. Each of the new departments would provide staff and funding to the embassies.

The Department of Security would bring together planning and operations to prevent and respond to such security threats as the rise of hostile states, terrorism, weapons proliferation, drug smuggling, and cyber attacks. (See Table 6.1 for the responsibilities that would and would not be assigned to the new Department of Security.)

As for the other departments that would be created in this approach, the Department of Economic Well-Being would bring together Treasury's bureaus for multilateral development, for economic and tax policies, and for domestic finance; Commerce's offices other than security; State's economic offices; USTR; and USAID. The Department of Health and Public Safety would bring together the departments of Health and Human Services (HHS), Housing and Urban Development (HUD), Education, and Veterans Affairs; the Social Security Administration; DHS's offices for domestic emergencies; and Justice's anti-crime offices. Places would still have to be

Table 6.1
Responsibilities of the Department of Security

Department/Agency	Current Responsibilities Included	Current Responsibilities Not Included
Department of Defense	All	
Central Intelligence Agency	All	
Department of Homeland Security	Counterterrorism, critical infrastructure, counterdrug activities	Disaster relief
Department of Justice/FBI	Counterterrorism, counterdrug activities	Law enforcement
Department of State	Counterterrorism, counterdrug, nonproliferation, political-military	Economic/trade, environment, human rights
Department of Energy	Nonproliferation, nuclear weapons	Domestic energy
Department of Commerce	Export controls	Trade promotion
Treasury Department	Terrorism and financial intelligence	International affairs, domestic finance, economic and tax policy

found in these or another new department for other agencies and departments such as the Environmental Protection Agency, the Departments of Agriculture and Transportation, and the State Department offices involved in public diplomacy, environment, promoting democracy, and refugees.

Establish a New National Security Department by Combining and Eliminating Staffs in the Department of State and DoD

The second approach is based on the view that in the new security environment, a division between domestic and foreign security responsibilities is appropriate, given the differences in the threats to Americans at home and abroad and in the methods needed to respond, e.g., law enforcement and military operations. What is needed, however, is a closer integration of overseas activities involving foreign policy and military operations. In this approach, the mission-related executive departments would be divided on the basis of domestic and overseas activities. DHS would encompass the counterterrorism activities of the Justice Department and the FBI. A single National Security Department would be created for international security activities, bringing under one roof the Department of State and DoD. The current roles and responsibilities of the DCI and the intelligence community would not change.

Consolidating State and DoD into a single Department of National Security would reduce duplication and enhance accountability. A single policy bureau would be created for each of the regions of the world (Europe, Near East, Africa, Asia) and for each of the main functional areas (economics, global issues, terrorism, nonproliferation). As the State Department has the lead in these today, the OSD staff would be folded into its bureaus, as would be experts in these areas from the Joint Staff and the military services. Regional and functional experts would exist only in the respective policy bureaus. Intelligence analysis would be housed in a single bureau, consolidating all DoD intelligence staffs and folding in experts from the State Department. Strategic planning would also be consolidated into a single staff, drawing together the current personnel from State, OSD, JCS, and the military services.

Steps would be taken to rationalize the structure and eliminate duplication among the other staffs of the Secretary of Defense, Chairman of the JCS, the secretaries and chiefs of the military services, and the combatant commanders. Only one civilian and one military staff would be designated for each of the defense functions. Responsibility would be given for weapons acquisition to OSD (Acquisition) and the Joint Staff; for program planning and budgeting to OSD (PA&E/Comptroller) and the Joint Staff; for operational planning to OSD (Policy) and the combatant commanders; and for personnel recruiting and training to OSD (Personnel Readiness) and the service secretaries, in consultation with the chiefs.

Beyond steps to combine and rationalize the Department of State and DoD, the logic of this approach would be to bring into this new department international activities from other departments—Treasury (International Affairs bureaus), Justice (FBI's International Operations Branch), and Commerce (Bureau of Industry and Security), as well as USAID and USTR.

Retain the State Department and DoD and Reform State
The third approach is based on the view that in the new security environment, responsibility should remain divided not only between domestic and overseas security activities but also between foreign policy and military operations. In a time of expanding international challenges, managing either the State Department or DoD is a formidable undertaking; combining the departments would be overwhelming. The mission-related departments in this approach would be defined, as today, in terms of the conduct of diplomacy (State) and of military operations (Defense). But the State Department would be reorganized according to the Volcker Commission's principle, to "create as few layers [as possible] between the top leadership and the operating units."

In 2001, the U.S. Commission on National Security/21st Century—known as the Hart-Rudman Commission—recommended a major restructuring of the State Department. It argued that "the State Department's own effort to cover all the various aspects of national security policy—economic, transnational, regional, security—has produced an exceedingly complex organizational structure." But "more fundamentally, the State Department's present organizational structure works at cross purposes with its Foreign Service culture." According to the commission, this is the case because the department's senior officials have functional responsibilities, whereas the foreign service expertise lies in terms of foreign countries and cultures. The result is an organizational structure that makes it difficult to develop a distinct State point of view or to speak for the department with one voice, thereby reducing the department's influence inside the government, in its interactions with Congress, and in its representation abroad.[7]

This approach adopts the Hart-Rudman recommendations, whereby responsibilities under the Secretary and Deputy Secretary of State would be divided among six substantive under secretaries overseeing the regions of Africa, Asia, Europe, InterAmerica, Near East/South Asia, and Global Affairs. Responsibilities of the Under Secretary for Management would not change (see Figure 6.2). The substantive under secretaries would be responsible and accountable for all foreign policy activities in their areas. They would orchestrate diplomatic strategies and crisis responses, oversee various assistance programs, provide a single point of contact for Congress, and represent the State Department overseas and on the Hill. Three functional bureaus would support each of these under secretaries: economic and transnational affairs, political affairs, and security affairs. USAID would be fully integrated into the State Department, with its programs divided among the under secretaries. This reorganization would rationalize the Secretary of State's span of control, individual accountability would be improved, and duplication of staffs would be reduced.

To the extent that the State Department could begin to function effectively by being able to integrate regional and functional perspectives into coherent policies, this reorganization could set the stage for

---

[7] U.S. Commission on National Security/21st Century, 2001, Chap. III, pp. 52–62 (available at http://www.nssg.gov/PhaseIIIFR.pdf). The author was Senior Study Group Advisor for the institutional redesign phase of the commission's work.

Figure 6.2
Proposed Organization of the Department of State

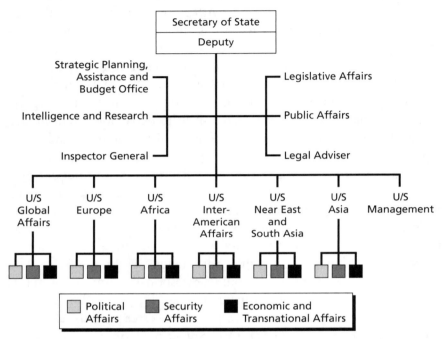

SOURCE: U.S. Commission on National Security/21st Century, 2001.
RAND *MG256-6.2*

pulling back into the department those responsibilities that have migrated elsewhere, e.g., international trade negotiations and international development programs. This could be a small step toward achieving another of the Volcker Commission's goals, that of bringing together in a single department similar activities.

Forgo Restructuring of the Departments and Reorganize the White House Staff

The fourth approach, like the first approach, views the new security environment as calling for a closer integration of foreign and domestic activities. But it contends that the breadth of government activities that contribute to the nation's security does not fit well into a limited number of executive departments. So this approach assigns to the White House staff responsibility, on behalf of the President, for achieving coordination, discipline, and accountability.

Today, three separate interagency coordinating processes and staffs in the White House have responsibility for aspects of national security policy: the National Security Council (NSC), the National Economic Council (NEC), and the Homeland Security Council (HSC). Coordination among the three is achieved by having overlapping membership in the councils, by having certain staff members (those responsible for international economics and counterterrorism) report to more than one of the assistants to the President, and by mandating through executive orders a sharing of responsibility, e.g., for defining requirements for foreign intelligence collection between the assistants for national security and those for homeland security.

The coordinating processes for economic and homeland security policies were created separate from NSC to give them political visibility and priority. But they make coordination more difficult, and they reinforce divisions between foreign and domestic activities, when often the need is to achieve closer integration, e.g., in the war on terrorism and in international financial crises. Multiple processes also present obstacles to achieving discipline.[8]

One way of remedying these problems would be to broadly define the activities that constitute national security and give the NSC responsibility for coordinating all their aspects, both foreign and domestic. Responsibility for setting priorities and ensuring discipline in the policymaking process would fall to the National Security Advisor. To be successful, this would require that his or her primary attention be given to managing the process, as an honest broker, rather than to operational activities, such as negotiating with foreign governments or acting as a public spokesperson.

To achieve the Volcker Commission's goal of accountability, the Assistant to the President for National Security would be confirmed by the Senate and available to testify before Congress. Today, this is

---

[8] For the arguments in favor of combining domestic and foreign coordinating responsibility for the war on terrorism in the NSC staff, see Davis et al., 2004.

the case for another member of the White House staff, the Director of the Office of Management and Budget (OMB). Such a requirement has the potential for undercutting the National Security Advisor's role as a personal adviser to the President, since it would mean having to share his or her advice publicly. But the alternative in this approach would be to place considerable power in the hands of a person who is not accountable to the American people, except through the President.

A Way Ahead

Cataloging the problems in the current U.S. government structure—and there are many—is reasonably easy to do. The approaches defined in this chapter address the problems specifically identified in the Volcker Commission report. To respond to the new security environment, domestic and foreign activities would be integrated in the creation of an entirely new Department of Security in the first approach and in a single White House security staff in the fourth approach. To address the problems of incoherence and immobilism in decisionmaking, as well as duplication, new departments focused on the mission of security would be created in the first and second approaches. To remedy the deficiencies caused by overlapping responsibilities and the lack of accountability, the Department of State would be reformed in the third approach. To improve coordination, discipline, and accountability within the government, the White House staff would be reformed in the fourth approach.

So, by design, each approach would improve the performance of the executive branch of the U.S. government. Quantifying the different benefits and costs of each approach is, however, very difficult, because the goals are so intangible. We can say that by eliminating duplication, all four approaches achieve a reduction in overall personnel and in administrative budgets.

There would also be certain costs to restructuring: personnel turbulence, financial expenditures, reduced effectiveness in decisionmaking until new processes are in place, and so forth. There would be other costs that are harder to define, such as overcoming the resistance of bureaucracies that are comfortable with existing processes and bases of power, of individuals in positions potentially vulnerable to change, of employee unions facing job losses, and so on. It would also be costly to gain political support for restructuring, as all but the reorganization of the White House staff would require congressional approval. None of these costs can be easily defined or quantified.

Therefore, any evaluation of restructuring proposals must be based on very subjective judgments. Given the uncertainties, it would be prudent for the burden to fall on those making the case for change. And that case needs to be made not simply in terms of a cataloging of problems. Some calculus must be made of "expected" benefits outweighing the "certain" costs.

Several questions are crucial to such a calculus of benefits and costs. How critical to successful national security policies in the future is the degree of integration of foreign and domestic activities *within departments*? How much difference would *streamlining the decisionmaking processes* actually make to the effectiveness of future national security policies? For each of these, further research would perhaps be useful. For example, one could examine case studies of good and bad decisionmaking and consider whether the new structure in the four approaches might have made a difference. Another avenue of research might be to engage former policymakers in a systematic consideration of the advantages and disadvantages of each of the approaches, drawing on their personal experiences.

Absent an affirmative answer to one or both of these questions, it is hard to make the case for the fundamental restructuring of the departments in the first approach, or even the consolidation of the Department of State and DoD in the second approach.

There is, however, a case to be made for undertaking both of the other restructuring approaches to improve the performance of the executive branch of the government. For the State Department to assume an effective role in policymaking within the U.S. government and in its representations to Congress and with foreign governments, it must be fundamentally reformed. Otherwise, DoD and the NSC staff will continue to exercise primary leadership on foreign policy, replicating the problems that have been evident in the recent failure to design a comprehensive political and military plan for postwar Iraq. There is also the need for better integration of foreign and domestic security activities throughout the U.S. government to enable it to respond effectively to the broad range of future threats. To this end, the President should create a single White House staff and give it responsibility for coordinating all national security policies both at home and abroad.

CHAPTER SEVEN

Using Public-Private Partnerships Successfully in the Federal Setting

Frank Camm

The Volcker Commission recommendations emphasize the value of (1) reorganizing the federal government to improve agency mission focus and (2) improving the operational effectiveness with which agencies pursue their missions. Effective use of public-private partnerships (PPPs) lies at the intersection of these two concerns. It provides a proven way to (1) get agencies out of the day-to-day business of providing services so that they can stay mission-focused on what the American public wants from its government, and (2) simultaneously assure or even improve the cost and quality of the services the government provides to the American public. This chapter describes how the federal government can improve its use of PPPs to effectively pursue these two high-level recommendations of the Volcker Commission.

The term *public-private partnership* is widely used, but it is not well-defined. A member of the European Commission with responsibility for PPPs, Frits Bolkestein, recently said, "There is no overarching definition for public-private partnerships. PPP is an umbrella notion covering a wide range of economic activity and is in constant evolution."[1]

---

[1] Bolkestein, 2002, p. 7. Consider the following examples: The government of Eire defines a PPP as a "partnership between the public and private sector for the purpose of delivering a project or service which was traditionally provided by the public sector. The PPP process recognises that both the public sector and the private sector have certain advantages relative to the other in the performance of specific tasks, and can enable public services and infra-

Most definitions include (1) a formal agreement between or
among public and private parties; (2) mutual sharing of resources,
information, risks, and rewards; and (3) formal links between output-
oriented performance measures and the allocation of risk and reward
among partners. Some PPPs treat all partners symmetrically; that is,
all partners work together to define goals, and they share the effort to
pursue these goals according to mutually agreed rules. These include
arrangements such as research and development consortia and investments in formal joint ventures. Other PPPs place one government
partner in charge. That partner defines strategic goals and uses its
standing procurement regulations to structure an agreement that en-
lists the aid of private sector partners in the pursuit of these goals.
These include a wide range of agreements in which private parties
provide services to a government agency or private parties use government assets, such as buildings or test facilities, for commercial
purposes. Both types of PPP are important.

This chapter focuses on the PPPs in which the government is
the lead partner. It gives special attention to the challenges likely to

structure to be provided in the most economically efficient manner by allowing each sector
to do what it does best" (Eire, "Public Private Partnerships: Supporting the Provision of
Infrastructure and Local Services," Department of the Environment, Heritage, and Local
Government (available at http://www.environ.ie/DOEI/DOEIPol.nsf/wvNavView/wwdPP
Partnership?OpenDocument&Lang=en, last accessed July 10, 2003). A U.S. Geological Survey study defines PPPs as "arrangements of public sector agencies, private corporations, research and technical institutions, and other non-governmental organizations created to coordinate and combine resources to achieve their separate objectives through joint pursuit of
one or more common objectives" (Parsons Brinckerhoff Quade & Douglas, 1998, p. 10).
The South Africa National Treasury defines a PPP as "a contractual arrangement between a
public sector entity and a private sector entity whereby the private sector performs a departmental function in accordance with an output-based specification. . . . It . . . involves a substantial transfer of all forms of project life cycle risk to the private sector. The public sector
retains a significant role in the partnership project" (South African Revenue Service, 2003, p.
8). For other useful definitions, see Hynes, Kirby, and Sloan, 2000; National Council for
Public-Private Partnerships website at http://ncppp.org/howpart/ (an excellent resource, last
accessed July 14, 2003); and Savas, 2000. DoD has a fundamentally different definition for
PPPs in depots, where a PPP allows a government depot to provide services to a private firm
in a particular way. Although such arrangements reflect many of the features discussed above,
they differ in intent from the type of PPP emphasized here, where the government is the
buyer. For details, see General Accounting Office, 1998 and 2003.

arise in such PPPs as the federal government uses its sourcing authority to align its private partners with its own public goals.[2]

In the United States, broad government interest in PPPs is manifested primarily at the state and local level. In 1992, Osborne and Gaebler recommended that governments tell their private suppliers *what* to do, but not *how* to do it.[3] As government buyers tried this, they discovered what their commercial counterparts had already learned as they increased their reliance on external sources—the better a buyer and seller understand one another, the easier it is for the buyer to focus on what it wants and the seller to focus on how to provide it (Moore et al., 2002). PPPs provide a good vehicle for fostering such understanding between public buyers and private sellers.[4]

Interest in the use of PPPs exists worldwide. The United Kingdom, in particular, has led the way in this practice since the 1980s,[5] and Australia, Canada, and New Zealand, among many others, have followed its lead.[6] As a result, a number of foreign governments are well ahead of most of their American counterparts in the application of PPPs. They tend to use them more often, with more aggressive arrangements, than U.S. government agencies do. International organizations have also found that private partners can provide implemen-

---

[2] "Sourcing" policy covers a wide range of topics associated with government use of external sources, including issues of public acquisition, purchasing, and supplier management policy.

[3] Gansler (2003) updates this logic to reflect the current federal policy context.

[4] Abramson and Harris (2003) provide a useful recent compendium of information on PPPs. See particularly the papers by Denhardt, Lawther, and Williams.

[5] Much interest in the UK grew from privatization efforts made by the Thatcher government. Pint et al. (2001) describes many of these efforts and provides references to British resources. The UK's Public Private Partnerships Programme (4ps) website at http://www.4ps.co.uk/ (last accessed July 10, 2003) is especially useful.

[6] Canada's Public-Private Partnership (P3) Office website at http://www.pppcouncil.ca/ (last accessed July 10, 2003) is a useful resource.

tation skills and capital not available within the organizations themselves to help them accomplish their global missions. [7]

The use of PPPs will continue to grow in the United States and should play an increasing role in the federal setting as interest in performance budgeting grows.[8] Performance budgeting deliberately separates what an agency does from how it does it, improving the agency's ability to see the potential for using a private source to execute its mission. And federal agencies will learn, as state and local governments are learning, that PPPs help foster the well-defined yet flexible environment a government needs to retain responsibility for and control over its mission while an outside source handles implementation.

The chapter opens with a brief description of PPPs and their key attributes. It reviews the factors that determine where it is most appropriate to use PPPs, then discusses a series of challenges that have arisen in recent federal government efforts to implement effective PPPs. It identifies several issues to monitor as government use of PPPs expands. Closing remarks summarize points important to ongoing efforts to help the federal government benefit from PPPs.[9] Descriptive examples of four very different kinds of federal PPPs are interspersed throughout the chapter to help explain what PPPs are and how their attributes work together to achieve their desired effects.

---

[7] See information on the United Nations' Development Programme's Public-Private Partnerships for the Urban Environment (PPPUE) at http://www.undp.org/ppp/ (last accessed July 14, 2003).

[8] Support for performance budgeting is growing fastest at the state and local level. The Bush administration seeks to apply performance budgeting through the Program Assessment Rating Tool (PART) that it uses to track agency performance against the President's Management Agenda. For details, see http://www.whitehouse.gov/omb/part/ (last accessed October 20, 2003) and Walker, 2002, on performance budgeting.

[9] This discussion draws primarily on recent empirical work done on PPPs at RAND and reported in studies listed in the bibliography. It also benefits from other work, especially the large body of studies on PPP from the General Accounting Office (e.g., General Accounting Office, 1998, 1999, 2001a, 2001b, 2002, 2003). Klitgaard and Treverton (2003) provide a recent overview of issues relevant to PPPs. Harbison and Pekar (1998) offer a practical guide to commercial alliances that includes many insights useful to public policy on PPPs. For further useful references beyond those listed here, see Clifton et al., 2002; Moore et al., 2002; and Camm, 2003.

Key Attributes of Successful PPPs

A successful PPP is basically a long-term relationship that allows the government to retain clear control over exactly what the partnership produces, in fact and in appearance, while giving all partners involved enough flexibility to take full advantage of their respective competencies.[10] Such relationships allow the government to focus more effectively on its own core competencies while taking as full advantage as possible of the core competencies of private firms.[11] For example:

- PPPs help the Department of Defense (DoD) focus its leaders and its in-house resources on the military core competencies in which it excels by giving DoD effective access to private organizations that excel in providing commercial-type activities and in providing capital outside the formal government budgeting process. DoD currently relies on PPPs to provide much of the life support for its deployed forces and even to provide worldwide materiel management for its frontline weapons, including the Navy's F/A-18-E/F aircraft (see Table 7.1). DoD also relies on private investors to pay for improved family housing at DoD installations.[12]
- Similarly, PPPs help other parts of the federal government, such as the National Park System and the Postal Service, focus on their inherently governmental activities while giving them access to private organizations that excel at more commercial-type activities (e.g., hospitality services and delivery services) and providing capital outside the formal government budgeting system. The government currently relies on PPPs to convert federal

---

[10] Hart (2003) discusses this idea in the more formal setting of the application of incomplete contracting theory to PPPs.

[11] Prahalad and Hamel (1990) first defined the concept of a core competency, a capability that is so critical to the future success of an organization in a competitive setting that the organization must excel in this competency to survive. Doz and Hamel (1998) help explain its implications for effective management of partnerships.

[12] Camm, Blickstein, and Venzor, 2004; Greenfield and Camm (forthcoming); General Accounting Office, 1998, 2003.

Table 7.1
Supplying Parts Needed by a Combat Aircraft Fleet

High-level public-policy goal	Cost-effective availability of serviceable parts for F/A-18-E/F
PPP approach	One contract to manage and redesign all parts against fleetwide metrics
Alternative, traditional approach	Separate contracts to pay for individual repairs of each part; in-house design and management of parts
Incentive for private partner	Paid for available parts, not cost of repairs
Public-partner advantage	Military operations specialist
Private-partner advantage	Supportability, supply-chain specialist; finances change
Formal agreements and arrangements	Contract with closely defined work scope; detailed process maps assigning roles, responsibilities; buyer-seller teams to run each process jointly; formal agreement to coordinate government depots
Public investments	Navy buys initial spare parts, repair facilities; invests in relationship
Private investments	Provider invests in design, installation of parts; repair facilities; relationship

SOURCE: Camm, Blickstein, and Venzor, 2004.

properties to higher-value uses and to use the value added to provide support services essential to the federal government free of charge (see Table 7.2).[13]

- PPPs can even play a role in transfer and social benefit programs. For example, where the government can define a program in terms of the *actual benefits* to be delivered, such as a training program to increase the likelihood that trainees will get good jobs, it can partner with a private expert to design and provide the training; the government can then focus its efforts on allocating appropriate levels of funds to this purpose and choosing who benefits from training (see Table 7.3).[14]

---

[13] General Accounting Office, 1999, 2001a, 2001b; Shenkar, 2003.

[14] This approach flows naturally from performance arrangements proposed by Gormley and Weimer, 1999, and Hatry, 1999.

Table 7.2
Building a New Government Building

High-level public-policy goal	Building and building-related services, provided cost-effectively at an appropriate level of quality
PPP approach	Provide government land and buildings in exchange for private financing of new buildings and private upkeep using commercial support standards
Alternative, traditional approach	Separate contracts with separate sources to (1) design, (2) construct, and (3) support building, using government support standards
Incentive for private partner	Paid based on characteristics of building and services, not cost of design, construction, and services
Public-partner advantage	Knows what building services it needs
Private-partner advantage	Building design, construction, and support specialist; finances change
Formal agreements and arrangements	Simple contract, because little money changes hands; complex memorandum of agreement to define performance specifications; commercial benchmarks for long-term support
Public investments	Government brings land and legacy facilities with alternative uses
Private investments	Provider invests in design, construction, and support plan

SOURCE: General Accounting Office, 1999.

In practice, such arrangements work best when buyer and seller have time to learn about one another. Through mutual experience, the buyer learns how best to communicate its needs to the seller; the seller in turn learns how best to bring its specific capabilities to bear on the buyer's needs. Such partnerships often expand in scope over time as buyer and seller find more and more mutually attractive opportunities for cooperation.[15]

---

[15] Austin (2000) provides a good discussion of how PPPs can evolve over time. Ryall and Sampson (2003) document evolutionary patterns by looking at how contractual forms change at different stages in a partnership.

Table 7.3
Training Unemployed People and Placing Them in Jobs

High-level public-policy goal	Cost-effective long-term placement in suitable jobs
PPP approach	Pay contractor for each person suitably placed; contractor designs and manages details
Alternative, traditional approach	Design training and placement program in-house; contract for execution of government-designed plan.
Incentive for private partner	Paid for each successful placement, not cost of program design, training, administration
Public-partner advantage	Knows what types of jobs the government should promote
Private-partner advantage	Training, placement specialist
Formal agreements and arrangements	Contract to define "success," fee; equitable adjustment for factors beyond provider control
Public investments	Government invests political capital to sustain funding
Private investments	Provider invests in design and provision of program

SOURCE: Measurement concepts in Gormley and Wiemer, 1999.

Such relationships tend to share several important characteristics:[16]

- The core competencies of buyer and seller differ. If they are too similar, competition grows between buyer and seller, creating continuing tension to choose between an internal and an external source. When a buyer depends on in-house and external sources for the same services—say, depot repair—concern persists about whether the buyer can treat the two fairly, and this disrupts efforts to share data and coordinate investments. When demand falls, for example, strong political pressures favor the internal source. Early efforts to foster buyer-seller cooperation in the Japanese automobile industry, for example, encountered this problem repeatedly and ultimately led the buyers to end competition between internal and external sources in order to create the basis for trust required to foster cooperation with external

---

[16] For more detailed discussion of these points and additional sources, see Anderson, 1999; Pint and Baldwin, 1997; Camm, 2002, 2003; and Ryall and Sampson, 2003.

sources.[17] A similar logic applies with even greater force to a public buyer.

- Buyer and seller try to maintain flexibility, but they do so within the confines of formally defined arrangements. In a federal setting, these arrangements must be compatible with the Federal Acquisition Regulation (FAR). This is less onerous than many believe, because the FAR is quite flexible in the hands of an expert. But until recently, procurement officials have favored conservative interpretations of the FAR in ways that limited flexibility in partnerships. Under acquisition reform in the Air Force in recent years, for example, high-level guidance has directed contracting personnel to stop using the FAR to "minimize risk" and, instead, to use it more creatively to "manage risk." This change sought to create the opportunity for flexibility required to shape new arrangements with a provider. The Defense Acquisition University is now changing its training to give relatively less attention to low-risk compliance with the FAR and more to using the FAR creatively in specific situations in pursuit of the buyer's strategic goals.

- One way to preserve flexibility is to state the goals of relationships at the highest levels possible. PPPs use the final customer's requirement specifications to the full extent to define goals. For example, in an agreement to document vehicle launches, the Air Force simply gave the provider its internal requirement documents and held the provider accountable for achieving them. The challenge here, of course, is that the provider must have enough authority to pursue the stated requirements. In Table 7.1, the buyer is really more interested in available aircraft than in available parts but, despite considerable effort, could find no practical way to hold the provider accountable for more than the availability of parts. PPPs attempt to state their goals at as high a

---

[17] Smitka (1991) provides a detailed history of how partnerships formed and evolved in the Japanese automobile industry. Bleeke and Ernst (1995) document the effects of more recent competition between internal and external sources from a broader, more strategic perspective in American industrial efforts to sustain partnerships.

level as possible, balancing definitions with the amount of
authority the provider has and hence can be held accountable
for.

• Partners all invest in and benefit from a PPP. At a minimum,
partners invest leadership focus and time to learn about their
partners' needs and capabilities. Government buyers bring specific assets, such as real estate, support equipment, and spare
parts.[18] Private providers bring liquid capital, which they invest
in assets that benefit the government but also generate income
streams for themselves. In a long-term relationship, such investment creates specific assets that the partners must work together to protect in order for the partnership to persist and
benefit them all. This works only as long as the partners continue to trust one another.

• The characteristics above ultimately yield less-than-arm's-length
relationships between the government and its partners. They
specialize in different capabilities, encouraging dependence.
They use broad agreements to learn about each other over time
and shape their expectations about what each brings the other.
They increasingly work toward common, very high level goals.
And they invest in tangible and intangible assets that will lose
value for both of them if the relationship ends.

When Does a PPP Make Sense?

A PPP is one of many sourcing options available to the government.
At one extreme, an agency can decide to provide a particular service it
needs in-house. At the other, it can decide to buy the service from an
external provider with a minimal contractual vehicle that requires little interaction between buyer and seller. A PPP is a choice in the

---

[18] Specific assets are assets that have more value in a specific, bilateral relationship than they
have anywhere else. As a result, they are "at risk" and can be exploited by an opportunistic
partner. Their status has proven to be the best single empirical predictor of sourcing arrangements that commercial firms choose. For details, see Williamson, 1985, and Masten,
1999.

middle, typically tailored to particular circumstances to take advantage of specific public sector and private sector capabilities. It usually takes time and resources to design a PPP. A PPP makes sense when (1) outsourcing is compatible with the buyer's broader strategic concerns and (2) the buyer and seller agree that the net benefits they can create together are large enough to justify their investments in the PPP.[19]

Government agencies must keep many activities in-house, even if a PPP could be a cost-effective alternative. Activities that require policy discretion, obligate the government to commit resources, affect the value of private interests through regulatory or judicial actions, or potentially involve the application of controlled military or police violence, for example, are "inherently governmental"; they cannot legally be outsourced.[20] Among the activities that involve policy discretion is the requirements determination that frames the goals for a PPP; the government cannot relinquish responsibility to determine its requirements to its partners. The government must sustain an experienced oversight capability in-house to participate effectively as a partner. To create and sustain this capability, it may be necessary to retain some activities in-house simply to train government personnel so that they can oversee external sources that provide these services as partners elsewhere in the government. Similarly, to grow the senior leadership it needs, the government may need to keep some activities in-house where junior personnel can prepare for future roles at a more senior level.[21]

---

[19] For more detailed discussions of the points made in this section, see Camm, 1996, 2002; and Moore et al., 2002. Other useful sources that discuss these issues include Lerner and Merges, 1998; Masten, 1999; Ryall and Sampson, 2003; Savas, 2000; Williamson, 1991; and Langlois, 2004. Salamon (2002) and Savas (2000) also provide typologies of government management tools that place PPPs in a broader public management context.

[20] Federal Activities Inventory Reform (FAIR) Act, 1998, Sec. 5.

[21] Recent changes in the personnel management policies of DoD and the Department of Homeland Security (DHS) create forms of flexibility that may reduce the government's need to "grow its own" leadership and contract oversight capabilities. But these policies are not yet in place, so their effectiveness has not yet been demonstrated.

Cost-effective PPPs are attractive only after a government agency has taken account of such constraints. For activities that are not inherently governmental or needed in-house for some other reason, the government must weigh the benefits and risks of using a PPP and the challenges of setting up a PPP. Partners can think about benefits from two different perspectives.

The easiest benefits to justify are positive *outcomes*. Experience with private partnerships and PPPs offers many examples in which they improve customer satisfaction and reduce costs. Improved customer satisfaction raises the price a buyer is willing to pay for a service. The increased price and lower costs create mutual benefits that a buyer and seller can split. For example, better coordination and information sharing supports integrated supply chains with reduced inventory costs and increased reliability of supply. Parallel decision-making and shared design responsibilities can shorten product cycles, simplifying a buyer's ability to match its product line to customer demands. Sharing of operational data facilitates product maturation that a provider can use to improve the reliability and maintainability of the spare parts it provides to a buyer. This cuts costs and reduces variability in the buyer's production processes. Data sharing can reduce transaction costs by reducing inspection requirements, reducing duplicative data entry, coordinating data protocols between buyer and seller, and transferring responsibility for transaction management to the partner with the best transaction management capabilities. Lower transaction costs mean cost savings that buyer and seller can share. And so on.

Such partnerships also improve *processes* in important ways. Although process improvements are worthwhile only if they ultimately yield positive outcomes of the kind listed above, partners often use process improvement as a proximate measure of merit. It is sometimes easier to link the existence of a partnership to a quickly observed process improvement than to an improvement in customer satisfaction or cost some time in the future. By freeing a buyer of day-to-day production responsibilities, for example, partnerships help the buyer think more strategically. By removing important fixed assets from the buyer's control and ownership, they improve his flexibility and responsiveness to change. By supporting trust, they increase a buyer's and a seller's abilities to solve problems together and learn from the mutual experience. By attracting commercial firms that prefer to work as partners, partnerships can give the government access to commercial capabilities that are simply not available through traditional government acquisition arrangements. By rewarding a provider for innovations that promote the buyer's interest, they give the government access to entrepreneurial and innovative capabilities not available in-house. By transferring appropriate responsibilities to providers and assuring future demand, they give the government access to private financial resources that providers can invest in a wide range of assets that the government needs. Used creatively, such private funds can reduce the budgetary constraints that government agencies face without partnerships. And so on.

By their very nature, the activities that generate these benefits present a government buyer with important risks.[22] Giving an external source discretion over activities too close to its core political concerns, for example, can limit the government's control over these activities, allowing an unscrupulous provider to exploit the discretion present in a PPP. This risk increases as the activities get closer to an agency's core political concerns—for example, high-dollar, high-visibility activities that are important to politically powerful constituencies. More generally, the government can expect partners to behave in a more mutually satisfactory way, and it is easy to replace unsatisfactory partners when numerous high-quality sources are available, performance and cost data are good enough to ensure accountability, and contracts are written to reward good behavior and to allow quick termination when behavior is unsatisfactory. The importance of these concerns depends on a wide range of factors that vary from one situation to another. The government should weigh these risks against the potential benefits described above to project the net benefits likely to be available from a PPP.

---

[22] Such risks are identified in Klitgaard, MacLean-Abaroa, and Parris, 2000, pp. 117–150.

Anticipated net benefits are often easier to achieve in a partnership than they are when a buyer retains provision of a service in-house or deals with external providers at arms length with limited information exchange or interaction. But they are not free. They take time to set up. Private partnerships often form over many years as buyer and seller test one another and build enough trust to drop one constraint after another or expand the scope of the partnership from one service to another, ever testing to verify that one partner does not try to squeeze too much from the other. Many firms give their suppliers different ratings and deal in a more open way with the suppliers who have proven through demonstrated performance to be more trustworthy. Partners—buyers and sellers—pay a lot of attention to the past performance of their counterparts before committing to partnership agreements; they give more attention in more-complex, higher-risk partnerships. Buyers use source selections specifically designed to allow in-depth data collection on a few high-quality alternative sources. Sellers conduct their own form of due diligence on the buyer before entering such source selections. Partners build increasingly complex governance structures for increasingly high-priority partnerships. These structures can involve the participation of personnel in both organizations from top to bottom and can even include personnel exchanges and joint training to increase the cultural compatibility of the partners. Data exchange requires careful preparations to design data protocols and to protect intellectual capital.[23] More-complex partnerships, with greater interaction and greater sharing of sensitive investment and information, typically require larger investments. They are worthwhile only if the expected benefits exceed the setup and maintenance costs.

Many case studies provide evidence of the net benefits available from partnerships. But the evidence is hard to extrapolate. Partnerships tend to be tailored to particular circumstances, including the exact identities of the partners. That said, it is possible to use the analytic "survivorship principle," in econometric studies or more

---

[23] These challenges are discussed in greater depth below.

metaphorically, to identify patterns of partnership use that have persisted in the private sector.[24] Competition over time favors cost-effective sourcing arrangements in the private sector and reveals the circumstances in which different arrangements tend to dominate. Figure 7.1 summarizes one highly regarded private company's views on these patterns.

The John Deere Co., like many other quality-management-based companies, stratifies the goods and services it buys along two dimensions. It distinguishes things it pays a lot for from things it does not pay a lot for (the horizontal axis). And it distinguishes things that present high risks to the performance of its final products—and the satisfaction of its final customers—from things that present few risks (the vertical axis). Thus, it uses different sourcing arrangements to buy goods and services with different characteristics. Figure 7.1 summarizes the kinds of arrangements it uses for different kinds of goods and services. The figure highlights references to partnerships that might suggest where PPPs could help government agencies buying similar goods and services.

John Deere prefers to create and sustain the most complex partnerships for "critical" goods and services (the upper right quadrant of Figure 7.1), which cost a lot of money and present high risks. If the risks get too high, it simply provides the good or service in-house. It uses simplified acquisition methods for "generic" low-risk goods and services that it does not spend a lot of money on. It uses less-complex partnerships, among many other less-complex methods, in the remaining two quadrants covering "commodities" and "unique," but noncritical products. This stratification is a direct result

---

[24] The survivorship principle states that entities or practices that persist in a competitive setting demonstrate that they dominate those that do not, in dimensions relevant to the competition. It allows one to predict where a practice such as a PPP is likely to dominate other sourcing alternatives, even in the absence of direct evidence on the relative cost or effectiveness of the alternatives. Shelanski and Klein (1995) and Masten (1999) provide useful surveys of many econometrics studies. The consulting literature uses a four-quadrant diagram like that in Figure 7.1 to help practitioners take advantage of more-formal empirical findings.

Figure 7.1
John Deere's Framework for Stratifying Sources of Goods and Services

High

Risk (source availability, response, quality)

Unique Products	Critical Products
• *Strategies:* Key suppliers; design to customer or supplier specifications; provide product/market differentiation	• *Strategies:* **Strategic supplier partnerships**; design customer or supplier specifications; provide product/market differentiation
• *Critical factors:* Manufacturing costs high when costs and/or quality problems occur; difficult to source	• *Critical factors:* Manufacturing costs high when cost and/or quality problems occur; very hard to source
• *Time horizon:* Variable	• *Time horizon:* Up to ten years
• *Management approach:* Simultaneous engineering and **some supplier partnerships**	• *Management approach:* **Supplier partnerships**
• *Methods:* Reduce number of products and suppliers	• *Methods:* Reduce number of suppliers
• *Agreement:* Contract or long-term agreement	• *Agreement:* Contract or long-term agreement
• *Tactics:* Decrease uniqueness of products unless competitive advantage is gained	• *Tactics:* Increase role of suppliers
Generics	**Commodities**
• *Strategies:* Standardize/consolidate	• *Strategies:* Leverage spend; preferred suppliers
• *Critical factors:* Cost of acquisition	• *Critical factors:* Cost of materials
• *Time horizon:* Up to a year	• *Time horizon:* Up to five years
• *Management approach:* Systems contracts; blanket orders	• *Management approach:* Volume contracting, and **some supplier partnerships**
• *Methods:* Reduce number of buys	• *Methods:* Reduce number of suppliers
• *Agreement:* Purchase order or credit card	• *Agreement:* Purchase order or long-term agreement
• *Tactics:* Increase use of technology	• *Tactics:* Increase business volume with fewer suppliers

Low ◄——— Value (cost, service, innovation, administration ———► High

SOURCE: Adapted in Moore et al., 2002, from John Deere, "Sourcing Strategies," *Supply Management Strategies*, 1997.
RAND *MG256-7.1*

of the reasoning outlined above. John Deere is willing to create and sustain complex and costly partnerships where the risks and the potential for cost savings are largest. It prefers simple, low-cost, arms-length arrangements where the risk is low and little opportunity exists to use a partnership to reduce cost.

This approach to stratification is quite common in the commercial sector, although each buyer thinks about cost and risks in a somewhat different way. A government agency can develop a similar stratification, which is likely to indicate that the agency should rely on simplified acquisition for low-cost, generic goods that are unlikely to significantly affect the quality of government services. It should develop fairly simple PPPs for some goods and services that it spends a lot of money on, even if they are unlikely to affect the quality of government services. Somewhat more complex PPPs make sense for acquiring certain specialized things that can affect the quality of government services, even if the government does not spend much money on them. The agency should give the greatest attention to selecting and nurturing partners that provide things likely to affect the quality of its services and that cost a lot of money.

Challenges of Using a PPP

Four types of problems have proven to be especially challenging in recent federal efforts to implement PPPs:

- Balancing partnership and control
- Exchanging information, ideas, and skills
- Coordinating partnerships with competition
- Changing the federal acquisition culture and skills in the federal workforce

Balancing Partnership and Control

Three factors are key to balancing partnership and control. First, the government must state clearly what it wants from an external partner. Second, it must remain practically engaged with its partners to ensure that it gets what it wants. Third, it must remember that its partners have goals as well and that they must be served.

Consider the Navy's current partnership with Boeing to provide materiel management for the F/A-18-E/F (Table 7.1). The Navy really wants a ready, available fleet of F/A-18-E/Fs, and this is what it sought at the beginning of negotiations to form the partnership. But Boeing could affect only materiel management, so the Navy agreed to set goals for Boeing that entailed only pursuing materiel availability, not fleet availability. Once these goals were set, it remained clear that Boeing would need detailed information on future plans, that the partners would have to exchange detailed information of changes in parts design, and that Boeing would have to depend on Navy depots to provide a portion of the materiel support that it was responsible for. The Navy and Boeing set up integrated process teams, co-led by Navy and Boeing personnel, to manage each process relevant to the partnership. Even though the formal contract increasingly shifts risk to Boeing over its lifetime, both sides recognize that Boeing has to make a reasonable profit to remain interested, so Boeing can obtain "equitable adjustment" for changes not anticipated by the formal agreement. It took four years to negotiate this agreement; these long negotiations succeeded only because both sides stabilized the teams involved and allowed them to develop personal relationships.

Despite the effort that went into this agreement, it is not the only way to do what the Navy and Boeing want to do together. The Air Force and Northrop Grumman have a partnership for similar "total system support responsibility" for the Joint Surveillance and Target Acquisition Radar System (JSTARS), with more-formal, less-flexible arrangements that limit Northrop Grumman's responsibility and authority. But in its own way, this agreement also states what the Air Force wants, keeps the Air Force closely engaged with Northrop Grumman through the life of the initial contract, and protects Northrop Grumman's interests, even as Northrop Grumman assumes risks traditionally borne by the government in a support agreement.

In partnerships like this, the government's role must remain paramount, because elements of the partnership involve inherently governmental activities. The government must retain responsibility for setting its own requirements, because these are instruments of public policy. It must retain control over the obligation of government funds and over the direction of government personnel. In a defense setting, it must retain all responsibility for executing military activities unique to combat. PPPs must reflect these legal requirements. Taken together, they make the federal government the dominant partner in any partnership providing goods and services to the government.

These requirements draw a clear distinction between PPPs and commercial joint ventures. For the most part, commercial joint ventures are mutual opportunities to make money together or develop valuable information together.[25] Such efforts can often work best when the partners operate at arm's length. For example, General Motors and Toyota created a separate company, Saturn, with a separate public image and capitalization, to meld their comparative advantages in an effort to bring Japanese production methods to a U.S. setting. If each made money and learned enough from the other and from the integration of their ideas through this partnership, it would be a success. Opportunities like this exist for the federal government as well, particularly in the realm of research and development.[26] But PPPs are more challenging when a government buyer must sustain its dominant role within the partnership.

The federal government of Australia is now experimenting with PPPs closer to commercial joint ventures by using a method it calls "alliance contracting."[27] In this approach, the government and private partners have more nearly symmetric responsibilities and authorities than U.S. federal arrangements would allow for the purchase of similar assets. Examples of completed applications include the design and construction of government roads, bridges, and buildings.[28] The Australian Navy is using this approach in its Project Djimini to design

---

[25] Clifton et al., 2002.

[26] Chang et al., 1999; Horn et al., 1997.

[27] For information, see http://www.defence.gov.au/dmo/lsd/alliance/alliance.cfm (last accessed October 20, 2003).

[28] Ross, 2003.

and manufacture a new torpedo.[29] In these arrangements, the Australian government does not start a project by stating its own requirements. Rather, each consortium negotiates a joint set of requirements that satisfies all the participants, somewhat as the management of Saturn designs new cars and manufacturing processes for the Saturn partnership, not for General Motors or Toyota per se. The Australian experience may ultimately show the way to use more symmetric roles in the United States as well, but it is too early to show that this approach would be appropriate for the U.S. government.

Exchanging Information, Ideas, and Skills

To learn about one another and improve their joint performance and cost over time, partners have to share information on a number of levels. At the most basic level, they share details on day-to-day operations. Even though formal agreements focus on improving performance and cost against high-level goals, they typically also give close attention to more detailed information about requirements, technical capabilities, and cost. For example:

- In its partnership with the Air Force to provide materiel support for aircraft engines, General Electric (GE) and the Air Force share data. Through the course of the contract, the Air Force gives GE detailed information on its planned flying hour program. GE uses its proprietary models to translate this information into predictions of future demands for parts and an inventory plan consistent with this demand. The Air Force maintains its own logistics models in-house. GE and the Air Force develop a consensus based on their respective models, which forms the basis upon which GE commits its own capital to buy parts for the Air Force, to be reimbursed only when the Air Force de-

---

[29] Jenkins, 2001.

mands these parts.[30] Close cooperation to get these forecasts right is critical to the long-term health of the partnership.

- Kellogg Brown and Root (KBR) shares detailed operational data with the Army as a standard part of their partnerships to support deployed U.S. forces. These data routinely give the Army proprietary data that are vital to the operation of the partnership but also leave KBR exposed if the data are not protected. To effect any change in work scope, KBR similarly provides additional proprietary information on its capabilities, even though the partnership does not require the Army to turn to KBR for changes in work scope. For example, in the Balkans Support Contract, which the U.S. Army uses to provide troop support and logistics services to deployed forces, the Army approaches KBR with a new task and asks for an execution plan and cost estimate. The Army pays KBR to develop these. KBR develops both, which serve as a basis for further discussions and ultimately an Army decision on whether to use KBR and, if not, whether to seek an alternative source for the services. The processes involved are scaled to the size of the new task; larger tasks get close review at a higher level.[31]

- Partners routinely use an "open books" policy to give government buyers access to detailed data on provider costs. Traditional arrangements under the FAR required private sources to provide detailed cost data in a standard government format. In principle, errors in these data could lead to criminal charges against private executives. Partnerships in the private sector rely on less-formal cost sharing. Partners can examine the internal accounts of a partner relevant to the partnership. Buyers typically accept provider formats. Their choice of a provider depends in part on whether they believe such an arrangement will be adequate. Recent efforts to incorporate fixed-price elements

---

[30] The formal contract is complex and does not leave GE this exposed, but it does shift risk to GE from the Air Force.

[31] For details, see Greenfield and Camm (forthcoming).

into government partnerships with private sources have complicated government access to provider records, since formal arrangements to use fixed-price terms in "commercial contracts" under FAR Part 12 explicitly limit the government's access to certified cost data. But government arrangements are likely to go in the same direction that private alliances have gone, where buyers have access to the seller's books, but cost data need not be provided on a regular basis or in a standard format.[32]

When government and private partners develop intellectual capital together, a different kind of challenge arises. For years, many private firms avoided research and development consortia with federal participation, because the federal government insisted on federal ownership of any ideas developed with its money. Companies feared that joint efforts to develop dual-use technologies could allow the federal government to benefit from their core technological capabilities with only a minor federal investment and, in the limit, could allow the government to appropriate a portion of those capabilities in new markets by claiming that federal participation had helped open the doors to these markets. This remains a problem as long as the federal government attempts to assert asymmetric authority in research and development consortia.[33]

Information exchange also occurs in a more latent form when partners allow their partners' employees to have close access to their own facilities, personnel, and databases; exchange personnel for several years at a time; or share training of their employees.[34] Such exchanges help partners learn about one another's cultures and processes, to their mutual benefit. They cement personal relationships

---

[32] Camm and Huger (2000) discuss these issues in greater depth.

[33] As noted above, this chapter focuses on PPPs with such asymmetric authority. This issue in intellectual capital offers an example of asymmetric authority not necessarily being in the federal government's best interest.

[34] Camm, Blickstein, and Venzor (2004) provide details on such exchange arrangements in six current federal PPPs. For a discussion of joint training programs in partnerships, see Resetar, Camm, and Drezner, 1998.

between individuals in the government and its partner firms, to their mutual benefit. One of the most important forms that personnel exchange takes today is the hiring of retired government personnel when the government outsources its activities to private firms. But good partnerships seek more systematic and strategic sharing within the context of a specific partnership.

Such sharing promotes development of what the Army calls a "habitual relationship" between its personnel and the personnel of its partners. The Army is now revamping its personnel assignment system precisely to build "unit cohesion" by letting individuals work together for longer periods. The same logic applies when the individuals in question are both inside and outside the government. Individual employees work together long enough and in close enough quarters to smooth the flow of ideas and cooperation between organizations. The Army believes that such habitual relationships are essential to the successful use of contractors on the battlefield. Without them, effective real-time information exchange and cooperation is impossible in the face of the chaos that characterizes the battlefield.[35] Habitual relationships pay off elsewhere in government as well. Navy and Boeing personnel involved in the F/A-18-E/F partnership described above emphasize that the partnership would never have come together if the Navy and Boeing participants had not remained in place over the four-year development period. Critical elements of the development required compromises on both sides, which succeeded only because the principals on both sides had come to trust one another as individuals. A similar theme also runs through many of the partnerships we have examined in the private sector, far from any military battlefield.[36]

---

[35] Camm and Greenfield (forthcoming) discuss Army views on habitual relationships on the battlefield in greater depth.

[36] Traditional government acquisition policy has often sought to discourage long-term relationships between government and contractor personnel, fearing that they would lead to corruption. This is another example of how a partnership tolerates important risks to create a setting conducive to mutual gain. See Klitgaard, MacLean-Abaroa, and Lindsey, 2000.

Coordinating Partnerships with Competition

Full and open competition is an integral part of federal procurement culture. The Competition in Contracting Act of 1984 formally states that all qualified sources should have an equal opportunity to do government work. Federal procurement culture maintains a strong belief that competition limits cronyism and the corruption that comes with it. It has faith that competition leads to higher performance and lower costs. These elements of federal procurement culture are so strong that competition has become a goal in its own right. Agencies have "competition advocates" who promote competition itself in government procurement.

PPPs can be seen as an assault on competition. They promote long-term relationships that limit the occurrence of competition. They often use "award terms" that reward good performance with contract extensions that put off the next competition. They promote less-than-arm's-length relationships that inevitably give incumbent contractors advantages relative to their competitors when recompetitions occur. In competitions that do occur, they inevitably use past performance as a prominent source selection criterion, simply heightening the advantage of partners who have performed well in the past. They promote habitual relationships that some see as an invitation to the cronyism that full and open competition attempts to prevent.

In the commercial sector, as buyers have discovered providers that perform well in partnerships, they have increasingly limited the number of providers included in competitions and limited the number of providers they do business with for any particular good or service. They have found that the quality of a competition is more important than the number of competitors.[37]

Commercial buyers have also found that they can use benchmarking within a partnership to induce and reward ongoing competition between standing partners and the partners' competitors without holding formal source selections. That is, the essence of competition—comparison of alternatives that rewards the best alterna-

---

[37] Moore et al., 2002.

tive—can occur without the formal instrument of competition, formal source selection. For example, the National Security Agency's (NSA's) Groundbreaker program uses a standard form of commercial benchmarking to determine the price of information service over the course of its PPP with the Eagle Alliance. NSA uses a third-party benchmarking specialist to compare the provider's costs and service level with those of relevant commercial analogs. The Groundbreaker source selection set the values of parameters to be used in this benchmarking process.[38]

PPPs do not have to eliminate formal source selection altogether to be effective. When more than one qualified partner is available, the federal government uses a formal source selection to choose its partner. For decades, DoD has used formal source selection to choose the partners that it will rely on to design and produce its weapon systems. Once chosen, these partners can expect a continuing relationship with the federal government over the life of the weapon system, which now can exceed 50 years. As federal *services* acquisition has become increasingly sophisticated in the past decade, it has incorporated subtle elements of the best-value competitions typical of weapon-system acquisition that are critical to making the right choice among available partners.

Once a partner is selected, formal competition can persist within a partnership. The government can use a formal source selection to choose a number of partners with broad capabilities in a particular area, such as the support of system development offices or the provision of information technology services (see Table 7.4). Then, over a period specified in the initial source selection (say, five to seven years), it treats these partners as prequalified sources, which can compete in quick source selections for specific task or deliver orders. The Army Rapid Response (R2) program and Air Force Flexible Acquisition and Sustainment Tool (FAST) program, for example, both support small numbers of partners that compete with one another in formal source selections that can be completed in less than three

---

[38] For details, see Camm, Blickstein, and Venzor, 2004.

Table 7.4
Using Competitions to Provide Rapid Access to Private Sources

High-level public-policy goal	Providing rapid, flexible access to high-quality sources for system program support services
PPP approach	Use full competition to "prequalify" sources and set contractual terms that can be used to serve task orders as they arise; use rapid competitions to select among "prequalified" sources for each task order
Alternative, traditional approach	Use a standard full competition to select a source and prepare contractual terms for each new task as it arises
Incentive for private partner	Simplified access to government markets; reduced transaction costs for rapid, task-order source selections
Public-partner advantage	Ensures compliance with federal acquisition and financial management rules in rapid acquisitions
Private-partner advantage	Matches especially qualified sources to government needs quickly; provides program integration and oversight
Formal agreements and arrangements	Formal contract with each "prequalified" source, with a funding ceiling and socioeconomic requirements; public and private program offices that share data and oversight responsibilities through clearly defined processes and information systems
Public investments	Government invests in information systems and procedures
Private investments	Provider invests in information systems and procedures

SOURCE: Camm, Blickstein, and Venzor, 2004.

weeks for any new work that a government buyer wants from one of the partners. The habitual relationship between these government buyers and their private partners supports a short acquisition lead time and effective oversight of a diverse set of unpredictable tasks.[39]

That said, in its PPPs, the federal government simply cannot go as far as commercial partnerships have in using benchmarking and past performance to limit their use of formal source selections. Formal source selection provides a degree of openness and fair process that federal procurement culture demands and benchmarking cannot provide. For similar reasons, the federal government is not as free as commercial buyers are to reward new work to proven performers on a

[39] For details on these Army and Air Force programs and the ways in which they differ from alternative approaches, see Camm, Blickstein, and Venzor, 2004.

sole-source basis when several qualified competitors are obviously available. That prevents the federal government from using one of the principal vehicles that commercial alliances use to grow and prosper. Nonetheless, as PPPs prove their worth to the federal government in improved performance and lower cost, the government is increasingly emulating commercial practice that substitutes PPPs for traditional competition in important ways.

Many contracts, for example, now have terms well beyond the five-year maximum allowed for services by the Service Contracting Act of 1965 (SCA). Partnerships for information technology and services have led the way, with terms of ten years not unusual. Some argue that longer terms are acceptable for complex services because contractors are committing such large private sums to capitalize the government's services. But the Army's partnership with KBR to support deployed forces, which focuses on mundane tasks such as cleaning laundry, cooking and serving food, maintaining trucks, and delivering the mail, has a ten-year contract. And the government can now extend service contracts governed by the SCA beyond five years by using award terms that dictate only five years of future work at any time but can slip that five years forward each year as the contract proceeds.

A certain tension can be expected to persist between PPPs and competition, just as a similar tension exists between the use of alliances or joint ventures and competition in the commercial sector. Economists are struggling with this tension as well. Traditional neo-classical economics keeps things simple by assuming arm's-length relationships and costless market transactions between buyer and seller. These assumptions empower competition as a powerful motivator that requires little information exchange to work. Transactions cost theory explains PPPs and other alliances as institutional arrangements where buyer and seller benefit from exchanging information, market transactions are costly, and long-term relationships can create incentives that support information exchange in a cost-effective manner.[40]

---

[40] Oliver Williamson has done the most to develop the details of this argument, offering the most complete statement of it in Williamson, 1985. Useful recent work on transaction costs

The success of PPPs and other alliances relative to traditional source selection suggests that the presumed superiority of competition, as defined in the 1984 Competition in Contracting Act (CICA), and the competition advocates' roles throughout the federal government deserves new attention.

Changing Federal Acquisition Culture and Skills in the Federal Workforce

A caricature of traditional practice in federal *services* acquisition could run something like the following.[41] To avoid any appearance of impropriety, government organizations should not seek to acquire any more than the lowest-cost service that provides acceptable support. That is, government activities should not reward offerors who promise to provide a higher level of quality, because a higher level would simply be inappropriate for government work. Hence, the government should seek low-cost providers. Doing so also avoids subjective judgments that are unavoidable in best-value competitions and hence makes the competitions more transparent and objective. Low-cost providers tend to have difficulty performing at the level promised and are likely to shirk or cheat. Government buyers must expect this and prevent it by using formal quality assurance surveillance plans to discover shirking or cheating and to ensure that the government does not pay for any services in which the provider cuts corners.

---

and institutional arrangements in partnerships includes Anderson and Sedatole, 2003; Das and Teng, 1999; Dekker, 2004; and Gulati, 1998.

[41] Those responsible for *systems* acquisition in DoD, in which the government acquires goods rather than services, long ago learned the value of giving product quality high priority and thereby avoiding low-cost providers and the problems they bring. DoD *services* acquisition is still struggling to balance quality and cost concerns. For example, it is quite common for major commands to program only enough money for military bases to acquire the level of service traditionally provided by low-cost services contractors. This complicates efforts at the base level to use innovative incentive arrangements, because these arrangements require the major commands to program for a higher level of quality than usual. If a higher level of quality cannot even be contemplated, bases cannot create source selections that attract better providers. This is one example among many of the challenge, discussed below, of coordinating all the government players relevant to services acquisition.

Such an arm's-length, adversarial perspective fits the legalistic nature of the due process that the federal government demands in any acquisition activity. It has a strong zero-sum presumption that anything that benefits a provider must cost the government buyer something. It does not fit the needs of partners well. When partners choose one another, they look for a relationship where the parties can share enough information to solve problems jointly and create enough value together so that they both benefit. They expect each other to be tough and demanding. But they also expect that a long-term relationship will be built on accumulating evidence of joint benefit. They share sensitive information—"open their kimonos"—expecting that the information will be used to solve problems, not to change the price when failures occur.

An open debate persists among federal procurement professionals about which view is more realistic and which is more appropriate in a federal setting. Those who prefer the traditional view are suspicious of partnerships and the less-than-arm's-length relationships they allow. They fear what can go wrong in such a setting enough to avoid the benefits the setting can generate. Periodic procurement scandals give them all the evidence they need to maintain the clampdown. Those who favor a more open approach argue that meaningful partnerships cannot exist under the traditional approach. Seeking partnership means managing risks rather than minimizing them. It means seeking offerors on grounds other than cost and accepting the degree of subjectivity that comes with this approach. It means punishing those caught abusing the system but not assuming that they are characteristic of the whole body of offerors chosen when proper criteria are used in source selections.

This debate is nowhere near being resolved. It puts offerors seeking partnerships with the federal government in an odd position. They may initially deal with government acquisition professionals who espouse the new approach and enter a relationship with the government expecting opportunities for mutual gains. To their surprise, they encounter other government acquisition professionals responsible for quality assurance who question the arrangements of a partnership and cripple it with restrictions. Alternatively, an oversight agency, which gets more credit for finding failure than for finding success, objects to the terms of the partnership and cripples it with inquiries that discourage risk taking.

At issue today are two approaches to government services acquisition that can each work on their own terms but do not work well when mixed. For a true partnership to work, the government has to select an offeror that can be a responsible partner and then must act as a responsible partner itself. To be a responsible partner, the government must (1) work with a provider to solve problems together, (2) oversee the execution of the contract enabling the partnership to support mutual problem solving, and (3) review the oversight role with a similar perspective. A different part of the government is often responsible for each of these three roles; for "the government" to be a responsible partner, all three government agencies must work together toward the goal. For example, in the Balkans Support Contract, (1) units deployed from the United States have the closest day-to-day contact with the contractor; (2) the Army command in Europe, the Army Corps of Engineers, and the Defense Contract Management Agency all play important, differing oversight roles; and (3) the congressional General Accounting Office has repeatedly reviewed how these organizations execute the contract with the contractor. These government organizations all have different roles, perspectives, and incentives in the services acquisition process.[42] Such cooperation is hard to achieve when the federal government has not resolved its ongoing debate about the two approaches to services acquisition. It is even harder to assure a responsible offeror, because a failure in any one of the roles can eliminate the gains the offeror wants from partnership.

Partnerships are succeeding in different places throughout the federal government, so groups of government professionals are finding ways to make the three roles work together. But controversy persists. A full shift from the traditional view to one more supportive of using partnerships will require a greater degree of agreement within

---

[42] For details, see Greenfield and Camm (forthcoming).

the federal acquisition community about where partnerships are worth the investment and risk taking required. Efforts are under way to help federal acquisition professionals understand better partnerships and the acquisition tools associated with them—strategic purchasing to target the appropriate activities of partnerships, best-value competition, performance-based contracts, incentives that extend contracts for good performance, and so on.[43] As a better consensus forms, government behavior as a responsible partner should improve, reducing the risks to high-quality private sources looking for opportunities to build mutual value in partnerships with the federal government.

Issues to Monitor

As the federal government expands its use of PPPs, two additional issues warrant special attention:

- How PPPs can affect mission focus
- Unintended effects PPPs can have on buyer and seller

How PPPs Can Affect Mission Focus

In an effective partnership, a buyer seeks to, and in fact must, give up day-to-day control over the activities it buys. To do this, the buyer must find more parsimonious, strategic ways to convey its intent. The better a buyer-agency understands its own mission, the better able it is to identify and demand appropriate elements of performance. And the better a private provider can take over day-to-day responsibility for execution, the more the provider can push the buyer to communicate parsimoniously and strategically about the key elements of the buyer's agency mission. In private-private partnerships, these factors lead to changes that we should expect to see in PPPs as they mature.[44]

---

[43] See, for example, recommended actions in Anderson, 1999.

[44] This discussion draws on interviews with best-in-class commercial buyer-seller pairs that underlie the findings in Baldwin et al., 2000, and Moore et al., 2002.

First, buyers become more attentive to differences between outcomes and the processes that generate them and increasingly focus on the outcomes. This frees time and resources for the buyers to think about whether these outcomes are compatible with their own higher-level missions. It even encourages entry of a new kind of manager into the buyer organization—someone more interested in thinking strategically and leading by formulating a clear, simple statement of intent than in executing day-to-day tasks and motivating the many individuals involved in specific elements of those tasks. Perceptive leaders in buyer organizations anticipate this change and seek new personnel who are mission-oriented.

Second, buyers become more attuned to communicating with providers through the accountability-oriented language of specific performance metrics, goals, and expectations. Effective partnerships require such a language to support communication between organizations that typically have different core competencies and hence often have differing cultures. Partners often find that such communication provides a degree of discipline not present between users and providers within a single organization. After choosing to use an external partner rather than an internal source, buyers often find a degree of purposeful communication and integration that had not existed between in-house user and provider. Ironically, in some cases, buyers say the formal accountability and communication methods imposed by using a formal partnership were more important to improved performance than the actual decision to use an external partner. That is, buyers benefited from partnership precisely because increased requirements for formal accountability led them to be clearer about their missions so that they could communicate them clearly to a partner; they could have done the same with an internal source if they had known how.

PPPs are likely to experience similar changes. If they do, PPPs could help public agencies understand performance-based accountability systems better and apply them not only in their PPPs but also in other parts of their internal activities. Efforts to implement performance-based budgeting, for example, should benefit. Better mission focus is an integral part of any agencywide performance-based accountability system.

Unintended Effects PPPs Can Have on Buyer and Seller

Much of the discussion above has drawn on experience in commercial partnerships to identify factors that are relevant to choosing to use PPPs and then structuring them. Unique characteristics of the public sector may induce unintended effects not likely to be observed in commercial partnerships.

First, as partners learn more about one another over time, aspects of their two cultures can be expected to seep across the boundary between them. Just as the border areas between two very different countries, such as the United States and Mexico, tend to display transition zones on both sides of the border that blend the core cultures of the countries, long-term partnerships could easily yield similar outcomes over time. Like two long-time spouses, two partners may easily grow to look more alike as they accommodate each other's peculiarities. PPPs are often touted as windows through which government agencies can see useful best practices and portals through which these practices can enter the government. But these windows and portals open in both directions. Over time, government contractors often become socialized, growing used to the complex acquisition regulations that govern their relationships with the government and promoting values that would not survive a pure market test in the commercial economy. Private firms like Boeing, Johnson Controls, and Ernst and Young divide down the middle, sustaining a government culture on the side of the firm that services the government and a commercial culture on the side of the firm that services commercial buyers. Whole communities of private sector competitors persist with a similar division down the middle and only limited communication across the divide. Over time, government agencies seeking private partners who can give them access to best commercial practice can find themselves in bed with "private" partners who have grown to look and behave very much like the agencies themselves.

Best commercial practice seeks to limit such effects by promoting broad benchmarking and by efforts to standardize internal processes across all customer classes. Acquisition reform in DoD seeks to emulate commercial practice precisely to achieve the same results. In all likelihood, government agencies will have to consciously stretch beyond their traditional partners to limit the partners' tendency to emulate government practice. Quality-based methods should help. But only time will tell whether these methods can survive in new PPPs that create truly habitual relationships between government buyers and providers that happen to be privately owned.

Second, private providers with political savvy and clout do not limit their influence on government agencies to the markets in which they deliver services to these agencies. We can expect providers to use political channels to protect and enhance their access to government buyers and users whenever they can. Where they are successful, such providers can limit an agency leadership's ability to align a provider's performance with the agency's mission in ways that benefit the providers. A really successful provider can induce an agency leadership to see the provider's well-being as a core part of the agency's mission. This can occur whether the provider is public or private. CICA sought explicitly to limit a private provider's ability to do this. PPPs that allow powerful private providers to limit competition, for example, in effect limit CICA's efficacious effects; they offer an opportunity for abuse. That said, public and private providers will continue to exercise political power where they can, whether PPPs exist or not. Experience will tell us whether government agencies can benefit from PPPs without opening the door to such abuse too widely.

Concluding Remarks

The government can use PPPs to improve its implementation of policy, but it cannot use PPPs to make substantive policy decisions. In any partnership implementing government policy, *the government must retain responsibility for setting the requirements the partnership will pursue.* In this way, the government always sits at the head of the table, no matter how equal other aspects of the partnership are.

PPPs are rhetorically easy to support: Who can be against the use of a "partnership"? In practice, however, *PPPs have proven to be difficult to implement effectively.* PPPs generate the largest benefits when partners with differing competencies find ways to partner with one another. Such differences usually mean differences in goals and cultures that must continually be overcome by the partners. Like a marriage, PPPs take a lot of commitment and work to ensure that all participants continue to benefit. Unlike marriage, they have little emotional glue to hold them together in bad times. As long as PPPs continue to work well, they can substitute for ongoing competition. But the threat and occasional reality of competition can help ensure that they continue to work well. Balancing such competition with incentives for partners to continue investing in one another is a continuing challenge, particularly in a public legal setting that strongly favors competition.

In the end, these challenges tell us that *PPPs are likely to be worth the effort only in certain places.* They are most attractive where the risks and cost savings associated with them justify the time and effort to put them in place. The most complex PPPs are likely to succeed where the government spends a lot of money on a source and the quality of the source's performance can have a large effect on the quality of core government services. Less complex PPPs will likely succeed in activities that involve smaller sums of money or directly affect less critical government services. PPPs are hardest to justify for generic services that the government can acquire easily and reliably at arm's length. PPPs need to be tailored to the government's needs in each situation and to the capabilities of private sector partners. If they work well, they can be expected to morph over time as the government's needs and the private partners' capabilities change. Reasonable markers exist today to suggest the best places to try PPPs,[45] but in the end, only the actual unfolding experience that the government has with specific partners will reveal whether the partnerships are worth continuing.

---

[45] For a discussion of such "strategic purchasing," see Moore et al., 2002.

We still have a lot to learn. The commercial sector has a great deal of experience with joint ventures, but join ventures seek different goals and behave differently than PPPs do. Federal sourcing culture will have to change to accept less-than-arm's-length relationships with partners and to state federal requirements without telling private partners how to meet these requirements. Mistakes will occur as the government experiments with partnerships. The federal government should seek to limit the damage from mistakes, to learn from them, and to avoid allowing mistakes to discourage the government from learning how to get full advantage from the potential that PPPs offer.

Additional policy analysis can assist this learning process. Decisionmakers in the public and private sectors would benefit from more-comprehensive and systematic empirical evidence on (1) what specific factors account for PPP performance in practice and (2) how factors that explain success and failure differ in public-private and private-private partnerships. Our empirical work to date indicates that the following factors deserve special attention in analyses directed at these two issues: (1) the types of activities in which PPPs are tried; (2) the general approach to services acquisition used where they are tried; (3) in particular, the strategic planning and market research used to prepare for the PPPs examined; (4) the specific forms, terms, and metrics used in the PPPs examined; (5) in particular, how a government partner combines competition, benchmarking, and incentive contracting to discipline the performance of its private sector partners; (6) the approach to coordinating all government agencies relevant to a PPP; and (7) the training that government personnel in these agencies receive to prepare for PPPs.

Volcker Commission Recommendation 2: Enhance Leadership

Improving Government Processes: From Velocity Management to Presidential Appointments

John Dumond and Rick Eden

We have two objectives in this chapter. The first is to substantiate the claim of the Volcker Commission that "governments and government agencies can change, even in ways that seem far-reaching, and those changes can produce significant improvements in efficiency and performance" (Chapter 2 of this volume, p. 26). In support of this claim, we present a case study (observed firsthand by us) in which governmental agencies worked together to achieve successful change. This study involved the Velocity Management (VM) initiative, which the U.S. Army began in 1994 to improve its order fulfillment and related processes, and which the National Partnership for Reinventing Government recognized with a Golden Hammer award in 1998.[1]

Our second objective is to suggest how the VM approach might be applied to other governmental processes. Because of the Volcker Commission's concern with the quality of senior governmental executives, we focus here on the presidential appointments process. As with military logistics processes, this process is complex, has both chronic and acute performance problems, and involves many stakeholders. The problems have been well described for decades, and many reasonable recommendations have been proposed. Nevertheless, the per-

---

[1] Another case of successful reform that we studied, Strategic Distribution, was a joint 1999 initiative of the U.S. Transportation Command (USTRANSCOM) and the Defense Logistics Agency (DLA) to improve the strategic distribution process serving all four services (see Robbins, Boren, and Leuschner, 2003). Both of these cases reveal dramatically improved performance in large and complex processes involving multiple agencies and organizations.

formance problems have continued to worsen to the point that the system is now considered to be in crisis. A proven approach to implementing and managing change through interagency cooperation may be the missing catalyst.

Part One: Improving Military Logistics Processes

In the commercial business world, the term *logistics* often refers simply to the distribution of material, particularly finished goods. In the military, the term has a broader meaning. Military logistics comprises the set of business processes that acquire and deliver the products and services needed by military units to operate. These processes include procurement, order fulfillment, distribution, inventory management, retrograde ("reverse logistics"), and maintenance—all with familiar commercial analogs.

The military logistics system is a far-flung supply chain whose customers are military units worldwide. Its providers, however, are not limited to the military. They include various agencies within the four services (such as the Army Materiel Command and the Air Force Air Mobility Command); other Department of Defense (DoD) agencies (such as USTRANSCOM and the DLA); non-DoD agencies (such as the General Services Administration [GSA]); and literally tens of thousands of both domestic and foreign commercial firms that design, manufacture, store, transport, maintain, modify, and dispose of all matter of items used by the military.

A Crisis of Performance—and Trust

At the end of the Cold War, the U.S. military logistics system needed to change for three primary reasons: to respond to environmental and structural changes, to correct chronic performance problems, and to address the fact that it had lost the trust of its customers, the warfighters.

By environmental and structural changes we mean changes that have occurred in the national security environment and U.S. force posture since the end of the Cold War. For instance, the military fielded a new generation of increasingly high-technology weapon systems, which presented consumption, failure, and maintenance profiles quite different from those of the weapon systems they replaced. These new systems could not be supported effectively and efficiently in the same ways. As forces were drawn down from their Cold War levels, demand for logistics support also declined, affecting the utilization and productivity of logistics resources. As the military shifted to a posture emphasizing basing in the continental United States (CONUS), the logistics supply chain had to be reconfigured to adjust for the changed locations of both many customers and many providers. The demand for logistics support also changed to reflect an increased emphasis on force projection and humanitarian missions. Finally, through much of the last decade of the twentieth century, the expectation of a "peace dividend" created pressure to reduce military costs in general and logistics support costs more specifically.

A second reason for needing change was that the military logistics system was suffering from chronic performance problems. The basic business processes (given above) were all slow and unreliable. Increasingly, the system's performance was being unfavorably compared to that of leading commercial firms engaged in similar business activities, such as FedEx for distribution and Wal-Mart for inventory management.

Third, the performance problems were causing a loss of trust. Military units were engaging in rational but inefficient behaviors, such as hoarding spare parts and other supplies, to protect themselves from the risks associated with slow and unpredictable processes. These behaviors further hurt system performance.

It is important to note that these chronic deficiencies in process performance persisted despite widespread recognition and despite waves of reforms attempted by talented experts and powerful leaders. Repeated failures to improve performance suggest that a new management approach may be needed to support a sustained and coordinated implementation of reforms across processes neither owned nor controlled by any single organization. Some of these deficiencies are visible in other areas of low-performance government, such as the presidential appointment process.

The Velocity Management Approach

A key realization that led to the Army's decision to use a process improvement approach to improve its logistics system was that no "process owner" had the authority or responsibility to undertake the needed improvement actions. Logistics processes such as order fulfillment and equipment maintenance have many stakeholders; therefore, the Army needed to form a coalition of military and civilian managers to build a consensus of purpose and a community for action. The coalition included both customer and provider representatives and extended outside the Army, since many organizations in the logistics system were not owned or controlled by the Army.

The Velocity Group (VG) has a broad membership.[2] The group is led by the general officers representing the three major logistics elements in the Army—that is, the Deputy Commander of the Army Materiel Command, the Deputy Chief of Staff for Logistics (now called the "G4"), and the Commander of the Combined Arms Support Command (CASCOM). Their organizations have responsibility, respectively, for decisions regarding wholesale-level logistics, policy and budget, and training and doctrine. The VG also includes representatives of the Army units that are the customers of the logistics system, including units in both the active and the Reserve components of the Army, both in garrison and deployed. Finally, the group includes other logistics providers in DoD, such as USTRANSCOM and the DLA.

The Commander of CASCOM acts as the executive agent for the VM initiative, and a small cell at CASCOM was given responsibility for coordinating the VM implementation and for serving as a clearinghouse for VM-related information (for instance, the cell manages a website devoted to the initiative: http://www.cascom.army.mil/adm/). Several times a year, the CASCOM people organize a systemwide meeting in which the VG receives updates on implementation progress and provides assistance and guidance. That does not

---

[2] This group was recently renamed the Distribution Management Board of Directors.

mean, though, that actions take place only to support the meet-ings—rather, the meetings take place to support the ongoing actions.

The managers in this coalition span the logistics system. To-gether they can create the conditions for changing it and can help to lower barriers to change. They can also provide a vision of the desired end state. But they need subordinate entities that are similarly cross-organizational in membership to identify and develop specific changes, implement them, measure their effect, and then report pro-gress toward goals. Because the Army logistics system crosses organi-zational boundaries and because every segment is technically com-plex, no single organization or individual has sufficient knowledge, control, or leverage to make dramatic change if operating alone. To improve a process in the logistics system, teams of technical experts and line managers drawn from all segments of the process must be established in order to develop and implement improvement actions that are not suboptimal to the system as a whole.

VM was implemented by teams of two types: Army-wide pro-cess improvement teams (PITs) and local site improvement teams (SITs) at each installation.

A PIT consists of technical experts representing all segments of a process. PITs are charged with walking through their respective pro-cesses to establish common, detailed definitions and understandings; developing processwide metrics and performance reports; and rec-ommending process changes designed to improve performance. The leader of each PIT is a general officer or civilian equivalent in the senior executive service.

A SIT is made up of local technical experts and managers at a specific site, and each major Army installation (i.e., fort) establishes its own VM SIT. These SITs are responsible for improving local processes and serve as a mechanism for the PITs to implement changes across the Army.

Define-Measure-Improve

Many organizations undertake improvement initiatives only to see them end inconclusively or quietly fail. One reason this occurs is that the organization has not prepared sufficiently to sustain the initiatives once the initial enthusiasm passes. Sometimes an organization addresses this problem by institutionalizing an improvement methodology to help sustain change. The two best-known examples of this are probably Toyota's four-step method (Plan-Do-Check-Act, sometimes known as the Shewhart cycle, after Walter Shewhart, the "father" of statistical quality control) and Motorola's six-step method. Embedding an improvement method into an organization's culture makes the expectation of and search for improvement a standard operating procedure—that is, an accustomed way of doing business.

As part of VM, the Army adopted a streamlined version of methods that had propelled successful change initiatives in large commercial firms. To improve the performance of the processes, three readily understood and executed steps are applied in what is called the DMI method: Define the process, Measure process performance, and Improve the process. These steps are cycled continuously. Figure 8.1 indicates the key activities encompassed within each of these steps.

Figure 8.1
Steps in the Define-Measure-Improve Method

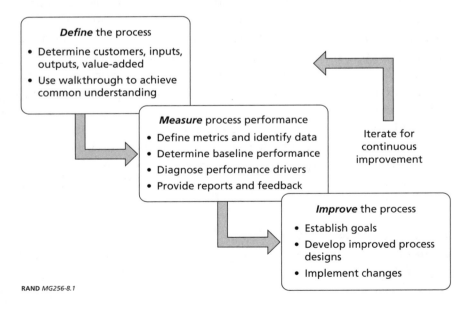

The application of DMI disciplines the impulse to make quick changes. In the DMI method, improvement is undertaken only after the organization has taken the preparatory steps of Define and Measure. These two steps improve knowledge about the process targeted for improvement, in terms of both the expertise of the individuals charged with changing the process and the quantitative data available to them regarding process performance.

Define the Process
The first step in the DMI approach, Define, focuses on understanding customer needs and the outputs of the particular process under study. Detailed walkthroughs of the process by teams of technical experts improve the organization's understanding of what procedures and actions are involved and how they affect performance. It is eye opening for the participants to discover that they all have different and limited views of the same process. Teams learn that previous improvement efforts focusing on particular segments of the process may have been working at cross-purposes. On the positive side, they learn that easy-to-fix issues can be immediately exposed during walkthroughs. These help to satisfy the desire to see quick action, and they build support for the improvement effort.

More important, though, is the fact that walkthroughs develop a cadre that collectively embodies new expertise. These individuals share an end-to-end understanding of the process, a common framework for assessing performance that focuses on customer satisfaction, well-informed hypotheses about the sources of performance deficits, and the collective authority to devise and recommend innovations to improve process performance.

Measure the Process
Like the Define step, the Measure step of the DMI method represents an investment that must be made before a higher level of performance can be reasonably expected.

The most critical aspect of measurement is the development and implementation of appropriate metrics that span the full process and reflect key customer values. Metrics are the *lingua franca* by which all stakeholders in a process communicate with one another regarding the goals and status of their improvement efforts. The choice of metrics is critical, because what gets measured is what gets attended to. VM advocates the use of multiple metrics to guide improvement on all dimensions of process performance—time, quality, and cost—and to ensure that improvements on one dimension (e.g., cost) are not achieved at the expense of others (e.g., quality). Because improvement aims to reduce the variability in process performance, metrics should, as a rule, measure both median performance and variance. Metrics for overall performance should comprise submetrics that permit diagnosis and analysis of the sources of poor performance (for example, total process time should be analyzable into time attributable to each subprocess).

Data sources to support the metrics must be identified and evaluated. To date, the VM implementation has been able to proceed utilizing data available from standard Army data systems, although these data have frequently been combined and used in innovative ways. A beneficial by-product of using data to support process improvement is that the data quality improves very quickly: Those who are trying to use the data uncover previously unnoticed quality problems, and those who are responsible for inputting and maintaining the data are alerted to the importance of their accuracy, completeness, and timeliness.

Measurement includes reporting, another activity critical to sustaining continuous improvement. Reporting helps to build support and maintain momentum over a long period. Measurement offers maximum benefit when the results are widely shared among stakeholders in the process. Improvement is difficult to guide and sustain unless performance feedback is consistent and rapid.

Because the DMI method depends centrally on the measurement of process performance, analytic support is needed for its use. For its analytic support, the VM initiative relied principally on RAND Corporation analysts conducting studies sponsored by the Army. The PITs counted RAND's analysts among their members, and their analyses helped to identify potential improvements to logistics processes and provided technical support as the changes were implemented and evaluated. RAND analysts also helped to develop metrics and reports, to analyze data, to diagnose performance problems, and to develop process changes and evaluate their implementation.

Improve the Process

The third step in the DMI method, Improve, capitalizes on the knowledge developed during the first two steps. In conducting the Define and Measure steps of the method, teams develop a better understanding of the performance deficits in a process and where reform might begin.

The measurements tell the teams which processes and subprocesses they should examine in more detail and which ones present the best opportunity for improvement. More fine-grained measurements give the team clues about what they should be looking for when walking through the process at a particular time or site. Generally, teams look for activities that are time consuming, error prone, or costly and that add little value, on scales large and small. For instance, they look for long periods of waiting, overprocessing, overproduction, multiple handling, duplication, unnecessary movement, and any action or item whose purpose the involved personnel cannot readily explain. In addition to looking for non-value-adding activities to eliminate, the teams look for ways to improve and streamline value-adding activities. Sometimes this might be accomplished through increased use of information technology—for instance, to place information in a shared dataset once it has been gathered, rather than to gather it several times in the course of a process.

The process experts also use metrics to articulate realistic but challenging goals for improved performance. Progress toward these goals, which operationalize the vision of the senior-level coalition, occurs incrementally. However, big payoffs can be produced early on by making a few quick, easy changes almost immediately to improve a process that is out of control and performing very erratically. For example, one might be able to reduce reliance on a provider whose service has been inordinately expensive. Besides providing benefits to performance, these initial improvements will build momentum for subsequent efforts. Metrics enable the improvement teams to measure whether performance improves after the implementation of process changes. Moreover, by comparing performance trends at these implementation sites to those at similar sites, the teams can create quasi-experimental demonstrations of the beneficial effects of a given intervention.

As performance of the process improves, the DMI cycle begins again, with repeated walkthroughs and a remapping of the changed process, continued measurement, and additional process changes.

The Army's Order Fulfillment Process

The Army's successful effort to improve spare parts support is a good illustration of the VM paradigm in action. In particular, it demonstrates how improvement teams employ the DMI method to build the collective expertise and coordination necessary to achieve and sustain dramatic improvement.

What was called the order fulfillment process had for decades been plagued by stubborn problems. Each segment of the process—from placing an order for a part to receiving the shipment—was slow and highly variable. Previous remedies had failed, and a chronic problem was becoming acute.

Figure 8.2 provides a schematic of the order fulfillment process for Army units in CONUS. The VG commissioned a PIT to focus on this process. The team was made up of experts representing each subprocess of the order fulfillment process.[3]

Defining the Order Fulfillment Process. The PIT began by defining the order fulfillment process. The outputs of the process are the parts needed to repair and support weapon systems; the customers are the maintainers of the systems and the supply clerks who manage local inventories of spare parts. As Figure 8.2 shows, the parts that were requested could be available at a number of locations through-

---

[3] These experts included maintainers, transporters, and inventory managers, as well as representatives from non-Army stakeholders such as the DLA, USTRANSCOM, and government contractors (e.g., J.B. Trucking, FedEx, and Emery). RAND provided researchers to guide the application of the DMI process and to provide analytic support.

Figure 8.2
Order Fulfillment Process for Army Units in CONUS

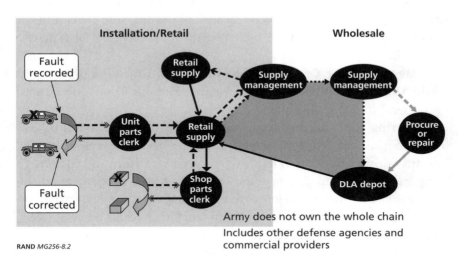

RAND *MG256-8.2*

out the Army. Some parts are available at local warehouses, called Supply Support Activities (SSAs), which are situated near the Army units and their maintenance facilities. These are usually the quickest source of spare parts, but they cannot carry all parts that might be needed. When an item is not available at a customer's SSA, another warehouse is asked to fill the order. If the part is unavailable at all nearby warehouses, the order is passed to what is referred to as the national, or wholesale, supply system, which includes commercial vendors.[4]

Members of the PIT and the SITs walked through each step of the process, including ordering, sourcing, picking, packing, shipping, delivery, and receipting. The PIT members spoke to customers about how the process worked. They looked at financial and information flows in addition to the more easily observable flows of materiel; they

---

[4] The PIT initially focused on the order fulfillment process for orders for spare parts that were filled by supply points in the wholesale system. This wholesale process can be defined as a cycle that begins at the SSA when a supply clerk places an order for a spare part to be filled by a wholesale supply depot or, rarely, by direct delivery from a vendor. The cycle ends at the same point when a supply clerk at the SSA retail supply organization receives the part.

also reviewed the software, scrutinizing "virtual" aspects of the process such as embedded algorithms, parameters, and thresholds. The activities of the Define stage produced a cadre of processwide experts in the Army's order fulfillment process, representing a new level of expertise not available before.

Measuring the Order Fulfillment Process. Once the process was defined, a determination had to be made about what constituted "goodness" in order fulfillment.

During the walkthroughs, members of the PIT and the SITs found that managers often focused on local effectiveness or efficiency but did not necessarily also focus on good service from the customer's perspective. For example, in some segments of the process, organizations sought to make efficient use of trucks, with the result that ordered materiel was delayed until a full truckload could be assembled. This "batching" of items in the process was done without regard for the urgency with which any given part might be needed by the customer many steps away in the process.

A process approach such as VM is typically concerned with three dimensions of performance—time, quality, and cost. Because of many complaints about delays, the PIT focused initially on the time dimension. The Army's dataset Logistics Intelligence File (LIF) contained time stamps for orders and deliveries of spare parts, and these data permitted time measurement of the process as a whole and of major segments.

The time from order placed to package receipted was referred to as order and ship time (OST).[5] LIF data were used to define a baseline against which to gauge subsequent success; the baseline period was from mid-1994 to mid-1995 (see Figure 8.3).[6] The Army knew

_____

[5] As an improvement effort progresses, the suite of metrics evolves. In the case of VM, OST was subsequently replaced by requisition wait time (RWT), in part to reflect later changes in the order fulfillment process and the Army's capabilities to measure it. In addition, RWT was complemented by customer wait time, a composite metric that represented the time needed to obtain parts from all sources of supply, rather than from the national-level supply system alone.

[6] See Girardini et al., 1996, for a detailed discussion of the development of metrics and the creation of a baseline measurement.

Figure 8.3
Order and Ship Time, Baseline Performance

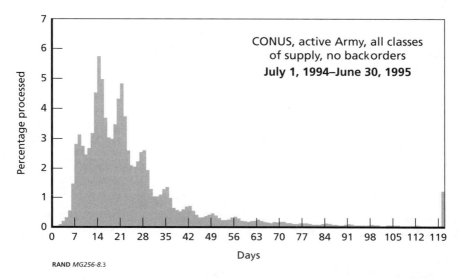

CONUS, active Army, all classes
of supply, no backorders
July 1, 1994–June 30, 1995

RAND *MG256-8.3*

that the average OST was very long—almost a month—and recognized how extremely slow this OST was compared to the rapidly improving order fulfillment times in the commercial sector (which widely advertised "overnight" and "next day" delivery). However, the Army had not recognized that its OST performance was also highly variable, with a long right-hand tail. This variability, more than slowness per se, was what had led to customer distrust of the process.

To cope with an unreliable process, mechanics were placing duplicate orders, hoarding parts, and finding alternatives to the supply system. This was their way to handle the fact that since a repair must wait until every needed part is at hand, even one part lying in the tail of the OST distribution could hold it up.

The PIT proposed three new metrics: the median OST (to measure "typical" rather than average speed of the process), the 75th percentile, and the 95th percentile. The purpose of the 75th percentile was to indicate the time by which three quarters of the filled orders had been received and receipted. The 95th percentile was useful for focusing attention on the "outliers" in the process that represent its worst performance. The new metrics for measuring OST perform-ance became standard in Army reports, which used overlaid bars to depict them graphically (see Figure 8.4).

Improving the Order Fulfillment Process. The VG used the met-rics to specify ambitious goals for improvement. The goals were feasi-ble yet challenging, and they signaled that dramatic improvement was needed. This encouraged an innovative and aggressive attitude toward developing and testing process changes.

The PIT and SITs discovered that many factors contributed to the long and highly variable OSTs. Some of these factors were easily fixed at the local level, without any investment in or increases to total process cost, and these resulted in quick "wins." For example, SITs helped their home installations strengthen oversight, simplify rules, improve the use of new requisitioning and receipting technologies (such as bar code scanners), reduce review processes so as to require

Figure 8.4
New Metrics for the Order Fulfillment Process: Median OST,
75th Percentile, and 95th Percentile

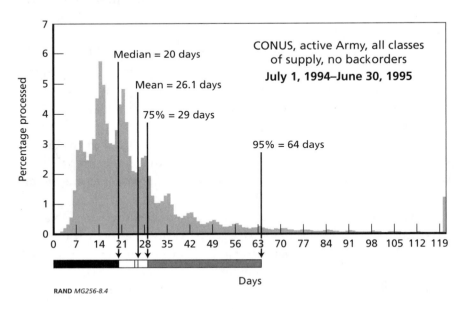

RAND *MG256-8.4*

fewer signatures, and streamline on-post delivery processes and routes.

Other changes required new coordination among organizations that controlled various segments of the order fulfillment process. Collaboration was facilitated by the relationships developed through the PIT. To take just one example, the Army had to work closely with the DLA, which operates many of the major supply depots, as well as with commercial trucking and small package delivery firms. The Army and the DLA worked together to establish a network of regularly scheduled trucks (similar to regular mail deliveries) as the primary shipping mode between DLA depots and large Army installations. Depending on how far the depot was from a particular installation in its customer region, these routes could provide at a very low cost a level of performance that was comparable to the relatively expensive "next day" service offered by small package air delivery firms. To capitalize on these routes, the supply depots started to increase the breadth of materiel that they routinely stocked for their major customers.

The new metrics, reported monthly, enabled everyone involved in efforts to improve the order fulfillment process to understand and monitor the effects of process changes. Two or three times per year, at meetings convened by the VG, the PIT and selected SITs could use the metrics to communicate their progress toward the goals.

The result of many improvements was a much faster, more reliable order fulfillment process (see Figure 8.5).

Part Two: Improving the Presidential Appointments Process

The presidential appointments process is the set of activities by which the executive branch of the federal government staffs most of the major management positions charged with executing the policies of an administration. Just like the Army's order fulfillment process before VM implementation, the presidential appointments process suffers long-standing performance deficits. Successive commissions and

Figure 8.5
Improved Order Fulfillment Process as a Result of Velocity Management Implementation

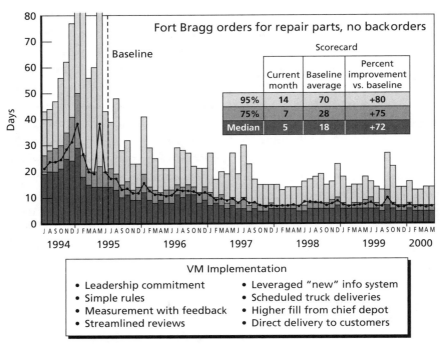

commentators have suggested well-conceived solutions for remedying the sources of the problems. However, these recommendations have not been implemented successfully and the problems have remained, only increasing in severity. The National Academy of Sciences complains that "the appointment process is slow, duplicative, and unpredictable" (Panel on Presidentially Appointed Scientists and Engineers, 1992, p. 5). The situation has grown worse with each administration of the past forty years, as shown in Figure 8.6. Between 1964 and 1984, the presidential appointment process rarely took longer than six months (Light and Thomas, 2000, p. 8). In the last two administrations—those of Bush and then Clinton—it averaged eight months (Brookings Institution, 2000).

Figure 8.6
Length of Presidential Appointments Process, Kennedy Through Clinton

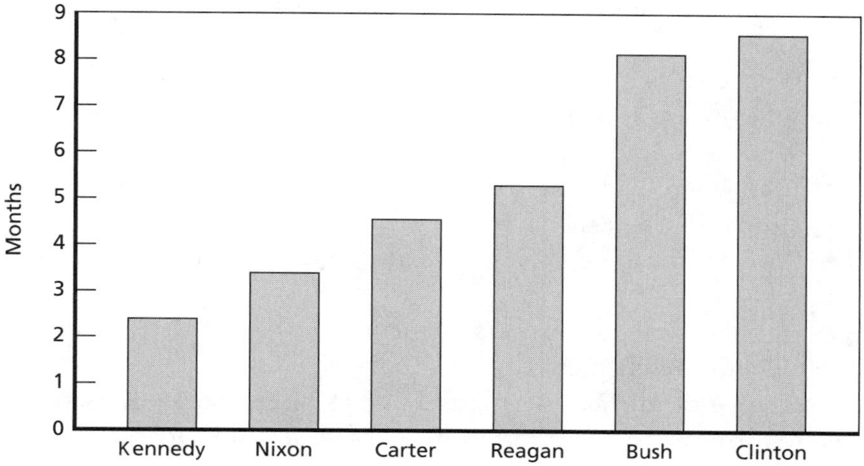

RAND *MG256-8.6*
SOURCE: Mackenzie and Shogan, 1996.

What was a long and unpredictable process has only become longer and more unpredictable. In fact, reform efforts may have backfired, exacerbating the problems they were intended to fix. According to a leading critic of the process, G. Calvin Mackenzie (1998), "The decades old effort to improve the process of selecting and confirming presidential appointees has produced an outcome directly opposite its intentions. It repels the appointees it ought to attract. It shortens the tenure in office it ought to sustain."

The history of failed reforms to date suggests that a new approach may be warranted in order to produce the "significant improvements in efficiency and performance" of the type sought by the Volcker Commission.

Might insights from Velocity Management be applied to this seemingly intractable problem? In considering the appropriateness of applying a VM-like approach to the presidential appointments process in order to improve it, we need to address questions such as the following:

- Can a case be made that there is an urgent need for change?
- Is there a vision of a better way?
- What does the vision suggest are the measures of goodness?
- Are there strong leaders committed to change?
- What coalition is needed to achieve change?
- What expertise must the process improvement teams have?
- What sites need improvement teams?
- Who will provide analytic support to the change initiatives?
- How will progress be reported?
- Where is the low-hanging fruit (the "now-term" initiatives)?

We begin to develop answers to many of these questions in the remainder of this chapter.

A sense of urgency may already be in place. Nancy Kassebaum Baker, former U.S. Senator from Kansas, testified to the United States Senate Committee on Governmental Affairs that "the current [presidential appointments] process desperately needs reform" (Baker, 2001). Paul Light of the Brookings Institution and New York University, and Virginia Thomas of the Heritage Foundation (Light and Thomas, 2000) have warned that "the presidential [appointments] process is broken in several places" (p. 11) and "now verges on complete collapse" (p. 3).

An effective case for change must include not only a compelling indictment of the present process, but also a vision of an improved process. The vision statement need not be detailed; in fact, it needs to be relatively broad in order to permit many competing perspectives to accede to it.[7] A vision statement such as this one, offered by Light and Thomas, might well be sufficient:

> [The presidential appointment process] should give nominees enough information so that they can act in their best interest throughout the process, move fast enough to give departments and agencies the leadership they need to faithfully execute the

---

[7] See Setear et al., 1990, for a discussion of what makes an effective organizational vision.

laws, and be fair enough to draw talented people into service, while rigorous enough to assure that individual nominees are fit for their jobs (2000, p. 7).

Even more succinctly, the Brookings Institution's Presidential Appointee Initiative (PAI) calls for "making the presidential appointment process easier, faster, and more respectful toward the people who have accepted the call to service" (Brookings Institution, 2000, p. 3).

In addition to a sense of urgency and a vision, the VM approach requires strong commitment and participation from all the organizations that are stakeholders in the process to be improved. It has long been recognized that no one organization owns or controls the presidential appointments process and that its reform will require the cooperation of the executive and legislative branches. For instance, Mackenzie writes that "since both the executive and legislative branches share responsibility for reducing the obstacles to public service, a bipartisan framework—that includes representatives of the executive branch, Congress, and the Office of Government Ethics—is needed to identify actions that should be taken by the President and Congress to broaden and deepen the pool of qualified persons willing to consider presidential appointments" (Mackenzie, 1998).

The Army's experience with VM suggests how to form and use a senior coalition to guide improvement. A standing coalition of stakeholders in the process would together act as the process owner and manager. The crucial political question is, of course, whether those now responsible for delay-making in opposing political parties would be willing to make a long-term agreement across several administrations to make up such a senior coalition. By analogy with the VG, what we might call a Leadership Coalition for the presidential appointments process would have responsibility for providing guidance and feedback to all those involved as to the focus and efficacy of their improvement efforts. Once they agree on the crisis, the vision, and the improvement approach, the members of the coalition can accomplish a great deal. This group would not be convened on an ad hoc or one-time basis; rather, it would constitute an ongoing management function focused on continuous improvement. It would develop metrics to measure the goodness of the process, establish goals in terms of those metrics, develop and implement process improvements, and monitor the process for progress toward goals.

A Leadership Coalition should include leaders from the key offices and agencies involved in the presidential appointments process. These would almost certainly include the senior managers of several White House offices (Office of Presidential Personnel and Office of Counsel to the President) and the Office of Government Ethics. The coalition should probably include high-level representatives from the agencies headed by the appointees, the Federal Bureau of Investigation (FBI), the Internal Revenue Service (IRS), and the Senate. And the coalition might even be extended to include participants from the many other organizations that play informal yet very powerful roles in the process, including the media, industries and their lobbies, watchdog and special interest groups, and the House of Representatives.

The Leadership Coalition will need to charter a PIT to develop and help execute specific actions to improve the presidential appointments process. Like the coalition itself, the PIT should be cross-functional in its membership, composed of experts drawn from the key organizations that perform the activities. The PIT would conduct walkthroughs of the process and work together to develop proposals for improvements that it would recommend to the Leadership Coalition. Each of the organizations represented in the Leadership Coalition and the PIT will also need to establish SITs to complement the PIT and to execute its recommendations.

Both the PIT and the SITs should use the Define-Measure-Improve (DMI) methodology to guide their activities. In the next three subsections, we outline the application of each step to the presidential appointments process.

Defining the Presidential Appointments Process

In the Define step of the DMI method, the PIT would identify the major activities of the presidential appointments process, its inputs and outputs, and its customers. This step would clarify for all PIT members the function of the process, its value, and its day-to-day detailed operation.

The outputs of the presidential appointments process are confirmed appointees. Each administration must fill approximately 1,000 managerial positions that require Senate confirmation and another 2,000 that do not.

There are many customers of the process. From one perspective, the customer of the process is the President, who needs executive managers to execute his policies. This is reflected in the term *presidential appointee*. From another perspective, reflected in the term *public service*, the customer of the process is the department or agency that needs a director to help execute its mission of serving the American public. The legislature is another stakeholder in the process, which cuts across executive and legislative branches. Key offices and agencies involved include several White House offices (Offices of Presidential Personnel and of Counsel to the President), the Office of Government Ethics, the agencies headed by the appointees, the FBI, the IRS, sixteen Senate committees, and the full Senate. Each of these might be a candidate for a SIT targeted to improve the site's activities related to the presidential appointments process. Many other organizations may play informal yet very powerful roles, including the media, industries and their lobbies, watchdog and special interest groups, the major political parties, and the House of Representatives.

The inputs to the process include the financial and personnel resources devoted to the process in the participating organizations. They also include information of various sorts, including information on the required outputs and on the pool of potential candidates. Much of the latter is provided by the selected candidates as the process unfolds.

Figure 8.7 diagrams the process from the perspective of the candidates. From this perspective, there are four stages, or what we call subprocesses: selection, clearance, nomination, and confirmation. Each subprocess is composed of activities performed by a number of participants. As Figure 8.7 suggests, these four stages vary in complexity. Whereas nomination is quite simple, almost clerical, Senate

Figure 8.7
Presidential Appointments Process from the Candidate's Perspective

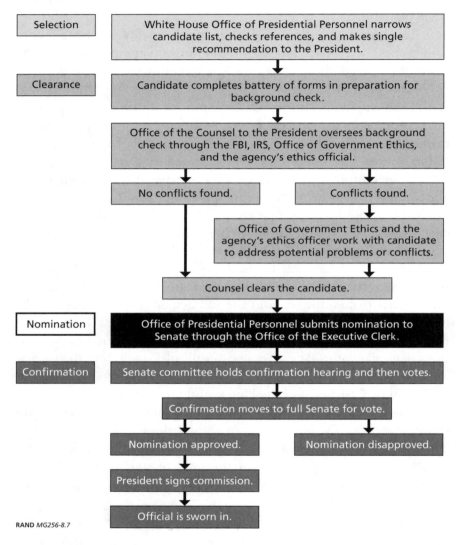

SOURCE: Adapted from Brookings Institution, 2000.

confirmation can range from straightforward to harrowing. The four subprocesses are described in order in the following paragraphs.

Selection. This first subprocess involves activities such as candidate identification, screening, interviewing, contacting, and recruiting. The main participants are the administration's transition team, the Office of Presidential Personnel, and the candidates themselves. The outputs of this subprocess are preferred candidates that can move to the next stage.

Clearance. Once a candidate is selected, he or she must be investigated to ensure that his or her background is "clear" of anything that might provide grounds for denying confirmation or creating political difficulties or embarrassment for the President. Examples of background items that are looked for are tax evasion, conflicts of interest, medical problems, and personal problems. The clearance subprocess is overseen by the Office of the Counsel to the President. A number of types of clearance are desired; thus, other major participants are the FBI, the IRS, the Office of Government Ethics, the ethics office of the agency where the appointment resides, and of course the candidate, who must fill out all the forms required by these entities. The outputs of this subprocess are names of qualified candidates that are suitable for nomination by the President.

Nomination. In this third subprocess, the cleared candidate is submitted to the Senate for confirmation. The major participants are the White House offices of the Counsel, of Presidential Appointments, of the Executive Clerk, and of the Press (for press releases). The outputs of this subprocess are nominations.

Confirmation. This last subprocess is overseen by one of sixteen Senate committees.[8] The chief activities are informal interviews ("courtesy calls") between the committee members and the candidate, together with formal hearings. There are separate votes by the committee and then the full Senate. As in previous subprocesses, the candidate is responsible for completing many forms; he or she also needs to develop detailed answers to specific policy questions pertaining to the position. The committee may undertake additional background investigations. The output of this subprocess is a list of confirmed

---

[8] The current status of candidates in the confirmation stage can be tracked at Senate website http://www.senate.gov/pagelayout/legislative/a_three_sections_with_teasers/nominations.htm.

candidates whose appointments the President completes by signing their commissions.

We have now sketched out the skeletal outline of the presidential appointments process by way of illustrating the Define step of the DMI method. If a VM improvement approach were applied to the presidential appointments process, a PIT would walk through the process from end to end. The walkthrough would consist of site visits by the team as a whole to each one of the organizations that participate in the process. At each site, experts responsible for that part of the process would describe and demonstrate how specific activities are performed. For most team members, this site visit would be their first opportunity to gain a detailed understanding of the other sub-processes of the process—that is, those subprocesses other than their own. It would also be their first opportunity to share with others their observations on how elements of the design or aspects of the execution of specific activities might bear on other activities upstream or downstream in the process.

Over the course of successive site visits, the members of the PIT would build a common and detailed understanding of the process from end to end. The goal of the walkthroughs is to build a team of experts who have the background, knowledge, and influence (through their mandate from the senior coalition) needed to begin measuring and improving the presidential appointments process.

Measuring the Presidential Appointments Process

Having mapped the presidential appointments process, we turn to Measure, the second step in the DMI method. The targeted process needs to be measured with respect to the dimensions of time, quality, and cost. The primary question here is, How might a PIT measure the goodness of the presidential appointment process along these dimensions?

Time Measures. Everyone seems to agree with Mackenzie: "It takes too long for a new president to staff the senior positions in the administration" (Mackenzie and Shogan, 1996, p. 73). Moreover, the growing delays are not confined to specific segments. According to Baker: "There is not a single stage of the appointments process—not one—where appointees do not say that it takes longer than it should" (Baker, 2001). For example, the clearance subprocess alone can take several months, and within that single subprocess, certification of the financial statements by the Office of Government Ethics can take two months (Brookings Institution, 2000, p. 42).

As these complaints suggest, obvious time metrics to consider in an improvement effort are total process time and total time within each of the four major subprocesses.[9]

Another lesson from VM is that measurement on all dimensions should address variability in performance as well as typical performance. Both very fast and very slow appointments may hold lessons for improvement efforts.

Quality Measures. When a process is long, unpredictable, and costly, quality must suffer. Measuring the quality dimension of process performance is usually more difficult than measuring the time dimension. One common strategy is to infer the quality of a process by measuring the quality of its outputs. But measuring the quality of inputs is also of interest, if one assumes that a good process can produce better outputs if it is given better inputs.

Critics usually tread lightly when complaining about the quality of the presidential appointees that finally emerge from today's very long process. For example, in describing the quality of appointees to science and technology leadership positions, the National Academy of Sciences states that "the quality of past appointees has been high" (Committee on Science, Engineering, and Public Policy, 2001, p. 3). Light and Thomas (2000) note that "it is difficult, if not impossible,

---

[9] Though the value of such metrics appears obvious, their precise definitions may not be straightforward and are subject to analysis and negotiation. It will be necessary for a PIT to stipulate for measurement purposes the beginning and end point of the process as a whole and of each subprocess. Moreover, care must be taken to leave no "air gaps" of unmeasured time for which no organization is accountable. Consider, for instance, the issues in defining when the process as a whole begins. For an individual candidate, one might say that the process begins with initial contact, typically by the White House transition team or Office of Presidential Personnel. This might also be the President's perspective. However, from the perspective of a department or agency needing its executive position filled, the process might be said to begin when the position becomes vacant. The department is clearly a customer of the process, and this would be the point at which a customer need is identified.

to know whether the quality of presidential appointments has changed with the passage of time" (p. 8). Nevertheless, the survey reported on by Light and Thomas did ask appointees to rate their colleagues as a cohort in order to determine appointee quality. The responses were lukewarm, with 79 percent of respondents describing Senate-confirmed appointees as "a mixed lot: some are highly talented, while others do not have the skills and experience their positions require" (p. 9).

One metric might be the percentage of first-choice candidates that are appointed. Several candidates for each position are identified in the selection stage of the current process, and it might be reasonable to assume that the first-choice candidates are considered higher quality. A similar metric might be the percentage of contacted candidates who agree to be considered for appointment.

To complement individual-level metrics of quality, one might develop metrics to assess the quality of a cohort of presidential appointments. For instance, cohort metrics might measure the quality of presidential appointments in terms of desired personal characteristics (such as diversity in religion, gender, age, race) or background characteristics (such as ideology, business experience, or previous public service).

In addition to measuring inputs and outputs, it is possible to measure outcomes and gauge the quality of a process on that basis. For example, an outcome-oriented quality measure for the presidential appointments process might be length of tenure in the appointed position. Using such a metric would be analogous to assessing the quality of the equipment repair process by measuring the length of time between needed repair actions: The implication is that the better a piece of equipment is repaired, the longer it stays fixed. The average tenure of presidential appointments is now only 24 months (see Figure 8.8).

Judged by the measure of length of tenure, the quality of the appointments process has fallen as the process has lengthened and become more burdensome:

Figure 8.8
Common Length of Service for Presidential Appointees (months)

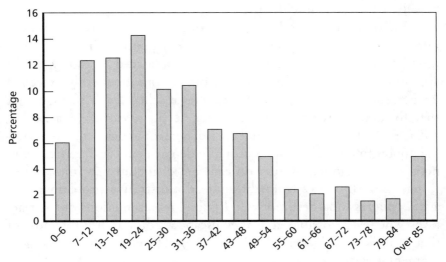

SOURCE: Mackenzie and Shogan, 1996, p. 45; based on General Accounting
Office analysis of period October 10, 1982, through September 20, 1991.
RAND *MG256-8.8*

Over recent decades, the average tenure of presidential appointees has been declining. A Brookings study of assistant secretaries
serving between 1933 and 1962 found an average tenure of 2.7
years. A study by the National Academy of Public Administration of Senate-confirmed appointees (excluding regulatory
commissioners who have fixed terms) found that tenure for the
period 1964–84 had declined to an average of 2.2 years. A General Accounting Office study in April 1994 found that the average tenure of contemporary political appointees was down to 2.1
years. In many positions tenure is even shorter. From 1981 to
1991, for example, there were 7 assistant secretaries for trade development in the Commerce Department and 7 deputy attorney
generals. The Federal Aviation Administration had 7 appointed
and 4 acting administrators in 15 years, the Federal Housing
Administration had 13 commissioners in 14 years, and the General Services Administration has 18 commissioners in 24 years
(Mackenzie and Shogan, 1996, pp. 4–5).

If such a metric were used to help improve the presidential appointments process, it would be important to measure variability in tenure as well as average tenure in office.

In addition to length of tenure, one might measure the vacancy rate for presidential appointments. Mackenzie notes that in the late nineties, "the administration as a whole experienced a vacancy rate in appointed positions in the executive branch that frequently exceeded 25 percent," whereas "judicial vacancies reached levels so high that the efficiency of the federal courts was deeply affected" (Mackenzie, 1998, p. 2). If it takes the better part of a year to complete a presidential appointment, it follows that many departments and agencies will need to limp along. "Acting officials are disinclined to initiate anything, they shy away from difficult administrative problems, they avoid congressional testimony and public representations of their actions whenever possible, and they escape accountability for most of their decisions" (Mackenzie, 1998, p. 13). The end result is that governmental performance suffers.

A quality metric similar to vacancy rate might be percentage of time that a position was filled by a confirmed appointee (that is, was neither vacant nor filled by an acting or temporary appointee). This metric reflects not only how quickly a new appointee arrives, but also how quickly the existing officeholder departs. As Mackenzie (1998) points out, "Many of those departing do not time their departures to coincide with the arrival of their replacement. They quickly move on, leaving their position vacant—often for months on end" (p. 13). Moreover, such early departures are exacerbated by the slowness and unpredictability of the replacement process: "Because the appointments process now moves so slowly, few departing officials are willing to peg their last day of work to their replacement's first day. They have lives to resume" (p. 13).

Cost Metrics. Costs are of many kinds. Government organizations have budgets for the appointments process. Within specific subprocesses, other proxy measures of cost are possible. For example, in the confirmation subprocess, one might be able to measure total hours devoted to confirmation hearings and to courtesy calls on committee members.

One reason to measure the cost of a process is to help identify and eliminate waste. Aside from duplication in the clearance stage, perhaps the most obvious kind of waste in the current presidential process is that created when a candidate removes him- or herself from further consideration. In such a case, the process must begin anew in order to fill the position for which the candidate was being considered. An analog in the military logistics system would be the need to submit a new order for an item because a shipment has been lost on route. One could use percentage of "lost candidates" as a cost metric of the presidential appointments process.

Costs are borne by the candidates, as well. Light and Thomas note that many appointees must incur thousands of dollars of lawyer and accountant fees in order to complete all the forms, and that a fifth of those surveyed spent more than $6,000 on such fees (2000, p. 7).

Throughout this discussion, our goal has been to illustrate the kinds and range of metrics that might be useful. In a VM-like improvement effort, it would be up to the PIT and the senior coalition to select metrics.

Moreover, metrics definition is not the end of the DMI process's Measure step. The PIT would also address related issues, such as how to define the population to be measured (being mindful that more candidates enter the process than emerge as appointees); what data exist or need to be developed; and how the data should be collected, integrated, analyzed, and reported. Once the PIT has identified a feasible measurement system, the senior coalition would approve its use to guide and monitor improvement actions.

This brings us to the third step of the DMI method.

Improving the Presidential Appointments Process

Participants in improvement efforts often wish to avoid tradeoffs. For instance, they would like to get a faster and higher-quality process without having to pay more. When a process is very much out of control, as the presidential appointments process appears to be, there are opportunities for synergy among performance improvements on multiple dimensions. That is, a PIT might be able to identify actions that not only speed up the presidential appointments process, but also reduce the number of errors and instances of waste—in other words, no tradeoff necessary.

A PIT could begin with some generic strategies for improving process performance. Two very broad strategies to help the process perform better are to redesign the process and to reduce demands on the process. The process can be redesigned by eliminating activities that do not add value and by streamlining those that do. It is possible to reduce demands on the process both by reducing or smoothing the requirements for its output and by improving the quality of its inputs. In this respect, a process can be thought of as a factory that works best when orders for its products are steady without straining its capacity and when it receives high-quality raw material from its suppliers. All of these strategies are aided by improved measurement of process performance.

Redesign the Process
When the PIT sets out to redesign the presidential appointments process, it is important to establish what degree of change is desired. If the process needs only to improve marginally, then minor modifications to evolve the current design may be sufficient. But if the process needs to improve dramatically, the PIT should consider more revolutionary design changes. The coalition should signal the degree of desired change by stating goals in terms of the metrics it has approved. Such goals will greatly influence the activities of the PIT. Consider, for instance, the time goal for the pro-cess as a whole once suggested: "The President should, in collaboration with the Senate, adopt the goal of completing 80–90% of appointments within 4 months" (Committee on Science, Engineering, and Public Policy, 2001, p. 2). Judged in the context of current process times, this time could probably be achieved without a radical redesign of the process. The challenge would be quite different if the coalition chose a still more challenging stretch goal and directed the PIT to design a process that completed most appointments in just two or three months. The hope is that a dramatically streamlined process would attract a

richer pool of highly qualified applicants, yielding "wins" in terms of not only time, but also quality and cost.

Eliminate activities that do not add value. The strategy of improving a process by eliminating activities that do not add value considers both their total elimination and their more selective use. Mackenzie's observation that "the appointments process has become a maelstrom of complexity, much of which serves little public service" (Mackenzie and Shogan, 1996, p. 7) suggests that value is not always added by the activities of the process as currently designed.

For example, Baker (2001) suggests that the final stage of the presidential appointments process, Senate confirmation, does not add value for whole classes of positions: "military, foreign service, and public health service promotions," as well as "part-time appointments to the government's many boards and commissions." For such positions, the requirement for Senate confirmation only adds delay and cost and may hurt quality by resulting in the loss of some highly qualified candidates. Eliminating the Senate confirmation stage for some positions might benefit the approval process for all positions. Those for which this stage is eliminated will shift to a shorter, simpler appointments process; and those remaining in the longer process should move along faster because of the reduced need for confirmations: "A simpler, more focused set of confirmation obligations can only yield a more efficient and more consistent performance of the Senate's confirmation responsibilities." These remaining positions, according to Baker's recommendation, would be restricted to "judges, ambassadors, executive-level positions in the departments and agencies, and promotions of officers in the highest rank . . . in each of the service branches."

Even for positions for which the Senate confirmation subprocess adds value, it may be possible to eliminate some activities within the subprocess. For instance, Baker (2001) suggests that a public hearing often adds no value: "For a great many nominations . . . confirmation hearings are little more than a time-consuming ritual." No value is added if the candidate has met privately with the senators on the confirming committee and if no issues have arisen. Scheduling these creates delays and adds costs—not just for the Senate, but also for the candidate and for his or her future department, which must prepare for the hearing. In such cases, Baker argues, public hearings could be eliminated. A PIT could consider such recommendations.

Another candidate for reform is the Senate practice of "holds": "Few features of the modern appointment process are as troublesome as the Senate practice [of holds] that permits any single Senator to delay indefinitely the confirmation of a nominee" (Baker, 2001). And holds do not add value to the appointments process, because "most of the holds have little to do with the qualifications of the nominees upon whom they are placed" (Mackenzie, 1998, p. 12). In addition, Mackenzie suggests that if holds cannot be eliminated, they should be limited in duration to "a week or ten days" (Mackenzie and Shogan, 1996, p. 18).

Mackenzie also suggests that clearances could be safely removed from the process for some posts: "FBI full-field investigations should be eliminated for some appointments and substantially revised for others" (Mackenzie and Shogan, 1996, p. 11). Other activities in the presidential appointments process add value, but need to be done only once. The elimination of duplicative activities makes the process faster and cheaper and eliminates a possible source of errors. From the candidate's perspective at least, there is a great deal of redundancy and duplication in the current process. For example, many agencies involved often need the same information regarding the candidate. Currently, they gather this information independently. Candidates resent the duplicative submission of information and "want the redundancy in data collection to stop. Presumably this duplication is amenable to a technological solution whereby candidates enter their information into a database once and it is then made available to all agencies that need it, as they need it" (Light and Thomas, 2000, p. 21). Mackenzie adds that "all parties to the appointment process should agree on a single financial disclosure form and one set of general background questions" (Mackenzie and Shogan, 1996, p. 13).

Some of the redundancy may reflect distrust. For instance, even though the executive branch conducts extensive clearance activities on each candidate, the Senate committee with jurisdiction over the candidate's nomination may sometimes undertake its own investigation.

The situation is analogous to the multiple inspections of a shipped item that can occur in a distribution process. The solution in logistics is to consolidate the inspections to a single activity that is fast, reliable, and efficient. Such consolidation can be achieved if the various stakeholders can cooperate in developing a trusted inspection activity that meets all their needs. The formation of a PIT can help build trust and cooperation among participating organizations, particularly because they all stand to gain from an improved process. Through the activities of the PIT, it may be possible to remove duplicative, non-value-adding activities from the gathering of information on candidate presidential appointees.

Streamline value-adding activities. Measurement of the presidential appointments process using time metrics can help the PIT to identify those steps that can be redesigned to speed up the process. Among the subprocesses plagued by delays, Senate confirmation is perhaps the worst. Baker (2001) proposes that the Senate limit how long this stage may take: "The Senate should adopt a rule that mandates a confirmation vote on every nominee no later than the 45th day after receipt of a nomination." More specifically, Mackenzie suggests that tighter control over the debates would help speed up the confirmation subprocess: "Confirmation debates on executive branch appointments should be granted "fast-track" status in the Senate to shield them from filibusters" (Mackenzie and Shogan, 1996, p. 18).

In any process, it is worthwhile to identify and reduce periods of time that constitute nothing more than waiting for the next value-adding activity to begin. In the order fulfillment process, orders can pile up on a desk as they wait to be processed, and packages can pile up on a loading dock as they wait for the arrival of a truck. Often, waiting periods are designed into the process intentionally, the thought being that processing a number of items together in a "batch" will be more efficient than processing them individually. This form of batching is evident in the presidential appointments process. Mackenzie (1998) highlights, for example, how the batching of candidates for regulatory positions slows the process for those appointments. The nominees move through the confirmation stage of the appointments process as a "team," which means that the time needed to confirm the most problematic of the nominees on the "team" defines the time needed for all nominees on the team. The elimination of batching might break up logjams in confirmation.

Reduce Demands on the Process

Reducing the demand for a process may permit it to operate more smoothly and quickly; this is particularly true if the demand is very "spiky" and surges to overwhelm the capacity of the process from time to time. This happens to the presidential appointments process at the onset of each new administration, and it doubles in difficulty if the new and old administrations are drawn from opposing political parties.

Reduce the needed outputs. Several critics of the appointments process have suggested that it is overly relied upon to fill senior executive positions in the government. For instance, Mackenzie suggests that the number should be reduced by about one third. Specifically, he recommends that "appointments to most advisory commissions and routine promotions of military officers, foreign service officers, public health services officers, except those at the very highest ranks, should cease to be presidential appointments" (Mackenzie and Shogan, 1996, p. 9).

Presumably, removing these positions from the regular presidential appointments process will permit the remaining positions to be handled more expeditiously.

Improve the quality of inputs. A fourth process improvement strategy is to improve the quality of inputs: personnel, capital, information, and infrastructure (including "virtual" elements of the infrastructure, such as the structure of relationships among key players).

The VM approach begins with activities intended to improve these inputs. For example, the formation of cross-functional teams improves the relationships among key players in the process, and as the players interact to perform the Define and Measure steps of the method, information about the process is also improved.

Light and Thomas (2000) focus on improving the candidates' information about the appointments process, something that should help candidates complete their activities more quickly and accurately, as well as improve their attitudes toward the process.

When candidates seek information about what is expected of them, they can encounter a great deal of variability, which may confuse them: "Variations in preemployment and postemployment requirements among agencies, departments, and congressional committees create an environment of uncertainty and inequity for appointees" (Committee on Science, Engineering, and Public Policy, 2001, p. 2). Mackenzie suggests that information about candidate requirements could be improved by having departments and agencies work to standardize requirements (Mackenzie and Shogan, 1996).

Conclusion: Moving to a New Approach

The presidential appointments process appears ideal for application of a process improvement methodology. It fails on all three dimensions of process performance: it is slow, it is costly, and it produces uneven quality. What is remarkable about the presidential appointments process is how long it has been ripe for reform, how visible and long-standing its problems have been, how firm a consensus exists on the causes of its failings, and how many excellent proposals have been advanced for its improvement. Yet the process has successfully resisted change even as its performance has continued to degrade.

This situation may be common in complex processes that cut across many organizations and lack a single owner or manager. In such processes, many organizations and individuals typically are working hard in multiple, well-intentioned improvement efforts. But due to the complexity of the process, their efforts are isolated, uncoordinated, and suboptimized. Often they may improve performance on one measure or in one part of a process while making performance worse on other measures or in other subprocesses. The organizations involved in the process simply lack sufficient capability and incentives to change it.

The VM approach offers a way to institutionalize new capabilities for change. The approach begins by building leadership coalitions of senior managers and by creating teams of experts in each of the process's major activities. Then it develops new sources of information through the Define and Measure steps of the DMI method. We have observed firsthand how this approach can help governmental agencies achieve the kind of "significant improvements in efficiency and performance" that the Volcker Commission has called for. Beyond good ideas for improvement, what is needed is a better management approach.

Of course, moving to a new management approach is not easy. It requires more than a few individuals with courage, vision, and persistence. The VM initiative, as well as the Strategic Distribution (SD) initiative,[10] benefited from the emergence of "inside champions" who were senior enough to be engaged, committed enough to dedicate a great deal of time and energy, and enough of a believer to take on challengers. These individuals enabled the initiatives to survive the first challenges of those who resisted change and to persist long enough to get positive change.

Both initiatives also benefited from the "behind the scenes" actions to get things started and move beyond the finger pointing that develops between organizations that share responsibility for a poorly performing process. In addition to the analytic role it played, RAND also served as an "honest agent" to seek out and develop the coalition for change. Because RAND had a reputation for being objective and had no stake in the process, it was able to help persuade a group of leaders to commit to making dramatic changes happen. When a critical mass "of the willing" was committed to trying this approach, a private meeting was held among the senior leaders of the various organizations to formally start the change process. Similar dealings might be required of leaders involved in the management of the presidential appointments process.

---

[10] As noted at the very beginning of this chapter, the SD initiative is another case of successful reform.

The VM approach is tailored to the reform of complex processes that cut across organizational boundaries. It can be used to improve the presidential appointments process so that it will be faster, cheaper, and able to produce better appointees.

CHAPTER NINE

Developing Leadership: Emulating the Military Model

Al Robbert

In its discussion of the foundation necessary for a high-performance government, the Volcker Commission frequently alludes to the need for federal managers, both career and political, to demonstrate stronger leadership and management skills (see Chapter 2 of this volume). The clearest message on this issue is in a discussion of Recommendation 7: The Senior Executive Service should be divided into an Executive Management Corps and a Professional and Technical Corps (p. 39).[1] The commission urges greater effort to "identify potential managerial talent early in employees' careers and to nurture it through adequately and consistently funded training, professional development, and subsidized opportunities for graduate education and work experience outside government" (p. 40). It offers the premise that the military services have evolved effective approaches to leadership development that can provide useful models for civilian agencies.

In this chapter, we examine that premise in detail. Are senior military officers generally better prepared for the positions they hold than senior career civil servants are? Are military organizations, ac-

---

[1] The recommendation itself is not groundbreaking. Statutory provisions exist for two types of senior scientific and technical positions that parallel the commission's recommended Professional and Technical Corps. In addition to the standard Senior Executive Service pay plan, agencies may establish scientific and professional positions under the authority of 5 USC 3104 and other senior-level positions under the authority of 5 USC 5108. In both cases, 5 USC 5376 authorizes agencies to fix pay for these positions within a range comparable to that of the Senior Executive Service. At least one agency, the Department of Defense (DoD), uses both of these alternative pay plans, designated ST and SL, respectively.

cordingly, managed to a higher level of performance than civilian agencies are? If so, what are the characteristics of military human capital management systems that make this possible?

The observation that senior military leadership is better developed and that military organizations perform at a high level must be accepted largely at face value. Comparative measures of individual and organizational performance that would allow a rigorous test of these observations do not exist. However, military organizations arguably are effective in accomplishing one difficult mission— developing large, technologically complex forces and systems and employing them effectively in hostile environments. To successfully meet the operational, technical, and logistical challenges inherent in this mission requires high performance and gives evidence of leadership that is, at minimum, consistently very good.[2] On that basis, let us accept the commission's judgment on the effectiveness of military leadership and turn to examining how it is developed.

We begin by examining the dimensions of the competencies the military services seek in their leaders. We then examine the processes through which these competencies are developed and the elements of the military human capital management environment that are favorable for development of these competencies. We conclude by identifying how civilian agencies will have to modify their human capital management practices if they want to more closely emulate the military model.

Senior Leader Competencies

The RAND Corporation has worked closely with senior leaders and senior leader management staffs of several of the military services in an effort to better understand the competencies required in senior leadership positions—those occupied by general officers and mem-

---

[2] The fact that DoD embedded members of the press with its units during Operation Iraqi Freedom, and thereby invited close scrutiny, indicates that DoD is confident in the performance of its leaders and their organizations.

bers of the Senior Executive Service. Through interviews and surveys of senior leaders regarding the competencies required for their positions, and critical reviews of their responses by both very senior leaders and research staff with relevant skills, RAND teams were able to identify multiple competency requirements that generally fit within the following dimensions.[3]

Domain Knowledge

In an important empirical study of general and senior functional manager effectiveness, Gabarro (1987) concludes that

> The all-purpose general manager who can be slotted into just about any organization, function, or industry exists only in management textbooks. Prior functional and industry experience does matter and it influences how a manager takes charge, the areas he is most likely to deal with effectively, and what problems he faces as he takes charge (p. 68).

He found, for example, that major organizational changes introduced by both general and functional managers typically involve their areas of prior functional experience, that individuals assuming management positions from within the same industry introduce many more fundamental organizational changes than managers from outside the industry do, and that lack of industry-specific experience characterized three out of four succession failures but less than half of the successes (pp. 39–50).

In our work on military senior leader competencies, we found that senior leaders' assessment of the domain knowledge required for their positions generally conformed to Gabarro's findings. Senior functional managers, quite naturally, identified experience in their specific function as critical. For senior line positions, such as chief of a service or commander of a major command, leaders tended to iden-

---

[3] These dimensions are not unique to military senior leader positions. Furthermore, this is but one among many available senior leader competency frameworks (see, for example, the U.S. Office of Personnel Management's list of executive core qualifications at http://www.opm.gov/ses/ecq.html).

tify experience in warfighting operations as critical, which is consistent with other research indicating that managers are selected to cope with an organization's critical contingencies (Salancik and Pfeffer, 1977) or that organizations tend to be led by individuals drawn from the organization's core elite professions (Mosher, 1982). In most positions, we found a need for *multifunctionality*—that is, experience in two or more operational or functional areas. For example, it is often advantageous for directors of system program offices to have prior acquisition management experience as well as prior operational experience either in or related to the system for which they are responsible.

An Enterprise Perspective

The more senior the position is, the more important it is for an incumbent to understand how his or her activity relates to the overall objectives of its larger organization and how the organization relates to its environment. Senior leaders generally are not closely supervised by their superiors (at this level, organizational autonomy, geographical separation, large spans of control, and other factors militate against close supervision). The interactions of their activities with other activities may be so complex that they cannot be coordinated hierarchically. Organizational effectiveness may thus depend critically on a shared sense of overall purpose and of how the parts of the organization must be aligned to achieve that purpose. The need for this shared perspective among senior leaders explains, in part, why organizations tend to fill their most critical senior positions with disproportionately high representation from core professions of the organization (Mosher, 1982). Individuals with such experience are more likely to have developed both a broad understanding of the organization's internal alignments and sensitivity to the interests of stakeholders and other features of the organization's external environment.

Leadership Skills

Effective leaders need to envision appropriate goals for their organizations, make decisions that will move their organizations toward their goals, and induce their followers to help realize the goals. Effectiveness in these roles typically depends on developing and employing certain sensing, communicating, motivating, and other interpersonal skills.

Management Skills

Leadership skills serve leaders well when they are engaged in setting organizational directions and shaping organizational behavior. In less complex environments, leadership skills may be sufficient to achieve these ends effectively. In more complex environments, however, leaders must find increasingly sophisticated ways to select among alternative paths toward their goals and to ensure effective implementation of their chosen paths. Typically, they must understand the factors that influence important outcomes, marshal information regarding those factors, establish criteria for choosing among alternatives, and choose those that make the best operational or business sense. Once alternatives are chosen, they must ensure that resources are made available as needed in the organization and establish feedback loops to determine if the organization is moving in the desired direction. These activities require management skills that can usefully be viewed as distinct from leadership skills.[4]

Tradeoffs and Interactions

Leaders rely on different mixes of these dimensions, depending on their circumstances. For example, if asked to assume a leadership role in a functional area where he or she has limited domain knowledge,

---

[4] Taxonomies of leadership and management skills are plentiful. For examples of respected sources in each of these categories, see Bass and Stogdill, 1990, on leadership skills and Mintzberg, 1973, on management skills. Such taxonomies tend to overlap—those focusing on leadership see management as a subset of needed leadership skills, while those focusing on management see leadership as a subset of needed management skills. I view the differences as a matter of emphasis. The most important roles of a leader or manager pivot around the making of decisions. Some roles are pre-decisional, setting a vision for the potentiality of the organization; some are decisional, choosing among alternatives so as to realize the organization's vision of itself; and some are post-decisional, marshalling resources and motivating individuals to support the decisions. Leadership skills are emphasized in the visioning and motivating roles; management skills are emphasized in the decisional and resource marshalling roles.

an individual with good leadership and management skills and a good enterprise perspective might be more effective than an individual with extensive domain knowledge but mediocre strengths in the other leadership dimensions. Alternatively, an individual selected from outside the organization to fill a senior leadership position might have very strong domain knowledge, a proven leadership and management record, and perhaps a very limited perspective on internal aspects of the enterprise, but might have an offsetting awareness of the external environment in which the enterprise operates. Weakness in any dimension, however, is likely to impair a leader's effectiveness.

Developing Senior Leader Competencies

Human capital, including senior leader competencies, may be developed using a variety of tools. While education, training, acculturation, mentoring, and experience are among the more recognizable of these, effects can also be achieved through recruiting/selection, promotion, and compensation policies and practices. In this section, we discuss how these tools relate to the dimensions of senior leader competency discussed above.

Developing Domain Knowledge

The fundamentals of a functional area are often gained through education or training. In domains that are strongly identified with a traditional profession,[5] an extensive educational foundation and continuing education and training are typically required. In other domains, individuals may function at a management level with an undergraduate education, not necessarily specific to the domain, and either an introductory training course or learning on the job, which may be conducted informally or through intern programs. Although

---

[5] Traditional professions include those occupations, such as medical doctor and lawyer, that require extensive graduate education. The term is increasingly applied to other occupations, such as financial management, human resource management, and acquisition management, that may require an undergraduate education, continuing training, and an objective certification process. See Mosher, 1982, for a discussion of the concept of professions.

the military services are a notable exception, most organizations invest little or no resources in providing the education or training required to enter a domain. Rather, through their recruiting and selection processes, they identify candidates who either possess the prerequisites or have potential for learning on the job. Regardless of the education or training required for entry into the domain, *depth* of domain knowledge is typically gained through experience in the domain, often supplemented by domain-specific training or continuing education (Morrison and Hock, 1986; McCall, Lombardo, and Morrison, 1989; Campion, Cheraskin, and Stevens, 1994).

In some domains, particularly scientific or technical fields, advanced academic education is an important component of development. In a favorable labor market, organizations may be able to recruit and select individuals with the appropriate advanced degrees. In other cases, organizations may need to sponsor advanced academic degree programs for their employees.

As mentioned above, we have found through our work on senior leader competencies that many senior leader positions require knowledge of more than one domain. To ensure that the required *multifunctionality* will be available in their senior leader corps, organizations need to systematically rotate promising future leaders through jobs in the appropriate functional areas during their mid-career years.

Developing an Enterprise Perspective

A thorough understanding of the internal and external environments of an organization is typically gained through experience and mentoring. Useful experiences might include serving in a variety of field and headquarters levels of the organization, as well as in the important operating environments of the organization. Mentoring typically involves a one-on-one transmission of knowledge, values, cues, proven responses, and other useful human capital from a senior leader to a protégé, often by placing the protégé in a position, such as executive assistant to a very senior manager, with a wide window on the enterprise. Education, training, and acculturation accomplished through enterprise learning institutions, such as professional military education schools, corporate universities, and programs such as the

Defense Leadership and Management Program (DLAMP), can provide systematic orientation to various aspects of the enterprise, helping to knit together the personal experiences of attendees.

Developing Leadership Skills

Researchers generally agree that leadership effectiveness is part nature and part nurture, the only debate being about the relative importance of innate abilities, formal education or training, and experience (Van Wart, 2003). Through education and training, individuals can acquire an academic appreciation of various leadership styles and techniques and a sense of their contingent efficacies—what styles and techniques tend to work in what circumstances. Education and training in leadership skills are typically delivered through the same enterprise learning institutions used to develop an enterprise perspective, but they may also be obtained through external programs such as those offered by the Center for Creative Leadership. These skills are honed through observation and practice—actual experience in seeking to shape the behaviors of organizations and the individuals within them, or in observing the efforts of others. One's ability to acquire and apply that knowledge also varies as a function of overall intelligence, charisma (Javidan and Waldman, 2003), and other innate personal characteristics. Thus, while leadership skills can be developed, organizations must also lay the groundwork for meeting their future leadership needs by insuring, through recruiting and selection processes, that a sufficient proportion of new hires have high leadership potential.

Developing Management Skills

Management skills are probably less dependent than leadership skills on innate personal characteristics, other than general intelligence, and thus are more readily developed than leadership skills. These skills are typically developed through academic programs—advanced degrees or continuing education in a classroom, seminar, or independent study setting. Typically, advanced degrees in business administration, public administration, engineering management, and decision sciences such as economics or operations research will systematically develop these skills. As with any learning, the skills tend to improve through usage and to atrophy without it.

Rewarding Development

Development of competencies in any of our four categories can be enhanced through promotion and compensation practices. If individuals expect that meaningful rewards will be associated with possession of these competencies or with organizational outcomes that rely upon them, they will be more likely to acquire them.

The Development Environment in the Military Services

The officer management environment in the military services uniquely favors development of senior leader competencies. As we discuss in this section, central management of human resource functions is often the key element that facilitates this development. Military officers are centrally recruited, selected, and initially educated and trained. They are centrally selected for reassignment, for important development programs, and for promotion. Their pay and allowances, as well as the costs of development programs, are borne by the service headquarters rather than by the subordinate organizations to which they are assigned. They incur service commitments as a result of education or training, which, combined with a culture that supports high retention even in the face of arduous duties, gives the services great flexibility in selecting individuals for job rotations, schools, and other development opportunities. In contrast, local supervisors often have a stronger voice, and also often incur significant costs, in the corresponding actions for civil service employees. Further, for reasons discussed below, a decentralized human resource management (HRM) system tends to create greater risk for civil service employees who take advantage of certain development opportunities.

In this section, we examine each facet of HRM separately. We describe the military environment and, where appropriate, contrast it with the civil service environment.

Selecting Career Entrants vs. Filling Entry-Level Jobs

When the military services recruit and select candidates for their commissioning sources, they do so with a career-long perspective on qualifications. Mindful that they are feeding a personnel system with virtually no lateral entries, they screen not only for the cognitive and motor skills needed for success in entry-level jobs, but also for evidence of the leadership skills that will be needed in the future. The screening process involves both psychometric instruments and personal interviews. For two of the three commissioning sources— service academies and Reserve Officer Training Corps (ROTC)— significant educational benefits are at stake, which tends to attract very strong candidates and make competition very stiff.[6]

Individuals may enter civil service at a professional or administrative level (encompassing jobs and responsibilities roughly comparable to those of military officer positions) through several routes. Most commonly, individuals completing college or graduate school apply for specific entry-level job vacancies. Less commonly, they apply for entry into the Office of Personnel Management's (OPM's) Presidential Management Intern Program or similar agency-sponsored Career Intern Programs—two-year apprenticeships that precede entry into the competitive civil service.[7] Others, with or without college degrees, enter professional or administrative levels by transitioning from clerical or technical occupations. Some enter laterally from the private sector or from other levels of government, although the civil service tends to be resistant to such entries. Of these sources, and ignoring the relatively small number of experienced lead-

---

[6] If special programs such as those for the medical, legal, and chaplain professions are excluded, each military department has three commissioning sources. In addition to service academies and ROTC, they each have one or more forms of officer candidate school or officer training school where individuals with college degrees—some earned while on active duty in the enlisted ranks—can earn a commission via a relatively brief training course of several months' duration. The Navy also has a limited duty officer program that allows some technically qualified enlisted members to advance to officer grades, but with limited promotion potential.

[7] Information on the Presidential Management Intern Program is available at http://www.pmi.opm.gov/index.htm. Information on the Career Intern Program is available at http://www.opm.gov/careerintern/index.htm.

ers accessed as lateral entries, the most likely to produce high-quality candidates comparable to those competing for military commissioning are the intern programs. The accelerated promotions and developmental attention featured in these programs provide incentives that facilitate recruiting. Moreover, in selecting candidates, agencies are allowed to employ a broad set of criteria that can include future leadership potential. In contrast, when selecting to fill ordinary job vacancies, selecting and appointing authorities are bound by law and policy to consider candidates only against requirements that are demonstrably valid for the specific job.

The military services screen against career-long criteria for virtually all of their officer-grade entrants. In contrast, the intern programs through which agencies can use career-long criteria typically represent a very limited proportion of their entry-level hires. Assuming these selection processes are efficacious, the military services start with a much broader base of highly qualified candidates from which to develop and select future senior leadership.

Heavy Investments in Education and Training

Service academy and ROTC curricula combine conventional academic offerings with programs to develop institutional awareness, leadership skills, personal and organizational management skills, ethical behavior, and other related knowledge, skills, behaviors, and attitudes. Other commissioning sources (OTC/OCS) seek to achieve similar objectives but in a more compressed period of time and without the academic content. These programs involve both theory, learned in the classroom, and practice, in the form of various cadet leadership responsibilities. The objective is not only to educate and train, but also to acculturate—to instill an appreciation for the history, traditions, values, and mission of the service and, as future officers, for the subculture of leadership within their service. Individuals emerge from these programs with a fundamental appreciation of the elements of leadership and a sense of what seems to work under various circumstances.

Following commissioning, the process of formal leadership education, training, and acculturation continues as part of the curricula of various professional military education (PME) programs, often resident, that vary in length from months to a full year. The most-promising candidates for future leadership attend a year of intermediate service school in about the 10-to-15-year point of their careers and another year of senior service school at the 15-to-18-year point. By bringing together individuals from various operational or functional communities and also providing curricula that touch on various aspects of service activities, these schools contribute significantly to their students' forming enterprise perspective and, depending on curriculum choices, may build management skills as well. Those not selected for resident PME have strong, promotion-related incentives to complete similar curricula by correspondence or seminar.

In addition to PME, the services also sponsor education at the master's and doctorate level, either through civilian institutions or their own schools, such as the Naval Postgraduate School and the Air Force Institute of Technology. These programs may be used to develop general management competencies or, in the case of technical or engineering degrees, to enhance domain knowledge.

Civil servants' comparable development opportunities are much more limited. Through programs such as DoD's Defense Leadership and Management Program, course offerings at OPM's Management Development Centers, the Federal Executive Institute, and the U.S. Department of Agriculture Graduate School, individuals may avail themselves of curricula that, in some respects, mirror the formal education and training available to military officers. A small number of civil servants from agencies with national security interests are accepted for attendance at resident military PME programs. Additionally, both military members and civil servants can seek agency sponsorship to attend leadership and management programs such as those offered by the Kennedy School of Government at Harvard University, the Maxwell School at Syracuse University, the Center for Creative Leadership, and other, similar sources. These programs, however, are collectively much more limited than military PME programs in terms of scope, intensity, and proportion of potential leadership cohorts impacted.

Moreover, through central selection processes for PME programs, the services can ensure that these rather significant investments in human capital are made in individuals with the highest potential for assuming future senior leadership positions. In contrast, participation in the roughly comparable civil service–oriented programs depends to a much greater extent on individual initiative and supervisor concurrence. For example, a civil service employee interested in a lengthy development program—such as attendance at a PME school, a congressional internship, or a resident master's degree program— must apply for and secure agency sponsorship and funding (of which, typically, the largest cost element is the employee's salary). To preserve the employee's post-development reemployment opportunity, the agency typically must either leave the employee's position vacant for the duration of the program or fill the position with an interim hire—options not particularly attractive to the local supervisor of the position, who may, depending on agency policies, hold a veto over the employee's participation. In this environment, local, short-term employee utilization needs can easily trump corporate, long-term development needs.

Military participants in PME or graduate education programs face no similar impediments. Because of frequent job rotations and a rank-in-person system,[8] military officers who enter lengthy development programs are more or less immediately replaced by other rotating officers. Upon completion of the program, they are reassigned to fill contemporaneous vacancies.

Another factor that makes such investments in human capital more attractive to the military services is the legal provisions that allow them to compel continued military service. While the military services have relied on an all-volunteer force since the draft was ended in 1973, volunteers nonetheless relinquish their right to separate at

---

[8] Military officers hold rank-in-person. Their appointment to a military grade is, except for the two highest general/flag officer grades (O-9 and O-10), independent of the specific job they hold. Civil servants, in contrast, generally hold rank-in-position. With certain exceptions, such as retreat to a lower-grade position as part of a reduction in force, a civil servant's grade is valid only for the duration of his or her appointment to a specific position in that grade.

will from military service. Officers attending costly or lengthy education programs typically incur a multi-year service commitment, ensuring at least a minimal return on the service's investment in human capital development.

Frequent Job Rotations

Job rotations, appropriately managed, often provide the most-powerful means of broadening and deepening domain knowledge and developing an enterprise perspective (Derr, Jones, and Toomey, 1989; Morrison and Hock, 1986; McCall, Lombardo, and Morrison, 1989; Gabarro, 1987; McCall, 1998; Campion, Cheraskin, and Stevens, 1994). Campion, Cheraskin, and Stevens found that surveyed executives identified the following as skills gained through job rotations: broader perspective on other business functions (46 percent), adaptability and flexibility (31 percent), leadership skills (19 percent), exposure to various management styles (15 percent), financial and planning skills (15 percent), building a network of contacts (15 percent), and interpersonal skills (12 percent) (1994, pp. 1520–1521). They also reported significant correlations between job rotations and career outcomes (salary, promotion), positive career affect (satisfaction, involvement, commitment), and perceptions of skill acquisition.

For military officers, frequent job rotations are the norm. While these rotations are often driven by needs unrelated to career development (e.g., completion of limited-duration overseas tours), they yield a rich array of career development experiences as a by-product. Additionally, the culture of the military services is such that most officers accept frequent rotations as an essential part of a military career. Special incentives are not needed. On the negative side, the tempo of military job rotations can be so high that individuals spend too little time in each position to reach full effectiveness as a manager (Gabarro, 1987) or to master key roles that are essential building blocks in a career pattern (Morrison and Hock, 1986).

With some exceptions, such as the State Department's Foreign Service, civil service environments have little of the built-in job rotation requirements found in military environments. If job rotations are needed for career development of civil servants, they must generally be initiated specifically for that purpose. Additionally, in order to induce civil servants to accept the career risks and personal/family displacements associated with job rotations that entail geographical relocation, strong incentives may be needed.

As with selection for education and training programs, selection of military officers for reassignment to new organizations or new occupations is typically done at the service headquarters level (or by the staff at a personnel operating agency that acts on behalf of the service headquarters). In these actions, the detailers/assignment officers seek to provide a number of critical experiences to high-potential officers, including the following:

- Core occupation-specific positions
- Higher headquarters staff assignments
- Command opportunities
- Joint tours of duty[9]

In many cases, the staffs responsible for assignment rotations have analyzed the flows through critical bottlenecks, such as command and joint billets, to find an optimal balance between tenure in the position and the size of the pools of officers who acquire the experience.[10] Occupation-specific development templates, describing both typical and high-potential career patterns, are not uncommon.[11] As

---

[9] In accordance with the Goldwater-Nichols Department of Defense Reorganization Act of 1986, officers must have served a tour in a designated position in a joint organization (e.g., the Office of the Secretary of Defense, the defense agencies, the Organization of the Joint Chiefs of Staff, or the staff of a joint combatant command) in order to hold flag/general officer rank or to serve in certain critical joint jobs.

[10] The longer the average tenure, the smaller the accumulated pool. Smaller pools result in less selectivity to fill senior positions that require the experience and in reduced motivation for junior officers who aspire to fill those senior positions. On the other hand, brief (less than two-year) tenures are associated with reduced individual and organizational performance (Gabarro, 1987).

[11] See, for example, branch-specific life cycle development models in Department of the Army Pamphlet 600–3, *Commissioned Officer Development and Career Management*, October 1, 1998.

discussed in the next section, responsible staffs also have strong cues to help them identify the high-potential candidates in whom the heaviest and most critical experience investments should be made.

For civil servants, the authority and responsibility for filling position vacancies are generally vested at the local level, often in the immediate supervisor of the position. When agency career management staffs play a role in the process, that role is typically limited to compiling certification lists of qualified candidates, with final selection remaining the prerogative of the local supervisor.[12] While the local supervisor's voice is important in ensuring a good person/position match, his or her local and immediate interests may not coincide with the agency's wider, longer-range career development interests. For example, the agency career management staff may wish to rotate selected individuals into new functional areas for broadening purposes and, accordingly, include them on certification lists for vacancies in the new functions. Supervisors may wish to avoid the learning curve associated with such assignments, favoring candidates from within the function instead. Additionally, individuals identified as candidates for developmental rotation to new geographical or functional areas are likely to be more willing to accept such assignments if they have reasonable prospects for eventually being rotated back from the developmental assignment. When supervisors have the final say, agency career management staffs cannot promise a return rotation as an incentive.

High-Potential Individuals Readily Identified

An essential step in developing high-potential individuals is to reliably identify them. Military officer personnel management, characterized

---

[12] See, for example, Air Force Instruction 36-601, *Air Force Civilian Career Management Program*, July 25, 1994, which describes one of the more well-developed agency programs. It specifies that the central career management staff "identifies and ranks candidates for all vacant career program positions" and "prepares Air Force-wide promotion, reassignment, or change to lower grade referral certificates" (p. 7). Supervisors "mak[e] selections for career program positions and . . . nominations or selections for training and developmental opportunities" (p. 9).

by very strong cohort identities, facilitates this task. Each "year group" (i.e., all officers commissioned in the same calendar year) progresses through the promotion system as a cohort. Officers who are promoted in "due course" (i.e., at the same pace as the majority of officers in their cohort are promoted) will always compete for promotion primarily against other officers in their original cohort. A relatively small proportion of officers are promoted earlier than the mass of their cohort, and another relatively small proportion are promoted later than the mass. Increasingly, as the cohort progresses to the higher grades, a significant proportion are not promoted. This regularized system makes it very easy to identify high-potential officers—they are the ones who are promoted faster than their peers. High-potential officers are also identified through their selection (typically by central selection boards) for attendance at professional military education in residence, command positions, or other prestigious assignments.

In the civil service system, identifying high-potential individuals is more difficult. Asch (2001) found that supervisor rating is not a good discriminator of quality because it has limited variance. Because of this and other known biases in supervisor ratings, she examined the use of promotion speed (similar to the primary indicator used to identify high-potential military officers) as a measure of quality. She noted that this measure is also problematic, in this case because it is driven by locality- and occupation-specific vacancies.[13] Thus, promotion speeds may reflect differential vacancy rates rather than differential personnel quality. In her analysis, she statistically controlled for these and other factors, which allowed her to use promotion speed more effectively as a measure of quality. Unfortunately, her analytic approach would be relatively inaccessible to career program managers routinely seeking to identify high-potential individuals.

---

[13] In contrast, military officers in the "line" promotion categories, from which most senior leaders are drawn, generally compete servicewide for promotion against all other line officers in their year-group cohort, without regard to occupation.

Emulating the Military Model

If leadership development among civil servants is to approach the effectiveness apparent among military officers, some features of the military HRM environment must be emulated in the civil service environment.

Expanded Use of Intern Programs

As noted above, of all available hiring modes, intern programs provide the closest approximation to selectivity based on career rather than entry-level job needs and to the initial acculturation achieved by the military services through their commissioning programs. Ideally, intern programs would be sized so that they build a pool of individuals with the potential to fill future leadership positions. Proper sizing would require some rudimentary modeling of the career progression pyramids in an agency. Such a model, or more likely a series of occupation-specific models, would consider the number of senior leadership positions, desired selectivity in filling those positions, retention rates at all stages, desired and expected cross-flow among occupations, expected influx of high-quality lateral entries, expected availability of leadership-potential entrants through nonintern hiring modes, and expected entry-level position vacancies at the time individuals emerge from the intern program.

Intern programs could be better integrated with job requirements. Under the current executive order governing these programs, individuals completing the normal two-year term of the program may be granted competitive civil service status but are not guaranteed further federal employment.[14] To remain employed, they must apply and compete for vacancies. Costs of intern programs, consisting mainly of the pay of the interns and their relocation expenses, are typically funded centrally by the agency, whereas other positions are funded locally. Nonetheless, the interns are a source of productive labor (possibly attenuated by the formal training and job rotation requirements of the intern program) for the local activities employing

---

[14] Executive Order 13162, July 10, 2000.

them. Expanding the intern programs to match analytically determined needs might be cost prohibitive if the intern programs are additive to conventional entry-level positions. However, if entry-level positions are reduced in number to offset the productivity supplied by additional interns, and the associated position funding shifted from local to central accounts, the marginal cost of expanded intern programs could be substantially mitigated. Further, the programs would become much more attractive if interns automatically reverted to competitive status in the same position at the end of the internship.[15] These program modifications would, however, require changes in the applicable executive order and possibly in Title 5, U.S. Code, also.

Greater Investment in Education and Training

In testimony delivered in May 2000 to the Subcommittee on Oversight of Government Management, Restructuring and the District of Columbia, Senate Committee on Governmental Affairs, Diane Disney, then Deputy Assistant Secretary of Defense for Civilian Personnel Policy, compared military and civil service personnel management in DoD and concluded that DoD must treat its civil service employees more like its military members—that is, it must invest more seriously and more systematically in their development. She attributed DoD's reluctance to make these investments to several perceptions, such as that civil service employees are expected to have requisite skills, knowledge, and abilities before being selected for a job. She acknowledged a need to overcome this reluctance.

To achieve parity with a military ideal, DoD and other departments and agencies would need to provide full-time, residential leadership development programs with a cumulative duration of between two and three years over the first twenty-five years of service for the most promising 10 to 20 percent of their middle- to senior-grade managers. For most, if not all, agencies, this would entail a significant increase in the resources devoted to leadership development.

---

[15] A possible disadvantage is that interns would have to be placed where vacancies were occurring rather than where their initial development might be optimized.

And even if the agencies were able to overcome their own reluctance, they might not find *takers* for this level of investment, unless they emulate another aspect of military HRM: rank-in-person. High-potential employees, in sufficient numbers, might be unwilling to exhibit the required mobility into and out of lengthy development programs without a reliable system in place to guide their career transitions and protect their economic interests, which are tied primarily to their grade levels. If their only option is to temporarily vacate, but retain, their old jobs during the course of development programs, their local supervisors will also be disinclined to see them enter such programs.

Career managers at the agency headquarters level can provide a virtual approximation of rank-in-person by assuming responsibility for continuity of employment of individuals on the development track.[16] As individuals depart their organizations to attend these programs, they would be permanently replaced, so there would be no need for disruptive gaps or temporary fills during their absence. As they complete the programs, they would be placed in other vacant positions, preferably those that can more fully exploit their recent development experience and also contribute to their further development. Agency-level career managers must anticipate or create vacancies in those positions as needed to bed down projected development program graduates, possibly by rotating incumbents (who would themselves be on a developmental track) to other, more demanding developmental positions. To make this feasible, agencies must centralize authority for the fill of key developmental positions, as outlined in the following discussion regarding mobility and job rotations.

Greater Mobility
In order to fully exploit the developmental benefits of job rotations, agencies must obtain a relatively high (by civil service standards) level of mobility among high-potential employees. Unlike managers of

---

[16] For a proposed concept for a real, rather than a virtual, rank-in-person system for civil service employees, see Kettl, Ingraham, Sanders, and Horner, 1996 (pp. 79–80).

military workforces, managers of civil service workforces cannot expect this mobility as a by-product of rotations driven by other needs. Instead, they will have to identify beneficial career progression patterns—sequences of jobs that develop combinations of competencies needed for specific senior leader positions—and commit the resources needed to channel high-potential managers into those patterns.

To provide agencies the leverage needed to maintain the required flow through developmental positions, individuals entering development-track jobs must sign mobility agreements that condition their continued employment on the acceptance of reassignment and relocation when directed by their agency.[17] When friction in this system prevents orderly successions, such as when no immediate vacancy exists to bed down an individual completing a lengthy educational program, funding must be available to double-billet or otherwise continue to pay those on the development track at their retained grade until a suitable vacancy can be offered. Individuals would remain in this development track as long as they continued to perform at a superior level and to accept the educational and job rotation assignments offered to them. They would opt out of the developmental pattern, without prejudice, by seeking a vacancy in a nondevelopmental job. Agencies would also centrally fund the development programs, including pay and allowances and relocation expenses for participants.

Procedures such as this would generally require an expanded HRM staff at the agency level, centralization of selection authority, and an expanded budget. More significantly, they would demand a change of culture among senior leaders, agency human resource managers, supervisors of key developmental jobs, and high-potential individuals on the development track. Senior leaders must assume personal responsibility for defining their agency's leadership develop-

---

[17] Statute and legal precedence have elevated federal civil servants' interests in their jobs to the level of a property right: They cannot be deprived of their jobs without due process. In signing mobility agreements, employees waive some aspects of their job-retention rights.

ment needs and insuring that programs are in place to meet them.[18] Agency human resource managers must develop the competencies required to understand and deliberately meet their organization's long-term leadership development needs. Supervisors of developmental jobs must accept higher turnover in those positions and less voice in selecting incumbents. High-potential individuals must commitment themselves to the greater growth, mobility, and professional challenges to be found on the development track.

Explicitly Identifying High-Potential Employees

As a prerequisite for using residential development programs and job rotations to cultivate pools of potential future leaders, agency-level civil service career management staffs must reliably identify their high-potential resources. Measures such as promotion-speed analyses can be used for some purposes. More generally, boards of senior leaders would be required to weigh individual records and supervisors' recommendations, either to identify individuals for special career monitoring or to select individuals for specific programs. The boards would function much like the formal promotion boards used to select officers for promotion or the less formal boards that select for command positions, resident professional military education, and other special opportunities.

In the military system, early promotion is such a distinct and universally recognizable signal that it is unnecessary to explicitly designate individuals on a high-potential list. In the civil service, with no similar clear signal, explicit lists may be necessary. Private-sector firms see advantages in keeping such lists secret, both from those on the lists and from those not on the lists (Derr, Jones, and Toomey, 1989). For reasons similar to those that compel confidentiality in performance reviews and salary setting, organizations do not want to

---

[18] While participation in this process by senior political appointees might be beneficial, the primary burden might more appropriately fall on career senior leaders—members of the Senior Executive Service or their intelligence community counterparts. The charters of executive resource boards, established per 5 USC 3393, can be usefully extended to serve this need.

denigrate and demotivate individuals by publicly acknowledging that they are not on a development track. Similarly, removing an individual from the list following a decline in performance is less disruptive if the lists are not publicly known. However, such secrecy may not be possible in a public-sector merit system that stresses "fair and open competition" in advancement and selection decisions.[19] Agencies and their employees will have to learn to deal with both the positive and the negative consequences of explicitly recognized differences in advancement potential, much as the military services have done.

Conclusions

The military services indeed have an enviable environment for developing military leaders. This environment can be usefully emulated to some degree in developing leadership competencies in civil service workforces.

The FY 2004 Defense Authorization Act amended Title 5, USC, to give the Secretary of Defense the authority to establish a National Security Personnel System (NSPS) that would replace other provisions of the United States Code and the Code of Federal Regulations in governing civil service workforces within DoD. At this writing, the elements of the NSPS are being developed. Similar flexibility was extended to the Department of Homeland Security (DHS) in the legislation that established it. Although the additional flexibility will be helpful to these agencies, particularly with respect to hiring and promotion selections, other agencies should not consider themselves blocked from taking effective action to improve their leadership development programs. Most of the steps outlined in this chapter can be implemented through aggressive and imaginative use of flexibilities available in the conventional civil service system.

What will be required in most agencies, including DoD and DHS, is a significant increase in the resources devoted to developing

---

[19] This and other merit system principles are codified in 5 USC 2301.

and managing the high-potential segments of civil service workforces. Increased funding will be needed for intern programs, subsidized education, and training programs, and to cover the salaries of high-potential employees engaged in agency-sponsored development activities.[20] New or enhanced information systems will be required to track workforce competency requirements, individual competencies, and development program participation. Increased staffing at central HRM activities will be required to analyze competency needs, identify and track high-potential individuals, administer development programs, and manage job rotations through competency-enhancing positions. To accomplish these strategic succession and competency management tasks, workers in traditionally transaction-oriented HRM staffs may themselves need to acquire a range of new competencies related to assessing requirements for, developing, and effectively utilizing critical workforce characteristics. Cultural change—inspired and carefully engineered by skillful, persistent, and attentive leaders at the highest organizational levels—will be needed both

---

[20] As examples of the kinds of costs agencies might encounter, consider the following. Leadership and management courses of a week or less generally cost under $1,000 (tuition only) at the Department of Agriculture Graduate School, $2,000 to $4,000 (tuition plus room and board) at the Federal Executive Institute, and $3,600 to $9,000 (tuition only) at the Center for Creative Leadership. Tuition for one- to two-month courses at the Harvard Business School ranges from $25,000 to $50,000. A two-year master's degree program at the Kennedy School of Government costs about $55,000 in tuition and fees, but this amount would be overshadowed from a sponsoring agency's perspective by the student's pay, other employment costs, and relocation expenses, which, for a mid-grade civil servant, could easily top $200,000.

An agency seeking to emulate the intensive development that the military services provide to their most-promising officers might provide two years of resident education (out of a 40-year career) to 20 percent of its mid-career workforce, incurring a 1 percent increase in pay and other employment costs (assuming that vacancies left by those attending such programs are backfilled). Cutting job tenures in half to provide more job rotations for a select 20 percent on a development track would increase relocation costs by 20 percent.

In principle, increased investment in leadership development should result in more-productive workforces. Increased productivity should allow workforces to be trimmed in size, perhaps more than offsetting the increased development costs. In practice, of course, productivity gains are difficult to detect. For planning purposes, most agencies might need to assume that increased organization performance, obtained through better leadership development, will come at an increased cost.

within HRM staffs and across agencies in order to successfully implement such changes.

The useful ideas outlined in this chapter are not the only steps needed to provide better civil-service leadership development. They merely allow agencies to exploit the lessons readily available from a respected military model. Other steps, not unique to this model, include identifying the necessary content of development programs, appropriately sizing the throughput, and designing agency-unique programs.

With additional effort and investment, agencies can do much to assure themselves stronger crops of future leaders. Returns on these investments in human capital will certainly be realized in the form of stronger organizational performance. The quality of leadership does make a difference.

CHAPTER TEN

Broadening Public Leadership in a Globalized World

Gregory F. Treverton

Two decades ago, a study looking at skills needed for America to exercise leadership in the world would have focused on the State Department, the Pentagon, the intelligence agencies, and a few other "international" departments of government. It would have concluded by bemoaning the paucity of area and language skills in the country, and might have called for crash national programs to increase the supply of those skills.[1] Leadership is still critical, for America's ability to shape the world in this century will depend on the quality of its leaders, as the Volcker Commission (see Chapter 2) emphasized.

Yet times have changed. The nature of "international" has changed and so has the meaning of "leadership." Recent RAND Corporation work surveyed the three sectors of American life— government, for-profit, and not-for-profit—asking what organizations in all three sectors look for in their future leaders and whether they find it.[2] The government did record some shortages in selected skill categories, given its constraints in paying and reaching out for talent. More important, though, is what we discovered across all sectors: The nation is producing too few future leaders who combine substantive depth with international experience and outlook. Also in

---

[1] A RAND Corporation study representative of this genre is S. E. Berryman et al., 1979.

[2] This chapter draws on my work with Tora Bikson, who spearheaded the project. The main report from the project is Treverton and Bikson, 2002. For more detailed results from this project, see Bikson et al., 2004; and Lindstrom, Bikson, and Treverton, 2002. All the tables and quotations in this chapter are from Bikson et al., 2004, unless otherwise indicated.

short supply are managers with a broad strategic vision in a rapidly changing world.

The first section of this chapter looks at the changes in the nature of leadership in a world where the distinction between "international" and "domestic" is blurring. The second reports what our interviewees said about the competencies they seek in the future leaders of their organizations. The third compares the three sectors in reaching out and developing leaders, and then turns specifically to the public sector, its obstacles, and its opportunities. The fourth section addresses the need to re-energize government. The final section outlines a specific agenda for improving future leadership. It includes a number of immediate and specific measures for the government, many of which are familiar and some of which are being enacted.

But actions by government alone will not be enough to ensure better leadership for government, so the agenda includes measures—both immediate and longer term—for all sectors, including higher education. All sectors will have a better chance of getting better leaders if all of them act, together. Government and higher education, foundations, intergovernmental organizations, and the for-profit sector need to come together to broaden intellectual formation, rooted in real world experience; to target career development, including exchanges among the sectors; and to open possibilities for "portfolio careers" across the sectors. For government, the implications are far reaching, not just for how it attracts, trains, and retains talent, but also for the laws and practices that govern conflict of interest in the United States.

Changing Leadership in Changing Global Circumstances

September 11th put a devastating punctuation point to the processes of globalization and its underside, the rise of terrorism. The two together have dramatically changed the nature of American leadership in the world. The United States confronts a world that is both networked and fractured, both full of promise and full of danger. In our interviews, government respondents saw their missions as most changed by globalization, as well as by September 11th.[3] Table 10.1 displays the results.[4]

Those public sector respondents saw a need for a fundamentally different approach to their agency missions, as illustrated in these comments by interviewees from different agencies:[5]

"In times past, foreign adversaries behaved in ways that corresponded to our systems. There were clear divisions between foreign and domestic, law enforcement and defense, civil and military. Now the situation is that foreign is impacting the domestic. It's a different reality—blurring the lines."

Table 10.1
How Have Globalization Trends Affected Your Organization in Recent Years?
(percentages)

Response Categories	Sector		
	Public	For Profit	Nonprofit
Few/negligible effects	2	24	6
Some/moderate effects	17	27	58
Many/major effects	81	49	36

[3] After reviewing existing studies, the project conducted some 135 interviews of line managers and human resource professionals across the three sectors, asking them, How has the promise of globalization and its underside, terrorism, changed the mission and activities of your organization? What new capacities do you seek in the professionals you hire? How hard is it to find them, and where and how do you look? How do you nurture talent once you recruit it? These interviews on the "demand" side were then supplemented by two dozen interviews on the "supply" side—that is, with deans of public policy, international relations, and business schools—and with people who have thought long and hard about America's needs for human capital and its means for producing it. The project was supported by funding from the Starr Foundation, the Rockefeller Brothers Fund, the United Nations Foundation, and RAND. It was guided by an advisory council made up of the leaders of major foreign affairs institutions—Council on Foreign Relations, American Enterprise Institute, American International Group, Inc., Brookings Institution, Carnegie Endowment for International Peace, Center for Strategic and International Studies, Heritage Foundation, Nixon Center, and U.S. Institute of Peace, as well as RAND.

[4] This table and all others in this chapter are from Bikson et al., 2004, unless otherwise indicated.

[5] All quotations in this chapter are from Bikson et al., 2004, unless otherwise noted.

"There is priority given in defense policy and international affairs policy . . . to not only the impact on foreign countries of the U.S. role abroad, but also the relationship to the domestic environment. This must now be calculated in very different ways."

"The bureaucratic structure of the government is not optimal for dealing with crises of the kind that occurred on September 11. There is increased emphasis on how to reorganize to efficiently and effectively deal with threats."

"Sharing will actually happen now. . . . The difference is that there has been a real effort toward more integrated steps between agencies that didn't happen before."

These comments emphasize the blurring of the line between "foreign" and "domestic" affairs, and they highlight the importance of new partnerships across many U.S. federal agencies. If in previous decades, international leadership was mainly viewed as the province of a few federal agencies, that is no longer the case. Now, a great many federal agencies have missions that incorporate significant and far-reaching international dimensions—Agriculture, Environment, Commerce, Health, and Labor, among others. Those agencies are, as Joseph Nye puts it, "embodied in a web of multilateral institutions that allow others to participate in decisions" (Nye, 2002, p. 17). As one consultant put it, today's problems are "bigger than any customer—no one agency, or even one nation, has these problems within its purview." Accordingly, respondents called attention to the need to join with other governments to accomplish their international missions, as well as the need for more flexible and agile processes to replace fixed, slow bureaucratic operations.

Nor is international leadership now for the government alone; it is exerted as well by corporations, non-governmental institutions (NGOs), and intergovernmental organizations. Thus, the need for a globally competent workforce spans these sectors, characterizing all organizations with an international reach. According to one respondent, globalization has meant that foreign policy now includes a whole host of actors: "It becomes a challenge to determine what the government should be doing and . . . what the comparative advantage of government will be." Also, as a second expert explained, "By now, the government needs to treat NGOs . . . as a normal part of making foreign policy." Summarizing neatly, a third expert said that you can "be a public leader without being in the public sector."

At the same time, organizational structures are changing. Levels of hierarchy are being reduced and stovepipes are being dismantled in efforts to create more agile, effective business processes. For instance, UN headquarters and other organizations in the intergovernmental community describe moves toward decentralization, with increased decisionmaking responsibility for field officers, and toward greater lateral cooperation across "silos." Further, new partnerships across organizations and across sectors have become part of the global land-scape. Operations abroad are more and more important, even if an institution's activities are still primarily "domestic." Our interviews underscored the need for competence at working across national boundaries and across cultures, including those within the United States.

In these global circumstances, leadership requires developing a broader and deeper understanding of the differing perspectives of people from other countries and other cultures, and learning to work effectively with people who differ in language, customs, and, in some cases, political and social values. The global role of the United States in the century ahead will demand greater understanding of the eco-nomic, political, and cultural forces that shape the world. It also means that high-level officers of public, for-profit, and nonprofit or-ganizations interact with one another across borders to arrive at nego-tiated decisions about issues that often blend advances in science and technology with policy concerns while blurring the distinctions be-tween foreign and domestic affairs. Moreover, globalization is not just concerned with economics and finance; it has significant political, legal, and cultural dimensions—both positive and negative.

The public sector got off to a slower start than the other two sec-tors did in coping with the broad and complex implications of glob-alization, but it has been moving quickly in the last several years to catch up. The other sectors became global faster as corporations sought new markets and nonprofits engaged new partners. The lag was also reflected in perspectives on the needs for personnel (see Table 10.2). Although the differences among the sectors are only marginally significant statistically, they suggest that public sector organizations, in comparison to organizations in the other sectors, perceive the effects of globalization on their human resource needs at present as being greater. This finding is consistent with the view that the public sector has come late to the issue of coping with globalization.

Competencies for International Leadership

The global role of the United States in the century ahead will require both breadth and depth. What, specifically, are America's institutions seeking as they recruit future leaders? Interviewees ranked nineteen different attributes. Table 10.3 displays the complete results.

Both the similarities and the differences across sectors are instructive. General cognitive skills and interpersonal skills ranked one and two overall. Personal traits were ranked as important by all sectors, as were ambiguity tolerance and adaptability—perhaps an indication of a more complicated, faster-moving world. Ability to work in teams was ranked highly in all sectors as well—higher than substantive or technical knowledge in a professional field.

Table 10.2
With Trends Toward Globalization, Does Your Organization Now Need Different Types of Employees?

Response Categories	Sector		
	Public	For Profit	Nonprofit
Few/no differences	24	47	31
Moderate differences	34	33	45
Major differences	42	20	24

Table 10.3
**What Makes a Successful Career Professional
in an International Organization?**

Attribute	Overall Rank	Overall Mean	Public Sector	For-Profit Sector	Nonprofit Sector
		Means for Rated Importance			
General cognitive skills (e.g., problem solving, analytical ability)	1	4.6	4.7	4.7	4.5
Interpersonal and relationship skills	2	4.6	4.6	4.5	4.6
Ambiguity tolerance, adaptivity	3	4.5	4.5	4.5	4.4
Personal traits (e.g., character, self-reliance, dependability)	4	4.4	4.5	4.3	4.4
Cross-cultural competence (ability to work well in different cultures and with people of different origins)**	5	4.4	4.3	4.1	4.6
Ability to work in teams	6	4.3	4.3	4.3	4.4
Ability to think in policy and strategy terms***	7	4.2	4.3	3.9	4.5
Written and oral English language skills*	8	4.1	4.3	4.0	4.0
Minority sensitivity	9	4.1	4.1	3.8	4.2
Innovative, able to take risks	10	4.0	4.0	4.2	3.8
Empathy, nonjudgmental perspective**	11	4.0	4.0	3.6	4.2
Substantive knowledge in a technical or professional field*	12	3.9	3.6	3.9	4.1
Multidisciplinary orientation	13	3.8	3.8	3.9	3.7
Knowledge of international affairs, geographic area studies***	14	3.6	3.9	3.2	3.8
Competitiveness, drive***	15	3.6	3.7	4.1	3.2
General educational breadth	16	3.6	3.6	3.5	3.7
Internet and information technology competency	17	3.5	3.5	3.5	3.5
Managerial training and experience	18	3.4	3.2	3.3	3.6
Foreign language fluency***	19	3.2	2.9	2.9	3.7

NOTES: n = 135. Each attribute was rated for importance, where 5 = very important, 1 = not important, and 3 = moderately important. The following annotations are used to indicate significance of differences in rated importance of attributes by sector: *p < .05; **p < .01; ***p < .001.

Not surprisingly, for-profits ranked the ability to think in policy and strategy terms as less important than the two other sectors did. Perhaps somewhat surprising, written and oral English skills were ranked as quite important by the government but much less so by the other two sectors. Empathy and a nonjudgmental perspective were much less important for the for-profits than for the other two sectors; and, correspondingly, drive and competitiveness were much more important to that sector than to the other two.

Knowledge of international affairs and of particular areas of the world was rated of medium to low importance, while fluency in a foreign language ranked at or near the bottom for all three sectors. The latter finding was a surprise, and it conflicted with comments made frequently in our interviews. The following samples are illustrative:

"We are in a multicultural world; the greater language capabilities we have, the better we can relate."

"You cannot work internationally without learning languages. It is critical for cultural understanding."

"It is hard to quantify the benefits of a foreign language, but there are real dividends."

"In many respects we don't need a second language, although it is an indicator of somebody with a broader global perspective."

"We get credibility when working on projects abroad if we can speak with our local counterparts—especially with those that are nonprofessional."

These comments suggest that becoming skilled in a second or third language is a proxy for the knowledge and attitudes that leadership in international domains will require. That is so despite participants' views that foreign language fluency, as developed and assessed by academic institutions, is typically not by itself sufficient to produce cross-cultural competency. Most university programs emphasize literary (e.g., reading and writing) rather than applied (e.g., spoken social or business interaction) uses of foreign languages. Thus, fluency in a specific foreign language may reflect academic mastery of literary usage that is not necessarily functional in real-world task contexts; serious negotiations will always require professional translators. As a result, language skills are valued not in and of themselves but, rather, for what they might indicate about a person's ability to work across cultures.

To give respondents a chance to emphasize skills they sought, we asked them what was missing from the list of nineteen competencies and had proved to be important in their organizations. For-profit sector respondents tended to emphasize individual attitudes; they seek, for instance, integrity, resilience, self-confidence, and initiative. Those in the nonprofit and public sectors, in contrast, paid more attention to social and political knowledge, skills, and attitudes. They frequently mentioned characteristics such as "diplomatic skills," "political savvy," "networking capabilities," and "ability to work in coalitions" (that is, across institutions). Additionally, respondents in both of these sectors underscored the need for people who could "sell ideas" and be "results oriented," attributes that have long been highly regarded in the for-profit sector.

Across all sectors, what emerges is an integrated cluster of competencies, including substantive knowledge, managerial ability, strategic vision, and experience at operating across cultures. All three sectors seek young professionals with broad experience, including across national cultures, and all three place broad experience above any academic or other pre-professional qualifications. To some extent, those competencies can be separated in different people, especially at lower levels of organizations. They cannot be separated for those at the top of organizations; rather, in leaders, the competencies need to come together.

Yet the practices of existing organizations do not produce enough such leaders—in fact, quite the contrary. And this is especially true in the federal government, where lateral entry from other sectors is almost nonexistent except at the very top, so its organizations deprive themselves of talent with experience outside the government. The for-profit sector, too, tends to hire young professionals primarily for their technical qualifications and then to grow them inside particular companies—but it later laments that the pool of broadly seasoned senior managers is small. Moreover, the interviews seem to reflect a gap between the international experience that organizations say they seek and the narrower technical criteria actually applied in hiring.

While new national initiatives to boost the supply of skills in science and technology, information, and critical languages might be welcome, they are probably less cost-effective than more-targeted innovations within organizations across all three sectors—and across the sectors themselves. If a government agency needs linguists in unusual languages and cannot hire such people directly, it might, for instance, offer fellowships in those languages in return for commitments to subsequently work at the agency. All three sectors need to explore, together, innovative career patterns across sectors. What might be called "portfolio careers" would produce senior leaders with skills and experience across sectors—and across national cultures. Shifts across sectors, from temporary secondments to more-permanent lateral shifts, need to be encouraged in law and practice, not discouraged. By contrast, such professional development efforts as now exist are usually ad hoc and initiated by employees. They neither reflect a strategic view of an organization's future needs, nor cumulate to produce the desired cadre of leaders.

Building Future Leaders: Comparisons Across the Sectors

Of the three sectors, the for-profit sector reports less difficulty, on the whole, finding the talent it seeks, and its advantages in the hunt are the mirror images of the government's obstacles. It sets the pay scales for technical expertise. When for-profits want expertise on China so they can enter the Chinese market, the answer is easy: hire Chinese. When expertise on, for instance, particular markets abroad is lacking, businesses sometimes can be patient, simply waiting until the right people are found. The government, by contrast, has no such luxury.

It cannot decide to wait to enter Afghanistan because it does not have enough experts.

The "not-for-profit" sector includes a varied set of institutions. In this study, it included international humanitarian and advocacy organizations, major foundations with strong international missions, and international organizations, such as the UN, which are nonprofit but not non-governmental. The number and roles of such organizations have grown dramatically in the last several decades. Most of those studied were global from their inception, so globalization for them mostly meant becoming more so, as well as moving into more specialized and technical activities. The not-for-profits have internationalized in the same way that the for-profits have, by hiring non-Americans. A generation ago, for instance, most of the leaders of the Ford Foundation abroad were Americans; now most of them are not. The MacArthur Foundation office in Moscow, with one American and a dozen Russians, works in Russian. The not-for-profits say they need people who combine technical expertise with international perspective, as well as people who identify with the organization's mission and can "sell" its ideas. The not-for-profits seek intellectual entrepreneurs who can articulate ideas and shape them into initiatives.

The three sectors all invest considerable time and money in training professionals once they hire them, but all are unenthusiastic about the contribution those efforts make toward producing leaders. As Table 10.4 indicates, career development opportunities are especially numerous in the public sector, and the gap between it and the other sectors grows at the mid-career stage.

Table 10.5 displays the evaluations of post-employment training, which were lackluster across sectors and across roles as well—that is, human resource officers and their counterparts in senior line management shared the same views.

The terms most frequently used to characterize later-stage career development activities were "self-initiated" and "ad hoc." While individual development plans are often filed as a part of performance review procedures or to establish that employee training objectives are

Table 10.4
Does Your Organization Offer Post-Employment Development Opportunities at Different Career Stages?
(percentages responding "yes")

	Sector					
	Public		For Profit		Nonprofit	
Response Categories	Early	Mid-Career	Early	Mid-Career	Early	Mid-Career
Few, none	6	13	7	40	10	35
Some	23	17	33	17	43	51
Many	71	70	60	43	47	14

NOTES: n = 126. Differences in development opportunities early in the career are not statistically significant; for mid-career and beyond, development offerings differ significantly by sector $(\chi^2 = 35.4; p < 0.0001)$.

Table 10.5
How Well Do Professional Development Programs Work at Different Career Stages?

	Means by Sector		
Career Stage	Public	For-Profit	Nonprofit
Early career	3.6	3.5	3.6
Mid-career and beyond	3.7	3.7	3.5

NOTES: n = 119. Effectiveness was rated on a 5-point scale, where 5 = very effective, 1 = not effective, and 3 = moderately effective.

being met, or both,[6] these person-specific efforts are unlikely to cumulate to yield the competencies critical to future international leadership. Moreover, short courses (the most widely used approach) are perhaps the least likely way of yielding the desired learning—

---

6 The Government Employees Training Act (GETA), which was passed in 1958, amended in 1994, and given a boost by the Government Performance and Results Act (GPRA), helps explain why the public sector reports an abundance of development offerings for employees at mid-career levels and beyond. However, it is not clear how extensively these options are used or how well they support organizational missions when employees take advantage of them. Most training is arranged by individual employees and their supervisors in individual development plans; typically, there is no higher-level link established between these and competencies implicit in either future workforce goals or agencies' strategic plans.

integration of substantive and managerial skills. As one for-profit sector interviewee explained, plenty of development programs are offered, but they need to be more structured and targeted. Respondents from the nonprofit sector complained about "no culture of training" and "no passion for training" at higher career levels.

All three sectors reported that they hire laterally to fill shortfalls in human talent. Overall, 45 percent of interviewees said this is a frequent practice in their organizations. It is most common in public sector agencies. As Table 10.6 indicates, when the sectors hire laterally, they all tend to do so within their own sector.

This tendency is most pronounced for for-profit organizations, which prefer to "grow from within": When they look outside, they look within the same sector, thinking there is too much risk in having top-level decisionmakers who are not thoroughly grounded in the industry's core business processes. Moreover, according to interviewees, the public and nonprofit sectors do not nurture the skills and attitudes valued in the for-profit sector.

The patterns of the nonprofit sector are more mixed. Like their for-profit counterparts, humanitarian and intergovernmental organizations in the nonprofit sector, when hiring laterally, tend to seek candidates from same-sector institutions engaged in similar lines of work. Foundation respondents, in contrast, said they seek to fill higher-level vacancies with individuals from other sectors who will bring energy and fresh perspectives. Said one foundation interviewee, "It is easy to get lax when you are in a giving position."

Table 10.6
When You Hire Laterally, How Frequently Would It Be
from the Same Sector?
(percentages)

Response Categories	Sector		
	Public	For-Profit	Nonprofit
Rarely, never	7	9	10
Occasionally	38	13	51
Often	55	78	39

The public sector falls somewhere between the practices of the other two sectors; over half the respondents indicated that when lateral hiring is involved, the senior manager or professional most often comes from another public sector agency. The existing Intergovernmental Personnel Act (IPA) makes it possible for employees to move across agencies but does not make it easy or especially desirable. In fact, the easiest way to fill a higher-level post is with a candidate from a parent agency, because so many of the hiring hurdles will already have been cleared.

In contrast, hiring promising leaders from outside is hard because of salary issues—an obstacle government agencies share with humanitarian organizations—and because of long hiring processes. Strong senior candidates with international expertise are often lost to the private sector during the wait. In many agencies, too, there is cultural resistance to welcoming outsiders who, as one interviewee described it, "haven't put in their time." It is, according to another government interviewee, "a difficult paradigm to break."

Despite all the hand-wringing over America's primary and secondary education, America's higher education remains the world's envy. The number of non-Americans who want to study here continues to rise, though the United States has recently been losing market share (primarily to Europe). Yet those impressive institutions are falling short in preparing leaders who can think strategically and who can integrate across cultures and move from technical knowledge to practical actions.

In part, the long debate over internationalizing university curricula continues, with ceasefires usually tending to favor technical or field knowledge over broadening. That may be all the more so because the traditional disciplines of internationalizing—language and area studies—are not highly prized by most prospective employers, who, like our interviewees, regard such knowledge at best as markers for some cross-cultural competency. Narrowness at U.S. universities is abetted by the "culture of AP," the high school Advanced Placement that permits many of the best freshmen to effectively skip a year of college, moving sooner into more-specialized majors.

Paradoxically, the very success of America's universities makes them less cosmopolitan than they might appear. They have, for instance, more and more non-American faculty members, but given the attractiveness of U.S. universities, the vast majority of those have U.S. Ph.D.'s. Their faces may differ from those of their U.S. counterparts, but their training is the same. Indeed, even taking a year or a semester to study abroad may be a less international experience than it would seem—American students often live in expatriate quarters and study with U.S. professors.

Finally, it is striking that while all three sectors of American life have cried out for leadership, that subject is only beginning to be studied and taught on American campuses. Traditionally, it was not academically respectable and thus was a regular feature only at the military academies, business schools, and a few venturesome public policy schools. Yet if leaders, like entrepreneurs (not to mention scholars), are partly born, they are also partly made. Leadership skills can be learned and developed, as Al Robbert points out in Chapter 9 (Van Wart, 2003).

Re-energizing Government

In the final analysis, shortages of desired competencies in future leaders were reported for all sectors, but the most acute shortage was the one in the public sector, as Table 10.7 indicates. And this pronounced shortfall exists despite the greater number of mid-career development opportunities the public sector provides its employees. By contrast, over two-thirds of for-profit sector respondents reported that few to none of the critical competencies required for their missions are lacking at higher organizational levels.

Although the severity of the shortfalls varies across sectors, the nature of the shortfalls is similar. One interviewee from the nonprofit sector said the need was for more "T-shaped" competency, referring to a combination of breadth in international orientation and in

Table 10.7
Are There Competencies for International Career Employees That You Find in Short Supply at Mid-Career Levels or Higher?
(percentages)

Response Categories	Sector		
	Public	For-Profit	Nonprofit
Few or no competencies lacking	29	71	32
Some competencies lacking	45	20	61
Many/major competencies lacking	26	9	7

NOTES: χ^2 = 22.1; p < 0.001.

managerial and interpersonal skills with depth in substance or technical expertise. A UN interviewee underscored the need for "national
U.S. decisionmakers who can 'play' at the international level." Public
sector respondents also emphasized the serious challenge of finding
people who have strong managerial skills, in addition to professional
competence and international experience. In particular, a broad perspective is missing for many people at middle and senior career levels:
"They understand their own job well but need a wider perspective on
the mission of the agency," commented one interviewee. Another observed that cultural competency is "always in short supply." As a result, some public sector participants called their organizations "neck-
less" because there was no senior level leadership cadre between top-
level officers and lower-level line employees.

The war on terrorism has driven home the need to re-energize
the government and has provided a rare opportunity to give the federal government better access to the talent it will need. The federal
government finds it very difficult to attract and keep substantive experts of all sorts. Young people are attracted by the work of government and by the opportunity to serve—almost all federal agencies
reported increases in interest immediately after September 11th—but
many of them find that public service simply imposes too great a
financial penalty in comparison to work in the private sector. The
high-technology collapse and the recession have been a boon for the
government, but managers who seek the best understandably shy

away from becoming the nation's employer of last resort. Moreover, a large fraction of the country's scientific and technological expertise resides in non-Americans, who are generally not accessible to the government, perhaps all the less so given the tightening of security regulations in the fight on terrorism.

A second concern that runs through the government sector is the thinness of middle management, which is a more specific form of "necklessness." The government downsizing of the 1980s and 1990s was not dramatic in overall numbers (it cut less than 10 percent of the federal government), but it was random, not strategic, tending to expel those having the least tenure, with no thought of the needs of the organization. In consequence, the government is facing enormous turnover—something over a third of civil servants will be eligible for retirement within five years—and lacking a cadre of experienced middle managers to serve as replacements.

But this challenge does not come without an opportunity. For a generation, the prevailing answer to the question, What should government, and federal government in particular, do? has simply been "less." Now, the question is more open. Citizens are asking their government to act. If America's governmental institutions, ones shaped by the Cold War, are to transform themselves to act, it will not be the patriotic people who have run those institutions for thirty years who will do it. Fresh blood is needed, and thus turnover can be a historic opportunity. The government needs to be quicker and better in bringing in talent, it needs to be richer at rewarding talent, and, critically, it needs to be much more open to bringing in leaders laterally, perhaps only for several-year tenures.

The interviewees were also eloquent in noting that many of the government's handicaps in attracting and keeping talent are self-inflicted. Those handicaps could be changed, and there is now an opportunity to change them. Hiring in the government takes too long and is too opaque and bureaucratic. The Office of Personnel Management (OPM) website, *USAjobs,* has for too long been easy to find but impossible to fathom, its job postings written in impenetrable bureaucratese. Government employment lasts a lifetime, is all or nothing, so lateral movements occur in only one direction—

out—except at the very top. Elaborate and dated civil service rules make bringing people in at mid-career very difficult. Moreover, the government has a very hard time reaching out to talent that is not American, and the pay is both uncompetitive and inflexible, often still keyed to seniority much more than to job or performance.

As Al Robbert observes in Chapter 9, the U.S. military has been relatively successful in preparing its senior officers for leadership. The military is entirely closed, with virtually no lateral entry, but what that means is that when young officers are brought in, they are brought in for a career. Those entrants know they can aspire to the positions of highest leadership, and the military can afford to make continuing investments in their career development, especially in those it judges as most promising. The military plans for officers to leave jobs at specified points in their careers and to spend a full year in training. And officers also move frequently, broadening their skill base and particularly their sense for the broader enterprise. They can have something of a "portfolio career" while remaining in the military.

Neither the Foreign Service nor the intelligence agencies match the military, but both have some of the same advantages. At the other extreme, the traditional civil service enjoys none of them. Promotion is competitive in theory only. The vast majority of senior positions at Commerce, Treasury, and Defense will be filled from outside, by political appointees. Not surprisingly, the civil service neither attracts nor retains the highest-quality people, and it produces few leaders.

Our public sector interviewees reported few development opportunities in early career (again, a situation in contrast to that of the military) but many at mid-career. However, it is not clear how extensively these opportunities are used, or how well they support organizational missions when employees take advantage of them. Moreover, most civil servants do not move frequently. If they seek training, their supervisors either have to hold positions for them or hire temporary substitutes, neither of which is an attractive option to either officials or their superiors. It is thus no surprise that most training tends to be short in duration. And civil servants change both jobs and locations much more rarely than their military counterparts do. They inhabit stovepipes within stovepipes, thus often acquiring little sense of the broader enterprise in which they are engaged, let alone the broadening that would let them take a strategic view of that enterprise.

The United States is not about to adopt—nor should it adopt—what the U.S. military resembles: a European-style closed civil service. But much can be done to increase opportunities for those in career government service. Robbert's agenda (see Chapter 9) fits well with the conclusions of our project, although, as he also notes, implementing some of those measures will be no mean feat. The civil service acquires entering talent in many more ways than does the military, but the one method most akin to that of the military is the intern program, either the Presidential Management Internship or the agency-sponsored Career Internship. These two programs let choices be made on the basis of careers, not just immediate agency needs, but both are small and special. Expanding them to provide a conscious pool of future leaders would be a natural.

If emulating the military in providing residential schools for year-long training is too expensive for the civil service, it should at least be possible to find ways to make leaving a job for training easier. It should also be possible for agencies to broaden their conceptions of human resources so as to take a more strategic view of training and other development opportunities. Finding ways to identify future leaders, as the military and many corporations do, will be harder for the public sector given the transparency of civilian, public employment, but that identification is part of a strategic view of human resources. Enabling agencies to move officials around was an issue in the legislation authorizing the Department of Homeland Security (DHS), but more mobility also makes sense in the interest of adding to officials' skills and broadening their outlooks. Most civilian agencies have no counterpart to the military joint chiefs of staff, but enhancing "jointness" by facilitating moves to sister agencies would also be broadening.

Recent legislation has freed both the DHS and DoD from many civil service constraints. Currently, more than half of the civilian employees of the federal government do not work under traditional civil service rules. Their managers now have much more latitude in rewarding performance. Yet the opportunity to reward promising future leaders also carries the responsibility of being held accountable for decisions, and the interviews suggest that managers are often reluctant to take advantage of the latitude they now have.

Finally, at the top of agencies, the gathering weight of measures—understandable as they are—to guard against conflicts of interest in the political appointments process has made that process slow, painful, and often humiliating. As a result, while America's involvement in the world and need for leadership grow, the pool of top-flight candidates ready to run the gauntlet shrinks. A recent review of four years of detailed assessments of federal agencies is instructive (Treverton, 2004). The agency leaders whose agencies were evaluated were "political"—that is, they served at the pleasure of the President. But, belying familiar stereotypes, most were actually qualified for the job, in training or experience.

Yet many of them had run the gauntlet already, either because they were politicians (Christie Todd Whitman, ex-governor of New Jersey, ran the Environmental Protection Agency) or because they had held similar jobs in state government (James Lee Witt had run disaster relief in Arkansas before taking over the Federal Emergency Management Agency; Kenneth Kizer, a doctor who had run California's Health Services Department, took over the Veterans Health Administration). Others—such as the Administration for Children and Families' Olivia Golden, the Federal Housing Administration's William Apgar, and the Immigration and Naturalization Service's Doris Meissner—were academic specialists in the substance they were appointed to manage. As such, they were less likely than others to suffer great hardship in taking government salaries, and probably found the conflict-of-interest portions of the gauntlet easier to run. By contrast, corporate executives were much rarer among the agency heads.

An Agenda for Building International Leadership

September 11th, like the launching of *Sputnik* two generations before it, led to bemoaning of gaps. Does America lag in learning languages, especially exotic ones, or risk losing the scientific and technological lead on which its primacy depends? If the answer is yes, the typical response is a broad national program (such as the National Defense Education Act of the early Cold War) to increase the supply pipeline. This time around, however, no such visible and specific gaps in total numbers were apparent. As a result, big national programs to subsidize supply are not so much wrong as they are indirect for meeting the needs that exist. For instance, information technology experts are not lacking in America; the government's problem is not the lack of total supply, but its limited access to the talent given the competition from the for-profit sector.

When government agencies have very specific needs, such as for people with knowledge of exotic languages or specific cultures, the right response is very targeted programs. First, the government should find ways to hire the experts, even if they are not American. Second, if the expertise needs to be nurtured rather than acquired, the government should build limited and focused programs, mostly at the graduate level, offering fellowships in critical areas in exchange for commitments to later (or simultaneous) government service.

The public sector, in particular, needs to reach out so that it reflects the diversity of the country—that need came through clearly in the interviews. Yet so did the challenges the government faces in doing so. Not only is the government hard-pressed to match the salaries that the private sector can offer to talented minority candidates, but the pool most readily available (from international studies or public policy graduate programs) is not itself all that diverse. It is important to keep in mind, all the more so now amidst the terrorist threat, that the United States also exercises global leadership through the non-Americans who come here to study and work. If they remain here, they add to the human resources on which the nation can draw; and if they return home or move back and forth, they become part of the web of connections that drive global society.

America's leadership in the 21st century will not be accomplished by government alone, however. From the interviews and analysis emerge an agenda for better positioning tomorrow's America to lead in a globalized world. Table 10.8 summarizes this agenda, which begins with the government and with immediate actions, some of them familiar and all in the spirit of the Volcker Commission. However, this agenda also includes actions by all three sectors, plus higher education—ideally in partnership. Some of those initiatives can have an effect in the short run; others will require that organizations be reshaped and new legislation be enacted. The for-profit sector will be the hardest to entice, but it should be drawn in by the national interest—and, ultimately, its own.

The following paragraphs elaborate on what this agenda entails for the government, not-for-profit, for-profit, and higher education sectors.

For government

- *Make the hiring process quicker and more transparent.* Promising applicants currently disappear for months into the black hole of silent delay. A start, one in which OPM is engaged, is to write job descriptions in plain English. The Central Intelligence Agency (CIA) has halved its hiring cycle of six to nine months by targeting its recruiting more tightly and by letting recruiting officers make conditional offers on the spot.
- *Make it easier for people to move across agencies.* In some areas, such as intelligence, it might be possible to mimic the experience of the military joint staff, making rotations to other agencies or "joint" appointments a requirement for promotion.
- *Look for ways to facilitate temporary movements of officials across sectors.* The existing Intergovernmental Personnel Act (IPA) makes it possible to move officials across sectors temporarily, but it does not make it easy to do so. It should be expanded, as should other programs that detail government officials to the Congress, to state and local governments, and to the private sector.

Table 10.8
Agenda for Building Future Leaders

	Time Horizon	
	Shorter Term—Developing Leaders	Longer Term—The Leadership Pipeline
Public	Increase and enhance use of intergovernmental personnel agreements Facilitate lateral movement inside and outside government Improve hiring processes Target robust career development programs Use the new latitude to reward promising future leaders	Expand internship and cooperative programs Narrowly target fellowships in areas of need Support and encourage portfolio careers Relax barriers to in-and-out careers (e.g., conflict-of-interest laws) Fund leadership development research Reserve some proportion of senior positions in any agency for the career service
For-profit	Support career exchanges with public and nonprofit sectors Target robust career development programs	Support and encourage portfolio careers Support internationalized master's in business administration programs
Nonprofit	Support career exchanges with public and for-profit sectors Heighten awareness of need for future leaders Improve hiring processes Target robust career development programs	Increase funding for producing dual (and treble) expertise Increase support for leadership study and training Articulate and support study of specialized human resource needs of international nonprofit organizations (both non-governmental and intergovernmental)
Higher Education	Promote and recognize real world study abroad Expand initiatives for internationalizing education at home	Internationalize graduate programs in relevant areas (e.g., master's degrees in public administration, public policy, business administration; and related doctoral studies) Rethink ways to internationalize other curricula Improve U.S. minority recruitment/retention in international programs Give leadership development a serious place in teaching and research

- *Develop ways to facilitate lateral entry from other sectors.* In particular, the existing government career structure makes it very difficult to bring in younger talent from outside at mid-career.

Ways beyond the IPA need to be found to permit such moves, for limited terms or beyond. In the long run, both law and practice will have to change if "in and out" careers are to be encouraged, not deterred.

- *Expand very targeted fellowship programs to nurture talent when it can be acquired no other way.* Graduate fellowships would be keyed to very specific government needs and granted in return for commitments to government service.
- *Reserve some proportion of senior positions—deputy assistant secretaries, especially—for permanent career officials.* This will not be easy, for it is precisely the political appointment process that leads to officials, even at the cabinet level, having very little incentive to worry about the state of the permanent government beyond their, usually relatively short, tenure. But nothing would do more to improve the morale, and in time the attraction, of the civil service.
- *Ask hard questions about why non-Americans cannot be hired for particular jobs.* The CIA's Foreign Broadcast Information Service, for instance, does hire non-Americans as translators and editors. Other agencies could find innovative ways to do so as well.
- *Start by making use of the new rules that make it possible to link pay to performance.* The rub here is that with opportunity also goes responsibility, which in many instances has made agency leaders reluctant to use the flexibility they now have available.
- *Look hard at some pay issues.* Pay needs to be looked at in general, but ways in which to reward people for performance and to recognize that the opportunity cost of federal service is much higher for some professionals than for others need to be looked at much more closely.

For the not-for-profit sector

- *Think about developing human resources.* Many institutions in this sector, especially startups, are run on a shoestring. They have had neither money nor time to develop their young professionals; they have been consumers of talent, not nurturers of it.

As the sector matures, though, it has both need and opportunity to develop human capital, for both its benefit and the nation's.

- *Develop more innovations in building specialized "dual expertise."* The Ford Foundation was the leader in developing area studies, and it later took the lead in building dual expertise—offering graduate students in one of two disciplines (for example, strategy and Russian studies) the opportunity to acquire expertise in the other discipline. The MacArthur Foundation is beginning a program to both train and employ a new generation of defense-minded scientists, replacing the generation that is now passing from the scene without a cohort of successors.

For the for-profit sector

- *Question the mismatch between leaders sought and hiring decisions.* This sector needs to ask whether there really is a mismatch between the strategic international leaders that organizations say they seek and the hiring decisions that actually result.
- *Assess the value of developing career paths that would produce "dual (or treble)-expertise" human capital.* The for-profit sector is in the best position to innovate in ways that will serve its human resource development needs—and those of the country—in this century.
- *Think of the other sectors as partners in developing broad-gauged leaders in a rapidly changing world.* This could range from joint, targeted mid-career training opportunities to longer postings across sectors.

For higher education

- *Rethink ways to give students a grounding in thinking and acting across cultures.* Requiring languages or area studies may not be the best way to achieve this grounding, in part because existing language programs are perceived by employers as emphasizing literary, not applied, skills. But there are many other ways. In particular, seek out answers to why so many college students arrive at college saying they intend to take a year of study abroad, but so few actually do so.

- *Internationalizing faculty is easier than international curriculums.* Non-Americans with U.S. Ph.D.'s are the beginning of internationalizing, not the end.
- *Treat leaderships as a serious subject.* Leadership is, on the cusp of the 21st century, neither pop psychology nor charging up San Juan hill. It is less an academic outcast than it used to be, as leadership programs have been created at the undergraduate and professional school levels. The question is their quality. Leadership can be taught, but how well are these new programs teaching it?

Actions taken by the sectors will be enhanced if they are taken together. For instance, government, and especially the military, makes significant investments in career development opportunities at mid-career. It and the for-profit sector could engage one another in increasing exchange opportunities to mutual benefit. Senior business leaders have recognized that their successors will not be like them, that they will instead be broader and more international. Making good on that recognition requires reaching out to the other sectors, not just as an occasional source of senior advice, but also as partners in developing future leaders.

Volcker Commission Recommendation 3: Create Flexible, Performance-Driven Agencies

CHAPTER ELEVEN

The Economic Complexities of Incentive Reforms

Beth J. Asch

Efforts are under way to create high-performance government by increasing accountability through strategic human resource plans, goal setting, and metrics of performance. The President's Management Agenda (U.S. Office of Management and Budget, 2002) requires that all government organizations increase performance through better management of its personnel, i.e., by attracting and retaining talented people and by tying pay to performance, thereby motivating them to use their talents in productive ways. The Department of Homeland Security (DHS) and the Department of Defense (DoD) both have broad new powers to design personnel and compensation systems. At the heart of these efforts are incentives for performance. Government is faced with questions of how to reward strong performers and respond to external market forces so that it can attract, retain, and motivate a qualified and talented workforce.

How might these goals be achieved? This chapter draws lessons from economics and management studies to help government leaders and federal managers as they move ahead with efforts to improve incentives in the federal government. Some key points made here are as follows:

- Pay-for-performance systems can be effective for motivating high performance and attracting high performers.
- Pay-for-performance systems have potential pitfalls associated with them, so care must be taken to recognize and address those pitfalls, if possible. These systems can lead to unintended conse-

quences because of difficulties in measuring individual performance, the presence of competing organizational goals, the pull from multiple decisionmakers, and the competing needs of various parties interested in organizational performance.

- There is no single solution to the problem of unintended consequences. Civil service managers should consider an array of available incentive mechanisms that can be tailored to various circumstances.

The chapter begins with an overview of the evidence on pay-for-performance, particularly in the federal government. It then describes the incentive problems that pay-for-performance mechanisms attempt to address, how explicit pay-for-performance systems solve those problems, and the unintended consequences that may arise. Next, it describes alternative approaches for providing incentives for performance, along with their advantages and disadvantages. Finally, the chapter concludes with a discussion of the implications for the federal civil service.

Overview of Evidence on Pay-for-Performance in the Federal and Private Sectors

The civil service compensation, classification, promotion, and staffing policies in the federal civil service are well defined in Title 5 of the U.S. Code. The published pay tables and the detailed processes for defining jobs promote clarity, openness, and predictability. However, various commissions and studies over the past decade have concluded that the civil service compensation and personnel systems are urgently in need of reform.[1] In 2001, the General Accounting Office (GAO)

---

[1] Just as the current Volcker Commission report (provided as Chapter 2 of this document) calls for reform of civil service, so, too, did the first Volcker Commission report (National Commission on the Public Service, 1990). Two examples of other commissions and studies are the Defense Science Board Task Force on Human Resources Strategy, 2002, and the *Naval Research Advisory Committee Report on Science and Technology Community in Crisis* (U.S. Office of the Assistant Secretary of the Navy, 2002).

added government performance and specifically personnel management to its list of "high risk" areas in government—i.e., those governmentwide areas that affect government's ability to serve the American public. As stated by GAO, "An organization's people—its human capital—are its most critical asset in managing for results. However, the federal government has often acted as if people were costs to be cut rather than assets to be valued" (General Accounting Office, 2001, p. 71).

The rigidity of compensation and personnel systems has costs in terms of attracting, retaining, and motivating talented personnel. For example, it typically takes up to three months to fill what are known as "competitive service" civil service positions, and even longer to fill other positions (General Accounting Office, 2003). In one survey, most federal employees called the hiring process slow and confusing, a quarter called it unfair, and more than two-thirds said the federal government was not good at disciplining bad performance (Light, 2001). According to the Office of Personnel Management (OPM), more than 75 percent of the increase in annual federal pay bears no relationship to individual achievement or competence. The director of OPM has called the General Schedule pay system an antiquated system that overly compresses pay as a result of an emphasis on internal pay equity rather than competitiveness (James, 2002).

Other evidence paints a less uniformly negative picture. Studies that focus on the recruiting and retention outcomes of the compensation system have found mixed evidence to suggest that personnel quality has declined in the civil service. For example, I found that high-quality civil service workers, measured in terms of supervisor rating and education level, were generally paid more and promoted faster than those of lower quality in DoD, when other characteristics, such as occupation, years of service, location, gender, and age, were held constant (Asch, 2001). I also found that DoD was having trouble retaining workers with advanced degrees. A related study (Gibbs, 2001) examined trends in the workforce outcomes of scientists and engineers who worked in laboratories in DoD in the 1980s and the first half of the 1990s, a group having many individuals with advanced degrees. That study found little evidence that DoD suffered a

declining trend in the quality of its science and engineering labora-
tory workforce, though it did not find evidence of an increase, either.
Similar results were found in an earlier study of defense workers (U.S.
Department of Defense, 1990; Crewson, 1995).

Studies comparing the pay of federal and private sector employees with similar "human capital" in terms of age, education, region,
and so forth found that federal pay exceeded private-sector pay from
the mid-1970s to 2000, though the gap declined somewhat for males
(Gyourko and Tracy, 1988; Krueger, 1988; Moulton, 1990; Borjas,
2002). However, the structure of compensation in the federal sector
relative to that in the private sector became more compressed, calling
into the question the ability of the federal sector to attract and retain
high-quality personnel in the future (Gibbs, 2001; Borjas, 2002).

In the past, several federal organizations were able to waive the
Title 5 civil service rules: the U.S. Postal Service, the Central Intelligence Agency (CIA), and other federal agencies. Within DoD, the
demonstration projects at the Naval Air Warfare Center in China
Lake, California, were also able to waive these rules. About half of
federal employees are in these exempt organizations (U.S. Office of
Personnel Management, 1998). Although the Volcker Commission
report does not recommend a specific replacement to the current civil
service system, it suggests that a good place to start is to model the
replacement on the system used in any of the successful demonstration projects. The new National Security Personnel System will be
built on the lessons learned from past demonstration projects (Federal
Register, April 2003).

The civil service waivers and demonstration projects have shown
promise but have not always lived up to their potential, according to
the available evidence. For example, OPM found that five of the 37
exempt organizations that it studied continued to follow Title 5 procedures for personnel classification and compensation because it was
easier to do so than to establish their own system (U.S. Office of Personnel Management, 1998). Gibbs (2001) studied the outcomes of
DoD laboratory scientists and engineers and found no evidence that
these other pay plans provided greater flexibility in personnel management. The Naval Research Advisory Committee report on the de-

fense science and technology community, which described reviews of the studies of these demonstration projects at various defense laboratories, concluded that the results of these projects could have been much better than they were and that many of the most promising or innovative initiatives for improving the civil service system were dropped due to problems in getting organizational approval (U.S. Office of the Assistant Secretary of the Navy, 2002). In summary, the evidence sketches a personnel system that is nonresponsive, bureaucratic, and failing to live up to its potential. But so far, neither demonstration projects nor the waiver of Title 5 rules has led to markedly better outcomes.

Calls for civil service reform universally include recommendations to more closely tie compensation to performance. For example, the 2002 President's Management Agenda calls for performance-based compensation where performance goals are linked to agency mission objectives. It also calls for better management of personnel, drawing on the best practices of the private sector, where personnel are viewed as a strategic resource of the organization.

Interestingly enough, available evidence from private sector establishments indicates that pay is often not closely tied to explicit measures of performance, such as sales or commissions. For example, a common finding is that time on the job, such as hours worked, is a stronger predictor of pay than is performance (Lazear, 2000a). Parent (1999) analyzed data from 1988 to 1990 on full-time workers ages 23 to 33 and found that only 9.4 percent overall are paid on the basis of piece-rate or sales and that 14.2 percent are paid bonuses, though these figures vary by industry. The rest were hourly or salaried workers. Other evidence indicates that workers who are rated the highest by supervisors earn only a few percentage points more in pay than those rated the lowest, suggesting that better performance often does not translate into substantially better pay (Medoff and Abraham, 1980; Baker, Jensen, and Murphy, 1988).

The evidence that pay is weakly linked to performance metrics in the private sector does not mean that incentives for performance are always weak or that employee performance is not responsive. As discussed in the management and economics literature, private sector organizations often rely on what appear to be egalitarian pay structures, such as promotion-based incentives systems. Under certain conditions, these alternatives can provide incentives that are just as powerful as those provided by direct pay-for-performance schemes. Private sector concerns use these alterative approaches because explicit pay-for-performance schemes have pitfalls.

Before turning to these pitfalls of the pay-for-performance schemes and to the alternative approaches, we first provide a brief definition of the incentive problems that pay-for-performance schemes are intended to address in the employment relationship between the employer and the employee.

Defining the Incentive Problem

Pay-for-performance is intended to solve the employer's twin problems of motivating high performance and attracting and retaining talented personnel when individual employee effort or ability is not readily measured or observed.[2] The potential for incentive problems to arise in the federal government seems great. Effort and output are often difficult to define and measure, because the nature of the work is generally complex, unique, and service oriented. Consider the following examples. Defense output is "readiness," so defense managers are faced with determining whether low levels of readiness are caused by low effort, lack of resources, or a poor quality workforce. Civil service output is often a result of team effort, and each individual team member's effort can be difficult to disentangle from the efforts of others. Projects can be extremely long term; for example, a NASA space mission is the culmination of the efforts of hundreds of individuals over several years. Whether or not an employee has characteristics that are particularly important for productivity (e.g., honesty, diligence, creativity, adaptability, entrepreneurship, collegiality) is

---

[2] In the literature, the employer is called the *principal* and the employee is called the *agent*.

often difficult to discern from entry test scores or even from resumes, and the civil service personnel and compensation systems may inadvertently attract employees with undesirable characteristics, despite screening based on test scores. Finally, the role of random factors in determining performance may be particularly important in some situations, because civil service projects may be "one-of-a-kind" or specific to the federal government, thereby preventing the use of "benchmarks" to compare performance (national defense and food safety come to mind in this context).

Explicit Pay-for-Performance Incentives[3]

The classic solution to the incentive problem is a piece-rate or direct pay-for-performance system that sets pay in direct proportion to either a metric of output (e.g., number of customers served) or the dollar value of output (e.g., commissions on sales). This approach solves the incentive problem in that workers who cut their effort also cut their pay. Performance-related pay systems also attract and retain better workers, because more-talented individuals prefer pay systems that explicitly reward them for their talent. Such systems induce the most-talented individuals to apply for employment and the least talented to leave.

The available evidence from private sector organizations that use commissions and piece rates supports this result. For example, Lazear (2000b), using individual-level data on the performance of workers who installed automobile windshields in the Safelite Glass Corporation, estimated that moving from a compensation system based on fixed salaries to one based on piece rates (pay per windshield installed) increased productivity by 44 percent, where productivity was measured as average output per worker. About half of the increase was due to increased effort on the part of installers; the other half was due to the higher ability of the installers that the company was able to

---

[3] The discussion in this section and the following one benefited from the input of Bogdan Savych (see Savych, 2004).

attract and retain. Prendergast (1999) reports that past studies have generally found that about two-thirds of the increase in performance was due to increased effort.

In the context of military recruiting, Asch and Karoly (1993) found that pay-for-performance had large effects on the productivity of Army recruiters, or job counselors, responsible for matching new recruits to Army jobs. Job counselors were organized into regional centers called recruiting battalions. They were not paid money for matching recruits to jobs, but were able to accumulate points as part of an incentive plan that rewarded points for achieving different types of productivity goals, such as meeting the battalion's monthly recruiting quota. Counselors who accumulated sufficient points earned awards, some of which led to faster promotion to higher pay grades. On average, counselors earned 77.5 points in 1989. Periodically, they had the opportunity to earn up to five bonus points if they filled a hard-to-fill occupation with a qualified recruit within a short time frame. We found that offering counselors five bonus points increased the fill-rate of these hard-to-fill occupations by 45 percent, other factors being equal. Moreover, this effect was larger than the effect of offering recruits enlistment bonuses worth up to several thousand dollars for choosing these occupations.

One disadvantage of pay-for-performance systems is that they expose employees to earnings variability caused by factors that are beyond their control. For risk-averse employees, the greater the random factors are, the weaker the incentives for performance and the greater the fixed component of compensation. Pay-for-performance systems generally specify a base level of pay and a component of pay that is a function of effort or performance. The optimum mix of the base and the risk component depends on the degree of risk aversion, earnings variability, and the worker's cost of effort.

In actual practice, few organizations directly tie pay to output in such a fashion or allow a large part of earnings to directly depend on performance. The provision of incentives is accomplished more indirectly, because explicit pay-for-performance systems have pitfalls connected to the high cost of measuring performance.

Measurement Costs with Pay-for-Performance

Pay-for-performance makes sense only when the gains in employee productivity associated with paying on the basis of performance exceed the costs of measuring output. Measuring output is likely to be the most costly when jobs are multidimensional or done in teams.

Multidimensional Performance. The simplest and arguably the best setting for pay-for-performance is one that has a single, easily measured output. The problem posed by multiple-dimensioned output is that employees can reallocate their effort toward those tasks that are measured and rewarded and away from those that are not (Holmstrom and Milgrom, 1991). That is, when pay is based on quantity and not based on quality, too little quality is produced. In this case, pay-for-performance schemes lead to unintended consequences.

Much empirical evidence supports this result. For example, in a RAND Corporation analysis of the productivity of recruiters, Polich, Dertouzos, and Press (1986) found that enlisting high-quality recruits (defined as youths who had at least a high school diploma and scored in the top half in the distribution of the Armed Forces Qualification Test) was four times as hard as enlisting low-quality recruits. They also found that recruiters who faced less than a 4-to-1 reward for enlisting high-quality recruits reallocated their effort toward enlisting low-quality recruits.

In a 1990 study (Asch, 1990), I analyzed how Navy recruiters reallocated some of their effort over time in response to an incentive plan that rewarded them on the basis of the number of people they recruited. Under this plan, performance was evaluated only at discrete and predetermined 12-month intervals. What I found was that recruiters increased their productivity when the 12-month date approached and reduced their productivity after the evaluation point. Similar results were found by Courty and Marschke (1997), who looked at job-training centers for individuals on welfare that were operating under the Job Training Partnership Act (JTPA). As part of the JTPA, training centers throughout the United States were placed under an incentive scheme that offered the center a bonus if it met a certain standard, which was measured in terms of the number of trainees gaining employment by June 1 of each year. The centers had discretion as to when trainees would graduate from the training program. What Courty and Marschke found was that center managers would strategically manage graduations throughout the year to ensure that they met, but did not exceed, the quota on June 1. A result of this strategic behavior was that trainees got jobs by June 1, though not necessarily well-paying or stable jobs. Courty and Marschke also found that centers focused their efforts on the most-qualified trainee candidates rather than on the most-needy.

The economics and management literature says that the greater the problems caused by these unintended consequences, the weaker the optimal link should be between pay and the explicit metrics of performance. In such circumstances, organizations may turn to alternative approaches to providing incentives (e.g., career-based incentives), as discussed in the next section.

One approach shown to reduce the problem of unintended consequences is to strategically design how job characteristics are bundled and assigned to workers (Holmstom and Milgrom, 1991). For the government setting, Dewatripont, Jewitt, and Tirole (1999) have recommended that specialists be employed for narrowly defined task sets. The use of high-powered incentives is then more feasible, because the workers have limited ability to reallocate their effort in unproductive ways. The Army uses this tactic for recruiting. Recruiters are grouped according to specialization (medical recruiters, reserve recruiters, active duty enlisted recruiters, officer recruiters, etc.), given an incentive plan specific to the group, and restricted to recruiting personnel for their group only. More generally, strategic job design can reduce the loss associated with workers taking undesirable actions or actions with unintended consequences.

Team Production. Problems with pay-for-performance systems can also arise when performance is the result of teamwork, and the contribution of each individual is thus difficult to identify. One solution in this situation is to base performance incentives on group performance. For example, the entire team may get a reward if some measure of group performance, such as a quota or a successful result, is met. In the private sector, profit-sharing, employee-owner organizations, and partnerships are different methods used to reward group performance (Gaynor and Pauly, 1990). In these schemes, the team shares in the residual revenue (after deducting costs), which serves as an inducement for the team to maximize net revenue. An advantage of incentive rewards based on team performance is that they foster cooperative behavior among team members, and this advantage can be critically important when cooperation is essential to team performance.

But the potential for "free-riding" (Holmstrom, 1982) in team-based incentive systems is a problem. If each employee's share of the reward is small relative to the difficulty of the work (or the cost of effort) and if effort is difficult for the employer to observe, each individual on the team has an incentive to shirk his or her work and free-ride on the efforts of others.

Several studies have documented this free-riding behavior in team-based incentive systems (see Prendergast, 1999, for a review). Asch and Karoly (1993) offer evidence suggesting that free-riding occurs among Army job counselors. Table 11.1 shows average point accumulations of counselors by the staff size of the battalion in which they worked. It can be seen that counselors in larger battalions earned fewer points on average. For example, counselors in battalions with four counselors earned 81.9 points on average, while those in battalions with nine counselors earned 71.1 points. Counselors could also

Table 11.1
Mean and Standard Deviation of Incentive Points Earned by Army Job Counselors, by Staff Size of Recruiting Battalion, 1989

Battalion Size (No. of Counselors)	Total Points	Bonus Points
2	88.6 (12.2)	31.0 (23.8)
4	81.9 (19.9)	28.7 (12.6)
5	79.2 (21.9)	26.3 (13.4)
6	79.2 (21.0)	25.1 (13.4)
7	76.3 (22.2)	23.4 (12.5)
8	75.3 (20.8)	22.7 (12.4)
9	71.1 (18.7)	21.5 (8.9)
11	77.3 (15.0)	20.7 (7.8)

SOURCE: Asch and Karoly, 1993.

320 High-Performance Government

earn bonus points; and here, too, the table shows that counselors in larger battalions earned fewer bonus points.

Team output is inefficiently reduced when free-riding occurs. One approach to avoiding this outcome is to encourage peer pressure and mutual monitoring among team members (Kandel and Lazear, 1992). Such mechanisms can induce team members to supply more effort than they might otherwise. Similarly, an organization that can successfully create a "corporate culture" of hard work and success can ameliorate the free-riding issue.

Another problem with team-based incentive systems is "regression to the mean." That is, performance of the least-able workers increases while that of the most-able declines. Weiss (1987) analyzes data on three plans operated by a large electronics manufacturer. All new production workers were initially paid by a piece rate that was based on individual productivity and was higher for overproduction than for underproduction. After about four months, these workers were moved to a team-based incentive plan in which the average size of the team was 126. Weiss measured the difference between individual output under the individual piece-rate plan and individual output under the team-based incentive plan. He found that individual output declined significantly, the biggest drop being for those workers who had been overproducers under the individual piece-rate plan. Consequently, the variance of output was lower under the team-based plan. Hansen (1997) found a similar result using data on telephone operators.

Clearly, much of the output of government reflects team effort. Performance and accountability measures that base rewards on metrics of team performance will run up against the free-rider problem. A government agency can attempt to counteract this behavior by adopting a "high performance" corporate culture. Alternatively, if it is feasible to do so, the agency can combine team-based incentives with individual incentive mechanisms. For example, the Army rewards its recruiters for meeting their individual enlistment quotas as well as for meeting their team or battalion recruiting quotas. By using a complementary incentive scheme that rewards individual performance, the Army is offsetting the negative effects of free-rider behavior while fostering the positive effects that team-based incentives have on co-operation.

Problems of Multiple Employers or Multiple Objectives

Multiple Employers. As noted earlier, the employment relationship is between the employee, or *agent*, and the employer, or *principal*. Defining the agent in this relationship is usually simple; defining the principal, however, may be difficult. Public sector organizations are often large and usually have multiple principals with very different objectives. For example, in the case of a middle manager in an executive branch agency such as DoD, the principals can include the DoD leadership, the White House and the OMB, members of Congress, the GAO, and different interest group constituencies, such as retired military members or civil service union members.

The problem posed by multiple principals is, again, one of unintended consequences: Efforts on behalf of one principal can divert efforts on behalf of other principals. The 1990s reform efforts in the DoD laboratories, which are documented in the Naval Research Advisory Committee Report (U.S. Office of the Assistant Secretary of the Navy, 2002), serve as a good example.

The purpose of the reforms in the 1990s was to allow the DoD laboratories to waive Title 5 requirements and to develop personnel and compensation systems that embedded more management flexibility and greater performance incentives. These reform efforts did not live up to their potential. They often conflicted with other reform efforts occurring at the same time, such as the National Performance Review initiative, which was being carried out throughout the federal government, and the Defense Management Review, which was being carried out within DoD. According to the Naval Research Advisory Committee Report, these other initiatives were often given preference. Furthermore, the laboratories required OPM to provide extensive justification before the Title 5 requirements could be waived.

The optimal incentive scheme when multiple principals have conflicting rather than complementary goals is one that weakly links pay with performance for any given activity (Dixit, 2002). The weaker link reduces the incentive to divert effort toward the goals of one principal at the expense of the goals of the others. Furthermore, the more that the efforts of the agent for the different principals are substitutes, so that effort on behalf of one principal takes away effort on behalf of another principal, the weaker the optimal link. Put differently, pay should be only loosely linked to metrics of performance tied to the specific objectives of different principals when those objectives cannot all be measured.

Obviously, having multiple principals is not a problem if the principals have common or complementary goals. And even when goals are not complementary, it may be possible to bundle the agent's tasks so as to limit the number of principals with an interest in any given set of tasks. For example, the Volcker Commission recommended that the federal government be reorganized by mission. If government agencies were "bundled" according to mission, the use of pay-for-performance incentives would become more feasible, because employees in the newly created agencies would have less scope to redirect their efforts to the missions of other principals.

Multiple Objectives. The objectives of public sector organizations are more diverse than those of most private sector businesses. The very reason why the activity is provided by the government may be motivated by the idea that profit maximization by itself will not result in the socially optimal allocation of resources. Public sector organizations often care about the ends *and* the means of their activities—i.e., about the outcomes *and* the processes of their activities. Thus, governmental organizations may have not only multiple principals, but multiple objectives as well (Tirole, 1994; Dixit, 2002; Wilson, 1989).

The problem with multiple objectives is similar to the problem of multiple dimensions. If only some objectives are measured and rewarded, pay-for-performance may lead to unintended consequences, especially if those objectives are not complementary. For example, suppose a pay-for-performance system is created at the Food and Drug Administration that ties the pay of employees to metrics of food safety. Such a system might induce employees to trade off safety at the expense of other objectives, such as food industry competitiveness. Representatives from the food industry will argue that food safety standards are too burdensome and the time to bring new products to market is too long. Alternatively, if pay at the FDA were tied to metrics related to "service to the customer," where the customer is defined as the food industry representatives, consumer groups would argue that the FDA is sacrificing food safety while "bowing to industry." Even if all agency objectives were measured or monitored with equal frequency, the question of what weights should be attached to the different objectives remains. Should food safety and industry competitiveness be given equal weight? The fact that the political process affects the goals of an agency means that goals will change with the election of a new administration or congress.

Related to the issue of multiple objectives is the concept of "fuzzy missions," which introduce uncertainty about what objectives agents are to pursue. As discussed by Wilson (1989) and developed more fully by Dewatripont, Jewitt, and Tirole (1999), vague objectives rather than clear missions result in lower performance because the uncertainty of the mission creates more uncertainty about the effects of effort, or worker talent, on performance.

Subjective Evaluations

Performance metrics can be quantitative, or *objective*, and/or qualitative, or *subjective*. (A subjective measure might be the ranking of an employee's performance based on a supervisor's expert opinion and experience.) The difficulties associated with measurement costs, multiple principals, and multiple objectives arise to some degree regardless of whether performance is assessed using objective or subjective metrics. For example, the contributions of specific individuals to team performance must be disentangled regardless of whether supervisors rely on subjective or objective metrics of performance. Subjective assessments do have an advantage over objective assessments in that evaluators can account for ill-defined dimensions of performance, such as collegiality. On the negative side, however, is the fact that the accuracy of the assessment with respect to ill-defined dimensions cannot be fully verified by outsiders (Baker, 1992).

Subjective performance assessments are valuable only if supervisors have an incentive to give assessments that are consistent with the organization's mission. But in a highly competitive labor market, private sector employers might have an incentive to reduce the company's wage bill. They thus might deny that the workers performed well in order to avoid paying higher wages (Landy and Farr, 1980).[4] In organizations such as the federal government, supervisors are not residual claimants: Claiming poor performance and denying workers increases does not increase the pay of the supervisors. In fact, just the opposite problem may occur. Supervisors may have an incentive to be lenient and give overly positive assessments so as to minimize complaints or maintain morale among employees (Milgrom, 1988; Milgrom and Roberts, 1988). In some organizations, supervisors have a fixed budget from which to allocate raises, which means that a higher raise to one employee ultimately has to be offset by a lower raise to another. In this case, employees have an incentive to influence the supervisor by lobbying for a better assessment and to induce the supervisor to give overly positive assessments.

The federal government has traditionally relied on subjective performance assessments. Supervisors rate employee performance, usually on a scale of 1 to 5. Those who score poorly do not receive a longevity pay increase (Federal Employees News Digest, 2002). The problem is that the overwhelming majority of employees in the federal government receive an acceptable rating, and most receive a rating in the top two categories. For example, in 1996, 85 percent of General Schedule employees in DoD received one of the top two ratings (author's calculations). The result is that virtually everyone receives a longevity increase, and the subjective performance assessments indicate little difference in employee performance. An empirical analysis of subjective evaluation systems in the private sector has also shown that ratings tend to be compressed and that the compres-

---

[4] This is a shortsighted strategy, however. An employer that cares about its long-term reputation in the labor market as a caring employer would eschew this strategy, and the competitive equilibrium would involve higher wages.

sion becomes more severe as the ratings become more important for setting pay (Prendergast, 1999).

As part of the move toward increased accountability, various federal organizations are using scorecards that rely on metrics of productivity. The use of scorecards based on quantitative assessments of whether a given metric or productivity was achieved enables these organizations to clearly articulate their goals, to measure their progress toward those goals, and to reward the performance when goals are achieved. However, for such approaches to be successful, the metrics must be meaningfully linked to productivity objectives, and supervisors must have an incentive to give accurate scores. Supervisors who inflate the performance scores to minimize complaints from their subordinates undermine the benefits of the accountability and metric system.

Thus, the use of subjective evaluation is subject to the problem of "grade inflation," while the use of objective metrics is subject to the problem of measurement cost associated with job complexity and the inability of managers to credibly specify all actions to be taken in all circumstances. Given these limitations, the simultaneous use of both approaches—each imperfect but still informative about performance—may be a good approach. For example, both subjective and objective evaluation methods might be used, with the weight assigned to each depending on the specific job, and with consideration of individual performance, team performance, and organization performance. The military uses test scores, education level, and other objective metrics of performance as input to the promotion process. In the lowest ranks, promotion is entirely based on these metrics. For more-senior promotions, when jobs become more complex and mistakes and poor productivity can have a larger impact on the organization, subjective supervisor ratings are used as input together with more job-related metrics of performance and skill. In the most senior ranks, subjective input from multiple sources receives considerable weight in determining who gets promoted. Another approach to addressing the problems associated with subjective evaluation is to require evaluations from multiple sources. For example, in the so-called

360 reviews, evaluations are solicited from both supervisors and subordinates.

Additional Approaches to the Provision of Incentives

The previous sections argue that pay-for-performance incentives are important but can lead to unintended consequences by inducing employees to divert their efforts toward rewarded activities and away from unrewarded activities. Unfortunately, there is no magic cure for the problem of unintended consequences. Instead, there are alternative approaches to the provision of incentives, including promotion-based incentives and career- or seniority-based incentives. These approaches appear "low-powered," because pay is tied to employee inputs, such as hours worked for blue-collar workers and time worked for salaried workers, rather than to output, such as the dollar value of sales for commissioned workers. Under certain conditions, however, these alternatives are "low-powered" in name only, because they can induce high effort levels. Furthermore, they may be preferred to direct pay-for-performance mechanisms because of monitoring costs. (The implications for the federal government are discussed in a section below.)

Promotion-Based Incentives

Promotion-based incentives rely on a pre-specified pay table where promotions to higher grades are based on performance assessed over several time periods (Lazear and Rosen, 1981). Like the pay tables of other public organizations, such as the military, the civil service's pay table specifies an employee's pay based on grade and years of service. Promotion-based systems are often viewed as egalitarian, because the table is publicly available and known to all, and pay, or "step," increases within a given grade are virtually automatic and occur as employees gain more years of service. Promotions to higher grades occur periodically in recognition of greater skill, experience, effort, and performance. Promotion usually means a job change as well as a pay change, and only occurs if a job opening is available in the higher grade. The promotion system is therefore not equitable in terms of its outcomes—after all, individuals receive different levels of pay after the promotion occurs, but individuals who are eligible for promotion have equal opportunities to achieve the promotion to a known and fixed level of higher pay.

For some employees, such as managers, promotion is the key source of pay growth. Over the course of a career, an employee "climbs" promotion ladders and is presumably motivated to perform well to the extent that promotions to higher grades are based on good performance, and good performance requires effort. Such promotion ladders are quite common in the public sector. While the federal government does hire laterally, it generally gives preference to current employees when filling most mid-grade and senior positions. Lateral hiring is more frequent in private organizations, as are career ladders (Baker, Gibbs, and Holmstrom, 1994).

Unlike the pay in explicit pay-for-performance methods, pay in promotion-based systems is not set in proportion to performance, since the pay table is fixed in advance. As an incentive scheme, the promotion process involves choosing, the objective being to choose those workers who have the best performance among those eligible for promotion in the next lower grade. In theory, those who perform better, all else being equal, are promoted faster on average and thus the expected pay over the course of their career is higher. The financial incentive to supply effort is affected by the probability of promotion and the financial return to promotion, given a promotion occurs. An increase in the return induces more effort, all else being equal. Increases in the probability of promotion (and therefore the expected return) raise effort up to a point. Beyond that point, the probability is so high that additional effort has little effect. In the extreme case, where the probability equals one and the return is received with certainty, there is no effort incentive.

Simulation modeling that was done for the Army illustrates these concepts.[5] Table 11.2 shows the estimated simulated effect of alternative personnel and pay policies on Army enlisted personnel outcomes, where the rows are the outcome variables and the columns reflect different policies. The first column is the steady-state base case under the Army's status quo policies; the second column shows the policy of reducing the probability of promotion to the top three pay grades of the enlisted pay table by 20 percent. (The other columns are discussed later.) Reducing the probability of promotion to the top ranks reduces the retention rate among those at years of service (YOS) 4 from .42 to .40 relative to the base case but raises retention among mid-career personnel (those at YOS 12). The overall productivity of

Table 11.2
Simulated Estimates of Effects of Pay and Promotion Policy Changes on Army Enlisted Personnel Outcomes

Outcome	Base Case (1)	Reduced Promotion Rates to E-7 to E-9[a] (2)	10% Across-the-Board Pay Raise[b] (3)	Skewed Pay Raise[c] (4)
Retention rate at:				
YOS 4	0.42	0.40	0.51	0.49
YOS 8	0.69	0.66	0.78	0.79
YOS 12	0.87	0.88	0.92	0.90
Mean performance of:				
Force[d]	100	92	124	153
Rank E-7	135	125	151	210
Force cost (billions $)[e]	12.6	12.1	15.3	15.3

SOURCE: Asch and Warner, 2001.
[a]This case reduces the annual promotion opportunity to ranks E-7, E-8, and E-9 by 20%.
[b]This means the same percentage pay increase (10% in this case) in all ranks and years of service.
[c]This means higher raises as rank increases, with force cost held constant and equal to the cost of the across-the-board pay raise.
[d]Since performance is measured in arbitrary units in the simulation model, whole force mean performance is normalized to 100.
[e]Force cost equals the annual cost of basic pay and the retirement accrual charge for the entire Army enlisted force.

[5] The modeling and simulation methodology, as well as the results, are discussed in Asch and Warner, 1994, 2001.

the force, measured by a performance index, falls from a baseline of 100 to 92, and effort among those in pay grade 7 falls from 135 to 125. Thus, reducing promotion tempo in the upper grades has a negative effect on performance.

Unfortunately, there is no comparable modeling capability for simulating the civil service retention, cost, and performance responses resulting from changes in promotion and pay in the civil service. However, available information on promotion speed across occupational areas in DoD suggests that despite the fixed General Schedule pay table, promotion speed varies considerably across these areas, as shown in Figure 11.1. Furthermore, having an outstanding supervisor performance rating increases the conditional hazard of first pro-

Figure 11.1
Cumulative Probability of Achieving First Promotion by Occupational Area, FY 1988 Cohort

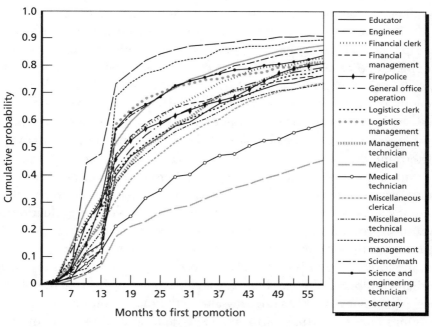

SOURCE: Asch, 2001.

RAND *MG256-11.1*

motion by 31 percent and of second promotion by 37 percent (Asch, 2001). However, because of compression of pay between grades in the pay table, an outstanding rating only increases real pay by 3 percent, all else being equal.

Promotion-based systems are equally as powerful as explicit pay-for-performance systems in terms of the incentives for performance they provide, if employees have the same attitudes toward earnings variability (Lazear and Rosen, 1981). Promotion-based systems only appear to be "low-powered" in terms of incentives because they have a fixed pay table, but the incentives for performance operate through the contest for promotion. However, if the contest is based not on performance but on favoritism or other factors unrelated to performance, then the incentive effect of the promotion system is diluted. If employees are averse to earnings variability, the effectiveness of promotion systems in providing incentives relative to explicit systems depends on the source of the earnings variability, from sources common to all employees or to individual-specific components such as ability.

Promotion systems are quite common in both the public and the private sector, in part because they often address some of the problems posed by explicit pay-for-performance methods (see earlier discussion). First, measurement costs are often much lower. What is required in a promotion system is that the supervisor determine who has the best performance, not the exact level of performance of each employee. It may be considerably easier to determine ranking than to determine the precise level of performance. Thus, when performance is multidimensional and some of the dimensions are ill defined, the most efficient approach to providing incentives is likely to involve the use of supervisor rankings, often together with subjective evaluations. Second, promotion systems can reduce the variability of employee earnings caused by random external factors if those factors common to all workers are important relative to those factors specific to individual employees. For example, if a weak economy affects all employees' performance in the same way and is the major component of the random factor affecting performance, a ranking of those employees' performance nets out the adverse effects on performance because all employees faced the same weak economy.

Third, the common pay table that forms the foundation of the promotion system helps ensure the transparency and credibility of the compensation system. Since the pay table is common knowledge, the employer cannot secretly renege and not pay the full amount to workers who hold various job positions and, similarly, employees cannot falsely claim that the employer reneged on its payments. The issue of reneging is a potential drawback of explicit pay-for-performance systems. It is also a criticism of "pay banding" systems, since managers in some pay banding schemes have discretion in varying pay within the band and, in the absence of oversight, can engage in favoritism and other types of misbehavior (Prendergast and Topel, 1996). Ensuring credibility of the pay banding system requires effective oversight within the organization as well as by external authorities.

For promotions systems to provide meaningful performance incentives, it is imperative that the organization maintain the integrity of the promotion system. Workers have an incentive to try to influence the outcome of promotion "contests" by either lobbying or otherwise influencing the supervisor who makes the promotion decision or by sabotaging (or spreading incorrect rumors about the performance of) competitors. In other words, a potential downfall of promotion systems is that employees have an incentive to engage in "industrial politics" and "influence activities" that increase their financial return but not their performance on the job. In fact, such activities may divert their attention and time from productive work and reduce their performance. The greater the expected return from promotion, the greater the incentive to engage in these activities. The U.S. military solves the problem of influence activities among midgrade promotions by relying on anonymous national selection boards. The problem of sabotage is ameliorated because service members compete against "the field," which is made up of all eligible members, who remain anonymous for the most part and are scattered throughout the world.

But in organizations where supervisors at the local work site make the promotion decisions, and those who make up an employee's group of competitors are usually known to him or her and consist of individuals working at the same site, the problems of influence and sabotage activities are more likely. If promotion is based on subjective performance assessments, supervisors can bias their assessments toward some individuals. Furthermore, supervisors may use promotion to solve personnel problems unrelated to promotion. For example, supervisors have been known to recommend employees for promotion because they were difficult to work with, and promotion was a way to remove them without having to fire them. Such behavior compromises the integrity of the system and undermines employee confidence about its fairness and accuracy.

An important policy implication of the economics literature regarding the structure of compensation in organizations such as the civil service and the military, where promotion-based incentives are used, is that the pay structure must be "skewed," with the differences in pay across grades rising with grade level (Rosen, 1982). For example, the difference in pay between the top two grades should be larger than the difference in pay between the two grades just below them. There are three reasons for this structure.

First, as individuals climb the promotion ladder, they have fewer remaining promotions left in their career, and their expected financial incentive to supply effort will therefore fall. Thus, the pay gain associated with each successive promotion must rise to maintain the same expected financial incentive.

Second, the probability of promotion declines as one moves up the ranks, thereby reducing the expected return to promotion. For example, the average promotion rate of DoD civil service employees in professional occupations in 1996 in grades General Schedule 6–7 was 80 percent, while the average rate for those in grades General Schedule 12 was 6 percent (see Table 11.3). Again, the pay gain associated with promotion must rise at higher grades to offset the negative effect on effort of lower promotion probabilities at those grades.

Third, higher-ranked jobs usually involve greater responsibility, so poorer performance at these jobs can have wider-ranging effects. Put differently, the value of filling a given position with a high-ability employee is greater in the higher-ranked positions. Thus, the pay gain associated with each promotion must increase to induce the most-

Table 11.3
Mean Annual Promotion Rates by Grade and PATCO Occupational Categories, General Schedule Full-Time Employees in the DoD Civil Service, 1996

PATCO	GS 1–5	GS 6–7	GS 8–9	GS 10–11	GS 12	GS 13	GS 14
Professional	N/A	0.80	0.29	0.17	0.06	0.03	0.04
Administrative	0.60	0.40	0.19	0.10	0.06	0.03	0.04
Technical	0.14	0.13	0.13	0.07	0.01	N/A	N/A
Clerical	0.15	0.10	0.08	N/A	N/A	N/A	N/A
White collar	0.19	0.08	0.18	0.06	N/A	N/A	N/A

SOURCE: Author's calculations.
NOTE: N/A means not applicable.

talented workers to stay in the organization and to seek advancement to the senior ranks, where their ability is valued most.

Table 11.2, shown earlier, illustrates the estimated effects on performance of skewed pay raises using a simulation model of the Army enlisted force that was built as part of a RAND Corporation project (Asch and Warner, 1994, 2001). Column 3 of Table 11.2 shows the effects of an across-the-board pay raise where every member receives the same percentage increase in pay, regardless of pay grade or year of service. Column 4 shows the effects of giving incrementally higher percentage pay increases to those in increasingly higher ranks—i.e., a skewed pay raise. The specific percentage pay increases were chosen to yield the same force cost as the across-the-board pay raise, $15.3 billion, and the same general retention profile. The skewed pay raise results in substantially greater effort or performance, raising the index of performance from 100 to 153 for the entire force and from 135 to 210 for those in pay grade E-7. For the same cost and retention, the across-the-board pay raise results in only an increase of the performance index to 124 for the entire force and 151 for E-7s. Clearly, the skewed pay approach is more efficient, raising performance for the same cost and retention outcomes. Beginning in 2000, military personnel began receiving both across-the-board pay raises as well as pay raises targeted to members at specific pay grades and experience levels. The targeted raises, especially for officers, were designed to increase the financial incentives associated with promotions, and hence performance, in the military, and importantly, the skewedness of the pay table, by ensuring that the pay gap between the top grades is greater than the pay gap between the bottom grades (9th Quadrennial Review of Military Compensation).

The federal government's pay structure is not skewed relative to that of the private sector for similarly skilled workers (Gibbs, 2001; Borjas, 2002; Katz and Krueger, 1991), implying that the government's promotion ladders do not provide as much financial incentive for performance as those in the private sector do. On the other hand, the degree to which the lack of skewedness has hurt retention and recruiting is unclear, as discussed at the beginning of this chapter. Furthermore, one important factor that diminishes the desired amount of skewedness in the federal sector is cooperation among employees. Reduced financial incentives associated with promotion in the upper grades can help engender a work environment or culture of public service. In contrast, a highly skewed pay structure with large financial incentives in the upper grades can also engender backbiting and sabotage behavior (Lazear, 1989).

Seniority-Based Incentives

Obviously, promotion-based incentives only make sense in hierarchical organizations where promotions are an important part of an employee's overall career path. But even in hierarchies, some occupational areas, such as highly technical workforces, have "flat" careers where employees enter at a high pay grade, reflecting their advanced education, advance slowly, and then spend most of their long career in just two or three grades. DoD has civilian occupations where this is true (Asch, 2001). Organizations that adopt a pay band structure also give the appearance of offering flat careers, because employees can spend relatively long periods of their career within just one or two bands. A key question is, How can these employees be motivated to supply effort in the absence of promotion-based incentives or explicit pay-for-performance incentives? This subsection discusses seniority-based incentive approaches.

Seniority-based incentives recognize that employees often stay with the same employer for long periods. In 1996, the median years of service among defense civil service workers was 13 years for General Schedule employees, 14 for Wage Grade employees, and 21 for employees covered by other civil service pay plans (author's calculations). When employees stay with one organization for much of their career, employers can motivate high performance by offering a reward later in the employee's career that is contingent on current levels of effort. One such approach is promotion-based incentives, which were described in the previous section.

Seniority-Based with a Pay Band. Another approach that seems well suited for careers within a narrow set of pay bands or other types of careers in the absence of promotion-based incentives is to vary pay within the band in such a way that employees are initially underpaid *relative to their productive worth* during the initial phase of their career. Later, when they are more senior, they are overpaid relative to their worth if they demonstrate high performance in the initial phase. In a real way, there is a "speed bump," or control point, within the pay band, beyond which an individual does not advance without adequate performance. The financial incentive for performance is based on the "carrot-and-stick" approach, with the promise of future overpayment providing a financial incentive to the more junior employees within the band. Over the course of a career in the band, the underpayment and overpayment cancel each other out, and expected pay equals the discounted value of productive worth. Those who fail to meet the performance standards when they are junior employees do not receive the promised higher future overpayment, and may even be dismissed. Thus, pay within the pay band grows faster than productivity, but only high-performing junior employees receive the overpayment when they become more senior employees.[6]

---

[6] One problem with this incentive scheme is that employees have no incentive to separate or retire when they are senior employees, because they are being paid more than their productive worth. Lazear (1979, 1983) discusses how mandatory retirement and nonactuarially fair pensions are important mechanisms to induce employees to retire involuntarily (as in the case of mandatory retirement) or voluntarily (as in the case of nonactuarially fair pensions).

An advantage of this approach is that performance can be assessed periodically, thereby saving measurement costs, given that employees are long-term employees.

Available evidence suggests that private sector organizations do offer such career paths. For example, using one firm's data on the earnings histories of office workers, sales employees, and managers, Kotlikoff and Gokhale (1992) found that productivity exceeded compensation while workers were young and fell below total compensation when they were older. Specifically, at age 35, productivity for male managers exceeded compensation by more than a factor of two, while compensation was over twice as high as productivity by age 57. Lazear and Moore (1984), using national data on self-employed individuals and those employed by a firm, found that pay profiles over the careers of these people were flatter for the self-employed than for the employed. This makes sense, because self-employed people have no incentive to shirk and do not require an upward sloping pay profile over their careers to motivate performance. Other evidence consistent with this approach includes that of Medoff and Abraham (1980) and Spitz (1991).

Career Concerns. Another approach recognizes that employees have career concerns and care how their performance in their current job influences their ability to get a future job in the internal or external market. If good performance on the current job leads to better future job offers from the external market or from other work groups in the internal market, employees have an incentive to work hard, even in the absence of explicit pay-for-performance contracts and even if they do not end up eventually changing jobs (Fama, 1980).[7]

---

[7] As discussed in Holmstrom, 1982, a problem with using career concerns as part of an incentive mechanism is that junior employees will work too hard (when the external market is still making judgments about the performance of workers and their entire career spans before them) and senior employees will work too little (because the market has already made its judgment and these workers have little of their career left before retirement). Gibbons and Murphy (1992) show that the optimal incentive scheme over workers' careers will involve a heavier reliance on career concerns and nonexplicit pay-for-performance schemes for junior and mid-career workers, but a weaker reliance on career concerns for senior workers. In fact, the optimal scheme for senior workers will rely more heavily on explicit pay-for-performance

The Economic Complexities of Incentive Reforms   337

Tirole (1994) discusses the importance of career concerns as a method of providing incentives in the public sector and notes that civil service personnel, especially political appointees, are often more concerned about the effect of their current performance on future promotions and on job prospects in both the government and the private sector. These career concerns provide a way to motivate performance when direct pay-for-performance systems are infeasible, and they are particularly amenable to the use of pay bands because pay bands do not rely on promotion to provide explicit pay-for-performance incentives. Drawing from earlier work by Holmstrom (1982), Tirole lists the four conditions necessary for career concerns in government to be an effective method of motivating high performance: (1) performance on any given task must be visible; (2) current performance must provide information about productivity in future tasks; (3) individuals must care about future outcomes (i.e., they must not discount future outcomes too much); and (4) both the external and the internal market must be able to learn about individual performance at a fairly low cost.

These conditions make clear that the employee's reputation, for good or poor performance, plays an important role in facilitating career concerns as a strong incentive for performance. Employees who gain a reputation for poor performance reduce their chances of getting a good job in the future. The military's use of the "dishonorable discharge" conveys information to future employers that the person's performance while in service was substandard. Consequently, members know that if they care about their post-service employment opportunities, they must perform at a level that ensures an honorable discharge. By the same token, organizations can earn a bad reputation for reneging on pay or treating employees poorly, thereby hurting their ability to hire high-performing workers in the future. If hiring high-quality employees is important, the organization has an incentive to refrain from such behavior.

---

incentive schemes, because career concerns are less relevant when there is little concern about external job opportunities.

Incentives to Attract and Retain Talent

The most efficient approach for achieving a high level of performance may involve structuring a pay system or using personnel policies to induce talented individuals to self-select or sort into the organization—seek employment and stay in the organization—rather than hiring a workforce of average quality and then devising a pay system that makes that workforce perform better.

There are a few approaches discussed in the economics literature to induce the self-selection of talented workers. One approach, discussed earlier, is to directly tie pay to performance. Talented workers are attracted to pay-for-performance systems because they can expect higher than average earnings. Another approach is to use apprenticeship or internship programs (Guasch and Weiss, 1981; Lazear, 1986). During the apprenticeship program, pay is set far below the apprentice's productive worth in order to discourage poorly qualified applicants. In the post-apprenticeship career, pay is set high enough to off-set the low pay earned in the apprenticeship period for highly qualified applicants. The civil service has a career intern program that serves this role. It could be expanded as a way to expand the screening of qualified recruits.

Another approach is for the organization to set pay higher than the average external alternatives of employees, thereby increasing the size and average quality of the applicant pool from which it can draw (Weiss, 1980), as well as the average quality of the personnel it retains. Arguably this has been the approach used by the federal civil service since the mid-1970s. As noted earlier, Borjas (2002) found that the real earnings of male full-time, full-year workers in the federal government exceeded the earnings of males with similar human capital characteristics in the private sector, though the earnings gap had declined. For females, Borjas found that the earnings gap was positive and relatively constant through 2000. Various studies have also examined the distribution of earnings in the federal and private sector. Borjas (2002), Gibbs (2001), and Katz and Krueger (1991) all argue that the compressed structure of earnings among those in the federal civil service relative to those in the private sector will likely hurt the federal sector's ability to recruit and retain highly talented personnel in the future.

Provision of Incentives in the Federal Government

Many federal organizations, including the DHS and DoD, are devising metrics, developing pay systems, and working toward introducing incentives for performance that are tied to the missions of their organizations. Though agencies are progressing in different ways in the early stages of these efforts, the fact that these efforts are occurring is a historic change. In the case of the DHS, the 15-grade General Schedule system is being converted to a pay band system with 10 to 15 pay clusters, based on occupation, such as management or science, with four pay bands for each cluster ranging from entry level to supervisor (General Accounting Office, 2004). DoD's new National Security Personnel System is likely to be similar. Pay within the bands and promotion across bands will be based on performance. But how pay will be connected to performance and the structure of incentives are being worked out. The discussion in this chapter can provide some guidance, and the following key points should be highlighted.

First, pay-for-performance has a number of pitfalls associated with it, all having to do with the high cost of directly measuring output and the resulting problem of the unintended consequences that can occur if pay is based on partial metrics of output. These pitfalls suggest that the amount of money at risk and directly dependent on performance at a point in time for a given employee should be relatively small. But while smaller financial rewards imply weak incentives, even weak incentives can be meaningful, especially if they are linked to important strategic goals of the organization. For example, information on military recruiters suggests that their productivity is responsive to rewards such as public recognition, even though the monetary value of the rewards is trivial. Thus, in the context of pay banding, performance-based pay is likely to be relatively small.

Second, other approaches can provide stronger incentives, though they will be less direct than explicit performance-based pay.

Furthermore, these incentive mechanisms can be implemented in conjunction with pay banding and can address a few but not all of the pitfalls of explicit pay-for-performance systems.

To illustrate and summarize these other approaches, Table 11.4 provides three examples of occupational pay clusters, the types of careers individuals typically have in those occupations, the incentive mechanisms that would likely be most dominant, and the pay structure that would be necessary for the provision of incentives. It is assumed that all groups are part of a pay banding system.

The first example is a group of managers, whose careers involve an upward climb of promotions. For them, the optimal pay structure within and across the four pay bands should be skewed, as discussed in an earlier section of this chapter. An advantage of a promotion-based system is that relative performance might be easier to measure than absolute performance. The second example is a group of scientists and engineers, who typically have horizontal careers that involve little promotion but the attainment of increasingly greater technical skills. For this group, incentives can be provided by a seniority-based system where pay is less than productivity until the employee hits the "speed bump," at which point pay exceeds productivity. Pay rises faster than productivity within the pay band and the speed bump

Table 11.4
Examples of Pay-Band Occupational Clusters, Incentive Mechanisms, and Pay Structure

Pay-Band Occupational Cluster	Type of Career	Incentive Mechanisms	Pay Structure
Managers	Upwardly mobile career	Promotion-based	Skewed pay structure within and across pay bands
Scientists and engineers	Horizontal career	Seniority-based	Pay within band rises faster than productivity
Political appointees, entry-level attorneys	Short-term "career"	Career concerns	Pay high enough to attract and retain talent

prevents low performers from earning the high pay. The third example is a group of political appointees and entry-level attorneys. These people enter the civil service either to serve the public or to gain civil service experience that is valuable in the private sector. Their incentive to perform is based on their focus on their external job opportunities—that is, they do not see the civil service as their career, and their motivation for working hard is their concern for how their current performance will affect their future private sector opportunities. Here the incentive approach is to set pay high enough to attract and retain talent, as discussed earlier.

The examples in Table 11.4 and, more broadly, the discussion in this chapter, suggest that civil service reform should permit flexibility to tailor incentives to specific circumstances. The circumstances in the table pertain to the occupational cluster, but as the discussion in this chapter makes clear, the circumstances could be defined by factors that influence the cost of measurement, the missions, or the objectives. Thus, whether the new system is pay band or another approach, a one-size-fits-all system is likely to be problematic if it is rigidly applied, because occupations have different careers, work environments differ, and missions differ.

It is important to recognize that incentive systems are not mutually exclusive. Evidence from the private sector indicates that when mechanisms are used together, productivity increases more than when individual mechanisms are used alone. Lambert, Larcker, and Weigelt (1993) compiled data from 303 large, publicly traded manufacturing and service firms in order to analyze which incentive model (promotion contests, pay-for-performance, and so forth) seemed to characterize these organizations. They concluded that their "results suggest that organizational incentives are most appropriately characterized by a combination of these models, rather than being completely described by a single theoretical description" (p. 438).

The third key point is that the discussion provides guidance on what questions to ask of future evaluations of current reform efforts. The types of questions future studies should ask about the move by the DHS and other agencies to improve incentives and implement pay-for-performance include the following:

- Did performance improve more in organizations with a simply defined output?
- Did performance improve more in organizations with more clearly defined missions?
- Did performance improve more in organizations with smaller teams?
- Were organizations able to attract and retain talent in key positions?
- Did performance improve more in organizations with fewer competing objectives?

In addition to these types of questions, future evaluations should ask questions about the implementation of the reform (including employee training) and about morale and the credibility of the reform. Without proper implementation, even a good incentive system may fail if administrators and employees do not understand how the new system works. Furthermore, without trust that the new reform will recognize high and low performers and reward them appropriately, employees are unlikely to be motivated by any incentive mechanism. Thus, evaluations of current reform efforts should provide assessments of employee attitudes toward the changes.

CHAPTER TWELVE

Measuring Performance

Jacob Alex Klerman

Introduction

Like several earlier reviews of government performance, the Volcker Commission endorses "new personnel management principles that ensure much higher levels of government performance" (see Chapter 2, p. 47). A key component is the aligning of personnel management with performance. That is, more-effective workers should be paid more and promoted faster; ineffective workers should be dismissed.

After a brief overview of performance management and the role of measurement, this chapter examines four issues: (1) net versus gross performance, (2) the precision of measurement, (3) which outcomes to reward, and (4) subversion of measurement. As we will see, the issues are interrelated. The chapter concludes with an iterative scheme for performance measurement.

The observations presented here primarily concern management of personnel in organizations in which dozens, hundreds, or thousands of line workers do relatively similar tasks—both across workers and from day to day. Such organizations and their personnel include schools and their teachers, police departments and their officers, courts and their judges, tax collectors and their auditors, the Social Security Administration and its disability examiners, armies and their soldiers, and (the organizations that I know best) welfare departments and their eligibility workers and employment caseworkers. The large numbers of individuals performing similar tasks make it possible to apply insights from statistics to the dual challenges of personnel management and performance measurement.

Roles and Goals

Before turning to technical issues of performance measurement, we should consider two logically prior issues: (1) the various ways that better measurement might lead to improved performance, and (2) the challenge of stating specific goals for public programs.

Measures of performance at the individual level might affect performance at the organizational level in three ways, each with a corresponding management strategy:

- *Remediation.* A popular view posits that "best practices" exist, and if government workers only knew about them they would follow them. Poor performers are benevolent, but ignorant. In this view, performance measurement serves two purposes. First, it can help identify both best practices and effective workers who implement (and perhaps implicitly define) them. Second, performance measurement can be used to identify worst practices and poorly performing workers, who can then receive remediation, such as additional training and mentoring. The pure version of this view posits that workers want to do the right thing, and therefore information and training—without any additional incentives—will suffice to improve performance.
- *Selection.* In another view, individual performance is viewed as more-or-less immutable. Some people are inherently better performers, and others are inherently worse. Performance measurement can be used to select the good workers, who are then kept or even promoted, and the bad workers, who are then terminated. This view recommends steps to make it easier for government managers to fire employees.
- *Incentives.* A third view posits that workers' performance is changeable, but higher performance is costly for them—more hours at work, more effort while at work (e.g., shorter breaks), more focus of effort on tasks directly related to the stated performance goals (see Milgrom and Roberts, 1992, Chaps. 6 and 7). Workers will perform better only if they are compensated in some way for their additional effort. That additional compensa-

tion could take several forms (see Asch, Chapter 11 in this volume). The simplest form of additional compensation is additional pay. In the extreme, this view leads to piece rates, a fixed payment for each unit of output. Another variant is a cash bonus for good performance. In addition to pay, other incentives are common and sometimes surprisingly effective: recognition—peer pressure for better performance, or small tokens (e.g., movie tickets). Less-direct incentives, such as faster promotion to positions of higher pay, can be based on performance measures and also yield better performance. Negative direct incentives are also used—slower promotion or dismissal.

We see examples of all three uses of measurement in public management, and of course they are not exclusive. Termination may be useful both as a device to select out recalcitrant workers and as a negative incentive for responsive workers. Even in the presence of incentives, identification of best practices and remediation may be a useful strategy for helping poorly performing workers focus additional effort toward better performance.

These three uses have something in common: They presuppose an operationally useful definition of *performance*. We can distinguish here various levels of performance: inputs (processes, what an agency does), outputs (its immediate products), and social benefits and costs (what happens as the result of citizens and clients doing that). Agreeing upon a simple set of performance measures is a chronic difficulty in public programs. Because public programs are established through a political process, they usually emerge as compromises, embodying multiple, often competing goals. And after a program is established, multiple stakeholders—the executive, the legislature, the bureaucracy, interest groups—continue to disagree about both broad program goals and operationally useful measures of performance toward those goals (e.g., Wilson, 1991, Chaps. 6 and 13). Some observers of government provision argue that government is specifically assigned the tasks for which goals are amorphous or difficult to measure (Wilson, 1991; Prendergast, 2003). The net result: Clear and accepted measures of performance upon which to find best practice (or worst), identify superb or atrocious workers, or build a system of incentives are not always available.

Nevertheless, experience shows that defining a clear operational goal is crucial for implementing performance-based management systems. In several leading examples of performance measurement and management in government, the crucial element was an explicit definition of performance. Sometimes this definition of a clear goal appears in the authorizing statute. As, for example,

- The ultimate goal of the federal Food Stamp Program is to improve the nutrition of the nation's poorest families. By contrast, the program's primary operational goal is defined in terms of proper paperwork: Is there proper documentation that benefits that were granted were deserved? This operational goal follows from the federal nature of the program: The federal government pays all benefits, and states determine eligibility. In the absence of such a paperwork definition, states have an incentive to provide benefits to the ineligible or to provide too many benefits to the eligible (see Rosenbaum and Super, 2001). Therefore, the federal government carefully tracks error rates, assessing penalties when it appears that states are not following the regulations in dispersing federal funds. High error rates can lead to federal penalties. This operational goal focuses on false positives, i.e., those who are getting benefits but should not. There is no penalty for false negatives, i.e., those who should be getting benefits but are not. The operational goal appears to focus the efforts of the workers (i.e., they make fewer errors). Whether those efforts address the ultimate goal (i.e., better nutrition) is less clear.
- The federal job training programs (from the 1980s, the Job Training Partnership Act/JTPA; from the 1990s, the Workforce Investment Act/WIA) state as their goal the provision of employment and training opportunities to "those who can benefit from, and are most in need of, such opportunities." The U.S. Department of Labor has translated this ultimate goal into an operational goal: employment and earnings shortly after the

completion of training (see Heckman, Heinrich, and Smith, 2002; Courty and Marschke, 1996). High performance on this measure can bring the training organization fiscal bonuses.

- Federal education funding—the 2001 reauthorization of the Elementary and Secondary Education Act/"No Child Left Behind Act of 2001" (NCLB)—states its goal as "to ensure that all children have a fair, equal, and significant opportunity to obtain a high-quality education and reach, at a minimum, proficiency on challenging state academic achievement standard and state academic assessments." In practice, implementing agencies have taken as their operational goal test scores in reading and mathematics (Hamilton, Stecher, and Klein, 2002).

- Traditionally, the goal of welfare policy has been to provide resources for the purchase of food, shelter, and clothing for the nation's poorest children and their families. Partially as a consequence of this amorphous goal, little performance-based management has been done in welfare programs. In 1996, though, federal welfare reform (the Personal Responsibility and Work Opportunities Reconciliation Act of 1996, replacing the Aid to Families with Dependent Children/AFDC program with the Temporary Assistance to Needy Families/TANF program) established an operational goal: the participation of welfare recipients in welfare-to-work activities. Furthermore, net declines in the welfare caseload were counted toward the participation rate, so that caseload decline became an implicit operational goal.

These are examples of the most mature implementations of performance-based management. The definition of an explicit operational goal appears to have been crucial to implementation. But we must go beyond the toting up of various measures of operational goals if we want true measures of the performance of individuals, offices, and programs. How might we assess net performance, or value added?

Net Performance

As we move from operational goals to measures of performance, we need to measure net performance, or value added; i.e., we want to assess performance *relative to what it would have been in the absence of the program*. For an individual worker, the corresponding concept is performance after his or her actions versus performance after the actions of some other worker. In the literature on program evaluation, this concept is sometimes referred to as the *impact* or the *net causal effect*, i.e., measuring performance, holding all else equal.

To understand the concept, consider the following: What would outcomes be if we assigned a given set of clients (e.g., students, trainees) all to Worker A (e.g., teacher, job counselor)? Alternatively, what would outcomes be if we assigned them all to Worker B? The better worker (i.e., the one who should be retained and compensated more) is the one who would achieve better outcomes with this common pool of clients.

It is not possible to observe what outcomes would have been if the same clients were assigned alternatively to Worker A and to Worker B. In practice, each worker has his or her own cases. Thus, comparisons of actual performance are comparisons of gross performance. Measures reflect a combination of (1) the effect of the worker (who might be better or worse, who might have provided more or less effort), (2) the effect of case mix and other factors that affect operational goals, and (3) chance. But, for the three uses of performance measurement (identifying best practices, selecting better workers, inducing more effort from a given set of workers), we want to isolate the first effect.

If most of the variation in observed gross output is due not to case-mix heterogeneity of chance, but instead to differences in worker effectiveness, the distinction between observed gross performance and net performance is not important. However, the available evidence suggests that much of the variation in gross performance is due to case mix and chance. For example, in public schools, much of the variation in students' test scores is due not to differences in teachers' performance or school inputs, but to differences in student background (Coleman et al., 1966). Much of the variation in job training outcomes is due to variation in the ex ante employability of trainees, not the quality of the training program. Much of the variation in the outcomes of welfare-to-work programs is due to variation in case mix and local economic conditions and not to how diligent the welfare caseworkers happen to be (Hamilton, 2002). Furthermore, in each of these examples, the number of cases is sufficiently small that simple "chance" (i.e., random variation) is also a major determinant of measured relative performance over short periods of time (perhaps several years).

How Gross Performance Measures Can Go Wrong

Misidentify best practices. Using gross performance measures identifies "best practices" that are simply those adopted by (or perhaps working with) the best clients (who would have performed well even in the absence of the program).

Misidentify best workers. Using gross performance measures identifies "best workers" who are simply those lucky enough to be working with the best clients.

Incentives to migrate. Using gross performance measures gives workers an incentive to move to sites with better clients.

Incentives to choose clients. Using gross performance measures gives sites an incentive to provide services only to better clients (the phenomenon of "cream skimming").

When heterogeneity is important, using gross performance measures will have undesired effects. First, it will result in misidentification of best practices (we will identify those practices that are applied to the best clients rather than those that have the largest net impact on a given set of clients).

Second, using gross performance measures will cause misidentification of the best workers (that is, we will identify those who happen to work with easy cases rather than those who might have the largest net impact on a given case). If we are using performance measurement for remediation, we will tend to choose the wrong workers as mentors and the wrong workers to be remediated. If we are using performance measures for selection, we will terminate the wrong workers. Finally, if we are using performance measures to provide incentives, we will reward the wrong workers and thus provide incentives for the wrong behavior (see below).

Third, using gross measures gives workers incentives to migrate to locations with ex ante better clients and to select better clients in any given location. In the case of schools and many other programs, such incentives often exacerbate the regressive nature of the programs. Insofar as better teachers (e.g., more senior teachers) can choose where to work, they often have incentives to work in better neighborhoods even in the absence of performance management (the schools are safer, the students are more like the teachers, parents are more supportive, the commute is shorter). Making management decisions based on gross performance gives teachers an even greater incentive to move schools in better neighborhoods.

Fourth, when a governmental organization has control over whether to serve cases at all, the problem is even more pernicious. In that context, using gross outcomes rather than net outcomes gives the governmental organization an incentive (perhaps a further incentive) to select for service those with the best prospects in the absence of the program, i.e., to practice what is called "cream skimming." Magnet schools will tend to select the best students rather than the students they can help the most. Training programs may train (or even advertise to) the most employable applicants rather than those whose income will be most increased by the training. Hospitals may choose to treat only the healthiest patients (Dranove et al., 2003).

Each of these considerations suggests that we want to make performance management decisions based on measures of net performance. Unfortunately, determining net causal effect is a fundamental problem of modern econometrics and a classic "hard problem" (see Angrist and Krueger, 1999; Hotz, Klerman, and Willis, 1997). The program evaluation literature suggests five successively less attractive approaches to estimating causal effects: random assignment, value added, regression adjustment, fixed effects, and cohort comparisons, or benchmarking. Here we consider each in turn.

Approaches to Estimating Net/Causal Effects

Random assignment. Remove discretion or systematic processes that assign cases to workers (or allow workers to select cases). Instead, use some type of approximately random assignment rule. Measure net effect as the difference across workers within the same assignment pool.

Value added. Measure performance for a given client before and after the governmental organization's intervention. Measure net effect as the pre-intervention/post-intervention difference.

Regression adjustment. Use some statistical method (often linear regression or its generalizations) to "handicap" performance on the basis of client pre-intervention outcomes. Measure net effect after handicapping.

Cohort comparisons. Measure performance for a cohort relative to that of some earlier cohort. Measure net effect as the change in output across cohorts.

Random Assignment. Random assignment is the "gold standard" in program evaluation and is equally attractive for performance management. When clients can be assigned randomly to workers, doing so assures that the cases assigned to each worker are nearly identical. Any remaining differences are due either to chance (which will average out over time, as discussed below) or to variations in performance across workers.

Sometimes random assignment is relatively easy to implement. In a social service system (for example, a welfare office), case assignment is handled by a clerk and proceeds independent of the characteristics of the case. In some systems, cases are assigned sequentially to each worker. In other systems, cases are assigned to the worker with the fewest currently active cases. In a school, students can be assigned at random to classes.

Assuming a large number of cases per worker (e.g., students per teacher, welfare recipients per caseworker), assigning cases independent of case characteristics will yield approximately equivalent case mixes across workers. Comparisons across workers will therefore estimate the relative effect of a particular worker versus that of other workers at risk for the same cases, i.e., the net effect. By the luck of the draw, some workers will draw easy cases, while others will draw hard cases. Such variation, however, will be random, and over (enough) time, it will average out.

The random assignment approach also controls for period effects. Welfare-to-work programs have better gross (and also net) effects when the economy is good. It is easier to find jobs for clients. Pay based on gross performance punishes caseworkers for being employed when the external economy is bad.

Finally, this approach exploits the assumed replicated nature of the organization—a large number of employees doing the same task. Net performance is determined by comparing output for one worker with the average for other workers doing the same task (on a nearly identical caseload). An example would be a large welfare office with several dozen caseworkers all processing the same type of cases. The larger the number of workers doing the same task, the better we can make comparisons. Having one particularly good or bad worker in the office does not radically change the evaluation of the performance of a given worker.

When the number of workers drawing cases from the common pool is smaller, this approach is less attractive. The approach would not work at all in a small elementary school with only one class per grade (the common assignment pool); it would work only poorly in a moderate-sized elementary school with perhaps two or three teachers per grade. When the number of other teachers/workers is small, one teacher/worker is being compared against a small number of other workers (in the extreme, one other worker), so that having a good co-worker makes one look bad. Sabotage of colleagues' work can make one look better.

Although random assignment has significant advantages, the conditions under which it works are limited. Random assignment will estimate net effects only for those drawing from the same case assignment pool. If variation across sites is large, randomization is not useful for comparing performance across offices, each with its own local service area. Thus, randomly assigning students to teachers within schools will give the relative causal effect for teachers within a school, but it will not allow comparisons of teachers across schools. It will not work for determining the relative performance of principals (or managers of local welfare offices), because randomly assigning principals to schools or office directors to offices yields ex ante equivalence (everyone has a chance of being assigned to a better site), but ex post, the manager has either a good site or a bad site. Since the variation across schools/offices is likely to be as large as or larger than the variation in performance across workers, we can infer relatively little about relative impact from relative performance. In the language of statistics, the signal-to-noise ratio is low.

Bureaucratic considerations sometimes subvert random assignment. Among the most important such bureaucratic considerations is specialization. Specialization of worker tasks destroys the comparability induced by random assignment. In a welfare organization, if a Spanish-speaking worker takes all the Spanish-speaking cases, it will not be possible to infer worse performance from worse outcomes; it may be that Spanish-speaking cases are simply harder to serve.

The Spanish-language case is probably extreme (though I once heard a manager proudly explain how she assigned welfare cases independent of language compatibility in order to preserve comparability across workers). It seems unlikely that a Spanish-speaking client can get even a minimal level of service from a non–Spanish-speaking worker. In less extreme cases, there will be a tradeoff between the direct benefits of specialization and the management benefits of random assignment. For example, an office handling disability claims could randomly assign the claims (and get a good measure of the quality of the workers) or it could assign all back-injury cases to one worker and all lung cases to a different worker (and perhaps get more equitable and efficient treatment of such cases).

How to weigh the tradeoff depends on the perceived benefits of specialization and the perceived benefits of having a good measure of the quality of a worker. Some organizations use random assignment early in a career (e.g., while a worker is on probation). Entry-level jobs are often relatively homogeneous, so it is easier to make interworker comparisons. Higher-level (perhaps post-probation) jobs tend to have more specialization and thus less opportunity for explicit interworker comparisons of performance. Note that this approach would be appropriate if the performance management problem is one of "selection." If worker performance is immutable (or at least the most important variation is in permanent worker characteristics—intelligence, personality, industriousness), establishing that someone is a good worker is sufficient. However, if the performance management problem is one of "incentives," this approach is less attractive. It gives strong incentives early in the career, but only weaker incentives later in the career.

Even when the problem is one of "selection," this approach is also less attractive when performance across jobs is not highly correlated. Consider personnel management in a welfare office. Entry-level workers are often assigned to the narrowly prescribed eligibility determination and benefits computations. There are often a large number of such workers, and their efforts are monitored through intensive quality-control procedures (e.g., the threat of federal penalties due to Food Stamp "errors"). Such positions are used as probationary jobs. In many welfare organizations, those who perform well on those jobs are promoted to positions as job specialists. These jobs are much less prescribed. They involve one-on-one interaction with clients, and their primary tasks do not have precisely defined regulations. Instead, those tasks involve motivating clients and matching clients to needed services. Usually, no rule book exists. The temperaments required are very different from those of successful eligibility workers, who are rule-oriented rather than people-oriented. With welfare reform in California, large numbers of job specialist positions were created. Counties that simply promoted their best eligibility workers often found that they performed poorly. This is an example of what is commonly known as the Peter Principle: Individuals are promoted to one level beyond their competence, to a level at which they are incompetent.

Specialization is not the only threat to random assignment. A classic problem is cream skimming. If workers select their own cases, they have an incentive to select the better ones. Consider a welfare office in which the worker who does initial screening is also assigned the case. Even if assignment of workers to the initial screening desk is random, the worker has an incentive to deem harder-to-serve cases ineligible or to discourage those clients from completing the application. Conversely, the worker has an incentive to encourage the most-able potential clients to complete their applications. Clotfelter and Ladd (1996) discuss the incentive for teachers to evaluate students as "unready for first grade" and therefore not included in the performance measures. Then note that in Dallas, some schools test less than 95 percent of their students. Perhaps, the poorly performing students "happen" to be sick or absent on the day of the test. The welfare example has a simple and generic solution: create special intake workers. More generally, arrange work flow such that the client who actually enters the program and is assigned to a particular worker is not under the control of the worker who will get performance credit for the outcomes. For the schooling example, do not allow teachers to exempt students from measurement through either formal or informal methods.

Other situations are more subtle and more difficult to handle. When workers know that assignments can be changed, they have an incentive to arrange to "lose" cases that would otherwise perform poorly. Poorly performing students are more likely to be reported as fighting with other students. Caseworkers will be more likely to report (or induce) irreconcilable differences with the clients least likely to succeed. Given the importance of worker-client/teacher-student interaction, such reassignments may improve performance. However, if workers use such reassignment differentially and strategically, reassignment has the potential to subvert the measurement scheme. A first step toward addressing this concern is to monitor case transfers for workers with abnormally high transfer rates.

In the evaluation literature, one approach to this problem is to base the analysis on the initial random assignment, regardless of the final assignment. In that case, standard intention-to-treat analysis using instrumental variables gives a valid estimate of program effects (see, for example, Krueger's analysis of the Tennessee STAR experiment, in terms of whether the student was randomized to the large class or the small class, regardless of the actual class attended [Krueger, 1999]). For the performance management case, the analogous approach would be to assign outcomes for each case to the initially assigned caseworker, whether or not a reassignment occurs. This assignment of outcomes to the initial worker would give the worker the right incentive: Only reassign the case if doing so would raise performance for the client. However, high-stakes performance measurement is different from standard evaluation. In standard evaluation, there is little additional incentive for workers to treat transferred cases differently. But in high-stakes performance measurement, knowing that caseworker A will get credit for any outcomes for the transferred client, caseworker B has little incentive to target effort on that client. The natural hybrid strategy would be to split credit for the case between the initially assigned worker and the worker actually dealing with the case. That approach would preserve some of the advantages of random assignment while retaining some incentive for the new caseworker to work with the client. I am unaware of any real-world attempt to implement such strategies.

Value Added. Recall that we are trying to determine what the outcomes would be for a given set of cases when two different workers handle the cases (teach the class, counsel the job seeker), given the concern that cases differ based on what their outcomes would have been even in the absence of the treatment. When random assignment is not possible, an alternative approach is to use each case as its own control.

To measure teacher performance, we can give individual students a test at the beginning of the year (or the end of the previous year) and another at the end of the year. We assume that the initial test score controls completely for the variation in initial student abilities. We can then take net performance to be the *improvement* in test scores over the year. For a training program, we would compare post-training earnings to pre-training earnings. This is a performance measurement analog of the fixed-effects estimator in the evaluation literature (Meyer, 1995).

In the simple version of the fixed-effects approach, teachers are compared on the basis of the improvement in the test scores of their students. Teachers with larger improvements in test scores are presumed to have performed better. Such simple value-added approaches must be used with care. They implicitly assume that we can compare test-score gains across teachers in different schools, even if they have widely different initial scores. This will not always be valid. If the test has "ceiling effects," students at the top of the score distribution cannot have the same improvement as students at the bottom of the score distribution. Conversely, there is some evidence that not only do some students start out higher at the beginning of the year, those students also (on average) advance more rapidly; in other words, good students perform better every year (Kane and Staiger, 2002b). Clotfelter and Ladd (1996) find that low-socioeconomic-status (SES) schools have smaller year-to-year gains. Conversely, if test scores have a large random component, we would expect regression to the mean—high scores will, on average, be followed by lower scores.

More-sophisticated versions of fixed-effects estimators can at least partially correct for these problems. One simple approach compares gains in scores among students with similar initial scores. This technique allows comparisons across apparently similar classes (based on initial test scores), but not across classes with different initial scores.

Active research in the education literature is developing more sophisticated approaches to value-added modeling. Those approaches allow the expected gain to vary, not only with the level at the beginning of the period, but also with other observed characteristics. Furthermore, they exploit the availability of multiple years of data, so that gains in a given year can partially be the result of teachers in previous years (McCaffrey et al., 2004a, b). Clotfelter and Ladd (1996) discuss an approach that uses regressions based on a quadratic function of each student's previous year's mathematics and English tests to predict expected outcomes for this year's tests with a correction for the school's SES. They also discuss another approach that adjusts for differences in the value added due to student race/ethnicity, limited English proficiency, gender, eligibility for free or reduced-price school lunches, school mobility rate, and degree of classroom overcrowding. They test this system by checking that the adjusted gain score is not related to any individual characteristic, e.g., it should not be more likely to have above-average value added if you teach richer children (who are less likely to receive free school lunches).

Regression Adjustment. Even when neither random assignment nor a value-added approach is possible, regression adjustment may be possible. Under regression adjustment, we compare workers of similar background characteristics (e.g., racial composition, previous work experience, time on welfare).

Consider the welfare example. If the outcome goal is speed of exit from welfare, the use of value added is not meaningful. Before treatment, all the clients are on welfare, so comparing outcomes relative to the baseline is a gross performance comparison. However, looking farther back (e.g., welfare receipt over the previous five years) or looking at other pre-treatment outcomes (e.g., average earnings) allows us to control for case mix.

Alternatively, consider a guidance counselor in a high school or college. Value added would not be useful for measuring net performance, because work experience during school is probably not a good proxy for work experience after completion of school. However, a manager might have other proxies for case mix, e.g., grade point average.

Regression adjustment is consistent in spirit with the Food Stamp Program's adjustment of error rates before assessing financial penalties, i.e., sanctions (see Rosenbaum and Super, 2001). Although there is no pre-intervention baseline on which to base a value-added measure, it is well known that some cases (e.g., immigrants and clients with earnings) are more error-prone than others. The Food Stamp Program computes a simple error rate. However, before a financial penalty is assessed, states are allowed to report alternative error rates that attempt to correct for changes in the program case mix, by showing that their rates computed according to the distribution of cases at some baseline year are lower than the national standard.

Regression adjustments are the modern standard in non-experimental program evaluation. They are used in some school performance schemes, and they are an implicit motivation for breaking out performance by racial subgroups. Perhaps minorities are "more difficult to serve," so performance is reported separately for whites and minorities. Actual formulas tend to be far from transparent, leading to resistance to their application.

An ongoing debate considers how well regression adjustment works (LaLonde, 1986; Dehejia and Wahba, 1999; Hotz, Imbens, and Mortimer, 1999; Hotz, Imbens, and Klerman, 2002). It appears that the ability of regression adjustment to yield proper estimates of net effects depends crucially on the richness of the available information. To what extent do the available measures of case mix control for the variation in outcomes that would exist in the absence of the program? From the literature, it seems clear that simple demographics (gender, race/ethnicity, age, parental education, and poverty or its proxy, receipt of a free school lunch)—are not enough. The debate concerns whether much more detailed past histories (e.g., pretests, history of welfare receipt, history of employment and earnings) are sufficient.

Fixed Effects. A related approach is the use of unit (e.g., school) fixed effects. With this approach, performance of principals, for example, can be evaluated by comparing average school test scores for a given year to average school test scores for the previous year. McCaffrey et al. (2004b) call this *the cohort-to-cohort gain approach* and note that its use was mandated by California's Public Schools Accountability Act of 1999. These comparisons are not pure value-added measures. The performance of a given group/cohort of students is not being compared over time. Rather, one cohort of students is being compared with another cohort of students (within a school, there will be some, but not complete, overlap). This design corrects for time-invariant heterogeneity in the units. Thus, on average, weaker school performance would be expected in schools located in high-poverty neighborhoods. It would therefore not be appropriate to compare outcomes in suburban schools with outcomes in inner-city schools. As long as neighborhood characteristics change only slowly, fixed effects that make comparisons over time in the same school should control for this bias.

Furthermore, this approach provides a rough correction for period effects. Comparing change over a common period across principals controls for common-period effects. Thus, if a crack epidemic (or its passing) depresses (raises) test scores approximately equally in all schools, comparing change scores across schools will control for that common-period effect.

The control using such fixed effects is imperfect. Since the baseline is itself affected by earlier performance, a new principal would not want to follow a "superstar." In the year-to-year change, the base year includes both the effect of the neighborhood and that of the superstar.

Benchmarking. Finally, we can compare organizational performance to the performance of similar organizations in other governmental units. These comparisons tend to be weak, since it is difficult to control for case mix, and period effects are less likely to be common. Moreover, output measures are rarely defined consistently, and differences in the definition often swamp true differences. The number of comparable units tends to be small, as does the number of comparable units examined. In net, it is hard to do regression adjustment.

In summary, it is useful to view these methods hierarchically. When feasible, random assignment is best; and it appears to be feasible, but unimplemented, in many government performance contexts. When random assignment is not feasible, value added, fixed effects, and regression can be useful, but less precise, alternatives. These approaches allow comparisons across sites that are not in the same random assignment pool or when the number of workers at a given site is too small to allow random assignment. Of the three, value-added approaches appear to provide better controls for case mix, while regression produces controls that are far from transparent (see Hanushek and Taylor, 1990, for a similar ordering in the context of student test scores). If none of these approaches is possible, benchmarking provides some information, but probably not enough or of high enough quality to be used as the basis for performance management.

Precision of Measurement

To do performance management, it is necessary to measure performance relatively precisely at the individual level and for every worker.
When person-to-person variation is large, individual measurements will be imprecise. Under such conditions, much of the variation between workers will be random. A worker with recorded performance in the bottom quartile may in fact be above average, and
vice versa. We have already discussed the need to correct for systematic differences in the assignment of cases to workers to allow the
measurement of net effects rather than gross effects. However, even in

---

Approaches to Improving the Precision of Measurement

Increase the number of clients measured. Precision will improve
as the number of cases measured increases. Thus, if measurements are being made on only a fraction of cases (e.g., survey follow-up), increase the fraction. Sometimes this can be accomplished by switching from separate data collection (e.g., surveys)
to measurement based on existing data (e.g., administrative records). If all cases are being measured, consider increasing the
time period over which measures are collected (e.g., two years of
student test scores rather than one year).

Increase the quality of the measurement. Some measurements
(e.g., higher-quality tests) are more precise than others. Computers (computer-aided testing, matrix sampling) can be used to improve the quality of measurement for given time allocated for
measurement. More related measurements per client (e.g., a
longer test) will also increase the quality of measurement. Do not
use order statistics (e.g., "best worker") or gain scores (e.g.,
"most improved worker"), as these measures are likely to have
very low precision.

Change the measure of performance. Multiple measures of performance tapping into the same outcome are often available.
Consideration of precision will sometimes make one measure
more attractive than others; it may have better intrinsic measurement properties, or it may be measured at less cost (e.g., as
part of the case management system or as part of some other
administrative data system).

the absence of *systematic* differences in the assignment of cases to workers, there will be *random* case heterogeneity.

Recall our description of random assignment: Cases are assigned to workers by a random device, independent of case characteristics (e.g., by flipping a coin, in rotation, or assignment to the worker with the smallest current caseload). Nevertheless, cases will still differ. Merely due to chance, some cases will be easier to serve than others (e.g., some students are smarter than others, some trainees have more work experience and better work habits). Furthermore, even for truly identical cases, subsequent outcomes may differ due to chance—one trainee happens to find a firm with an available job, another does not; one trainee becomes ill, another does not.

The smaller the number of cases for each worker and the larger the random variation across clients, the larger will be the random variation in the measures of performance for each worker. In many government operations, such variation is large. Random-assignment evaluations for welfare-to-work programs appear to imply that most of the variation in outcomes is due to random factors related to the client (see Hamilton, 2002, on the NEWWS experiments; see also Greenberg, Michalopoulos, and Robbins, 2001; Bloom, Hill, and Riccio, 2001). In education, Kane and Staiger (2002a,b) argue that student-to-student variance is too large and class sizes too small to allow reliable estimation of the true effect of being a student in a given classroom and perhaps even of being a student in a given school district. Other analyses suggest more-optimistic conclusions (Sanders and Horn, 1998; Rogosa, 2003; Hanushek, 1992; Rivkin, Hanushek, and Kain, 2002).

Recent work by McCaffrey and his colleagues (2004a, b) comes to an intermediate conclusion: They note that the statistical precision required for ranking teachers (where ranking is a prerequisite for rewarding) is much higher than that required for research on whether teachers matter and which teacher characteristics matter. In an exploratory study applying multiple models to a small dataset, McCaffrey et al. found that 20 to 40 percent of the variation in teacher performance is due to random factors. According to their calculations, this is two to four times too large to allow ranking of teachers. Their carefully worded statement conveys the nature of the uncertainty: "We identified between one-third and one-fourth of teachers as distinct from the mean—that is, the probability that the teachers' effect was greater than zero was either very high (greater than 0.9) indicating that the teacher was likely to be less effective than average, or very low (less than 0.1) indicating that the teacher was likely to be more effective than average" (McCaffrey et al., 2004a, p. 108).

This is a discouraging finding. Nonetheless, such estimates may still be useful in medium-stakes (not high- or low-stakes) performance-based management. For example, with these results, it seems reasonable to identify the top 10 to 20 percent of teachers as "better"—using them as mentors, giving them recognition and even financial incentives. Conversely, it seems reasonable to identify the bottom 10 to 20 percent as "worse"—providing them with remediation, not promoting those at the beginning of their careers from probation to permanent positions, putting those later in their careers on a "watch list," with the possibility of termination if there is not significant improvement.

It is unclear whether McCaffrey's results hold in other contexts. The situation in education is arguably worse, because the variation across students is large and the number of students is small. Both of those factors increase the random variation. On the other hand, the measures in education are of high quality and have been carefully studied.

The message here is intended to be cautionary, but constructive. Statistical tools are available to shrink the random variation in measurement (see Kane and Staiger, 2002a, for a related list). First, increase the fraction of cases that are measured. Since measurement is expensive, it is tempting to measure performance for only a sample of the population. This leads to the standard message on call-center interactions: "This call *may* be monitored for quality control purposes" (emphasis added; note that call centers—or call-center-like operations— are a common government operation). Random variation can be cut by increasing the fraction of calls that are monitored. A larger fraction of paperwork can be checked for errors by supervisors (or quality-control teams). Rather than giving a customer service survey to only a sample of clients, give the survey to all of them; rather than testing some students, test everyone.

In some cases, technological changes have made more-intensive measurement considerably less expensive. In earlier periods, the high costs of tabulating outcomes or surveying clients limited performance management. In some areas, computer advances have significantly cut the cost of measurement (Hamilton, Klein, and Lorié, 2000), as in the automated scoring of multiple-choice tests.

More broadly, social service programs (e.g., welfare-to-work programs) increasingly record process measures and some outcomes in computer systems as part of the regular case management task. Insofar as those case management records are computerized, entries are more structured than simple narratives, and record keeping is accurate (as might be expected as part of good case management), it is relatively easy to tabulate the outcomes recorded in the system. This allows us to track the number of meetings or contacts. In some cases, additional outcomes can be collected at relatively low cost by matching to other computerized data sources, e.g., welfare receipt from welfare program records, earnings from firm filings for the administration of state unemployment insurance programs (see Hotz et al., 1998).

Performance often has a strong quality component, and quality can be expensive to measure. Sometimes the cost can be reduced by shifting from measuring inputs to measuring outcomes. Returning to the training example, it is likely to be difficult to measure the quality of training provided. Also, the process might involve observing the training, which would be expensive. Since it is usually cheaper to measure outcomes, in the training example, we can use administrative data to measure employment and earnings for all trainees.

Second, performance can be aggregated over longer time periods. Statistical variation decreases as the sample size increases. For example, using the average of outcomes over four months rather than the average of outcomes over a single month can cut random variation in half. In practice, this means that it may not be possible to measure short-run variation in performance. Elementary school teachers teach only a small number of students (perhaps 30) each year. To distinguish high-performing teachers from low-performing teachers, it may be necessary to combine outcomes for students across several years.

Third, in some contexts, changes in measurement for a given client can reduce random variation. In the school context, tests with more items have lower variability. Furthermore, Computerized Adaptive Testing (CAT) makes it possible to tailor specific test items to previous answers so that good students do not spend a lot of time answering questions that they can easily answer correctly, and bad students do not spend a lot of time working questions that are very difficult. In net, this allows more-precise measures of achievement in a given testing period (Wainer et al., 1990).

Similarly, careful consideration of the exact performance statistic can sometimes cut random variation. Order statistics (e.g., the best-performing worker in a given month) have high variability. When workers are relatively similar, even small variation will change the ordering of performance. Thus, pay bonuses and promotions should be based on averages over time rather than the number of periods in which a worker was the best performer (or among the five best performers). More generally, it is better to base rewards on average performance than on order statistics. Finally, management should not be based on *improvement* in worker performance (e.g., on the "most improved worker" or consistent improvement over several years); managing based on client outcomes will usually have better precision. Although properly measured improvements in worker performance might be a better motivator, period-to-period changes in performance are particularly subject to random variation; and in implementing performance-based management, reducing random variation in measurement is crucial.

Given the costly and noisy measures, some form of *sequential sampling* will often be appropriate. The term comes from quality control in manufacturing, where a fraction of the product is tested. If there appears to be a problem, more of the product is tested until it can be verified that the first measurement was due to random variation or that there truly is a problem. The application of sequential sampling to performance measurement would proceed as follows: Make additional measurements for workers who appear to be poor performers (or perhaps good performers) according to the standard measurement system before any decision is made. For example, in a call center, if the occasional measurements suggest a problem with a particular worker, the monitoring fraction for that worker could be increased for a few more periods. Verify that the problem continues to be observed in the larger sample. Perhaps, make additional measurements along some alternative dimension; for a teacher, these might include moving beyond standardized tests to evaluation of essays or observation of classroom performance. The latter step is likely to be part of any remediation plan. Together, such steps will increase the precision of measurement and thus to improve the chance that workers identified as bad or good truly are. Such precision is a necessary condition for increasing the role of formal measurement and consequences for outcomes in performance management.

Which Outcomes to Reward

The issue of net versus gross effects is a narrow part of the broader issue of selecting performance measures that align with ultimate program goals (see Klitgaard, Fedderke, and Akramov, Chapter 14 in this volume). With respect to choosing outputs, the adage "you get what you pay for" applies (Holmstrom and Milgrom, 1991). Performance management systems are intended to focus effort on particular outcomes. Focus on the measured and compensated outcomes often causes less effort to be directed toward unmeasured or uncompensated goals (Hart, Schleifer, and Vishny, 1997). Thus, if performance in English and mathematics is tested (as in the vision of No Child Left Behind), science, social studies, music, and art will get less attention (see Stecher and Barron, 1999; Hamilton, Stecher, and Klein, 2002).

Pure-quantity goals exemplify this issue most clearly. If the output measure is pure quantity, workers will ignore quality, often not

---

Which Outcomes to Reward

Choose net outcome measures. We care about net effect, so do not reward gross effect.

Choose measures with high precision. Workers should be judged on the basis of their true input, not the random variation in outputs. Therefore, choose measures with relatively little random variation.

Choose outcome measures that cover all outcomes of interest. Workers will work toward the incentives provided by the measures. Consider quality as well as quantity. Note, however, that performance management works best when the goal is simple. Hard choices about goals are at the core of performance management. Can outcomes be viewed as "secondary" and therefore be assessed using some less formal procedure?

Choose outcome measures that are as close as possible to ultimate outcomes. Candidate operational measures are not always closely (or even positively) related to ultimate outcomes. In general, choose outcome measures that are closer to ultimate outcomes. The extent to which this is a problem is an important research question. Track research on this issue, perhaps by considering much earlier performance that can now be evaluated after a much longer follow-up interval.

Choose outcomes that cannot be gamed. Regularly monitor outcomes for evidence of gaming. Are workers modifying their behavior in ways that get them higher performance measures but are neutral or negative with respect to the ultimate outcomes (e.g., changing the timing of claiming performance, coaching students on the exact structure of the test)? When such problems are identified, modify the measurement accordingly.

---

the desired outcome. In welfare programs, caseload should probably not be used as the only output measure. After all, the welfare caseload can be cut by simply closing down the program or denying benefits. Instead, some "quality" condition should be put on welfare case exits, e.g., welfare exits to full-time employment. It should be noted, however, that the Personal Responsibility and Work Opportunities Reconciliation Act of 1996 (the recent major welfare reform legislation) does use the (for these purposes) unadjusted welfare caseload as its output measure, and there are potentially large penalties for failure to meet the stated goals. There is no quality correction. There is also no net-impact correction, so states were rewarded for the booming economy of the late 1990s and are being punished for the recession of the early 2000s.

The natural approach to a disjunction between ultimate goals and measured performance is to use the ultimate goals as performance measures. But in practice, that is not feasible. For performance management, it must be possible to measure performance at a reasonable cost and within the decision cycle of the performance management system. Thus, for example, even if the ultimate goal of a training program is to increase lifetime earnings, for the purposes of performance management, we cannot wait until the ultimate outcomes are realized to make management decisions (e.g., who should mentor and who should be mentored, who should receive a bonus, who should be promoted, and who should be terminated). Such considerations lead schools to focus on end-of-year test scores, and in this case, the correlation with long-term outcomes appears to be quite good. Test scores in high school are significantly correlated with adult (mid-20s through mid-30s) earnings, even after controlling for background variables (Neal and Johnson, 1996; Murnane, Willett, and Levy, 1995; Zax and Rees, 1998). Currie and Thomas (1999) present new estimates based on test scores of much younger children (age 7). They also find a correlation with adult earnings, even after controlling for other factors, including father's SES, father's and mother's education, and maternal grandfather's education. These correlations lend additional confidence to the assumption that increasing learning—as proxied by test scores—in elementary school or high school will lead to better labor market outcomes in adulthood.

The situation for job training programs (including those within welfare programs) is different. These programs traditionally manage based on short-term (13 weeks after training) measures of employment and weekly earnings. Heckman, Heinrich, and Smith (2002) consider the extent to which such measures are correlated with longer-term measures of labor market success for a large training program (JTPA), where *longer term* is defined as approximately two years after the short-term measures (18 to 30 months after randomization). Their results are distressing. In many cases, the actual relation is negative—better short-term performance predicts *worse* long-term performance. Their results are not unique. They survey similar analyses of job training, many of which find similar results.

The extent to which the education example or the training example is more common is unclear. The closer the performance measure is to the ultimate outcomes, the less likely this disjunction is to occur.[1] Such considerations often lead to longer evaluation cycles—the outcomes are simply not available quickly enough for short evaluations. But it is possible to place at least some weight on longer-term outcomes. Thus, while short-term evaluations and new employees must rely on short-term (e.g., one quarter) outcomes, for longer-term employees, longer-term outcomes (two quarters, one year, even longer) can be reviewed and compensated.

Military recruiting provides a useful example. The ultimate goal of military recruiting is to provide successful soldiers. Clearly, we cannot base compensation for recruiters on the recruits' entire military careers. We need not, however, go to the other extreme and give credit for merely signing a contract. It is possible to track whether a recruit actually enters the service, whether the recruit completes basic training, and even whether the recruit finishes the first term of service (two to three years). Recruiters could get additional credit for recruits who pass each career point.

A related issue concerns the possibility of "gaming" the performance measure. A good performance measure should encourage performance without distorting it. However, many apparently plausible performance measures can be gamed. The best known example of this is "teaching to the test," where teachers focus their instruction narrowly on the form of the test, rather than on mastery of the material (Koretz, 2002, esp. Figure 3). In one much-quoted example, the test

---

[1] This line of argument builds on Wilson's (1991) insightful classification of jobs by whether staff actions and ultimate outcomes are well defined and easily observed. In Wilson's schema, these two considerations define a four-way classification of jobs: coping (neither actions, nor outcomes), procedural (actions, but not outcomes), craft (outcomes, but not actions), production (actions and outcomes). The argument in the text urges managers to try to change the definition of performance and its measurement to allow movement toward managing based on outcomes, rather than actions.

asked students to add numbers vertically. When an alternative test presented the numbers horizontally, performance dropped from 86 percent to 46 percent (Koretz, 2002, p. 759). More generally, Koretz shows that test scores (against a national norm) improve from year to year as a school district uses a given test. Then, when the district switches to a new test, test scores (again, against a national norm) drop, often sharply. Evidently, teachers are teaching not merely the broad domain, but also the specific material covered on the test.

In another variation of gaming the system, performance systems with threshold values may induce time-shifting of performance. Asch (1990) describes the Navy Freeman plan, which gave awards to Navy recruiters who exceeded a performance threshold in a given month. In practice, military recruiters have considerable discretion over exactly when a military contract is signed. A potential recruit can be urged to come in a little earlier (before the end of the month), or an interested recruit can be deferred a few days (into the next month). In such a situation, a performance threshold gives recruiters (or any worker facing a threshold reward) an incentive to accelerate performance if he or she is near the threshold or to defer performance if he or she is past one level of the threshold and far from the next level.

Similar issues occur with respect to rank-ordered performance, i.e., bonuses for the highest performer. In periods in which one performer is doing very well, others have less incentive to perform. If the high performer is far enough ahead, even he or she has less incentive to perform. These considerations suggest another reason for basing performance on a continuous measure. In the case of recruiting, the reward can be adjusted continuously with the number of contracts, rather than relative to some threshold. In the case of relative performance, rewards can be based on performance relative to average performance (rather than on rank).

As we noted earlier, poorly designed performance measures give workers and their organizations incentives to skew their entry rules or their labeling of clients. If learning-disabled or non–native-English speakers are excluded from the performance measure, the worker or organization has an incentive to label hard-to-serve clients in a way that excludes them from that measure. In the extreme, such performance measures give workers and organizations an incentive to avoid treating the hardest-to-serve clients. A first approach to this problem is to remove the decision about who is included in the performance measure or who receives services from the individual or organization whose performance is being measured. Depending on the situation, it may be necessary to audit such decisions, e.g., to determine whether a student truly met the learning-disabled criteria.

The TANF program took an alternative approach. Under its predecessor, the JOBS program, states had been allowed to determine which clients were not employable. Those clients were deemed ineligible for services and were excluded from both the numerator and the denominator of the performance measure. The net effect of this exclusion was to raise measured performance, and states were perceived to have done so. In response, TANF eliminated any credit for the unemployable. Instead, everyone was included in the denominator of the performance measure, and the target rate was lowered to account for some nonemployables.

Finally, despite our guidance to identify a narrow set of numerical performance goals, some attention must usually remain on other dimensions of performance. In education, tests rarely cover all of the domains. In social service organizations, professional courtesy toward supervisors, colleagues, and clients is valued. Most jobs have at least some teamwork component. A narrow relative performance measure gives workers an incentive to sabotage the work of their colleagues. These secondary performance goals are also important, and they appear sometimes to be dealt with adequately with other, less formal evaluation procedures. Thus, professional performance is evaluated on the basis of formal quantitative evaluation criteria and a narrative discussing other issues. Workers are informed that a minimum level of performance on the secondary performance goals will be required in order to receive whatever rewards are available. This is the policy in many welfare-to-work offices running formal performance management systems. Oken and Asch describe a similar system in Navy recruiting: "Awards were distributed at the discretion of the district commander and could be denied if other attributes of the individual's performance, such as conduct or personal appearance, were not satisfactory" (Oken and Asch, 1997, p. 21). As long as the most important performance measures are tracked quantitatively, such more informal methods sometimes appear to be sufficient to prevent wanton disregard of secondary goals.

Errors, Cheating, and Auditing

In many performance measurement systems, the workers themselves record performance. In a survey field operation, for example, performance is measured by surveys recorded by the interviewer. In a school, teachers usually supervise their students' tests. In the Food Stamp Program, workers both collect the information from the applicant and make the eligibility determination. In a social services delivery system (e.g., a welfare-to-work program or a welfare benefits computation), workers record that they met with clients, what the clients reported, and the actions they took based on those reports.

When workers' own records of their actions are used to measure their performance, incentives are introduced for shading the truth and even for outright fraud. The higher the stakes in the measurement, the greater the temptation to cheat. Jacob and Levitt (2003) show that the degree of teacher cheating increases as the importance (to the teacher) of the test increases (see also Koretz, 2002, pp. 768–769; Clotfelter and Ladd, 1996, pp. 45–46).

Teachers are certainly not the only groups subject to such pressures. I once ran a focus group with welfare caseworkers in which one participant said that he had figured out what to enter into the computer system to "get his supervisor off his back"; then he went and did the casework that he thought was most appropriate for the clients. Dresselhaus, Luck, and Peabody (2002) provide evidence consistent with fraud in medical outcomes. In survey interviewing, this process is known as "curbstoning." An interviewer walks up to the front (the curbstone) of the designated address (if even that) and guesses the answers a family living in this household would give.

Not all cheating behavior is so blatant. A performance management system that measures the quantity of cases "resolved" gives workers a strong incentive to dispose of cases quickly, not necessarily correctly. A doctor performs an incomplete exam or rushes through the (unrecorded) conversation with the patient.

Given these incentives, performance measurement requires that claims of output be verified. The appropriate verification/auditing strategy should balance multiple considerations. The economic literature on deterrence (Becker, 1968; Ehrlich, 1996; Stigler, 1970) suggests a tradeoff between the penalty and the probability of detection. When the penalty is higher, the probability of detection can be lower, and vice versa. Government has large penalties available, including loss of employment and criminal prosecution. However, verification and auditing is not cheap. This suggests sequential sampling (see the earlier discussion of sequential sampling in the identification of high and low performers in the presence of random variation). At some regular interval, a few randomly selected cases from each worker are audited, but far from all cases. This approach can be sufficient to detect gross cheating and should help with uncovering overemphasis on quantity at the expense of quality. If the penalty for discovered cheating or shorting quality is large enough, this will also be enough to discourage cheating.

However, there also needs to be a concern about false positives. Finding one error may simply indicate an honest mistake. Perfect record-keeping is not a cost-effective standard. Severely penalizing even a single honest mistake would have the effect of inducing workers to double- and triple-check their work, an inefficient use of their time. Some form of sequential sampling is probably more appropriate. Under sequential sampling, when an error is detected, drastic penalties are not immediately assessed; rather, a more intensive review is initiated. Additional cases handled by the worker are pulled and scrutinized for a systematic pattern of errors. If the broader review finds few additional cases, the worker receives a notice, but not a negative action. If the broader review finds systematic problems, more serious action is taken. The optimal initial sampling rate and the size of the second-stage samples constitute a formal statistical problem that we leave for more technical forums.

In practice, this type of sequential-sampling system is likely to be multi-tiered. Here, the Food Stamp Program quality-control process is exemplary. A similar process is in place with respect to claims for the Work Activity Participation Rate in welfare/TANF. For the Food Stamp Program, primary auditing is done by each state according to a set of criteria precisely defined by the federal government. Specifically, the sample size is set large enough to estimate the error rate to a given level of precision. Furthermore, the states' auditing efforts are verified, and states are required to have a clearly defined and auditable audit process. Federal auditors then audit the states' procedures to verify not the error rate, but that the audit process was properly implemented.

This state and federal audit is almost exclusively an ex post quality-assessment procedure. In practice, the error rates are set so low that states need to devote considerable attention to them, i.e., assuring that individual workers know the rules and apply them properly. Doing so requires an ex ante process in which the efforts of individual caseworkers are monitored, problems are identified, and remediation or termination occurs. In principle, this monitoring should be a part of the regular ongoing tasks of supervisors. In practice, supervisors are busy, and their own procedures are not always perfect. In response, individual offices (and perhaps counties or states) must audit their supervisors to verify that they have actually audited their caseworkers and that they are themselves applying the rules properly.

Some equivalent form of auditing is necessary whenever workers record their own performance or when performance may be error-prone. The audit must review enough of the process to establish that it was done properly. The Food Stamp Program case is relatively simple. A proper decision is defined by what is in the case file. In survey operations, performance is checked by reinterviewing a subset of households. At the reinterviews, the supervisor verifies that the households are truly as interviewed and that the recorded responses are consistent across the two interviews. In the school setting, full auditing requires retesting students.

A Multi-tiered Auditing System

Workers do their work in an auditable way. Workers should have an auditable paper trail of their work and their claims. However, paperwork is not the main task of most workers, and it is clearly possible to spend too much time on paperwork. Thus, it is not appropriate to require perfect paperwork. Minor paperwork errors should not be punished severely.

Supervisors should audit their caseworkers in an auditable way. Such auditing is a basic function of a supervisor. It is important primarily because it is a step toward continuous quality improvement and assurance of equal treatment of clients. It also serves as a check on cheating and substandard quality (i.e., overemphasis on quantity). The auditable record makes it possible to check the work of supervisors. To prevent collusion between supervisors and workers (which might be attractive if supervisors are evaluated on the basis of their workers' efforts), cases for audit should be chosen by the central audit group.

Managers should audit supervisors. If the organization has enough layers of management, managers should check supervisors' auditing records and independently check some individual cases.

A central auditing group should audit all levels. The central auditing group selects cases to be audited by supervisors, managers, and the central auditing group. It also audits each level's audits.

Any auditing system probably needs to be multi-tiered. Supervisors can and should be doing regular reviews as part of their regular supervisory responsibilities. These audits serve both as a disciplinary device (i.e., to detect or at least discourage fraud) and also as continuous on-the-job training (work is reviewed, failure to follow official procedures or to do proper data input is noted, better practices are suggested). However, when a supervisor is busy, it is just too easy to let case audits slide. Therefore, in addition to supervisor audits, some central staff group needs to audit supervisor audits, and supervisors must be required to provide a paper trail of their audits: How were cases selected? Which cases were selected? What was the result of the audit? With a formal paper trail, the central audit group can easily verify that supervisors are doing the audits and that the audits are being done correctly.

Conclusion

The gains in performance that can be achieved by implementing a performance management system for personnel are potentially large: Workers can be remediated, so identifying poorly performing workers and counseling them is worthwhile. Some workers are better than others, so selection—terminating poor performers and attracting better performers—is potentially important. Finally, workers respond to incentives with more effort, so measuring performance and rewarding it is potentially important.

But implementing a performance management system requires a system for measuring performance. And as we have seen, the challenges of implementation are daunting: measuring net performance, measuring performance in a way that minimizes random variation, aligning performance with ultimate outcomes, and auditing performance claims to discourage cheating.

How should one proceed? The needed steps are summarized below. A crucial insight is that setting up a performance measurement system is not a one-time task, but an ongoing effort. Even with the best preparation, initial implementation is likely to be problematic. Measurements will have a random component; measured performance will not align perfectly with ultimate outcomes; workers will find ways to "game" the system, leading to unintended consequences. In short, any initial system will almost certainly be imperfect. In the textbook theory of performance management (see, e.g., Milgrom and Roberts, 1992), each of these considerations implies "lower-powered incentives," i.e., weighing formal measurements less (relative to informal, conventional management practices) in making decisions about remediation, selection, and compensation.

Steps to Implement a Performance Management System

1. *Start somewhere*
- Define a small set of ultimate goals.
- Identify measurable short-term outcomes that are plausibly related to the ultimate outcomes.
- Put in place a system to measure those short-term outcomes (e.g., testing).
- Record the results in a data system.
- Distribute the results—to the workers, to their supervisors, to senior management.

2. *Evaluate the measurements*
- Are the measurements properly recorded in the data system?
- Are the measurements consistent with the impressions of observers (e.g., do they yield rankings of workers that are similar to the informal rankings of supervisors)? If yes, good. If not, why not? (See below.)
- Explore the measurement properties of the system. Informally, are the rankings of workers roughly consistent over time? Unstable ranking over time is informal evidence of measurements with a large random component. Perhaps conduct a formal statistical evaluation of the measurement properties of the system. Consider changing the measurement system. Consider devoting more resources to measurement (e.g., testing more students, testing more frequently, longer tests).
- Search for perverse incentives. Ask workers and supervisors (perhaps informally, perhaps anonymously) to describe perverse incentives; some of them may complain loudly even without being asked. Revise the measurements to eliminate the perverse incentives.

3. *Put in place an auditing program*
- Establish an auditing group (perhaps from some existing internal control operation).
- Have the auditing group randomly select (but keep private) three sets of cases for audit by supervisors, by managers, and by the auditing group (exact details would depend on the structure of the hierarchy). As a rule of thumb, the audit should be sufficiently intense to identify gross malfeasance (e.g., lying about one-fourth of the cases) relatively quickly, but no more intense than necessary (auditing is time-consuming and expensive).
- Require line workers to have auditable records for all cases.
- Have supervisors audit the selected cases and require auditable evidence of their audits. Identify and remediate casework problems. Forward evidence of cheating to the audit group for official review.

- Have managers audit the auditable records of their supervisors' audits and a new sample of individual cases (to prevent supervisors and line workers from conspiring to ex post fix the audited records). Identify and remediate casework problems (with the supervisor, who then remediates his or her entire staff). Remediate auditing errors. Forward evidence of cheating to the audit group for official review.
- Have the audit team audit its sample of cases, a sample of the cases audited by supervisors, a sample of the cases audited by managers, the audit records of supervisors, and the audit records of managers.
- When evidence of potential malfeasance is discovered, audit more cases.
- When evidence of malfeasance is confirmed, punish it severely. It is important not to punish minor errors in paperwork—it is clearly possible for caseworkers to allocate too much effort to perfect paperwork, at the expense of real casework. However, evidence of gross malfeasance needs to be followed up and, as confirmed, sanctioned.

4. *Use the measurements (more)*
- Use the measurements for monitoring organizational performance.
- Use the measurements as a component in remediation decisions.
- Use the measurements as a component in termination decisions.
- Use the measurements as a component in compensation and promotion decisions.

5. *Repeat*
- Review the ultimate goals, the measurable outcomes, and the measurement recording system, and adjust as appropriate.
- Reevaluate the measures and adjust as appropriate.
- Review the audit program and adjust as appropriate.
- Increase the importance of the measurements in monitoring organizational effectiveness, remediation, termination, and compensation/promotion.
- Repeat.

If performance management is viewed as an ongoing effort, it should be possible to make progress in addressing each of the challenges. Better measurement instruments and increasing resources devoted to measurement should shrink the random component in the measures. Measurements can be adjusted to eliminate ways to game the system. Auditing systems can be put in place to detect and therefore deter fraud. Long-term research can identify short-term measurements that are more highly correlated with long-term, ultimate outcomes. As progress is made toward addressing these challenges, the quality of measurement will improve, and it will be appropriate to rely more heavily on the formal performance measurement system in making management decisions. The research evidence suggests that the combination of performance measurement and management based on that measurement will improve performance.

CHAPTER THIRTEEN

Lessons from Performance Measurement in Education

Laura Hamilton

The Volcker Commission's report calls for better performance measurement and accountability. One of its main conclusions is that attempts to reform government must be characterized by a heightened emphasis on effectiveness. Several aspects of the commission's vision for the government of the future are captured in this statement:

> The government we envision would be organized around critical missions, with management *keyed to performance.* It would be a dynamic government, prepared to meet the multifaceted and evolving needs of a complex modern society. Federal employment would appeal to highly competent people because it would *encourage and reward their best efforts* (Chapter 2 of this volume, p. 57, emphasis added).

Implicit in this vision is the need for a clear and agreed-upon set of performance standards, as well as accurate measures of performance, for organizations and for individuals working within those organizations. A system that involves setting standards, measuring progress toward those standards, and imposing consequences for meeting or failing to meet the standards may be called a performance-based accountability (PBA) system. Most PBA systems are intended not only to measure and reward, but to create incentives that will promote certain kinds of practices within the organization. For such a system to be effective, the measures must motivate the desired behaviors while minimizing the likelihood of undesirable responses, and they must be perceived as fair and accurate by those to whom they are applied.

Although the government's personnel systems have been criticized for their failure to motivate and reward good performance, the idea of performance-based measurement in government is not new. Systems for measuring, rewarding, and sanctioning performance have existed in some form in the U.S. government for over a century, but few of them have achieved widespread success (White, 1958), though there is evidence of benefits in some cases (see Asch, Chapter 11). This failure of performance-based personnel systems to lead to fundamental improvement stems in no small part from faulty assumptions about how employees and managers will respond to such systems and from a failure on the part of system designers to anticipate and prevent unintended consequences (Larkey and Caulkins, 1992). The debates that surrounded proposals for performance-based personnel systems in the Department of Homeland Security (DHS) and the Department of Defense (DoD) illustrate some of the concerns arising from past, unsuccessful attempts to create such systems. In particular, observers worry that the incentives will be too weak and the quality of measurement too poor. Future proposals to implement PBA in government should be based on what we have learned from past attempts in both the public and the private sector.

This chapter explores PBA in one sector of government, the public education system that serves students in kindergarten through grade twelve (i.e., the K–12 education system). It provides insights on the design of effective performance measurement systems and proposes a research agenda to examine the implementation and effectiveness of such systems in government. The chapter is not intended to be an exhaustive review of what is known about measuring performance; rather, it summarizes selected key findings, points out ways in which these are relevant to the broader federal government setting, provides some guidelines for promoting good measurement, and identifies areas in need of additional evidence.

How Are Educators Held Accountable?

Many of the commission's recommendations taken together may be thought of as promoting a system that holds staff accountable for their performance—in other words, a PBA system. The emphasis on clarity of mission, high standards, flexibility, and rewards for good performance is consistent with the kinds of PBA systems that have been implemented in education at the state and district levels. In general, such systems involve four major components:

- *Goals*, which specify the desired outcomes.
- *Measures*, which are used to determine the extent to which the goals are met.
- *Targets* for performance on the measures, which correspond to the desired level of goal attainment.
- *Consequences* for performance, which reward and motivate effective performance while discouraging ineffective performance (Hamilton and Koretz, 2002; see also Stecher, Hamilton, and Gonzalez, 2003).

In education, these components take a specific form called a test-based accountability (TBA) system. Goals are represented by published content and performance standards that specify what students need to know and be able to do (content standards), as well as what level of attainment of those goals is expected (performance standards). The goals typically focus on key short-term objectives of schooling, such as increasing the number of third-grade students reading at grade level, rather than on long-term objectives related to postsecondary education and labor market outcomes. This is due in large part to the impracticality of measuring long-term objectives, as well as to an almost universal belief that attainment of the short-term goals is a necessary condition for promotion of the long-term goals.

The measures used in TBA systems are typically standardized achievement tests in core subjects such as reading and mathematics. Targets may take the form of levels of performance to be reached (e.g., 80 percent of a school's students should test at the proficient level or above) or gains in performance (e.g., schools must demonstrate an average annual gain of five percentile points). Consequences vary across systems, but they typically include financial rewards and other forms of recognition for good performance and threats of intervention, school takeover, or loss of resources for poor performance. The federal education legislation, the No Child Left Behind Act of 2001 (P.L. 107-110, H.R. 1) (NCLB), embodies all of these components and includes consequences that are designed to empower the consumers of education (parents and students): Schools that fail to meet their targets two years in a row must offer school choice, and after three years of failing to meet the targets, schools must provide parents with options for supplemental instructional services, both at district expense.

Test-based accountability is only one form of accountability affecting public school educators. Other forms include market accountability, in which schools are directly accountable to families as a result of parental choice in some contexts (e.g., voucher and charter school programs); bureaucratic accountability, which emphasizes compliance with rules and regulations; professional accountability, which relies on the professional norms and expertise of educators, tempered by external controls, including credentialing and professional development requirements; and political accountability, which results from the relationship between voters and elected officials (Adams and Kirst, 1999; Armstrong, 2003; Finn, 2002). These models often operate together, and as discussed below, some of them (e.g., market accountability) may hold promise for improving the effectiveness of PBA systems both in education and elsewhere.

We know from experience with PBA systems in education as well as in other sectors that the measures and the way they are implemented will have a significant influence on how participants in the system respond. In the next section, we present some lessons learned from the K–12 public education system to illustrate ways in which measurement matters. The chapter concludes with a discussion of guidelines for promoting effective performance-based accountability and a brief summary of future research needs.

What We Know About Performance-Based Accountability in Education

Many of the problems the commission report addresses are similar to those faced by the public education system; these problems have served as an impetus for the current focus on accountability in education. Policymakers and private individuals have expressed concerns that spending on public schools has increased dramatically over the past several decades but has not been accompanied by a corresponding increase in student achievement. For example, in describing the need for a fundamental reform of the system, the Department of Education noted that while real spending on K–12 education has grown substantially over the past ten years, academic achievement as measured by the National Assessment of Educational Progress (NAEP) has barely budged for most groups of students (U.S. Department of Education, 2003). Such comparisons of trends are often used in policy debates as arguments in favor of imposing new forms of accountability on educators rather than continuing to "throw money at schools."

In addition, there are concerns in education about ineffective personnel management procedures. For the most part, the selection and management of teachers have been characterized by an emphasis on years of training and experience rather than on quality, a lockstep salary scale that fails to distinguish between excellent and poor performers, problematic relationships between labor and management, and a failure to recognize differences in market value across specialties (for example, teachers' unions have expressed resistance to the idea of paying more for science and mathematics teachers, who are in short supply and often face attractive career options outside the public education system, than for teachers of other subjects for which there is no shortage). High levels of attrition among public school educators have been attributed to poor working conditions, lack of rewards for hard work, and low salaries that do not compete with those offered by the private sector. Various merit pay schemes have been proposed and, to a lesser extent, tried in several states and districts, but most of these have been met with resistance by collective bargaining groups and have ultimately been abandoned (Cornett and Gaines, 1992; Murnane and Cohen, 1986). In general, the culture of public education tends to be resistant to any type of performance measurement, in large part because of a lack of trust in the validity of the measures that would be used.

At the same time, state and federal education policy has increasingly emphasized performance measurement at the school level, and efforts to rank schools and publicize their test results and also to hold schools accountable for those results are becoming widespread. In the 2002–2003 school year, 49 states and the District of Columbia published report cards on every public school's performance. In 23 states, test results were being used to make decisions about whether students would graduate from high school or be promoted to the next grade,[1] and 24 states used results as a basis for school closure or reconstitution (Skinner and Staresina, 2004).

Has Test-Based Accountability Worked?

Arguably, the primary purpose of K–12 public education is to promote student learning, and the primary goal of TBA in education is to improve the level of learning that schools produce. The evidence regarding whether accountability has in fact resulted in increased learning is mixed.[2] Advocates of TBA have pointed to gains in scores on state tests after those states introduced accountability systems. Both Texas and North Carolina have been cited as examples of states that enacted successful TBA systems, as evidenced by dramatic score improvements (Grissmer and Flanagan, 1998; Texas Education Agency, 2000). Some research supports the link between accountability and student achievement on the test that is used in the accountability system, particularly when the system includes high-school exit exams (Fredericksen, 1994; Winfield, 1990). Gains are often the greatest for students attending low-performing schools,

---

[1] The use of tests for grade-retention or graduation decisions explicitly holds students accountable for their performance but imposes a great deal of pressure on educators as well.

[2] See Hamilton, 2003, for a more comprehensive review of the effects of high-stakes testing.

which tend to face more pressure to improve than do other schools (Roderick, Jacob, and Bryk, 2002).

Studies of the extent to which scores on high-stakes tests generalize to measures other than the specific test used in the accountability system have produced mixed results. Some studies have attributed improvements on nonaccountability tests such as NAEP to states' implementation of TBA systems (Carnoy and Loeb, 2002; Grissmer et al., 2000). Similarly, a comparison of countries and Canadian provinces with and without exit exams showed that middle-school-aged students in schools with such exams had higher average achievement on external tests than those in schools without them (Bishop, 1998). Despite these positive relationships between gains on accountability tests and score changes on other tests, however, the increases on NAEP and other nonaccountability tests have typically been significantly smaller than the increases on the high-stakes tests (Koretz and Barron, 1998; Jacob, 2002). Consequently, inferences about the *magnitude* of improvement in student learning may be misleading if they are based solely on the high-stakes test, even if the direction of change is the same on high- and low-stakes tests.

These studies illustrate one of the primary threats to the validity of test-score information in education: score inflation, or "increases in scores that are not accompanied by commensurate increases in the proficiency scores are intended to represent" (Koretz, 2003, p. 9). In other words, the gain on the state test may produce misleading information about the degree to which student learning has actually improved. This phenomenon first received widespread attention when a physician named John Cannell (1988) observed that most school districts and states were reporting average achievement test scores that were above the national average as defined by test publisher norms. Subsequently Linn, Graue, and Sanders (1990) showed that performance as measured against test publisher norms had increased throughout the 1980s for most published tests, but these gains were not replicated on NAEP. Recent research has confirmed the tendency for increases in standardized test scores to fail to generalize to other tests of the same subject matter (Koretz and Barron, 1998; Koretz et al., 1991). To the extent that test scores are affected by score inflation, the validity of the information those tests produce is compromised, and the inferences that users of the data (including policymakers and the general public) make are likely to be inaccurate. Score inflation also may break the presumed link between attainment of short-term objectives (higher test scores) and longer-term objectives such as college admission or successful participation in the labor force after graduation.

Why Are Scores Inflated?

One of the primary reasons for score inflation appears to be a reallocation of effort and resources toward content that is measured and away from content that is not measured. For example, teachers report spending more time on tested topics and less time on untested topics as a result of high-stakes testing programs (Jones et al., 1999; Koretz et al., 1996; Shepard and Dougherty, 1991; Smith et al., 1991; Stecher et al., 2000), as well as emphasizing particular formats or styles of test items in their instruction (Koretz and Hamilton, 2003; Pedulla et al., 2003; Romberg, Zarinia, and Williams, 1989; Smith et al., 1991). For example, Shepard and Dougherty (1991) found that in two districts with high-stakes writing tests, teachers of writing said that, as a result of the format of the writing test used in those districts, they emphasized having students look for mistakes in written work rather than produce their own writing.

To the extent that the measure captures all aspects of performance that are considered important, this type of reallocation may not be problematic. In most cases, however, tests are capable of tapping only a limited array of the skills and knowledge that society values, and they tend to measure achievement using specific formats (such as the multiple-choice question) that may encourage narrowed instruction. In addition, districts and schools have sometimes manipulated results by excluding certain students from the testing system or retaining low-performing students in grade (Figlio and Getzler, 2002; Jacob, 2002). Even policies that are designed explicitly to prevent schools from shortchanging specific groups of students may lead to unexpected and undesirable incentives. Kane and Staiger (2002) demonstrated that the requirement to report performance for separate racial/ethnic and socioeconomic groups of students, a requirement that many states put in place to ensure attention to these groups, results in more-diverse schools facing an increased chance of failing to meet targets simply because of sampling error. As a result, districts may be tempted to segregate their schools to avoid having multiple subgroups in any one school. Instances of cheating and other inappropriate behaviors tend to increase as the stakes attached to performance become higher (Jacob and Levitt, 2003).

These attempts to "game the system" are not limited to the K–12 public education system. The Job Training Partnership Act (JTPA), passed by Congress in 1982 to improve the employment prospects of disadvantaged youth and adults by providing job training and other services, created performance standards and incentives for training centers. The need for low-cost measures and timely reporting resulted in a focus on short-term labor-market measures and consequently led to actions that may have been in conflict with long-term goals (Heckman, Heinrich, and Smith, 2002). Problematic responses included (1) selecting participants who were most likely to enhance short-term goals but who may not have had the greatest need for the program and (2) manipulating reporting dates to enhance measured performance (Kirby, 2004; see also Chapter 11).

In general, organizations and the people who work in them often focus on short-term, measurable objectives even when these are in conflict with the longer-term goals the system is intended to promote, and this type of response is exacerbated when members of those organizations believe the goals are difficult or impossible to attain (see, e.g., Koretz, 2003). Therefore, it is critical to devise appropriate measures and set targets that are viewed as attainable, as discussed below.

The Need for Capacity-Building

Rowan (1996) identifies three main factors that affect employee performance: the employee's motivation to perform the job, his or her job-relevant skills and abilities, and the situation in which the job is performed. Most TBA systems emphasize the first of these three conditions and assume that teachers and other educators will work harder and more effectively if they are motivated to do so. There is some recognition that in some cases, educators may need help figuring out how to improve: NCLB and most state systems have provisions for districts and/or states to provide technical assistance to schools that repeatedly fail to meet targets. However, these technical assistance provisions are often insufficient to address the severity of the capacity problems and the broader context in which the poor-quality work is performed. Capacity problems may include insufficient material and financial resources, lack of knowledge and skills needed to improve practice, and lack of understanding of how to allocate time and effort more appropriately. In particular, few professional development or teacher training programs sufficiently prepare teachers to engage their students in intellectually demanding work (Cohen, 1996), and such preparation is likely to require much more time than is available from state and district providers of technical assistance. Exacerbating this lack of preparation is a more general lack of knowledge among the education community about how to improve practice. Aside from a few well-documented findings, the field's understanding of effective practices is limited, though efforts are under way to promote scientific research in education that should ultimately lead to a stronger knowledge base (National Research Council, 2002).

The problem of lack of capacity extends beyond individual knowledge and skills to encompass organizational climate and culture. Experience has shown that only a small minority of schools respond to incentive systems in constructive and effective ways (Cohen, 1996), and those that respond effectively do so as a result of highly effective leadership, strong levels of trust among staff (including between teachers and principals), and professional norms that make effective responses possible (Bryk and Schneider, 2002; McLaughlin and Talbert, 1993). Professional staff in education and in other fields are often strongly motivated by the standards of work developed by their own work groups (Friedson, 1984; Talbert, 1991), but the organization must support the emergence and propagation of these standards. These forms of organizational capacity are not easy to instill and may be especially difficult to achieve in low-income and low-performing schools, those that tend to be most in need of improvement (Cohen, 1996).

The Attribution Problem

Systems that reward and sanction educators for their students' performance embody a belief that educators are the primary factor controlling how much students learn. Although no one doubts the importance of an effective and dedicated teacher, it is the students themselves who must put forth the effort to learn the material with which they are presented, and a number of factors may limit the extent to which students exert this effort. Students' attention is drawn in many directions, and school does not always rank as their highest priority. This is particularly the case in the United States, where students may be distracted by work and extracurricular activities, and where the rewards for hard work in school are not as apparent as they are in other nations (Bishop, 1989; Powell, 1996).

Parents, too, have a clear role to play in the messages they send regarding the importance of learning, the environment they create to support learning in the home, and the ways in which they interact with their children around schoolwork and other activities; Schneider, Teske, and Marshall (2000) note that families and students are co-producers (with teachers) of educational outcomes. Some aspects of this co-production may be manipulated somewhat through policies that impose additional accountability on students or parents, but others, such as the well-known differences in the quality of the educational environments students experience before they enter the school system (Hart and Risley, 1995), are not as easy to address. As a result of these outside-of-school influences, systems that hold educators accountable for student outcomes are likely to produce inaccurate attributions much of the time and will be perceived as unfair by many of the employees who are subjected to their provisions. Staff who are risk-averse are especially likely to reject such systems if the systems subject a large portion of their compensation to outside influences (see Chapter 11). Moreover, such systems create incentives for teachers and other school staff to avoid taking positions in schools with hard-to-teach student populations, possibly exacerbating the existing gap in teacher quality between wealthy suburban schools and poor inner-city schools.

This brief overview summarizes some of the key findings from research on TBA systems and reform in education. The following sections attempt to apply this evidence to the problem of performance-based measurement in government.

How Can Government Promote Effective Performance-Based Accountability?

As the research summarized above suggests, simply setting clear goals and measuring progress toward them are insufficient for producing the desired responses. Certain conditions must be met for PBA to work as intended. This section discusses some general guidelines that government should follow as it seeks to create an effective system of performance measurement and accountability.

Produce High-Quality Measures

A frequently repeated axiom in education is that you get what you test, and you do not get what you do not test (Resnick and Resnick, 1992). In other words, the measure in large part determines how actors in the system will respond, especially when consequences for performance are significant. Although the notion that measurement can fundamentally influence instruction has been challenged (Firestone, Mayrowetz, and Fairman, 1998), evidence suggests that testing does in fact shape educators' behavior in fairly significant ways. Performance measures, therefore, need to be designed not only with an eye toward measuring the appropriate outcome, but also with consideration for how the nature of the measure will affect the behaviors of system participants.

Clearly, it is not possible to provide a specific set of recommendations that would be applicable across departments and organizations. However, two general guidelines may be offered: First, even the best-designed measurement system may lead to inappropriate reallocation of effort, since no single system is likely to capture all behaviors that are considered important. One way to avoid this narrowing is to supplement the primary measure with some sort of audit mechanism. Some of the education studies cited earlier used NAEP as an audit test, and the NCLB legislation requires states to participate in NAEP for this purpose. Auditing may be done on a periodic basis and with a sample of respondents rather than the entire population. Users of the audit data need to be provided with assistance to help them interpret the results, since a simple comparison of trends may not be the most appropriate strategy for understanding what the results mean. It is critical that the audit test not involve stakes for individuals; otherwise, it may be subject to the same type of inflation that affects the primary measure. Instead, information from the audit should be used by high-level managers and others responsible for overseeing performance to determine whether there is a need to change the primary measurement system or to make other kinds of workplace changes in response to inappropriate narrowing of behaviors or activities.

Second, a measurement system that includes a combination of outcomes and practices may minimize the likelihood of inappropriate responses. The narrowing of instruction described earlier was detected through measures of classroom practices. By monitoring practices, it may be possible not only to discourage excessive emphasis on a limited set of behaviors, but also to send a clear message about the kinds of behaviors that are valued. There are a number of ways to measure practices, depending on the nature of the job involved. These include direct observation of performance, questionnaires, interviews with staff about their own practices as well as those of their colleagues, supervisor ratings and reports, and logs or time diaries. Measuring practices is not likely to be easy; the diversity of practice across contexts, the possibility for response bias (particularly if survey-based methods are used), the likely political backlash in some sectors, and high costs are all impediments to implementing a large-scale system that measures practice (Koretz, 2003). But imperfect as such a system is likely to be, it has the potential to minimize undesirable consequences and provide a more balanced basis for evaluating performance than does a system that relies exclusively on outcome measurement. Measurement of practices also may provide a way for accountability systems to address longer-term goals that are not amenable to outcome measurement but that are clearly associated with particular practices.

At the same time, where possible, systems should not rely exclusively on measures of practice, which tend to be based on ratings that are subject to various forms of distortion such as the tendency for managers to assign high ratings to all employees and the differences in severity among raters (Larkey and Caulkins, 1992). Despite the numerous problems associated with the use of tests for high-stakes purposes in education, it has proven to be politically more palatable for school and teacher ratings to be based on achievement test scores than on supervisor ratings of performance, in large part because the former can be defended as reasonably objective and comparable across sites. It may not be possible in all government contexts to create a measure analogous to the standardized tests used in education, but where feasible, performance measurement should be based on more than subjective ratings by employees or their supervisors. And when such ratings are used, they should be subjected to efforts to validate them and make them comparable (perhaps through statistical adjustments) across raters.

To the Extent Possible, Use a Performance Index That Reflects Actual Performance

As discussed above, some education accountability systems rely on levels of performance, whereas others emphasize some form of gain in performance. There is increasing interest in devising education accountability systems that utilize value-added measures of performance, particularly for the purpose of measuring individual teacher effectiveness (Sanders and Horn, 1998; Webster et al., 1998). Much of this interest stems from the attribution problem discussed earlier (although this problem cannot be solved entirely through value-added measures). Most systems that utilize a value-added approach use a fairly sophisticated mixed-models approach, which addresses some of the problems associated with raw gain scores but introduces some additional costs. Decisions about whether to use a value-added approach, a simpler gain-score method, or performance levels can dramatically affect the rankings of schools or other institutions (Clotfelter and Ladd, 1996), as well as the messages that are sent to staff about what they are accountable for accomplishing. In addition, these decisions are likely to influence the kinds of behaviors in which organizations engage to "game" the system; an educational measurement approach that focuses on performance levels creates an incentive to serve the highest-performing students, whereas one that uses a value-added approach may increase the willingness of schools to serve lower-performing students (though only to the extent that school staff believe these students are capable of high rates of improvement).

While the use of value-added measures is likely to produce more-accurate inferences about performance and to create more-effective incentives than does a focus only on levels of performance, it is not a straightforward task to devise a measure that isolates performance from other contributing factors such as student background characteristics (McCaffrey et al., 2003). To isolate the effects of schools, it may be necessary in some cases to adjust explicitly for student background. Besides the statistical and measurement problems inherent in this type of adjustment, there are political problems: Does adjusting for student socioeconomic status (SES), for example, send a message that we expect less of low-SES students? This may be one of the reasons NCLB focuses on raw levels (schools are required to meet targets for performance that are uniform across schools and not based on prior performance) rather than on change or on adjusted scores; proponents of the legislation have emphasized the importance of ensuring that *all* students, regardless of personal circumstances, are given the opportunity to achieve high standards. In addition, the use of complex value-added measures or other statistical adjustments lacks transparency and therefore may be difficult for some staff to accept; it may even invite legal challenges (Cohen, 1996). Compared with the available alternatives, however, some sort of value-added measurement will in most cases be the most desirable approach to ensuring a fair and valid system for education and for other government activities in which the difficulty of attaining the goals is affected by the tasks that workers are assigned.

Do Not Rely Exclusively on the Measure to Communicate Goals

In the test-based accountability systems described above, content and performance standards are intended to be the primary vehicle through which goals are conveyed, whereas the tests are intended to serve as the measure of whether those goals have been attained. In many schools and districts, however, staff use the test rather than the standards as the key source of information about what they are expected to accomplish (Clarke et al., 2003). This is a rational response, given the stakes attached to test performance and the lack of mechanisms to ensure attention to the standards. However, it undermines the goals of the system because the test typically captures only a narrow range of the outcomes of interest. The standards are designed to be comprehensive, to include material that is difficult to measure through a paper-and-pencil test, and to reflect some consensus on what is considered important for students to learn. Thus state and district administrators need to make efforts to ensure that educators are paying attention to the standards in addition to the tests if they want the goals of the system to be reached. Such efforts often include professional development and translating the standards into information that is useful for instructional planning—e.g., by linking specific standards to descriptions of sample lesson plans or student work.

The same principles are likely to apply in other sectors of government. The saliency of the measurement instrument will tend to make it the main source to which staff turn for information about what is expected of them. To avoid excessive focus on a single measure, the broader goals of an organization must be clearly communicated, and efforts must be made to help staff figure out how to adopt these goals. As in education, the efforts are likely to involve some combination of staff development and provision of materials or other resources that help make the goals concrete and understandable.

**Create Targets for Performance That Are Perceived
as Fair and Attainable**

Performance-based accountability systems often assume that performance will improve simply as a result of the increased motivation those systems instill. But increased motivation does not necessarily result from the imposition of goals, rewards, and sanctions. To be motivated by externally imposed goals and incentives, employees must to some degree accept the goals, view the incentives as significant, and believe that the goals are attainable through their own efforts (Rowan, 1996). In fact, if staff believe that the goals are unattainable or that the system is somehow biased against them, the level of motivation is likely to decrease, and the likelihood of inappropriate responses may increase (Koretz, 2003). The tendency to rely on shortcuts to achieve goals is in part a result of the uncertainty inherent in a system of goals that is perceived as too ambitious; employees need some assurance that they can, in fact, attain the goals by working effectively. Common sense is critical in setting goals that will be perceived as attainable, but it would also be valuable to seek feedback from employees to understand how they perceive the goals and whether they are responding in appropriate ways. Employees not only need clear information regarding what the goals are, they should also be offered assistance in understanding how to attain them.

Create an Incentive System That Promotes Effort and Teamwork
In the public education system, rewards and sanctions are typically targeted to schools rather than to individual employees. This reflects, to some extent, concerns expressed by teachers' collective bargaining organizations, which typically try to avoid merit pay schemes that require evaluation of individual teacher performance. But the school-level reward system also reflects a recognition that teachers are most effective when they are working with their colleagues to promote the welfare of the school and that fostering competition among teachers within a school may be harmful to morale and, ultimately, to student learning.

In organizations where teamwork is critical, it may be desirable to create a set of incentives that balances individual-level rewards or sanctions with organization- or department-level consequences such as bonuses or flexible funds. This type of system recognizes the importance of fostering a cooperative culture but may mitigate problems such as free-riding that are likely to occur when only group incentives are used (see Chapter 11). In addition, research suggests that to be effective at motivating staff, incentives must be significant enough to compensate for the perceived costs of working toward the goals (e.g., increased stress) and must be based on clearly specified, noncompeting goals and an ongoing system of feedback (Kelley et al., 2000). Designers of incentive systems should also recognize that monetary compensation may not be the strongest motivator of performance, particularly for those who have chosen to work in the public sector (Larkey and Caulkins, 1992). Other forms of recognition, promotions, or improvements to working conditions may be more attractive than bonuses or salary increases to many employees, especially when the monetary rewards are modest in size. Asch (Chapter 11) provides an extensive discussion of alternative compensation schemes. It may be necessary to gather information from employees to understand what motivates them and to adopt multiple incentives to address variability in that motivation. It is not possible to ensure that all employees will accept and choose to work toward the goals imposed on them, but managers can create the conditions that will maximize the likelihood that goals will be accepted and that incentives will be perceived as significant.

One problem with many current accountability systems is that they provide extra resources to schools that fail to meet their targets. While these resources may be entirely appropriate and may ultimately help the schools improve their standing, the systems may in fact create incentives for school staff to behave in counterproductive ways. Accountability systems must be carefully designed to ensure that needed resources are provided, while still offering incentives for staff to adopt the goals of the system.

Provide Accessible and Transparent Reporting, Including to the Public

Clear reporting is not only necessary for making effective management decisions, it can enhance employee performance by providing feedback and can promote public understanding and acceptance of the organization's goals. In some cases, it may also create an additional layer of accountability, particularly to the extent that users of the information are empowered to make choices among providers

and can exert market pressure (e.g., when there is competition between the public sector and the private sector in the provision of
some service). An effective reporting strategy requires multiple reports
at different levels of aggregation—for example, employees need clear
information on their own performance, whereas for public reporting
purposes, aggregate measures across employees within an organization
would be more appropriate. Some form of value-added reporting may
be most effective, provided it can be presented in a way that is accessible to all interested parties. The Volcker Commission report (Chapter 2) notes a lack of public confidence in government. Increasing the
transparency of reporting may ultimately contribute to an increased
level of public trust and support by encouraging more effective performance on the part of government employees while making those
performance improvements evident to the public.

Use Performance Measurement as a Tool for Organizational Improvement

Much of the attention devoted to high-stakes testing has focused on
its role as a punitive mechanism. But most educational accountability
systems also include provisions for using test scores to drive school
improvement. NCLB, for example, requires districts to provide technical assistance to schools that fall short of their performance targets.
Good measures can provide information that can guide improvement
efforts at both the individual and the organizational level. They can
help foster a shared vision and common goals, identify strengths and
weaknesses, and help employees determine whether their actions are
producing the intended results. For measures to serve in this role,
managers must have access to the information in a usable format, as
well as guidance to help them use it effectively.

Promote Local Flexibility

The commission recommends that "agencies . . . have maximum
flexibility to design organizational structures and operating procedures that closely fit their missions" (Chapter 2, p. 32). In some ways,
TBA programs in education have sought to provide this kind of flexibility by specifying the outcomes that schools are expected to achieve

but allowing local personnel to make decisions regarding instruction, curriculum, and other aspects of schooling that contribute to those outcomes. Despite ostensibly having such flexibility, many school personnel have complained that the specificity of the outcome measures (i.e., the standardized tests used to measure achievement) has resulted in a reduction in local control, as teachers and principals have felt compelled to institute practices that closely resemble these measures. In other words, even though it may be possible for a variety of instructional approaches to lead to test-score improvement, school staff tend to rely heavily on approaches that mimic the format and content of the tests. Requiring employees to achieve a large number of very specific goals may limit flexibility and creativity, as employees struggle to make sure they are addressing every objective. Managers can create an organizational structure that encourages flexibility and experimentation, provided the goals are clearly specified and not too numerous.

By providing local flexibility, managers can instill a sense of empowerment in their staff, which could enhance morale. When work rules are imposed from outside, by people who do not engage in the job for which rules are being imposed, a sense of alienation can result (Adler, 1993). The commission report notes the critical need for the government to attract motivated, creative professionals; therefore, any attempt to impose a performance measurement system must be accompanied by efforts to ensure that these kinds of people are not deterred from government service as a result of a perception of excessive external control. Barney and Kirby describe the effects of this form of local empowerment on workers:

> Empowering workers in this way has a number of important advantages. . . . It ensures that all jobs are designed by the people who are most familiar with them, so specific knowledge is fully utilized, and worker buy-in is enhanced. It increases workers' motivation and interest in their own improvement. In addition, a system that grants local authority for problem-solving allows solutions to be found quickly while problems are still small and localized, with minimal loss of needed information (Barney and Kirby, 2004, p. 40).

A combination of clearly specified, externally imposed (for the most part) goals, and a means of permitting local staff to determine how they will meet those goals should enhance accountability without detracting from workers' sense of professionalism. Local flexibility may be especially important in fields such as education, where the raw materials vary and there are no commonly agreed-upon prescriptions for addressing most problems. To the extent that the research base allows policymakers to determine what practices are effective, the use of those practices should be encouraged—if not required. But for many types of government work, there may be little evidence to support the use of specific methods definitively, especially given the diversity among contexts in which government employees work.

Expand the Role of the Private Sector in Government Operations, but Impose Transparency Requirements

The NCLB law provides for an enhanced role of the private sector in public education. Most notably, when schools fail to make adequate yearly progress for three consecutive years, districts are required to pay for supplemental services such as tutoring, and these services may be offered by private, for-profit companies. Some critics as well as supporters of NCLB have also noted that the law's reporting and adequate yearly progress requirements will generate increased public support for opening up K–12 public schooling to the private sector, as the public becomes disillusioned with the progress being made by traditional public schools. In addition to NCLB, numerous school voucher programs have been instituted in districts and states across the country, and a recent Supreme Court decision paves the way for expansion of these programs.

Predictably, these efforts at privatization have met with resistance from many public school educators. Their objections reflect not only concerns about job security, but also the perception that private providers may be given an unfair advantage in some systems. In particular, many advocates of TBA assert that the testing and reporting requirements imposed on public schools should not be extended to private schools, even under publicly funded voucher systems (see, e.g., Greene and Winters, 2003). They argue that market competition will weed out unfit private providers, whereas public schools do not face such competition (however, under a voucher or other choice system, schools face more competition than they do under a traditional neighborhood-assignment system). But if only public schools are required to report on their performance, consumers are left with incomplete information and may not make the most effective choices, with the result that public schools may not be given due credit for improvements in performance.

To create a level playing field, provide adequate information to interested members of the public, and maximize buy-in from affected government employees, efforts to involve the private sector in any government operation should be accompanied by a reporting system that ensures transparency, as noted by the commission (Chapter 2, p. 55). To the extent that private companies are engaged in activities similar to those performed by government, and particularly when those companies receive public funds, the performance reporting requirements imposed on government organizations and employees should be required of the private companies as well. Although these requirements may diminish the supply response to the extent that private companies find the requirements burdensome, in many contexts they are necessary for promoting effective collaboration between public and private agencies and for ensuring public support.

Research Should Be Built into Accountability Systems

Although the suggestions presented above are consistent with many experts' recommendations regarding performance measurement in education, the empirical literature on the effectiveness of these strategies is, in most cases, inadequate for determining with any level of confidence whether they will lead to the intended outcomes. Despite a sizable body of research and writing on accountability in education, few studies have collected the data required to examine the empirical links among accountability policies, personnel practices, and student outcomes. Beyond education, there are few evaluations of PBA in government, and most of the existing research focuses on surveys of attitudes and beliefs of employees rather than attempting to evaluate outcomes (Larkey and Caulkins, 1992). In education as well as in the broader government context, would-be evaluators are impeded by a lack of access to research subjects (resulting in no small part from a strong incentive on the part of managers and others to avoid evaluation) and by the absence of appropriate outcome measures and comparison groups. It is critical that researchers find ways to overcome these hurdles and gather information on how well various instantiations of PBA systems are working, so that future designers of such systems can benefit from the mistakes and successes of the past.

Efforts to implement performance measurement in public education and in other sectors of the government should be accompanied by careful tracking of both the behavior changes that the system induces and the ultimate outcomes that eventually result from performance measurement. The inclusion of an audit measure of outcomes, as discussed above, is likely to be necessary in many cases for evaluating the effectiveness of organizational changes in a PBA system, since corruption of results on the primary measure may threaten the validity of inferences that are based on that measure alone.

Of particular importance is a comparison of changes in performance on the short-term measures that are used to monitor individuals' progress with changes in the longer-term outcomes that are associated with the organization's core mission and objectives. Because of the difficulty inherent in collecting longitudinal data on individuals, as well as the short time frame permitted for most research studies, little evidence is currently available on which to base judgments about the extent to which the test-score gains that many states and districts have achieved recently are associated with improvements in ultimate goals of schooling, including placement in jobs and in postsecondary education. Collecting the data needed to understand the validity of short-term performance measures will require extensive resources, as well as patience on the part of those interested in the results.

Research and evaluation must recognize the role that context plays in determining whether a particular approach to performance measurement will be effective. In education, teachers' motivation, practices, and responses to incentive systems vary as a function of school and classroom context characteristics, including the ability levels of students in their classes and the SES of students at the school (Raudenbush, Rowan, and Cheong, 1993; Talbert, McLaughlin, and Rowan, 1993). For many government activities, factors such as the nature of the work (e.g., the amount of collaboration involved), the presence of unions, and the quality of relationships between staff and managers will affect the accountability system, so it is important to conduct research in a variety of settings to understand how these contextual factors interact with the system and the outcomes it produces (National Research Council, 1991). This suggests the need for a broad agenda of coordinated studies across sites, with an effort to integrate the findings in a way that will inform future development of PBA systems.

Now Is the Time to Act

Polls show strong public support for accountability in education. Parents, and the public more generally, tend to believe that personnel in the education system should be held accountable for their performance, and they support frequent measurement of students' achievement (Public Agenda, 2003). This sentiment carries over into other sectors of government, as suggested by the commission report. The implementation of a PBA system for government is likely to receive broad support, and the lessons we have learned from education and other sectors provide some guidance that can help get the system off to an effective start.

At the same time, it is important for policymakers and others to refrain from pinning too many hopes on a single approach to reforming government. The other recommendations offered in the commission report should be considered along with the institution of performance measurement. And other forms of accountability, such as those that rely on markets or professional organizations rather than on outcome measurement, should be explored as ways to supplement PBA systems and mitigate their negative effects. Finally, capacity-building efforts must accompany performance measurement systems so that employees are not only motivated to perform but have the requisite skills and knowledge to do so. It may be possible to build into the incentive system some mechanism for encouraging employees to seek out the most effective forms of professional development (Firestone, 1994; Odden, 1996). In many cases, simply providing outcome-based incentives is unlikely to induce the desired changes, because employees may not be able to figure out how to make those changes on their own. In short, a well-designed PBA system has the potential to improve productivity in government, but only if it is implemented sensibly and combined with other efforts to ensure its success.

CHAPTER FOURTEEN

Choosing and Using Performance Criteria

Robert Klitgaard, Johannes Fedderke, and Kamil Akramov

Introduction

The Volcker Commission calls for performance-driven public management. Which performance measures should be chosen? And how should the chosen measures be used?

This chapter looks at a current example, the Millennium Challenge Account, but its goal is more general. It shows how to use performance measures to select a few among many candidates (countries, agencies, programs, people) for special benefits. Choosing and using performance measures has four effects:

1. Allocative efficiency
2. Distributional effects
3. Incentive effects
4. Fundraising effects

Those choosing and using performance measures should analyze all four effects—something that is apparently seldom done in practice or in the academic literature.

Governance and Development

This chapter illustrates the use of governance measures to allocate additional foreign aid. In February 2003, President George W. Bush sent Congress a bill that will increase foreign aid by 50 percent over the next three years by creating a Millennium Challenge Account (MCA) for a select group of poor countries. In March 2002, President Bush said the MCA will

> reward nations that root out corruption, respect human rights, and adhere to the rule of law . . . invest in better health care, better schools and broader immunization . . . [and] have more open markets and sustainable budget policies, nations where people can start and operate a small business without running the gauntlets of bureaucracy and bribery.[1]

By early 2004, the Bush administration had identified 63 countries eligible to compete for MCA funds because their per capita income (GDP p.c.) was below $1,415 and they were not "sponsors of terrorism." These countries were then rated on 16 performance measures.[2] To receive MCA funds, a poor country has to score above the median on the anticorruption indicator and above the median in half the indicators in each of three domains of performance.[3]

---

[1] Remarks by the President on Global Development, March 14, 2002, Washington, DC: Office of the Press Secretary (available at http://usinfo.org/wf-archive/2002/020314/epf409. htm).

[2] The measures (with sources), "chosen because of the relative quality and objectivity of their data, country coverage, public availability, and correlation with growth and poverty reduction, will be used to assess national performance relative to governing justly, investing in people, and encouraging economic freedom." They are: Governing justly: civil liberties (Freedom House); political rights (Freedom House); voice and accountability (World Bank Institute); government effectiveness (World Bank Institute); rule of law (World Bank Institute); control of corruption (World Bank Institute).

Investing in people: public primary education spending as percent of GDP (World Bank/national sources); primary education completion rate (World Bank/national sources); public expenditures on health as percent of GDP (World Bank/national sources); immunization rates: DPT and measles (World Bank/UN/national sources).

Promoting economic freedom: country credit rating (Institutional Investor Magazine); inflation (IMF); three-year budget deficit (IMF/national sources); trade policy (Heritage Foundation); regulatory quality (World Bank Institute); days to start a business (World Bank) (available at http://www.whitehouse.gov/infocus/developingnations/millennium. html).

[3] Exceptions will be allowed by recommendation of the MCA board of directors to the President. Once chosen, recipient countries will sign three-year contracts with the United States, and the effectiveness of their efforts will be judged by the results.

In both scale and design, the MCA has been called the first major foreign aid initiative in more than 40 years. Its underlying logic is that aid can help countries with good governance but will make little difference in countries with bad governance.[4] This is a view expressed in developing countries themselves. For example, the New Economic Partnership for African Development (NEPAD), originated by four African presidents, defines improvements in governance as essential for economic development (United Nations Economic Commission for Africa, 2002; Zirimwabagabo, 2002). For a Latin American example, consider the remarks of Jorge Castañeda, the former Foreign Minister of Mexico:

---

[4] See, for example, Dollar and Pritchett, 1998; Dollar and Kraay, 2000; and Easterly, Levine, and Roodman, 2004. The U.S. Agency for International Development (USAID) has translated these insights into policy pronouncements:

> When development and governance fail in a country, the consequences engulf entire regions and leap across the world. Terrorism, political violence, civil wars, organized crime, drug trafficking, infectious diseases, environmental crises, refugee flows, and mass migration cascade across the borders of weak states more destructively than ever before. They endanger the security and well-being of all Americans. . . . Indeed, these unconventional threats may pose the greatest challenge to the national interest in the coming decades (USAID, 2002, p. 1).

> For the past several decades the conventional and, until recently, the predominant perspective on development in the international donor community has been that countries are poor because they lack resources, infrastructure, education, and opportunity. By this logic, if rich countries and international institutions could only transfer enough resources and technology, improve human capacity enough, and support health and education enough, development would occur. To be sure, greater public resources, better physical infrastructure, and stronger public health and education are essential for development. But they are not enough, and they are not the most crucial factor.

> No amount of resources transferred or infrastructure built can compensate for or survive bad governance. Predatory, corrupt, wasteful, abusive, tyrannical, incompetent governance is the bane of development. Where governance is endemically bad, rulers do not use public resources effectively to generate public goods and thus improve the productivity and well-being of their society. Instead, they appropriate these goods for themselves, their families, their parties, and their cronies. Unless we improve governance, we cannot foster development (USAID, 2002, p. 33).

> Only if governance becomes more democratic and accountable will development occur in the poorly performing countries. And only with a comprehensive, consistent "tough love" from the international community is political will for governance reform likely to emerge and be sustained (USAID, 2002, p. 51).

For a long period, authoritarian regimes were disguised as presidential ones, states of order were disguised in states of rights, imposing one group's will onto another was disguised under consensus, perpetuating oligarchies were disguised in regimes of altering and the semi-colonial foreign presence and penetration disguised in legal defense of sovereignty (Castañeda, 2003).

Better governance is the key to the solution of the economic problems, adds Castañeda: "This for one simple reason: the only way to pursue structural reforms—if this is the goal to achieve—or to impose a human face to neoliberalism—if this is what is wanted—or to build an alternative to the Washington Consensus—if this is what one wishes—is through institutions which are both democratic and functional, something which Latin America, with rare exceptions, has never benefited from and that is urgent to build" (Castañeda, 2003).

What will the effects be if we choose one or another set of performance criteria for selecting the countries that will receive additional aid?

Abstracting the Problem

This sort of question is not confined to foreign aid. When federal or state governments stress accountability in schools, they hope that rewarding some schools for good performance will create better incentives for districts, schools, teachers, and students. In Pennsylvania, for example,

> The Performance-Incentive Grant Program was created in 1997 to reward individual schools that improve on their own past performance in two primary categories: achievement and effort. Improvement in student achievement is determined from the Pennsylvania System of School Assessment (PSSA) reading and mathematics scores and job-related placements (for Area Vocational Technical Schools), while improvement in effort is measured by increases in student attendance rates. Consistently high-performing schools also are eligible for awards. . . . Recognized schools may use the monies for a wide variety of purposes, selecting those best suited to meet their particular school's educational needs (Pennsylvania Department of Education, 2002).

Allocation by performance measures may mean giving funds to some schools above a threshold of performance but not to those below, as was done, for example, in Florida in the 1980s (Darling-Hammond and Berry, 1988, pp. 51–68).

An abstract version of the problem posits three stages: a legislature (funder) provides money to an executive, who then dispenses the money across recipients (activities, agents). The legislature decides the budget, and the executive decides on the allocation criteria according to measures of performance among recipients.

The legislature maximizes a utility function that is a function of

1. Some results among the agents (Y) and some other dimension of agents' behavior or results (g).
2. The allocation formula eventually chosen by the executive (which may matter apart from 1, say, as a signal of good management) ($k = k(g)$).
3. The size of the budget (k).

See Table 14.1 for examples.

For simplicity, consider g to be a performance measure that is an imperfect predictor of the value of k in terms of later Y: dY/dk is a positive function of g, with an error term.[5] We might say that Y is produced through an interaction of g and k, along with other factors and with error. We expect that there will be diminishing returns to k to a given agent—otherwise, the executive would give all the aid to the agent with the highest g.

Let us assume the position of the executive. Our task is to choose a set of recipients based on a performance measure g such as to maximize U(Y, g, k), given how agents and our legislature (funder)

---

[5] The legislature, the executive, and the recipient may also value g for its own sake, in addition to g's (imperfect) effect on (later) Y. In the governance example, g might be a measure of democracy, which might be valued as an objective in its own right, as well as an imperfect long-run facilitator of economic development. Similarly, in an educational example, the legislature, the executive, and the schools may all value academic learning for its own sake, as well as for its role as an imperfect contributor to longer-term economic advance, equity, and political development.

Table 14.1
Examples of Choosing and Using Performance Measures

Funding Area	Recipients or Agents	Goal (Y in the future)	Performance Measure or Proxy (g right now)	Investment Based on g (k)
Foreign aid	Countries that receive aid	Economic development	Governance	Foreign aid
Education	Districts or schools	Well-educated citizens	Test scores (or gains in them)	State or federal funding
Health care	Health care providers	Healthy citizens	Proxies for quality of health care, or short-run health indicators	State or federal funding or percentage of reimbursement
A federal agency	Employees	Better public service by employees	Proxies and short-term indicators of employee output	Bonuses, "gain-sharing," and other incentive schemes

will react to our choice and use of g. Our choice and use of performance measures will have several effects:

1. By allocating investments to the agents with higher g, the productivity of k increases in period one. So, compared with equal allocation across agents, there is more Y. The allocation of k that maximizes Y defines efficient static allocation.

2. The selected group may contain a disproportionate number of agents from a particular population of interest. This may lead to accusations of unfairness or bias.

3. Dynamically, agents have an incentive to increase g in order to capture more k in the next round of investment. This has two positive implications: Y will grow more in the future as a function of that higher g, and the marginal impact of each dollar of investment dY/dk in the next round will likely be greater than it was in the first round. But problems may also ensue if agents shift their performance away from productive but unmeasured activities toward measured ones or if they try to "fiddle" the measures of g we use.

4. Our funder may increase (or decrease) our investment budget k in the future because we condition investments on g. The funder may value g for its own sake. The funder may (also) consider that our using the g is evidence that the investments made in the agents will not be wasted. And returning to point 2 above, the funder may react to "inequities" across those selected and those not selected to receive aid.

Analysis for the Case of Foreign Aid

We present our analysis of the use of performance criteria for foreign aid in five parts. First, what measures of governance performance exist, and what are their statistical properties?

Second, how can we analyze efficient static allocation of aid, depending on the way performance measures are used to select a few among many countries for the extra help? If we use g to choose a subset of countries, how much gain in Y can we expect compared with, say, randomly choosing the subset of countries?

Third, how can we examine the representation of groups (of countries, in this case)? How can we portray the tradeoffs of including more members of underrepresented groups?

Fourth, how can we analyze the incentive effects on countries of allocating aid according to governance?

Finally, how can we analyze fundraising effects? Does evidence suggest that aid donors will give more when countries improve their governance?

Measuring Governance

Governance is a popular term, yet defining it is not easy.[6] The term is applied to corporations, universities, and civic associations; in this

---

[6] The Oxford English Dictionary (2d ed., 1989) defines *governance* as 1. The action or manner of governing. b. Controlling, directing, or regulating influence; control, sway, mastery. To govern: 1. *trans.* To rule with authority, esp. with the authority of a sovereign; to direct and control the actions and affairs of (a people, a state or its members), whether

chapter, we concentrate on governments. Most usages include such aspects as popular sovereignty, the size of government, the efficiency of government, the inclusiveness of political and administrative processes, and sometimes political stability. "Good governance" is democratic, limited, efficient, little affected by corruption, open to all members of the population, and stable. "Bad governance" is dictatorial and arbitrary, sweeping in its powers, inefficient, highly corrupt, closed to all but a privileged few, and unstable.

We have collected what we believe are all the publicly available measures of governance, some 40 in all.[7] They differ in coverage, concept, source, and clarity. Little information is available about their reliability or validity, as some scholars have lamented for years (for example, Bollen, 1991, and Inkeles, 1991). We also find little concern with how these different kinds of information might be used together.[8] As a result, we see a phenomenon experienced in many "new areas" of the social sciences: an explosion of measures, with little progress toward theoretical clarity or practical utility.[9]

Confronted with a multitude of possible performance measures, how should we proceed? One question is, How closely related are the various measures? If we have one of them, do we in effect have all of them? Or are they measuring quite different things? After many statistical explorations, including considerable attention to long-tailed distributions, outliers, and bimodality, we find that the many measures of governance are correlated across all the countries in the world in the 0.6-to-0.9 range, with the exception of several of the newer, so-called second-generation governance measures. We also examined the

---

despotically or constitutionally; to rule or regulate the affairs of (a body of men, corporation).

[7] A full description is available from the senior author of this chapter, Robert_ Klitgaard (gaard@prgs.edu).

[8] An exception is the work of Daniel Kaufmann and his colleagues (1999a,b, 2002).

[9] This phenomenon finds a parallel in the early stages of work on measures of personality. Large numbers of psychologists developed their own, relatively untheorized measures of this-or-that angle of personality, tried the measures out on batches of their students, and published the results and the instrument. Only later did other scholars examine the validity, reliability, and interrelationships among the various measures.

correlations among the six composite variables[10] derived in the best data reduction exercise to date (Kaufmann et al., 1999a,b). Using data from 2001–2002, we found that the bivariate correlations among the six composite variables ranged from 0.73 to 0.92. For example, "government effectiveness" and "control of corruption" have a correlation of 0.89. As another example, the correlation between two rival indices of country competitiveness in the World Economic Forum's annual Global Competitiveness Survey—the Growth Competitiveness Index originally developed by Jeffrey Sachs and John MacArthur and the Business Competitiveness Index pioneered by Michael Porter—is above 0.9.[11] Using data through the early 1990s, Klitgaard and Fedderke (1995) found correlations exceeding 0.8 between measures of democracy and measures of corruption.

How might we interpret these correlations? These are imprecise measures. Each suffers from (unknown) measurement error. For normally distributed data, the observed correlation between two variables is equal to the "true" correlation between such variables if perfectly measured times the square root of the product of the reliability coefficients for each variable. Suppose two variables are each measured with a reliability of 0.8, and we observe a correlation of 0.6 between them. Our best guess of the "true" correlation is the observed correlation divided by the square root of the product of the reliability coefficients, or 0.6/0.8 = 0.75. For many social data, reliability is not above 0.8 to 0.9. Thus observed correlation coefficients of 0.6 to 0.8 are high, given the unreliability of measurement. Putting it another way, we would be hard-pressed to say that these highly correlated variables are measuring very different things.

Two of these variables are available for many countries over a long time period (1972 to today): the measures of political rights and of civil liberties developed by Raymond Gastil and now continued by

---

[10] The six composite variables are voice and accountability, political stability, government effectiveness, regulatory quality, rule of law, and control of corruption.

[11] World Economic Forum, 2004. The correlation is from the 2001–2002 report.

Freedom House. These measures correlate between 0.55 and 0.92 with the six composite measures of Kaufmann et al. The canonical correlation between the six Kaufmann measures and the two Gastil measures is 0.95. In our analysis of the broader set of 40 governance measures, we transformed many of the variables to prepare them for factor analysis. In these analyses, a single factor consistently explained "most" of the variance, and the two Gastil measures consistently "correlated highly" with this factor.

However, among developing countries only—a narrower sample—the two Gastil measures do not correlate as highly with important governance variables such as corruption. Among developing countries, the two governance variables based on data from a long period of time—political rights and civil liberties—are correlated with but do not fully capture variables related to the rule of law or the prevalence of corruption. For example, consider the 16 countries selected in May 2004 in the first round of the MCA. Recall that this selection was made on the basis of 16 different variables, including political rights and civil liberties (see footnote 2). If we rank eligible developing countries on the basis of only these last two variables, the top 22 countries—i.e., those with scores of 6 or less on political rights plus civil liberties—include 13 of the 16 countries chosen under the MCA. But they also include nine countries not chosen by the MCA.[12] The agreement is not perfect. So, to check our results, we report below the results of additional statistical analyses that include a larger set of governance variables but over a shorter time period (necessarily so, because of data limitations).

---

[12] The 16 countries selected in May 2004 under the MCA are Benin, Cape Verde, Ghana, Lesotho, Madagascar, Mali, Mozambique, and Senegal in Africa; Mongolia, Sri Lanka, and Vanuatu in Asia and the Pacific; Bolivia, Honduras, and Nicaragua in Latin America; and Armenia and Georgia in Eastern Europe and Central Asia. If we use only the sum of the two variables (political rights plus civil liberties) among countries eligible for the MCA, the 21 best-governed countries (with combined scores of 6 or under) would be found to be these 16 minus Mozambique, Armenia, and Georgia. The best-governed 21 would also include Kenya, India, Kiribati, Papua New Guinea, São Tomé e Principe, Solomon Islands, Guyana, and Albania.

Rewording these results for other performance indicators: First, we have been considering a case where we do not have a strong theory on which to define *performance*, so we have to proceed empirically and examine carefully many possible measures. In the process, we take account of outliers, long-tailed distributions, bimodality, measurement error, and other troubling features of the data.

Second, factor analysis and other multivariate techniques can be useful for determining which measures agree how well, and for exploring whether "performance" appears to be multidimensional.

Third, when one factor captures most of the variance, we may wish to select a few measures that correlate highly with that factor and are widely available.

Finally, if we do choose just a few measures, we sacrifice information. We should examine how some performers deviate from the rest of the population along certain dimensions. And we should compare our results with those obtained using a broader set of measures.

Allocative Efficiency

Once we have tentatively chosen measures of performance based on their theoretical and statistical properties, we turn to the question of their use. Our analysis has four parts: allocative efficiency, representation of groups, incentive effects, and fundraising effects. In this section, we consider the first part. How might we analyze the static efficiency of choosing some countries and not others to receive additional aid?

Fedderke and Klitgaard (1998) showed that various development outcomes and various governance measures go together—although in light of undertheorized models and scant data, it was impossible to establish causality. Barro and Sala-i-Martin (2003, Chap. 12) found that across all countries (not just poor ones), Gastil's two measures have a weak, perhaps curvilinear relationship growth when many other economically relevant variables are taken into account (middling democracies have slightly higher growth than very strong or very weak democracies). They found that a measure of rule of law is positively associated with growth, other things equal (their rule-of-law measure is not publicly available).

In background work for this chapter, we reexamined the relationship between governance and growth (this work will be fully reported in future publications) and found that countries differ. Cointegration analysis of time series for growth and Gastil's governance measures revealed quite different patterns of relationships across developing countries. Thus we cannot readily assume that the relationship between governance and growth is the same in all developing countries.

Using new techniques of panel data analysis across countries, we discovered a useful stratification of the data: For developing countries with ratings higher than 11 on a sum of political rights and civil liberties—in other words, countries with poor governance—we found that investment was lower and the marginal product of each dollar invested was also lower, compared with those of countries with ratings below 10. Our findings supplement the literature. The so-called growth competitiveness index developed by Sachs for the World Economic Forum selects the governance indicators with the highest correlations with growth, holding constant a few other variables (World Economic Forum, 2004). In contrast, we address a different question. In addition to allowing a direct impact of governance on output, we also allow for the possibility of an impact of governance on the level of investment as well as the marginal product of investment.

We examined a population of 66 developing countries from 1972 to 2000. (A number of countries from our earlier analysis of governance measures had to be excluded for lack of data about investment.) The pooled mean group (PMG) estimator we employed exploits the improved power characteristics of a panel by imposing a homogeneous long-run equilibrium relationship across all countries constituting the panel, while allowing for heterogeneity in the dynamics of the specification, as well as fixed effects.[13] Accordingly, we

---

[13] Note that the solution to the implied difference equation for each country can imply a quite distinct steady state. The advantage of the PMG estimator is that it has greater efficiency than estimators that allow for greater heterogeneity in the panel (e.g., the mean group estimator). Estimators that impose excessive homogeneity on the panel (say, by imposing

test for the presence of long-run homogeneity by means of a Hausman test.[14]

In estimation, we are explicit in recognizing the possible existence of nonlinearities in the association between governance and output, through the possibility of an impact of governance on both the level of investment and the marginal product of capital.[15] Col-

---

homogeneity in both the long run and the dynamics and allowing for only fixed effects, as does the dynamic fixed effects estimator) risk introducing bias and inconsistency in estimation. See the discussion in Pesaran, Shin, and Smith, 1999.

[14] In estimation, we impose a maximum lag length of 3 and choose the lag length for each individual country in the panel by means of an information criterion.

[15] Suppose that

$$Y = f(K,g), \tag{1}$$

such that the level of output depends on a (vector of) standard factors of production such as capital. It also depends on the level of governance. Suppose further that technology has the standard feature that $Y_K>0$, $Y_{KK}<0$, $Y_g>0$, $Y_{gg}<0$. It follows that

$$dY=Y_K dK + Y_g dg, \tag{2}$$

such that output growth depends on governance—or improvements in governance. Estimation of equation (2) subject to an error term may be subject to at least two potential complications. First, accumulation of capital may itself depend on governance:

$$K = K(g), \tag{3}$$

For analytical clarity, assume $K_g>0$, $K_{gg}<0$, such that

$$dY = Y_K dK + (Y_g + Y_K K_g)dg. \tag{4}$$

The impact of any change in governance on output will be both direct ($Y_g dg$) and indirect by altering the *level* of investment ($Y_K K_g dg$). Given the assumptions of $Y_{KK}<0$, $K_{gg}<0$, the impact of changes in governance will be nonlinear in both the level of governance and the level of capital intensity of production. Specifically, at high levels of governance and at high levels of capital accumulation, improvements in governance will have less impact on output than they will where governance or capital stock are low. Second, suppose the marginal product of capital is contingent on the quality of governance. A unit of capital under good governance may contribute more to output than would one under bad governance. Thus we have $Y_K(g)$, and suppose that $Y_{Kg}>0$, $Y_{Kgg}<0$. Then

$$dY = (Y_{Kg} dg + Y_K)dK + Y_g dg. \tag{5}$$

Again the impact of any change in governance will be both direct and indirect—direct through $Y_g dg$, indirect by changing the *impact* any investment has on output, via ($Y_{Kg} dg + Y_K$)dK. Nonlinearity again follows, in this instance across levels of governance. The impact of investment in physical capital on output rises with the level of governance, though at a declining rate. We address these issues through two alternative estimation strategies. Testing for the impact of governance on the marginal product of capital follows immediately by estimating the interaction effect implied by equation (5). Yet this does not serve to identify the umn (1) of Table 14.2 reports the results from a panel of 66 developing countries.

Columns (2), (3), (6), and (7) report the results for countries with fair or better governance, defined as having scores less than 8 (or less than 10 in columns (3) and (7)) on "governance" (here, a sum of civil liberties and political rights). Columns (4) and (8) give the results for countries with relatively bad governance: Their average scores were above 11. Comparing these columns yields two important findings relevant to the impact of aid.

First, the *impact* on growth of a dollar of investment is higher in countries with good governance than it is in countries with bad governance.[16] Second, results are consistent with a positive association

---

nonlinearity that equation (4) implies. Hence we also proceed by estimating both equations (4) and (5) in a stratified sample of countries: for low, mid-level, and high governance levels. Where governance affects the *level* of investment, we should see statistically significant changes in the coefficient on changing governance. Where governance affects the *impact* of investment, we should see statistically significant changes in the coefficient on investment.

We used data on gross investment in constant 1995 U.S. dollar terms. Strictly, we would like a measure of the change in the capital-labor ratio, given the use of per capita output as the Y variable. However,

$$k = K/L$$

$$dk = (1/L)dK - (K/L^2)dL$$

$$(1/L)dK = dk + (K/L^2)dL.$$

Since $(K/L^2) \to 0$, it follows that $(1/L)dK \to dk$; and we are therefore able to estimate dk from the gross investment data modified by population size.

[16] Note that the coefficient on investment in columns (2) through (4) captures the combined effect of the marginal product of investment, as well as the impact of changes in governance on the marginal product of capital (see equation (5) of footnote 15). By contrast, in columns (5) through (8), the coefficient on investment should isolate the marginal product of capital across the groups of countries, while the explicitly included interaction term now identifies the impact of changes in governance on the marginal product of capital. Comparing columns (2) through (4) in the developing countries with fair or better governance (g<10 and g<8), the impact of investment on growth is statistically significant and two to three times larger than it is in countries with g>10. Columns (5) through (8) report findings with an interaction term between governance and investment. With better governance, the marginal product of capital increases, with the impact of investment under sound governance being roughly twice that which holds under poor governance. The interaction term shows that improvements in rights increase the marginal product of investment. What is more, the strongest impact obtains among countries with the worst governance (g>11), which have a coefficient roughly ten times as large as that for countries with better governance (g<8)—contrast the coefficients for X3 in columns (6) through (8). The efficiency of investment

between better governance and increases in the *level* of investment.[17] Good governance thus appears to bring a double benefit in the form of higher levels as well as higher productivity of investment.

To check these results, we carried out another analysis using a wider range of right-hand-side variables over a shorter time period (because of data limitations over time). When we stratified the countries by measures of governance, once again the impact of investment on changes in per capita income is higher in countries with good governance (better political rights and civil liberties) than in those with bad governance. For countries with good governance, the coefficient on investment is between 0.80 and 0.98, depending on model specification and included covariates, while for countries with poor governance, it is between 0.29 and 0.46. (These results will be reported fully in a future publication.)

These results support the underlying idea of the MCA. In terms of the productivity of additional investment (such as aid), countries with poor governance do seem different from countries with good governance. If one wishes to select some among many developing countries for additional aid and one has the goal of allocating the aid to produce the most growth, a solution is to omit countries with poor governance.

How much additional growth would be obtained by using one or another performance criterion to select the subset of recipient countries? We have been considering here allocative efficiency, without yet taking into account incentive effects. In this vein, one could

---

improves with governance, with the strongest increase obtaining for moving out of the worst-possible-governance category.

[17] Note that where governance impacts the level of investment, the coefficient of governance captures both its direct marginal impact on output and the indirect impact via changes in the level of physical capital stock (see equation (4) of footnote 15). Given our finding that the marginal product of capital increases with improvement in governance, and presuming standard concavity of output in governance, the expectation is of a decline in the absolute magnitude of the coefficient on governance, if the level of investment rises with improvement in governance, though under strong concavity assumptions. The evidence of both columns (2) through (4) and columns (6) through (8) can be shown to be consistent with this prior.

Table 14.2
Investment, Governance, and Growth

	(1)	(2)	(3)	(4)	(5)	(6)	(7)	(8)
Estimator	PMGE	PMGE	PMGE	PMGE	PMGE	PMGE	PMGE	PMGE
	Full Sample	Governance <8	Governance <10	Governance >11	Full Sample	Governance <8	Governance <10	Governance >11
Info Crit:	AIC(3)	AIC(3)	AIC(3)	AIC(3)	ARDL(3,3,3)	ARDL(3,2,0,1)	ARDL(3,2,0,1)	ARDL(3,1,1,3)
Y:	Growth	Growth	Growth	Growth	Growth	Growth	Growth	Growth
X1: Investment	0.005*	0.006*	0.005*	0.002	0.007*	0.007*	0.005*	0.003
	(0.001)†	(0.002)†	(0.002)†	(0.005)†	(0.002)†	(0.002)†	(0.002)†	(0.005)†
X2: dGovernance	0.000	-0.001	-0.001*	-0.010*	0.000	-0.003*	-0.003*	-0.075*
	(0.001)	(0.001)	(0.001)	(0.005)	(0.001)	(0.001)	(0.001)	(0.023)
X3: X1*X2					-0.002*	-0.002*	-0.001*	-0.019*
					(0.001)	(0.001)	(0.001)	(0.007)
N	66	29	43	21	64	29	43	21
δ	-1.03*	-0.97*	-1.05*	-0.82*	-0.85*	-0.81*	-0.93*	-0.77*
	(0.04)	(0.06)	(0.06)	(0.08)	(0.05)	(0.07)	(0.06)	(0.11)
h-test	3.88	1.03	1.10	3.96	2.79	3.85	1.38	X1:1.39[0.24]
	[0.14]	[0.60]	[0.58]	[0.14]	[0.43]	[0.28]	[0.71]	X2:1.51[0.22]
								X3:2.05[0.15]
Constant	0.02*	0.02*	0.02*	0.007*	0.02*	0.02*	0.02*	0.01*
	(0.002)	(0.004)	(0.003)	(0.002)	(0.002)	(0.004)	(0.003)	(0.003)
dY(-1)	0.04	0.03	0.06	-0.09	-0.03	-0.07	-0.02	-0.06
	(0.03)	(0.04)	(0.04)	(0.07)	(0.04)	(0.05)	(0.04)	(0.06)
dY(-2)	-0.01	-0.02	-0.02	-0.054	-0.07*	-0.06	-0.04	-0.05
	(0.02)	(0.02)	(0.02)	(0.044)	(0.03)	(0.04)	(0.03)	(0.06)
dX1	0.14*	0.15*	0.14*	0.12*	0.13*	0.15*	0.15*	0.11*
	(0.01)	(0.02)	(0.01)	(0.03)	(0.01)	(0.02)	(0.01)	(0.03)

Table 14.2 (continued)

	(1)	(2)	(3)	(4)	(5)	(6)	(7)	(8)
Estimator	PMGE	PMGE	PMGE	PMGE	PMGE	PMGE	PMGE	PMGE
	Full Sample	Governance <8	Governance <10	Governance >11	Full Sample	Governance <8	Governance <10	Governance >11
Info Crit:	AIC(3)	AIC(3)	AIC(3)	AIC(3)	ARDL(3,3,3)	ARDL(3,2,0,1)	ARDL(3,2,0,1)	ARDL(3,1,1,3)
Y:	Growth	Growth	Growth	Growth	Growth	Growth	Growth	Growth
dX1(-1)	0.02* (0.01)	0.01 (0.01)	0.02* (0.01)	0.03 (0.03)	0.02* (0.01)	0.01 (0.01)	0.02* (0.01)	
dX1(-2)	0.01* (0.004)	0.01* (0.01)	0.012* (0.005)		0.01 (0.01)			
dX2	0.001 (0.001)	0.000 (0.002)	0.000 (0.001)	-0.01 (0.01)	0.01 (0.02)			0.07 (0.04)
dX2(-1)	0.000 (0.001)	0.001 (0.001)	0.000 (0.001)	-0.01 (0.01)	-0.01 (0.01)			
dX2(-2)	0.001 (0.001)	0.000 (0.001)	0.000 (0.001)	0.00 (0.01)	0.003 (0.01)			
dX3					-0.01 (0.02)	-0.01 (0.01)	-0.005 (0.004)	0.03 (0.02)
dX3(-1)					-0.01 (0.01)			0.001 (0.002)
dX3(-2)					0.01 (0.01)			0.000 (0.001)

NOTE: Y = growth in real per capita GDP. Governance = the sum of the two Gastil measures (political rights + civil liberties, where 2 is best and 14 is worst). Investment = the rate in real physical capital stock. δ = the difference operator. * = significance at the 5% level. ** = significance at the 10% level. † = the variable concerned was under natural logarithmic transform. N = number of countries in group. δ = speed of adjustment to long-run equilibrium. h-test = the Hausman test for long-run homogeneity. Round parentheses denote standard errors; square brackets denote probability levels carry out simulations of the growth that would follow from using various performance measures to allocate the aid. These simulations would be based on econometric estimates such as those we have been considering: If we use these performance criteria to select the k countries among N possible recipients, the result would be a Y percent increase in growth.[18] Psychometrics provides another method for assessing the efficiency of a selection. For simplicity, suppose we are to select a proportion k/N or π of N countries (and the countries are of equal size). It is proposed that we use g, an indicator of each country's (governance) performance now, which we value solely as a predictor of a valued objective in the future (Y). How much of an increase in Y will we get by selecting π using g?

Applying selection theory under normality, the gain per country turns out to be

$$\Delta E(Y) \text{ per country} = r\sigma_Y \phi/\pi.^{[19]}$$

---

[18] Simulations based on our estimations, accounting for possible nonlinearities between governance and output growth, suggest that other things being equal, growth increases from 0.5 percent per annum to 3 percent per annum as countries move from the worst level of governance (>11) to midrange governance (>7, <10) and that growth then settles down to roughly 1.5 percent for good governance (<7).

[19] For simplicity, assume the data are well-behaved; that g is normalized so it has a mean of 0 and a standard deviation of 1; and that we end up with a partial correlation r of Y and g given k. Suppose we define $\mu(Y)$ as the mean of Y among all developing countries. Then the regression of Y on g (after adjusting for other variables) is

$$Y = \mu Y + \beta g + e, \tag{1}$$

where e is a random error term.

If we select recipient countries *on the basis of g* (not randomly), what is the average Y of the selected group of recipients?

$$E(Y_s) = E(\mu Y) + E(\beta g_s) + E(e), \tag{2}$$

where the subscript s means *in the selected group*. Since $E(e) = 0$ and μY and β are constants, this becomes

$$E(Y_s) = \mu Y + \beta g_s E(g_s). \tag{3}$$

Since $\beta = r(\sigma Y/\sigma_g)$, where σY is the standard deviation of Y of all recipients and $\sigma_g = 1$, $\beta = r\sigma Y$. Thus

$$E(Y_s) = \mu Y + r\sigma Y E(g_s). \tag{4}$$

For normally distributed data,

$$E(g_s) = \phi/\pi, \tag{5}$$

Here $\Delta E(Y)$ is the change in expected Y, r is the correlation we compute between g and Y in the entire sample (not just the π selected), σ_Y is the standard deviation of Y in the population of countries, π is the proportion of countries we wish to select, and φ is the ordinate of the standard normal distribution corresponding to that.[20]

Statistical analyses of this genre could help us estimate the allocative efficiency of different ways to allocate foreign aid. We could examine what might happen to total GDP across all aid recipients if we allocated more aid to countries with good governance and less to countries with bad governance. In addition to the "best guess" about these effects of allocative efficiency, we would report the uncertainties surrounding the predictions.

Representation and "Fairness"

There is a second point in the use of performance measures: group representation. If certain groups differ in their scores on a performance measure, then using that measure to select will lead to an underrepresentation of lower-scoring groups. For example, the MCA will exclude a disproportionate number of African countries (Brainard and Driscoll, 2003). Predictably, this will lead to accusations of "unfairness" to Africa.

The MCA seems to anticipate underrepresentation by degree of poverty. It segments the poor countries into two groups, poor and very poor. Otherwise, on the basis of governance measures, "too few" very poor countries might be selected. Too few in what sense? Per-

---

where φ is the ordinate of the standard normal distribution corresponding to a π probability of being selected.

To compare the expected increase in Y from using g to select π, we would take equation (4) and subtract the expected Y if selection were random, which is μY. Thus, the gain per country is

$$\Delta E(Y) \text{ per country} = r\sigma_Y\varphi/\pi. \tag{6}$$

[20] As an example, suppose we find r = 0.4. Suppose we select one in five countries to receive aid, so π = 0.2. The normal tables tell us that for π = 0.2, φ is 0.28. Thus φ/π = 1.4. What about σ_Y? Recall that this is the standard deviation of Y in all countries. If Y is GDP growth and σ_Y = 3 percent, then the gain per country selected in expected Y is 1.68 percent. Just by selecting countries with better governance, we will end up with countries with higher GDP growth.

haps not in terms of allocative efficiency or incentive effects on the countries, but too few in some dimension of representation or fairness.

The phenomenon of underrepresentation is quite general in selection models and allocation models. Around the world, we are familiar with this problem with regard to personnel selection, merit pay, and university admissions, where the use of merit ratings leads to the underrepresentation of certain disadvantaged groups (Klitgaard, 1986; Klitgaard, 1990, Chaps. 10–12; Sowell, 2004).

Policymakers often face a tradeoff between efficient selection and underrepresentation. The tradeoff depends on value judgments—how much do you value a such-and-such percentage increase of members of group A among those selected? But it also depends on factual matters. How much do you give up in performance to get more members of group X among those selected? Answers can be provided in terms of g and in terms of forgone Y.

The Appendix provides a tool to help decisionmakers understand possible tradeoffs between efficient allocation and group representation. The tradeoffs depend on specific features of the particular selection problem, such as the strength of the predictive relationship r, the proportion π of agents chosen, the differences among groups in the performance measures g, the shares of the various groups among the agents, and the value we give to later outcomes Y.

Incentive Effects

The third dimension of using performance measures concerns the incentives created for recipients (agents, programs). What might recipient countries do if we choose to allocate new aid to countries with good governance?

Milgrom and Roberts studied a general version of this problem. They found that "the strength of incentives should be an increasing function of the marginal returns to the task, the accuracy with which performance is measured, the responsiveness of the agent's efforts to incentives, and the agent's risk tolerance" (Milgrom and Roberts, 1992, p. 240). Transferring this to our problem, how strongly we should condition aid on performance (governance) is an increasing function of the marginal returns to Y of the recipient's "effort" (for which g is a performance measure), the accuracy with which g is measured, the responsiveness of the countries to the incentives, and countries' attitudes toward risk.

These conditions will vary across countries. One might speculate that the most recalcitrant countries will be those where

- Geography, poor human and physical capital, and instability mean that better governance will have a small payoff in terms of growth.
- Leaders and citizens are so poor that they will resist entering any new aid scheme in which they might lose resources.
- Leaders and perhaps citizens deny the validity of Western concepts and measures of "good governance."
- It is easy to dissimulate good governance or to manipulate the performance measures used.
- Aid is a small part of the recipient's total budget.
- Leaders benefit personally from bad governance.

Thus, in terms of the incentives created, under some conditions a donor should give great weight to governance performance criteria in allocating aid, but under other conditions the best choice is an amount of aid that does not vary with performance. Table 14.3 illustrates some extreme cases.

Note that the incentive effects depend on the particular governance measures we choose. Suppose we have several measures with more-or-less equivalent predictive power. If we choose a measure that is beyond a country's control, then of course it will have no incentive effect (except frustration). For example, Acemoglu, Johnson, and Robinson (2001) found that differences across countries in the extent of property-rights enforcement can explain the bulk of the differences in income per capita. But they argue that the underlying cause is different colonization experiences and that these differences led to different institutional developments that still affect economic out-

Table 14.3
When Recipients Will Respond Positively to Allocating Aid by Governance

Recipient Characteristic	Responsive When	Unresponsive When
Marginal benefit of more effort by recipient on future GDP	Better governance leads to rapid economic growth	Because of other constraints in the country, better governance has little effect on economic growth
How accurately governance predicts future GDP growth	Governance can be measured accurately and cheaply (and without controversy); governance is highly correlated with the country's "development effort"; performance measures cannot easily be dissimulated or manipulated	Governance measures are inaccurate, expensive, and controversial; governance is only weakly correlated with a country's "development effort"; performance measures can easily be dissimulated or manipulated
Responsiveness of recipient's effort to governance-based aid incentives	Recipient is responsive to governance-conditioned aid—perhaps because aid is a large part of the recipient's budget, perhaps because improvements in governance are valued by the recipient	Governance-conditioned aid is a small part of the recipient's budget; improvements in governance are not in the interests of the recipient's leaders
Recipient's risk aversion	Recipient countries are almost risk-neutral	Recipient countries are very risk-averse, perhaps because they are poor

comes. Suppose an unwise reader of their conclusions decided to use colonial heritage as a measure of governance. Since a country today has no control over that variable, using this measure would have no incentive effects. In contrast, a country can affect such measures as political rights, civil liberties, and corruption.

Some measures may be more easily manipulated or dissimulated than other measures. The chapters by Asch, Hamilton, and Klerman in this volume describe how performance measures can be gamed or corrupted.

Finally, incentives are particularly powerful right around the "cut point," where a country is selected or not. If a country is far below the cut point, it may feel little incentive to improve, because it can't conceive of improving enough to be chosen. Studies of affirmative action have noted this theoretical possibility.

When choosing performance measures, we should take into account a variety of incentive effects as well as allocative efficiency. And a final dimension, how our funders will respond, should also be considered.

Fundraising Effects

Actors besides the donor and recipient are often important in choosing and using performance measures. For example, the aid USAID allocates is part of the State Department's budget, submitted by the President and approved by Congress; in some sense, the budget is ultimately affected by voters' preferences. How well USAID spends the money—the impact the aid has, the accountability USAID demonstrates—influences how much money USAID gets in its next budget.

In our illustrative example, the budget we have is a function of the performance criteria we use for allocation. We call this the *fundraising effect*. This effect can emerge for two reasons: First, the administration, Congress, and the people may value good governance for its own sake, as an objective of aid apart from GDP growth. This is probably especially true for measures of political rights and civil liberties. And second, they may believe that the leakage of aid will be lower if we give it only to countries with good governance. This is probably especially true for measures of rule of law, government efficiency, and (low) corruption.

Fundraising effects arise in other examples of allocation according to performance criteria. For example, if an education agency puts a strong emphasis on allocating educational budgets according to performance on standardized tests, one result may be that the legislature and the people decide to spend more money on education.

This point has been recognized by economists and political scientists in the literature on poverty targeting, but to our knowledge, it has not been explicitly included in analyses of performance-driven allocation systems. Nichols and Zeckhauser (1982) pointed out that food stamps may be more efficient for the poor than theoretically optimal lump-sum transfers if those providing the budget for aid to the poor value food-based aid. Gelbach and Pritchett (1997) created a model in which the policymaker chooses the performance criteria for aid allocation, but the budget for aid is determined through majority voting. Most voters do not like the idea of a program benefiting only the poor, so the majority oppose targeting aid. If we ignore political feasibility and assume that the budget is fixed, we will choose full targeting of transfers. But in response to this choice of "performance"-based allocation, in the Gelbach/Pritchett model, the legislature reduces the budget, and consequently the poor receive little. In contrast, when we recognize budgetary endogeneity, we give aid to everyone, and the aid budget grows. The poor actually do better under this scheme than they do under an allocation formula that seemingly favors them.

How does this analysis apply to foreign aid? Note that it undercuts critiques of tied aid (aid that a country insists its nationals provide, even if nonnationals can provide the good or service more cheaply). Critics point out that untied aid gives a recipient access to lower prices and higher quality through an unrestricted market, and some estimates put the gains at 20 percent of the aid received. But the critics ignore the likelihood that untied aid would win fewer votes in Congress. The aid budget might plummet, leading to fewer goods and services being available to recipients.

For the case of governance and foreign aid, we wish to know how the State Department, the administration, Congress, and the citizens of the United States will respond to the MCA. Will the conditioning of additional aid on governance lead to more support for this aid? Put another way, if the MCA's conditioning on governance were scrapped, would the additional aid be scrapped as well? The answers go beyond the bounds of this chapter. But in the analytical spirit of this discussion, it is useful to consider a related question and to consider what one can infer from historical data. Do donor countries and international financial institutions give more aid to countries with better governance, other things being equal?

We have analyzed bilateral aid flows from 1975 to 1999 from 21 donor countries (including the United States) to 144 recipient countries, using two dependent variables: the chance a country would receive aid and the amount of aid it would receive. The independent variables included the country's governance[21] and a variety of other factors, including population, GDP p.c., colonial ties to the specific donor, continent, aid from other countries (to measure a "bandwagon effect"), and trade flows to the donor relative to GDP. Akramov used a variety of estimation techniques and specifications.

We found that in most donor countries, the quality of a recipient's governance has *not* been an important driver of foreign aid decisions. In only four of the 21 donor countries (Canada, Denmark, Sweden, and the United States) does the governance variable have a statistically significant positive effect on the probability of giving foreign aid. In only three of the donor countries (Belgium, Germany, and New Zealand) does the governance variable have a statistically significant positive effect on per capita aid flows—and again, the effect is only mildly important. These results suggest that only seven bilateral donors seem to reward good governance one or another way (however, those seven donors provide about 46 percent of total bilateral foreign aid).

The case of the United States is of course of most relevance to this chapter. The analysis suggests that a country moving from the mean level of governance among recipients to one standard deviation above the mean raises the probability that the United States will give that country aid by 71 percent. But once the United States decides to give a country aid, the amount is not a function of the recipient's governance.

What can we conclude from this historical analysis for current U.S. policy regarding the MCA? Especially compared with other donors, the United States has for the past quarter-century already been giving governance considerable implicit weight in selecting the recipients of bilateral aid. The MCA is new in many ways, but the United States has already been selecting recipients on the basis of political rights and civil liberties.

---

[21] Governance was measured using a combination of g1 and g2 (political rights and civil liberties) constructed through a canonical correlation with the six Kaufman et al. composite measures.

What can we infer about the likely behavior of American aid in the future? Arguably, not much, because times have changed, in the United States and elsewhere. To predict the fundraising effects of the MCA's emphasis on good governance, we would like to know how much Congress' willingness to fund a 50 percent increase in aid depends on the use of "tough love." Without thresholds in areas such as corruption and democracy, would Congress be likely to agree to the MCA, or might the agreed-upon budget be much smaller?

By announcing our selection criteria, we send several kinds of signals and create several kinds of incentives. We signal a policy of broader import in our administration ("we allocate by results"). We signal to our international partners (donors, recipients) our values of democracy and good government, which matter, for example, in foreign policy. We support subsets of countries that are undertaking governance reforms, including NEPAD.

How large will these effects be? These results cannot tell us. The point in doing the econometric work is rather a methodological one, perhaps applicable for other contexts. Sometimes we are looking at problems in which times have not changed, and we can examine the apparent preferences of the legislature (the funder) over time. This will give us ideas about whether our use of performance mea-sures might lead to an increase (or a decrease) in funding for the next period. We quickly learn, however, that estimating the funder's decisions is not easy, either theoretically (many factors matter) or empirically (ideally, we would need data from many time periods). But econometric modeling can help as an analytical guide to the questions we should be asking directly of the funder(s).

Implications for Choosing and Using Performance Measures

The Complexities of Aid Policies

As we turn to policy implications, we must emphasize the limited scope of the foregoing discussion of foreign aid. We have been analyzing development assistance, which is conventionally separated from humanitarian or relief aid, from military assistance, from private philanthropic activity, and from commercial credits. In the real world, the separation is not stark. Military assistance has developmental impacts, not always good ones; so do food aid, disaster relief, and export or investment credits.

Even with development assistance, our country's objectives are numerous and complicated. The legislature and the executive want to increase growth, reduce poverty, enhance human rights and dignity, protect vulnerable groups and cultures, prevent illegal migration, strengthen democracy, reduce global warming, improve international understanding, and create nations capable of resisting terrorism. At last count, the U.S. Foreign Assistance Act of 1961 as amended posits 33 different development goals and 75 priority areas; each USAID project has to say what it will do for the environment, women, children, and so forth. *Development* means many things, not necessarily tightly connected and not necessarily agreed upon among "us" or "them."

For these things, the relevant utility functions are surely non-linear. We value a $100 increase in average annual income much more between $200 and $300 than between $3,000 and $3,100. The utility functions may also have national and continental subscripts. For example, even if it were possible to reduce more poverty by focusing only on India and Nigeria (say), we might want to make sure that at least some aid is going to every continent.

As the United States allocates foreign assistance, it has always recognized that aid is (or should be) more than simply money. When the United States decides how much to give to whom, it should also ask *what* it should give—for example, technical assistance. What is the United States especially good at providing, compared with the recipient's needs and with other donors' capabilities? And *how* should the aid be provided? The United States may condition aid on actions by the recipient: "You only get the aid if you do this and that." Conditionality may offend the recipient as interference. On the other hand, conditionality is well known in the private sector, where venture capitalists may invest only if certain conditions are met, even a requirement to give the investor a seat on the board of directors.

Sometimes conditionality has been welcomed by the recipient, even if not publicly.[22]

So aid policy is more complex than our simple allocation problem above (see Table 14.4). With aid, we are trying to achieve many objectives, only one of which is growth. We weight growth by a country's level of income and perhaps by other geographical factors. We are giving not just money, but factors of production (technologies, knowledge, skill) that may have a value in the country much greater than our cost or than a certain amount of money (because the country would allocate money in other ways). How we give the aid matters, for example, in the conditions we attach that help or hinder local commitment.

Implications

In this chapter, we have forgone the complications of aid policy to emphasize points sometimes overlooked in discussions of choosing and using performance measures.

Table 14.4
Reality Check

Characteristic of Aid	Simple Allocation Problem	Real-World Problem
Objective	Maximize recipient income	Complicated by multiple developmental objectives and nonlinear utility functions
For whom	All countries (all poor countries)	Country and regional subscripts may matter
What is given	Money	Skill, technology, knowledge, and other things, meaning that the donor's comparative advantage matters
How it is given	A gift (a check)	Conditional assistance, perhaps in the form of a project or a contract

[22] In the 1960s, Peruvian President Fernando Belaúnde Terry wanted land reform but was blocked by the oligarchs in parliament. The Alliance for Progress worked with Belaúnde Terry to create a set of conditions for Peru to receive the alliance's aid. One of the conditions was land reform. In public and in parliament, Belaúnde Terry protested mightily against this condition. But in private he welcomed it, as it enabled him to win a bargaining game with his own parliament.

First, as in our problem, performance is often "undertheorized" in many areas of public policy, meaning that we have no agreed-upon set of measures to use for selecting recipient countries—or in related problems, for selecting schools, health programs, or employees for special funding. Statistical analysis can help clarify the relationships among proposed indicators of performance. We have learned that across all countries, most measures of g are highly correlated. In our main econometric work, we used two among 40 possible governance measures because those two were correlated with the others and because data about the two were available for many years and many countries. Nonetheless, some countries and groups of countries may perform differently on different measures, so using only a few measures is an imperfect convenience.

Second, we have shown how heterogeneity may matter—and how it can be analyzed. Heterogeneity here implies that the relationship between the performance measure now and what we value later—between governance and later GDP p.c.—is not the same across countries. We used cointegration analysis for individual developing countries to show that our governance measures and GDP p.c. do not go together in the same ways across countries. Then, in panel data analysis, we employed a method that allows for heterogeneity and discovered that countries with "worse governance" are different from countries with "better governance." The results enable us to get a better idea of what might happen if aid recipients were selected according to their governance. Along the way, we separated two issues that are often confused: the marginal effect of additional aid on Y given g, which is not the same thing as the marginal effect of an increase in g on Y. For other examples of choosing and using performance measures, these same lessons may be important: pay attention to heterogeneity, use estimation techniques that take it into account, and focus on the right question of allocative efficiency (the productivity of the additional funds in terms of Y, given each recipient's performance measure g).

Third, the choice of performance measures may have effects on the representation of certain groups of recipients among those selected. If we select countries on the basis of their governance, we get a group in which investment is more productive. However, we also may get too few countries from certain groups of interest, such as the very poorest countries, or from a particular region. We may want to define our selection procedure to give weight to such factors or to stratify the selection. In the case of the MCA, it is likely that African countries will be underrepresented among those that meet the governance criteria for selection. How we might trade off efficiency and representation is the subject of the Appendix.

Fourth, allocative efficiency is not all that matters when we choose and use performance measures. We should also care about the incentives our performance measures create. A simple model here yields interesting qualitative results that seem to have general applicability. The power of the incentives we create for recipients depends on four factors: the marginal returns of the agent's "effort" to future output, the accuracy with which effort is measured by our performance measures, the responsiveness of the agent's effort to incentives, and the agent's risk tolerance. Agents will change their behavior as the result of performance incentives when

- Their efforts to improve performance measures have a significant effect on valued outcomes in the future.
- Agents are not so risk-averse that they will resist entering any new incentive scheme where they might lose resources.
- Given their own objectives, agents accept the validity of the performance measures.
- It is not easy to dissimulate good performance or to manipulate the performance measures used.
- The performance incentive is a significant proportion of an agent's total budget or paycheck.
- Agents do not benefit personally from bad performance (e.g., via corruption).

We can translate these ideas to other domains besides foreign aid, such as schools, health programs, and federal employees.

Fifth, the performance measures we choose have fundraising effects. Our funders may approve (or disapprove) of the measures we use. We have considered the perhaps surprising theoretical result that targeting aid in certain ways may lead to a reduction in the budget due to voter response; this may leave those whom we target worse off than if we didn't target at all. More to the point of the foreign aid problem, there is historical evidence that the United States has chosen aid recipients on the basis of political rights and civil liberties. One might conjecture that the MCA will enable an increase in aid by extending and formalizing this historical trend. But this is only conjecture; more generally, we emphasize that the choice of performance measures should consider the effects not only on recipients but also on our sources of money—thus the moniker, *fundraising effects*.

How might all these considerations be taken into account? They are still not sufficient for the complications of the foreign aid problem, as we have seen; data are too scarce, theory is too weak, and complications are too many. And yet, even in their relative simplicity, combining them exceeds the powers of statistical analysis and formal modeling.

Despite their limitations, the factors we have presented can still be used to guide discussion among policymakers, legislators, and recipients. The following questions might be asked when choosing and using performance measures:

- What performance measures could we use to select those who receive additional help or incentives? What are the statistical properties of these measures? Do they tend to go together? Do they cluster in certain groups?

- How well do various performance measures predict more ultimate outcomes that we value? How does using one set of measures or another affect the impact of an additional dollar of investment? Do these predictive relationships vary across agents or groups of agents? If so, can we take heterogeneity into account when we assess the value of using one performance scheme or another?

- Will some groups of recipients be underrepresented among those selected? How might we trade off efficiency and representation in the way we use performance measures?

- What incentives are created for recipients by the performance measures we choose and how we use them? How might we enhance the good incentives and dampen the nefarious ones?
- What will be the reactions of donors and recipients to the performance measures we choose and the way we use them?

The models presented here provide ways to get rough estimates of possible results—methods that can also be used to encourage a dialogue among policymakers, recipients, and legislators. We hope this combination of analysis and dialogue will improve the ways we choose and use performance measures, both in foreign aid and more generally.

APPENDIX
A Model for Trading Off Efficiency and Representation in Selection[23]

The indented boldface sentences are *Mathematica* commands. The indented plain-face sentences and the graphics are *Mathematica* output. The particular parameters chosen are for illustrative purposes only. Read in graphics and statistics packages if needed.

Needs["Statistics'ContinuousDistributions'"]

Needs["Graphics'ImplicitPlot'"]

Define the probability density functions f_A and f_B of the performance measure for groups A and B. A performance measure could be a test score, such as a SAT or GRE score, or a measure of productivity, such as citations per time period.

f_A[t_] : = PDF[NormalDistribution[μ_A, σ_A], t]

f_B[t_] : = PDF[NormalDistribution[μ_B, σ_B], t]

Define the cumulative distribution functions F_A and F_B of the performance measure for groups A and B.

F_A[t_] : = CDF[NormalDistribution[μ_A, σ_A], t]

F_B[t_] : = CDF[NormalDistribution[μ_B, σ_B], t]

---

[23] The *Mathematica* code for this appendix was prepared by Prof. Michael Mattock of the Pardee RAND Graduate School.

Define functions g_A and g_B that transform performance measures into outcome measures. For example, a function could transform a SAT score into expected college GPA.

$g_A[x\_]$:= $\alpha_A + \beta_A\ x$

$g_B[x\_]$:= $\alpha_B + \beta_B\ x$

Define functions h_A and h_B that are the inverses of g_A and g_B.

$h_A[o\_]$ = x/ . Solve [$g_A[x]$ == o, x] [[1]] // Simplify

$$\frac{o - \alpha_A}{\beta_A}$$

$h_B[o\_]$ = x/ . Solve [$g_B[x]$ == o, x] [[1]] // Simplify

$$\frac{o - \alpha_B}{\beta_B}$$

Define a group of example parameters; n_A and n_B are the numbers of applicants in groups A and B, respectively.

Parameters =

{ $\mu_A \rightarrow$ 50, $\sigma_A \rightarrow$ 10, $\alpha_A \rightarrow$ 0, $\beta_A \rightarrow$ 1/2, $\mu_B \rightarrow$ 60, $\sigma_B \rightarrow$ 10, $\alpha_B \rightarrow$ 0, $\beta_B \rightarrow$ 3/4, $n_A \rightarrow$ 20, $n_B \rightarrow$ 80 }

$$\left\{ \mu_A \rightarrow 50, \sigma_A \rightarrow 10, \alpha_A \rightarrow 0, \beta_A \rightarrow \frac{1}{2}, \mu_B \rightarrow 60, \sigma_B \rightarrow 10, \right.$$
$$\left. \alpha_B \rightarrow 0, \beta_B \rightarrow \frac{3}{4}, n_A \rightarrow 20, n_B \rightarrow 80 \right\}$$

Plot the distributions of the performance measure for the two groups. The dashed line represents group A, and the solid line represents group B.[24]

---

[24] The Mathematica instructions are written to generate output in color, as indicated by RGB in the code. For this volume, we have substituted line styles for color.

Plot[Evaluate [{f$_A$[t], f$_B$[t]} / . Parameters],

    {t, 0, 100}, PlotStyle → {{RGBColor [1, 0, 0], Thickness [0.01]},

        {RGBColor [0, 0, 1], Thickness [0.01]}},

        AxesLabel – > {Performance, ρ}]

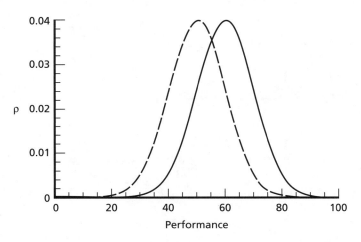

Plot the distributions of the outcome measure for the two groups. The dashed line represents group A, and the solid line represents group B.

$$\textbf{Plot[Evaluate}\left[\left\{\frac{f_A\,[h_A\,[t]]}{\beta_A},\ \frac{f_B\,[h_B\,[t]]}{\beta_B}\right\}\ /\ .\ \textbf{Parameters}\right],$$

    {t, 0, 100}, PlotStyle → {{RGBColor [1, 0, 0], Thickness [0.01]},

        {RGBColor [0, 0, 1], Thickness [0.01]}}, AxesLabel – >

        {Outcome, ρ}, PlotRange – > {0 , 0.08}]

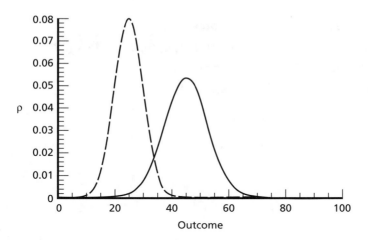

Plot the distributions of the outcomes for the two groups according to their relative sizes. The dashed line represents group A, and the solid line represents group B.

$$\text{Plot[Evaluate}\left[\left\{n_A\,\frac{f_A[h_A[t]]}{\beta_A},\,n_B\,\frac{f_B[h_B[t]]}{\beta_B}\right\} / \text{. Parameters}\right],$$

$$\{t, 0, 100\}, \text{PlotStyle} \rightarrow \{\{\text{RGBColor [1, 0, 0]},$$

$$\text{Thickness [0.01]}\}, \{\text{RGBColor [0, 0, 1]}, \text{Thickness [0.01]}\}\},$$

$$\text{PlotRange} -> \{0, 4.5\}, \text{AxesLabel} -> \{\text{Outcome}, \rho\}]$$

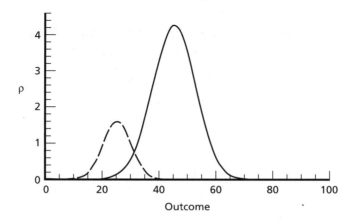

Define f, the combined probability density function over outcomes for the entire population.

$$f[t\_] = \dfrac{n_A \dfrac{f_A[h_A[t]]}{\beta_A}}{n_A + n_B} + \dfrac{n_B \dfrac{f_B[h_B[t]]}{\beta_B}}{n_A + n_B} \quad // \text{ Simplify}$$

$$\dfrac{E^{-\frac{(-t+\alpha_B+\beta_B\mu_B)^2}{2\beta_B^2\sigma_B^2}} n_B\beta_A\sigma_A + E^{-\frac{(-t+\alpha_A+\beta_A\mu_A)^2}{2\beta_A^2\sigma_A^2}} n_A\beta_B\sigma_B}{\sqrt{2\pi}(n_A + n_B)\beta_A\beta_B\sigma_A\sigma_B}$$

Plot the distributions according to their relative sizes. The dotted line represents the total population distribution, while the dashed line represents group A, and the solid line represents group B.

Plot[Evaluate

$$\left[\left\{n_A \dfrac{f_A[h_A[t]]}{\beta_A}, n_B \dfrac{f_B[h_B[t]]}{\beta_B}, (n_A + n_B)f[t]\right\} / . \textbf{ Parameters}\right],$$

{t, 0, 100}, PlotStyle → {{RGBColor [1, 0, 0],

  Thickness [0.01]}, {RGBColor[0, 0, 1], Thickness[0.01]},

  {RGBColor [0, 1, 0], [Thickness [0.01]}}, PlotRange −> {0, 4.5}]

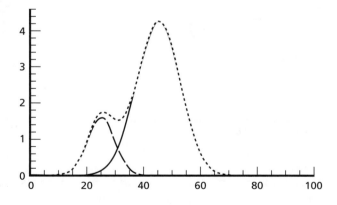

Define F, the combined cumulative distribution function for the performance measure for the entire population.

$$F[b\_] = \frac{n_A F_A[b]}{n_A + n_B} + \frac{n_B F_B[b]}{n_A + n_B} \quad \text{// Simplify}$$

$$\frac{\left(1 + \text{Erf}\left[\frac{b - \mu_A}{\sqrt{2}\,\sigma_A}\right]\right)n_A + \left(1 + \text{Erf}\left[\frac{b - \mu_B}{\sqrt{2}\,\sigma_B}\right]\right)n_B}{2(n_A + n_B)}$$

Plot the cut score (ignoring representation) C_T versus π, the fraction of the total applicant population to be selected.

ParametricPlot[{(1 – F[t] / . Parameters), t}, { t, 0, 100 } ,
   AxesLabel – > {π, C_T}, AspectRatio – > GoldenRatio,
      PlotStyle – > {{RGBColor [1, 0, 0], Thickness [0 .01]}}]

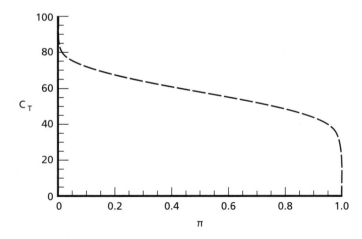

Solve for the cut score for group A given that *m* total applicants are to be selected and that the desired representation of group A is p.

$C_A [p\_, m\_] = C_A /. Solve [n_A (1 - F_A [C_A]) == p\ m, C_A] [[1]]$

Solve: : ifun : Inverse functions are being used by Solve, so some solutions may not be found.

$$\mu_A + \sqrt{2}\ \text{InverseErf}\left[0, 1 - \frac{2mp}{n_A}\right]\sigma_A$$

Solve for the cut score for group B given that m total applicants are to be selected and that the representation of group A is p.

$C_B [p\_, m\_] = C_B /. Solve [n_B (1 - F_B [C_B]) == (1 - p)\ m, C_B] [[1]]$

Solve: : ifun : Inverse functions are being used by Solve, so some solutions may not be found.

$$\mu_B + \sqrt{2}\ \text{InverseErf}\left[0, \frac{-2m + 2mp + n_B}{n_B}\right]\sigma_B$$

Define a utility function for differences in marginal performance.

$U[o\_] := 200o$

Plot the cost at the margin in terms of the difference in performance versus the representation of group A.

$Plot[Evaluate [U [g_B [C_B [p, 20]] - g_A [C_A [p, 20]]] /.$
$\quad Parameters], \{p, 0.00, 0.20\}, PlotPoints \rightarrow 40,$
$\quad\quad PlotRange \rightarrow \{2000, 5000\}, AspectRatio \rightarrow GoldenRatio,$
$\quad\quad\quad AxesLabel \rightarrow \{p, \text{"U[}g_B [C_B] - g_A [C_A]]\text{"}\}, PlotStyle \rightarrow$
$\quad\quad\quad\quad \{\{ RGBColor [1, 0, 0], Thickness [0.02]\}\}]$

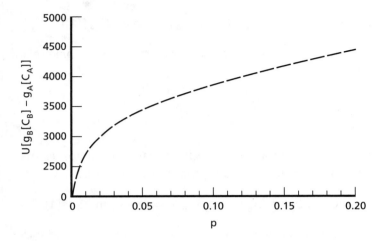

Bibliography

Aberbach, J. D., and B. A. Rockman, *In the Web of Politics: Three Decades of the U.S. Federal Executive*, Washington, DC: Brookings Institution Press, 2000.

Abramson, Mark A., and Roland S. Harris III (eds.), *The Procurement Revolution*, Lanham, MD: Rowan and Littlefield, 2003.

Acemoglu, K. Daron, Simon Johnson, and James Robinson, "The Colonial Origins of Comparative Development: An Empirical Investigation," *American Economic Review,* Vol. 91, No. 4, 2001, pp. 1369–1401.

Adams, J. E., and M. W. Kirst, "New Demands for Educational Accountability: Striving for Results in an Era of Excellence," in American Educational Research Association (ed.), *Handbook of Research in Educational Administration*, Washington, DC: American Educational Research Association, 1999.

Adler, P. S., "Time-and-Motion Regained," *Harvard Business Review*, January–February 1993, pp. 97–108.

Akaka, Daniel K., U.S. Senator, "Civil Service Reform and the Rights of Federal Employees," *Congressional Record*, June 19, 2001, at S5767.

Alberta Teachers' Association, *Assessment, Accountability and Performance Incentives*, Research Monograph No. 36, August 1999 (available at http://www.teachers.ab.ca/publications/monographs/assessment/assessment03.html).

American Bar Association and the Federal Bar Association, *Federal Judicial Pay Erosion: A Report on the Need for Reform,* Washington, DC, February 2001.

Anderson, Frank J., Jr., Brig. Gen, USAF, *A Plan to Accelerate the Transition to Performance-Based Services: Final Report of the Section 912(c) Working Group for Review of the Acquisition Training, Processes, and Tools for Services Contracts*, AF903T1, Washington, DC: USD(AT&L), June 1999 (available at http://www.acq.osd.mil/dpap/Docs/servrpt.pdf, last accessed May 5, 2003).

Anderson, S. W., and K. L. Sedatole, "Management Accounting for the Extended Enterprise: Performance Management for Strategic Alliances and Networked Partners," in A. Bhimani (ed.), *Management Accounting in the Digital Economy*, Oxford, UK: Oxford University Press, 2003.

Angrist, Joshua D., and Alan B. Krueger, "Empirical Strategies in Labor Economics," in Orley Ashenfelter and David Card (eds.), *Handbook of Labor Economics*, Vol. 3a, Chap. 23, Amsterdam: Elsevier, 1999.

Armstrong, J., *What Is an Accountability Model?* Denver, CO: Education Commission of the States, Issue Paper, 2003.

Arquilla, John, and David Ronfeldt, *The Advent of Netwar*, Santa Monica, CA: RAND Corporation, 1996.

Asch, Beth, "Do Incentives Matter: The Case of Navy Recruiters," *Industrial Labor Relations Review*, Vol. 43, 1990, pp. 98–107.

Asch Beth J., *Navy Recruiter Productivity and the Freeman Plan*, Santa Monica, CA: RAND Corporation, R-3713-FMP, 1990.

Asch, Beth J., *The Pay, Promotion, and Retention of High-Quality Civil Service Workers in the Department of Defense*, Santa Monica, CA: RAND Corporation, MR-1193-OSD, 2001.

Asch, Beth, *The Defense Civilian Workforce: Insights from Research*, Santa Monica, CA: RAND Corporation, CT-208, 2003.

Asch, Beth, Steven Haider, and Julie Zissimopoulos, *The Effects of Workforce-Shaping Incentives on Civil Service Retirements*, Santa Monica, CA: RAND Corporation, DB-404-RC, 2003.

Asch, Beth, and Lynn Karoly, *The Role of the Job Counselor in the Enlistment Process*, Santa Monica, CA: RAND Corporation, MR-315-P&R, 1993.

Asch, Beth, and John Warner, *A Policy Analysis of Alternative Military Retirement Systems*, Santa Monica, CA: RAND Corporation, MR-465-OSD, 1994.

Asch, Beth, and John Warner, "Incentive Systems: Theory and Evidence," in David Lewin, Daniel Mitchell, and Mahmood Zaidi (eds.), *Handbook of Human Resource Management*, Greenwich, CT: JAI Press, 1996, pp. 175–215.

Asch, Beth, and John Warner, "A Theory of Compensation and Personnel Policy in Hierarchical Organizations with Application to the United States Military," *Journal of Labor Economics*, Vol. 19, No. 3, 2001, pp. 523–562.

Austin, James E., *The Collaboration Challenge: How Nonprofits and Businesses Succeed Through Strategic Alliances*, San Francisco, CA: Jossey-Bass, 2000.

Baker, George, "Incentive Contracts and Performance Measurement," *Journal of Political Economy*, Vol. 100, 1992, pp. 598–614.

Baker, George, Michael Gibbs, and Bengt Holmstrom, "The Wage Policy of the Firm," *Quarterly Journal of Economics,* Vol. 101, 1994, pp. 921–955.

Baker, George, Michael Jensen, and Kevin Murphy, "Compensation and Incentives: Practice vs. Theory," *Journal of Finance*, Vol. 43, 1988, pp. 593–616.

Baker, Nancy Kassebaum, *A Bipartisan Plan to Improve the Presidential Appointments Process: Testimony Before the United States Senate Committee on Governmental Affairs*, April 5, 2001 (available at http://govt-aff.senate.gov/040501_kassebaumbaker.pdf, accessed September 21, 2004).

Baldwin, Laura H., et al., *Strategic Sourcing: Measuring and Managing Performance*, Santa Monica, CA: RAND Corporation, DB-287-AF, 2000.

Bankes, Steven C., "Exploratory Modeling for Policy Analysis," *Operations Research,* Vol. 41, No. 3, 1993, pp. 435–449.

Bankes, Steven C., Robert J. Lempert, and Steven W. Popper, "Computer-Assisted Reasoning," *Computing in Science and Engineering*, 2001, pp. 71–77.

Bardach, Eugene, *Getting Agencies to Work Together: The Practice and Theory of Managerial Craftsmanship*, Washington, DC: Brookings Institution, 1998.

Bardach, Eugene, "Developmental Dynamics: Interagency Collaboration as an Emergent Phenomenon," presented at the Fifth National Public Management Research Conference, College Station, TX, December 2–4, 1999.

Barney, H., and S. N. Kirby, "Toyota Production System/Lean Manufacturing," in B. Stecher and S. N. Kirby (eds.), *Organizational Improvement and Accountability: Lessons for Education from Other Sectors,* Santa Monica, CA: RAND Corporation, 2004, pp. 35–50.

Barro, Robert, and Xavier Sala-i-Martin, *Economic Growth* (2nd ed.), Cambridge, MA: MIT Press, 2003.

Bass, Bernard M., and Ralph M. Stogdill, *Handbook of Leadership: Theory, Research and Managerial Applications,* 3rd ed., New York: Free Press, 1990.

Bauer, Francis X., et al., "A Call for Competency: Report to the [First] National Commission on the Public Service by the Education, Training and Development Task Force of the Management Development Center," written testimony submitted to the first commission, September 1988.

Becker, Gary S., "Crime and Punishment: An Economic Approach," *Journal of Political Economy,* Vol. 76, No. 2, March–April 1968, pp. 169–217.

Behn, R., "Creating Leadership Capacity for the Twenty-First Century: Not Another Technical Fix," in J. D. Donahue and J. S. Nye, Jr. (eds.), *For the People: Can We Fix Public Service?* Washington, DC: Brookings Institution Press, 2003, pp. 191–224.

Bell, Richard W., National President, Classification and Compensation Society, letter submitted to the commission, August 20, 2002.

Bemelmans-Videc, Marie-Louise, Ray C. Rist, and Evert Vedung (eds.), *Carrots, Sticks, and Sermons: Policy Instruments and Their Evaluation,* Somerset, NJ: Transaction Publishers, 1998.

Ben-Haim, Yakov, *Information-Gap Decision Theory: Decisions Under Severe Uncertainty,* Academic Press, 2001.

Benjamin, Daniel, and Steven Simon, *The Age of Sacred Terror,* Random House, 2002.

Bennett, James C., *Network Commonwealth: The Future of Nations in the Internet Era,* forthcoming.

Bernstein, Jared, et al., "Any Way You Cut It: Income Inequality on the Rise No Matter How It's Measured," Economic Policy Institute Briefing Paper, September 2000 (available at http://www.epinet.org/printer.cfm?id=840&content_type=1, last accessed February 13, 2004).

Berryman, S. E., et al., *Foreign Language and International Studies Specialists: The Marketplace and National Policy,* Santa Monica, CA: RAND Corporation, R-2501-NEH, 1979.

Bikson, Tora, Gregory Treverton, Joy Moini, and Gustav Lindstrom, *New Challenges for International Leadership: Lessons from Organizations with Global Missions,* Santa Monica, CA: RAND Corporation, MR-1670-IP, 2004.

Birch, Elizabeth, Executive Director, Human Rights Campaign, statement submitted to the commission, June 15, 2002.

Birchman, Bruce, Legislative Chairman, Forum of United States Administrative Law Judges, paper submitted to the commission, June 13, 2002.

Bishop, J., *Incentives for Learning: Why American High School Students Compare So Poorly to Their Counterparts Overseas,* Ithaca, NY: Cornell University Center for Advanced Human Resource Studies, 1989.

Bishop, J., *Do Curriculum-Based External Exit Exam Systems Enhance Student Achievement?* Philadelphia, PA: Consortium for Policy Research in Education, CPRE Research Report RR-40, 1998.

Bleeke, Joel, and David Ernst, "Is Your Strategic Alliance Really a Sale?" *Harvard Business Review,* Vol. 73, No. 1, January/February 1995, pp. 97–105.

Blinder, Alan, *Paying for Productivity: A Look at the Evidence,* Washington, DC: Brookings Institution, 1990.

Bloom, Howard S., Carolyn J. Hill, and James Riccio, *Modeling the Performance of Welfare-to-Work Programs: The Effects of Program Management and Services, Economic Environment, and Client Characteristics,* New York: Manpower Demonstration Research Corporation (MDRC), 2001 (available at http://www.mdrc.org/Reports2001/EffectsofPrgmMgmt-WkgPpr/EffectsPrgMgmt-Method.pdf).

Bobbitt, Philip, *The Shield of Achilles: War, Peace, and the Course of History*, New York: Knopf, 2002.

Bolkestein, Frits, speech presented at 3rd Annual Public-Private Partnership Global Summit, Commission Européenne, Brussels, Belgium, November 8, 2002 (available at http://europa.eu.int/comm/commissioneres/ bolkestein/docs/speeches/20021108-public-private_en.pdf, last accessed February 4, 2004).

Bollen, Kenneth A., "Political Democracy: Conceptual and Measurement Traps," in Alex Inkeles (ed.), *On Measuring Democracy: Its Consequences and Concomitants*, New Brunswick, NJ: Transaction Publishers, 1991, pp. 3–20.

Bonosaro, Carol, President, Senior Executives Association, "The Federal Workforce: Legislative Proposals for Change," written testimony submitted to the U.S. Senate Governmental Affairs Subcommittee on International Security, Proliferation, and Federal Services, March 18, 2002.

Borjas, George, "The Wage Structure and the Sorting of Workers into the Public Sector," Cambridge, MA: National Bureau of Economic Research, Working Paper 9313, October 2002.

Brainard, Lael, and Allison Driscoll, "Making the Millennium Challenge Account Work for Africa," Washington, DC: Brookings Institution, Policy Brief 123, September 2003.

Brookings Institution, *The Presidential Appointment Initiative: A Survivor's Guide for Presidential Nominees*, Washington, DC: Brookings Institution, November 2000 (available at http://www.appointee.brookings.org/ survivorsguide.htm, accessed September 21, 2004).

Bryk, A. S., and B. Schneider, *Trust in Schools: A Core Resource for Improvement*, New York: Russell Sage Foundation, 2002.

Burnside, Craig, and David Dollar, "Aid, Policies and Growth," *American Economic Review*, Vol. 90, No. 4, 2000, pp. 847–868.

Camm, Frank, *Expanding Private Production of Defense Services*, Santa Monica, CA: RAND Corporation, MR-734-CRMAF, 1996.

Camm, Frank, "Strategic Sourcing in the Air Force," in Zalmay Khalilzad and Jeremy Shapiro (eds.), *Strategic Appraisal: United States Air and Space*

Power in the 21st Century, Santa Monica, CA: RAND Corporation, MR-1314-AF, 2002, pp. 397–435.

Camm, Frank, "Adapting Best Commercial Practice to Defense," in Stuart E. Johnson, Martin C. Libicki, and Gregory F. Treverton (eds.), *New Challenges, New Tools for Defense Decisionmaking*, Santa Monica, CA: RAND Corporation, MR-1576-RC, 2003, pp. 211–246.

Camm, Frank, Irv Blickstein, and Jose Venzor, *Recent Large Service Acquisitions in the Department of Defense: Lessons for the Office of the Secretary of Defense*, Santa Monica, CA: RAND Corporation, MG-107-OSD, 2004.

Camm, Frank, and Victoria A. Greenfield, *How Should the Army Use Contractors on the Battlefield? Assessing the Comparative Risks of Sourcing Decisions*, Santa Monica, CA: RAND Corporation, MG-127-A, forthcoming.

Camm, Frank, and Cynthia Huger, "Prevailing Patterns of Using Time-and-Materials Methods in Commercial Services Acquisition," Santa Monica, CA: RAND Corporation, unpublished research, 2000.

Campion, Michael A., Lisa Cheraskin, and Michael J. Stevens, "Career-Related Antecedents and Outcomes of Job Rotation," *Academy of Management Journal*, Vol. 37, No. 6, 1994, pp. 1518–1542.

Cannell, J. J., "Nationally Normed Elementary Achievement Testing in America's Public Schools: How All 50 States Are Above the National Average," *Educational Measurement: Issues and Practice*, Vol. 7, No. 2, 1988, pp. 5–9.

Carnoy, M., and S. Loeb, "Does External Accountability Affect Student Outcomes? A Cross-State Analysis," *Educational Evaluation and Policy Analysis*, Vol. 24, 2002, pp. 305–331.

Castañeda, Jorge, article in *El País* (Spain), 2003.

Castel, P. Kevin, President, Federal Bar Council, statement submitted to the commission, October 28, 2002.

Center for Strategic and International Studies, Seven Revolutions Project (available at http://www.csis.org/sevrevs).

Chandler, Alfred D., Jr., *Strategy and Structure: Chapters in the History of the American Industrial Enterprise*, Cambridge, MA: MIT Press, 1962.

Chang, Ike Yi, Steven E. Galing, Carolyn Wong, Howell Yee, Elliot I. Axelband, Mark Onesi, and Kenneth P. Horn, *Use of Public-Private*

Partnerships to Meet Future Army Needs, Santa Monica, CA: RAND Corporation, MR-997-A, 1999.

Chronicle of Higher Education, "Facts and Figures" (available at http://chronicle.com/stats/990/2001/results.php3?Carnegie_Type=doc).

Clarke, M., A. Shore, K. Rhoades, L. Abrams, J. Miao, and J. Li, *Perceived Effects of State-Mandated Testing Programs on Teaching and Learning: Findings from Interviews with Educators in Low-, Medium-, and High-Stakes States*, Boston, MA: National Board on Educational Testing and Public Policy, 2003.

Clifton, Chris, et al., "Alliance Contracting: A Resource and Research Bibliography," Melbourne, Australia: University of Melbourne, December 3, 2002 (available at http://www.civag.unimelb.edu.au/epmg/content/Alliance_Bibliography.pdf, last accessed October 20, 2003).

Clotfelter, Charles T., and Helen F. Ladd, "Recognizing and Rewarding Success in Public Schools," in Helen F. Ladd (ed.), *Holding Schools Accountable: Performance-Based Reform in Education,* Washington, DC: Brookings Institution, 1996, pp. 23–63.

Cohen, D. K., "Rewarding Teachers for Student Performance," in S. H. Fuhrman and J. A. O'Day (eds.), *Rewards and Reform: Creating Educational Incentives That Work,* San Francisco, CA: Jossey-Bass, 1996, pp. 60–112.

Coleman, James, et al., *Equality of Educational Opportunity*, Washington, DC: Department of Health, Education and Welfare, 1966.

Committee on Science, Engineering, and Public Policy, National Academy of Sciences, National Academy of Engineering, and Institute of Medicine, "Science and Technology in the National Interest: The Presidential Appointment Process," Washington, DC, National Academy Press, 2001 (available at http://books.nap.edu/html/ presidential_appointments/pres_app_bklt.pdf, accessed September 21, 2004).

Corbett, Thomas, "Changing the Culture of Welfare," *Focus*, Vol. 16, No. 2, Winter 1994–1995.

Cornett, L. N., and G. F. Gaines, *Focusing on Student Outcomes: Roles for Incentive Programs, The 1991 National Survey of Incentive Programs and Teacher Career Ladders*, Atlanta, GA: Southern Regional Education Board, 1992.

Courty, Pascal, and Gerald Marschke, "Moral Hazard Under Incentive Systems: The Case of a Federal Bureaucracy," in Gary Libecap (ed.), *Advances in the Study of Entrepreneurship, Innovation and Economic Growth, Vol. 7, Reinventing Government and the Problem of Bureaucracy*, Greenwich, CT: JAI Press, 1996, pp. 175–190.

Courty, Pascal, and Gerald Marschke, "Measuring Government Performance: Lessons from a Federal Job-Training Program," *American Economic Review*, Vol. 87, 1997, pp. 383–388.

Crewson, Phillip, "A Comparative Analysis of Public and Private Sector Entrant Quality," *American Journal of Political Science*, Vol. 39, No. 3, 1995.

Culkin, Charles, Executive Director, Association of Government Accountants, letter submitted to the commission, July 15, 2002.

Currie, Janet, and Duncan Thomas, *Early Test Scores, Socioeconomic Status, and Future Outcomes*, New York: National Bureau of Economic Research, NBER Working Paper 6943, 1999.

Darling-Hammond, Linda, and Barnett Berry, *The Evolution of Teacher Policy*, Santa Monica, CA: RAND Corporation, 1988.

Das, T. K., and B. Teng, "Managing Risks in Strategic Alliances," *Academy of Management Executive*, Vol. 13, No. 4, 1999, pp. 50–62.

Davis, D. A., M. A. Thomson, A. D. Oxman, and R. B. Haynes, "Changing Physician Performance: A Systematic Review of the Effect of Continuing Medical Education Strategies," *Journal of the American Medical Association*, Vol. 274, No. 23, 1995, pp. 1836–1837.

Davis, Lynn E., *Globalization's Security Implications*, Santa Monica, CA: RAND Corporation, IP-245-RC, 2003.

Davis, Lynn E., Gregory F. Treverton, Daniel Byman, Sara Daly, and William Rosenau, *Coordinating the War on Terrorism*, Santa Monica, CA: RAND Corporation, OP-110-RC, 2004.

Dawes, Robyn M., *Rational Choice in an Uncertain World*, San Diego, CA: Harcourt Brace College Publishers, 1998.

de Cooman, G., T. L. Fine, and T. Seidenfeld, *Proceedings of the Second International Symposium on Imprecise Probabilities and Their Applications*, The Netherlands: Shaker Publishing, 2001.

Dehejia, Rajeev, *Was There a Riverside Miracle? A Framework for Evaluating Multi-Site Programs*, New York: National Bureau of Economic Research, NBER Working Paper 7844, 2000.

Dehejia, Rajeev, and Sadek Wahba, "Causal Effects in Non-Experimental Studies: Re-Evaluating the Evaluation of Training Programs," *Journal of the American Statistical Association*, Vol. 94, No. 448, December 1999, pp. 1053–1062.

Dekker, H. C., "Control of Inter-Organizational Relationships: Evidence on Appropriation Concerns and Coordination Requirements," *Accounting, Organizations, and Society*, Vol. 29, No. 1, 2004, pp. 27–49.

Demaio, Carl D., Adrian Moore, and Vincent Badolato, *Designing a Performance-Based Competitive Sourcing Process for the Federal Government*, Reason Foundation and Performance Institute, October 2002.

Denhardt, Kathryn G., "The Procurement Partnership Model: Moving to a Team-Based Approach," in Mark A. Abramson and Roland S. Harris III (eds.), *The Procurement Revolution*, Lanham, MD: Rowan and Littlefield, 2003, pp. 59–86.

Department of the Air Force, *Air Force Civilian Career Management Program*, Air Force Instruction 36-601, 25 July 1994.

Department of the Army, *Commissioned Officer Development and Career Management*, Pamphlet 600–3, 1 October 1998.

Derr, Brooklyn C., Candace Jones, and Edmund L. Toomey, "Managing High-Potential Employees: Current Practices in Thirty-Three U.S. Corporations," *Human Resource Management*, Vol. 27, No. 3, Fall 1989, p. 275.

Dewar, J., C. H. Builder, W. M. Hix, and M. H. Levin, *Assumption-Based Planning: A Planning Tool for Very Uncertain Times*, Santa Monica, CA: RAND Corporation, MR-114-A, 1993.

Dewatripont, Mathias, Ian Jewitt, and Jean Tirole, "The Economics of Career Concerns, Part II: Application to Missions and Accountability of Government Agencies," *Review of Economic Studies*, Vol. 66, No. 1, Special Issue: Contracts, 1999, pp. 199–217.

Dimasi, J. A., R. W. Hansen, and H. G. Grabowski, "The Price of Innovation: New Estimates of Drug Development Costs," *Journal of Health Economics*, Vol. 22, No. 1, 2003, pp. 51–85.

Disney, Diane, "Educating and Training Civilian Employees in the Department of Defense," testimony before the Subcommittee on Oversight of Government Management, Restructuring and the District of Columbia, Senate Committee on Governmental Affairs, May 18, 2000.

Dixit, Avinash, "Incentives and Organizations in the Public Sector: An Interpretative Review," *Journal of Human Resources*, Vol. 37, No. 4, 2002, pp. 696–727.

Dollar, David, and Aart Kraay, *Growth Is Good for the Poor*, Washington, DC: World Bank, 2000.

Dollar, David, and Lant Pritchett, *Assessing Aid: What Works, What Doesn't, and Why*, Washington, DC: World Bank, 1998.

Doz, Yves L., and Gary Hamel, *Alliance Advantage: The Art of Creating Value Through Partnering*, Cambridge, MA: Harvard Business School Press, 1998.

Dranove, David, Daniel Kessler, Mark McClellan, and Mark Satterthwaite, "Is More Information Better? The Effects of 'Report Cards' on Health Care Providers," *Journal of Political Economy*, Vol. 111, No. 3, 2003, pp. 555–588.

Dresselhaus, T. R., J. Luck, and J. W. Peabody, "The Ethical Problem of False Positives: A Prospective Evaluation of Physician Reporting in the Medical Record," *Journal of Medical Ethics*, Vol. 28, 2002, pp. 291–294.

Dumond, John, Marygail K. Brauner, Rick Eden, John R. Folkeson, Ken Girardini, Donna J. Keyser, Eric Peltz, Ellen M. Pint, and Mark Wang, *Velocity Management: The Business Paradigm That Has Transformed U.S. Army Logistics*, Santa Monica, CA: RAND Corporation, MR-1108-A, 2001 (available at http://www.rand.org/publications/MR/MR1108/, accessed September 21, 2004).

Easterly, William, Ross Levine, and David Roodman, "New Data, New Doubts: A Comment on Burnside and Dollar's 'Aid, Policies, and Growth,'" *American Economic Review*, Vol. 94, No. 3, 2004, pp. 774–780.

Eden, Rick, "Faster, Better, Cheaper: U.S. Army Manages a Logistics Revolution," in *RAND Review*, Santa Monica, CA: RAND Corporation, CP-22-0204, Spring 2002 (available at http://www.rand.org/publications/randreview/issues/rr.04.02/faster.html, accessed September 21, 2004).

Ehrlich, Isaac, "Crime, Punishment, and the Market for Offenses," *Journal of Economic Perspectives*, Vol. 10, No. 1, Winter 1996, pp. 43–67.

Eisner, Neil, Chair, Section of Administrative Law and Regulatory Practice, American Bar Association, letter submitted to the commission, October 9, 2002.

Ellsberg, Daniel, "Risk, Ambiguity, and the Savage Axioms," *Quarterly Journal of Economics*, Vol. 75, 1961, pp. 644–661.

Executive Office of the President, National Performance Review, *From Red Tape to Results: Creating a Government That Works Better and Costs Less,* Washington, DC: Government Printing Office, 1993.

Fama, Eugene, "Agency Problems and the Theory of the Firm," *Journal of Political Economy*, Vol. 88, 1980, pp. 288–307.

Fedderke, Johannes, and Robert Klitgaard, "Economic Growth and Social Indicators: An Exploratory Analysis," *Economic Development and Cultural Change*, Vol. 46, No. 3, 1998, pp. 455–489.

Federal Activities Inventory Reform (FAIR) Act, 112 STAT 2382, P.L. 105-270, 1998.

Federal Employees News Digest, *Federal Employees Almanac 2002*, 49th Annual Edition, Reston, VA, 2002.

Federal Register, "Science and Technology Reinvention Laboratory Personnel Management Demonstration Program; Notice," Vol. 68, No. 63, April 2, 2003, pp. 16122–16142.

Feinberg, Wilfred, Circuit Judge, U.S. Court of Appeals for the Second Circuit, written testimony submitted to the commission, July 9, 2002.

Figlio, D. N., and L. S. Getzler, *Accountability, Ability and Disability: Gaming the System,* Cambridge, MA: National Bureau of Economic Research, NBER Working Paper w9307, 2002 (available at http://papers.nber.org/ papers/w9307, last accessed August 7, 2003).

Finn, C. E., "Real Accountability in K–12 Education: The Marriage of Ted and Alice," in W. M. Evers and H. J. Walberg (eds.), *School Accountability*, Stanford, CA: Hoover Institution Press, 2002.

Firestone, W., "Redesigning Teacher Salary Systems for Education Reform," *American Educational Research Journal,* Vol. 31, 1994, pp. 549–574.

Firestone, W., D. Mayrowetz, and J. Fairman, "Performance-Based Assessment and Instructional Change: The Effects of Testing in Maine and Maryland," *Educational Evaluation and Policy Analysis,* Vol. 20, No. 2, 1998, pp. 95–113.

Fountain, Jane E., *Building the Virtual State: Information Technology and Institutional Change*, Washington, DC: Brookings Institution Press, 2001.

Fredericksen, N., *The Influence of Minimum Competency Tests on Teaching and Learning*, Princeton, NJ: Educational Testing Services, Policy Information Center, 1994.

Freedman, Stephen, Lisa Gennetian, Jean Knab, and David Navarro, *The Los Angeles Jobs-First GAIN Evaluation, Final Report on a Work First Program in a Major Urban Center,* New York: Manpower Demonstration Research Corporation, 2000.

Friedlander, Daniel, David H. Greenberg, and Philip K. Robins, "Evaluating Government Training Programs for the Economically Disadvantaged," *Journal of Economic Literature*, Vol. 35, No. 4, December 1997, pp. 1809–1855.

Friedson, E., "The Changing Nature of Professional Work," *Annual Review of Sociology,* Vol. 10, 1984, pp. 1–20.

From Reorganization to Recruitment: Bringing the Federal Government into the 21st Century, hearing before the Committee on Government Reform, House of Representatives, 108th Cong., 1st Sess., Washington, DC: Government Printing Office, 2003.

Frost, Ellen, "Globalization and National Security: A Strategic Agenda," in Richard L. Kugler and Ellen L. Frost (eds.), *The Global Century: Globalization and National Security*, Vol. I, Washington, DC: Institute for National Strategic Studies, National Defense University, 2001.

Fukuyama, Francis, *The End of History and the Last Man*, New York: The Free Press, 1992.

Gabarro, John J., *The Dynamics of Taking Charge*, Boston, MA: Harvard Business School Press, 1987.

Gansler, Jacques S., *Moving Toward Market-Based Government: The Changing Role of Government as the Provider*, Arlington, VA: IBM Endowment for the Business of Government, June 2003.

Gaynor, Michael, and Michael Pauly, "Compensation and Productive Efficiency in Partnerships: Evidence from Medical Group Practice," *Journal of Political Economy*, Vol. 98, 1990, pp. 544–573.

Gelbach, Jonah, and Lant Pritchett, "More for the Poor Is Less for the Poor: The Politics of Targeting," Washington, DC: World Bank, Policy Research Working Paper 1799, 1997.

General Accounting Office, *Defense Depot Maintenance: Use of Public-Private Partnering Arrangements*, GAO/NSIAD-98-91, Washington, DC, 1998.

General Accounting Office, *Public-Private Partnerships: Key Elements of Federal Building and Facility Partnerships*, GAO/GGD-99-23, Washington, DC, 1999.

General Accounting Office, *High-Risk Series: An Update*, GAO-01-263, January 2001.

General Accounting Office, *Public-Private Partnerships: Factors to Consider When Deliberating Governmental Use as a Real Property Management Tool*, GAO-02-46T, Washington, DC, 2001.

General Accounting Office, *Public-Private Partnerships: Pilot Program Needed to Demonstrate the Actual Benefits of Using Partnerships*, GAO-01-906, Washington, DC, 2001.

General Accounting Office, *Military Housing: Management Improvements Needed as the Pace of Privatization Quickens*, GAO-02-624, Washington, DC, 2002.

General Accounting Office, *Depot Maintenance: Public-Private Partnerships Have Increased, but Long-Term Growth and Results Are Uncertain*, GAO-03-423, Washington, DC, 2003.

General Accounting Office, *Results Oriented Government: Shaping the Government to Meet 21st Century Challenges*, GAO-03-1168T, September 2003.

General Accounting Office, *Human Capital: Preliminary Observations on Proposed DHS Capital Regulations, Draft*, GAO-04-479T, February 2004.

Gibbons, Robert, and Kevin J. Murphy, "Optimal Incentive Contracts in the Presence of Career Concerns: Theory and Evidence," *Journal of Political Economy*, Vol. 100, No. 3, 1992, pp. 468–505.

Gibbons, Robert, and Michael Waldman, "Careers in Organizations: Theory and Evidence," in Orley Ashenfelter and David Card (eds.), *Handbook of Labor Economics*, Amsterdam: Elsevier, 1999, pp. 2373–2428.

Gibbs, Michael, *Pay Competitiveness and Quality of Department of Defense Scientists and Engineers*, Santa Monica, CA: RAND Corporation, MR-1312-OSD, 2001.

Girardini, Kenneth J., William Lewis, Rick Eden, and Earl S. Gardner, *Establishing a Baseline and Reporting Performance for the Order and Ship Process*, Santa Monica, CA: RAND Corporation, DB-173-A, 1996.

Glennan, Thomas Keith, Susan J. Bodilly, Frank A. Camm, Kenneth R. Mayer, and Timothy Webb, *Barriers to Managing Risk in Large Scale Weapons System Development Programs*, Santa Monica, CA: RAND Corporation, MR-248-AF, 1993.

Gormley, William T., Jr., and David L. Weimer, *Organizational Report Cards*, Cambridge, MA: Harvard University Press, 1999.

Greenberg, David, Robert Meyer, Charles Michalopoulos, and Michael Wiseman, *Explaining Variation in the Effects of Welfare-to-Work Programs*, Madison, WI: University of Wisconsin, Institute for Research on Poverty, Discussion Paper 1225-01, 2001.

Greenberg, David H., Charles Michalopoulos, and Philip K. Robbins, *A Meta-Analysis of Government Sponsored Training Programs*, Baltimore, MD: University of Maryland, Baltimore County, 2001.

Greene, J. P., and M. A. Winters, "Forcing the FCAT on Voucher Schools Is a Bad Idea," *Tallahassee Democrat*, op-ed, March 31, 2003.

Greenfield, Victoria A., and Frank Camm, *Risk Management and Performance in the Balkans Support Contract*, Santa Monica, CA: RAND Corporation, TR-108-A, forthcoming.

Grimshaw, J. M., "Towards Effective Professional Practice," *Therapie,* Vol. 51, No. 3, 1996, pp. 233–236.

Grissmer, D. W., and A. Flanagan, *Exploring Rapid Score Gains in Texas and North Carolina*, Washington, DC: National Education Goals Panel, 1998.

Grissmer, D. W., A. Flanagan, J. Kawata, and S. Williamson, *Improving Student Achievement: What State NAEP Scores Tell Us,* Santa Monica, CA: RAND Corporation, MR-924-EDU, 2000.

Guasch, Luis, and Andrew Weiss, "Self-Selection in the Labor Market," *American Economic Review*, Vol. 71, No. 3, 1981, pp. 275–284.

Gulati, R., "Alliances and Networks," *Strategic Management Journal,* Vol. 19, No. 4, 1998, pp. 293–317.

Guttman, Dan, "Who's Doing Work for Government? Monitoring, Accountability and Competition in the Federal and Service Contract Workforce," written testimony submitted to the U.S. Senate Committee on Governmental Affairs, March 6, 2002.

Gyourko, Joseph, and Joseph Tracy, "An Analysis of Public-Private Sector Wages Allowing for Endogenous Choices of Both Government and Union Status," *Journal of Labor Economics*, Vol. 6, 1988.

Hamilton, Gayle, *Moving People from Welfare to Work: Lessons from the National Evaluation of Welfare-to-Work Strategies*, Washington, DC: U.S. Department of Health and Human Services, U.S. Department of Education, 2002 (available at http://www.mdrc.org/project_publications_21_11.html).

Hamilton Gayle, et al., *How Effective Are Different Welfare-to-Work Approaches? Five-Year Adult and Child Impacts for Eleven Programs*, New York: Manpower Demonstration Research Corporation (MDRC), 2001.

Hamilton, L. S., "Assessment as a Policy Tool," in R. Floden (ed.), *Review of Research in Education,* Vol. 27, Washington, DC: American Educational Research Association, in press.

Hamilton, Laura S., S. P. Klein, and W. Lorié, *Using Web-Based Testing for Large-Scale Assessments*, Santa Monica, CA: RAND Corporation, IP-196, 2000.

Hamilton, L. S., and D. M. Koretz, "Tests and Their Use in Test-Based Accountability Systems," in L. S. Hamilton, B. M. Stecher, and S. P. Klein (eds.), *Making Sense of Test-Based Accountability in Education*, Santa Monica, CA: RAND Corporation, 2002, pp. 13–49.

Hamilton, Laura S., Brian M. Stecher, and Stephen P. Klein (eds.), *Making Sense of Test-Based Accountability in Education*, Santa Monica, CA: RAND Corporation, MR-1554-EDU, 2002.

Hansen, Daniel, "Worker Performance and Group Incentives: A Case Study," *Industrial Labor Relations Review*, Vol. 51, 1997, pp. 37–49.

Hanushek, E. A., "The Trade-Off Between Child Quantity and Quality," *Journal of Political Economy*, Vol. 100, No. 1, February 1992, pp. 84–117.

Hanushek, Eric A., and Lori Taylor, "Alternative Assessments of the Performance of Schools: Measurement of State Variations in Achievement," *Journal of Human Resources,* Vol. 25, No. 2, 1990, pp. 179–201.

Harbison, John R., and Peter Pekar, Jr., *Smart Alliances: A Practical Guide to Repeatable Success,* San Francisco, CA: Jossey-Bass, 1998.

Harcourt, Bernard, *Illusion of Order: The False Promise of Broken Windows Policing*, Cambridge, MA: Harvard University Press, 2001.

Hart, B., and T. R. Risley, *Meaningful Differences in the Everyday Experience of Young American Children,* Baltimore, MD: Brookes Publishing, 1995.

Hart, Oliver, "Incomplete Contracts and Public Ownership: Remarks, and an Application to Public-Private Partnerships," *Economic Journal*, Vol. 113, No. 486, March 2003, pp. C69–C76.

Hart, Oliver, Andrei Schleifer, and Robert W. Vishny, "The Proper Scope of Government: Theory and an Application to Prisons," *Quarterly Journal of Economics*, Vol. 112, No. 4, 1997, pp. 1126–1161.

Hatry, Harry P., *Performance Measurement: Getting Results*, Washington, DC: Urban Institute Press, 1999.

Heckman, James J., Carolyn Heinrich, and Jeffrey Smith, "Assessing the Performance of Performance Standards in Public Bureaucracies," *American Economic Review*, Vol. 87, No. 2, 1997, pp. 389–395.

Heckman, James J., Carolyn Heinrich, and Jeffrey Smith, "The Performance of Performance Standards," *Journal of Human Resources*, Vol. 37, No. 4, 2002, pp. 778–811.

Hirshon, Robert E., President, American Bar Association, "Statement on the Need for Judicial Pay Reform Submitted to the National Commission on the Public Service," paper submitted to the commission, July 2002.

Hix, W. M., *Taking Stock of the Army's Base Realignment and Closure Selection Process*, Santa Monica, CA: RAND Corporation, MR-1337-A, 2001.

Hofmeister, Kent S., National President, Federal Bar Association, letter submitted to the commission, October 17, 2002.

Holmstrom, Bengt, "Managerial Incentive Schemes—A Dynamic Perspective," in *Essays in Economics and Management in Honour of Lars Wahlbeck*, Helsinki: Swenska Handelshogkolan, 1982.

Holmstrom, Bengt, and Paul Milgrom, "Multitask Principal-Agent Analyses: Incentive Contracts, Asset Ownership, and Job Design," *Journal of Law, Economics, and Organization*, Vol. 7, Special Issue, 1991, pp. 24–52.

Horn, Kenneth P., Eliot I. Axelband, Ike Yi Chang, Paul Steinberg, Carolyn Wong, and Howell Yee, *Conducting Collaborative Research with Nontraditional Suppliers*, Santa Monica, CA: RAND Corporation, MR-830-A, 1997.

Hotz, V. Joseph, Robert Goerge, Julie Balzekas, and Francis Margolin (eds.), *Administrative Data for Policy-Relevant Research: Assessment of Current Utility and Recommendations for Development*, A Report of the Advisory Panel on Research Uses of Administrative Data of the Northwestern University/University of Chicago Joint Center for Poverty Research, Chicago, IL, 1998.

Hotz, V. J., G. Imbens, and J. A. Klerman, "The Long-Term Gains from GAIN: A Re-Analysis of the Impacts of the California GAIN Program," New York: National Bureau of Economic Research, NBER Working Paper 8007, November 2002.

Hotz, V. J., G. Imbens, and J. Mortimer, *Predicting the Efficacy of Future Training Programs Using Past Experiences*, New York: National Bureau of Economic Research, NBER Working Paper T0238, April 1999.

Hotz, V. J., J. A. Klerman, and R. Willis, "The Economics of Fertility in Developed Countries: A Survey," in M. Rosenzweig and O. Stark (eds.), *Handbook of Population and Family Economics*, Amsterdam, Netherlands: North Holland, 1997.

Huntington, Samuel P., "The Clash of Civilizations?" *Foreign Affairs*, Vol. 72, Summer 1993, pp. 22–49.

Huntington, Samuel P., *The Clash of Civilizations and the Remaking of World Order*, New York: Simon & Schuster, 1996.

Hynes, Michael, Sheila Nataraj Kirby, and Jennifer Sloan, *A Casebook of Alternative Governance Structures and Organizational Forms*, Santa Monica, CA: RAND Corporation, MR-1103-OSD, 2000.

Ink, Dwight, President Emeritus, Institute of Public Administration, "Suggestions for Consideration of the National Commission of the Public Service," paper submitted to the commission, July 2002.

Inkeles, Alex (ed.), *On Measuring Democracy: Its Consequences and Concomitants*, New Brunswick, NJ: Transaction Publishers, 1991.

Jacob, B. A., *Accountability, Incentives, and Behavior: The Impact of High-Stakes Testing in the Chicago Public Schools,* Cambridge, MA: National Bureau of Economic Research, NBER Working Paper 8968, 2002.

Jacob, Brian A., and Steven D. Levitt, "Rotten Apples: An Investigation of the Prevalence and Predictors of Teacher Cheating," *Quarterly Journal of Economics*, Vol. 118, No. 3, 2003, pp. 843–878.

Jacobson, Louis, "Soaring Salaries," *National Journal*, Vol. 13, March 30, 2002, pp. 919–930.

James, Kay Coles, "A White Paper, A Fresh Start for Federal Pay: The Case for Modernization," Washington, DC: U.S. Office of Personnel Management, April 2002.

Javidan, Mansour, and David A. Waldman, "Exploring Charismatic Leadership in the Public Sector: Measurement and Consequences," *Public Administration Review*, Vol. 63, No. 2, 2003.

Jenkins, Chris, "Project Djimindi Alliance: An Industry Perspective," briefing at Defence and Industry 2001 Conference, Australia (available at http://www.defence.gov.au/dmo/lsd/alliance/alliance.cfm, last accessed October 20, 2003).

Johnson, Ronald N., and Gary D. Libecap, *The Federal Civil Service System and the Problem of Bureaucracy: The Economics and Politics of Institutional Change*, NBER Series on Long-Term Factors in Economic Growth, Chicago, IL: University of Chicago Press, 1994.

Jolly, E. Grady, President, Federal Judges Association, letter submitted to the commission, July 2, 2002.

Jones, G., B. D. Jones, B. Hardin, L. Chapman, T. Yarbrough, and M. Davis, "The Impact of High-Stakes Testing on Teachers and Students in North Carolina," *Phi Delta Kappan*, Vol. 81, No. 3, 1999, pp. 199–203.

Jones, Reginald M., President, Council of Former Federal Executives, letter submitted to the commission, July 19, 2002.

Kamarck, Elaine Ciulla, *Applying 21st-Century Government to the Challenge of Homeland Security*, Arlington, VA: PricewaterhouseCoopers Endowment for the Business of Government, 2002.

Kamarck, Elaine Ciulla, "The End of Government as We Know It," in John Donahue and Joseph Nye, Jr. (eds.), *Market-Based Governance*, Washington, DC: Brookings Institution, 2002.

Kandel, Eugene, and Edward Lazear, "Peer Pressure and Partnerships," *Journal of Political Economy*, Vol. 100, No. 4, 1992, pp. 801–817.

Kane, Thomas J., and Douglas O. Staiger, "The Promise and Pitfalls of Using Imprecise School Accountability Measures," *Journal of Economic Perspectives*, Vol. 16, No. 4, 2002a, pp. 91–114.

Kane, Thomas J., and Douglas O. Staiger, "Volatility in School Test Scores: Implications for Test-Based Accountability Systems," in D. Ravitch (ed.), *Brookings Papers on Education Policy*, Washington, DC: Brookings Institution, 2002b, pp. 235–269.

Kanouse, D. E., J. D. Kallich, and J. P. Kahan, "Dissemination of Effectiveness and Outcomes Research," *Health Policy*, Vol. 34, No. 3, 1995, pp. 167–192.

Katz, Lawrence, and Alan Krueger, "Changes in the Structure of Wages in the Public and Private Sectors," New York: National Bureau of Economic Research, Working Paper No. 2667, 1991.

Kaufmann, Daniel, Aart Kraay, and Pablo Zoido-Lobaton, "Aggregating Governance Indicators," Washington, DC: World Bank, World Bank Policy Research Working Paper 2195, 1999.

Kaufmann, Daniel, Aart Kraay, and Pablo Zoido-Lobaton, "Governance Matters," Washington, DC: World Bank, World Bank Policy Research Working Paper 2196, 1999.

Kaufmann, Daniel, Aart Kraay, and Pablo Zoido-Lobaton, "Governance Matters II," Washington, DC: World Bank, World Bank Policy Research Working Paper 2772, 2002.

Kelley, C., A. Odden, A. Milanowski, and H. Heneman, *The Motivational Effects of School-Based Performance Awards,* Philadelphia, PA: Consortium for Policy Research in Education, CPRE Policy Brief RB-29, 2000.

Kelling, George L., Catherine M. Coles, and James Q. Wilson, *Fixing Broken Windows: Restoring Order and Reducing Crime in Our Communities,* Reprint edition, Free Press, 1998.

Keohane, Robert O., *After Hegemony: Cooperation and Discord in the World Political Economy,* Princeton, NJ: Princeton University Press, 1984.

Keohane, Robert O., and Joseph S. Nye, *Power and Interdependence,* Boston, MA: Little, Brown, 1973.

Kettl, Donald F., Patricia W. Ingraham, Ronald P. Sanders, and Constance Horner, *Civil Service Reform: Building a Government That Works,* Washington, DC: Brookings Institution Press, 1996.

Keynes, John Maynard, *The Economic Consequences of the Peace,* New York: Harcourt, Brace and Howe, 1920.

Kirby, S. N., "The Job Training Partnership Act and the Workforce Investment Act," in B. Stecher and S. N. Kirby (eds.), *Organizational Improvement and Accountability: Lessons for Education from Other Sectors,* Santa Monica, CA: RAND Corporation, 2004, pp. 51–63.

Kirshenberg, S., "Base Closings: What's Ahead in 1995?" *Public Management,* Vol. 77, February 1995, pp. 4–8.

Klerman, Jacob A., et al., *Welfare Reform in California: State and Country Implementation of CalWORKs in the Second Year,* Santa Monica, CA: RAND Corporation, MR-1177-CDSS, 2001.

Klitgaard, Robert, *Choosing Elites,* New York: Basic Books, 1985.

Klitgaard, Robert, *Elitism and Meritocracy in Developing Countries,* Baltimore, MD: Johns Hopkins University Press, 1986.

Klitgaard, Robert, *Adjusting to Reality: Beyond "State vs. Market" in Economic Development*, San Francisco, CA: Institute for Contemporary Studies Press, 1990.

Klitgaard, Robert, and Johannes Fedderke, "Social Integration and Disintegration: An Exploratory Analysis of Cross-Country Data," *World Development*, Vol. 23, No. 3, 1995, pp. 357–369.

Klitgaard, Robert, Ronald MacLean-Abaroa, and H. Lindsey Parris, *Corrupt Cities: A Practical Guide to Cure and Prevention*, Oakland, CA: ICS Press, 2000.

Klitgaard, Robert, and Gregory F. Treverton, *Assessing Partnerships: New Forms of Collaboration*, Arlington, VA: IBM Endowment for the Business of Government, March 2003.

Knight, Frank H., *Risk, Uncertainty, and Profit*, Boston, MA: Houghton Mifflin, 1921.

Knott, J. H., and G. J. Miller, *Reforming Bureaucracy: The Politics of Institutional Choice*, Englewood Cliffs, NJ: Prentice-Hall, Inc., 1987.

Koretz, Daniel M., "Limitations in the Use of Achievement Tests as Measures of Educators' Productivity," *Journal of Human Resources*, Vol. 37, No. 4, 2002, pp. 752–777.

Koretz, D., "Attempting to Discern the Effects of the NCLB Accountability Provisions on Learning," paper presented at the Annual Meeting of the American Educational Research Association, Chicago, IL, 2003.

Koretz, D. M., and S. I. Barron, *The Validity of Gains on the Kentucky Instructional Results Information System (KIRIS)*, Santa Monica, CA: RAND Corporation, 1998.

Koretz, Daniel M., S. Barron, K. Mitchell, and B. Stecher, *The Perceived Effects of the Kentucky Instructional Results Information System (KIRIS)*, Santa Monica, CA: RAND Corporation, MR-07920PCT/FF, 1996.

Koretz, D. M., and L. S. Hamilton, *Teachers' Responses to High-Stakes Testing and the Validity of Gains: A Pilot Study*, Los Angeles, CA: Center for Research on Evaluation, Standards, and Student Testing, CSE Technical Report 610, 2003.

Koretz, D. M., R. L. Linn, S. B. Dunbar, and L. A. Shepard, "The Effects of High-Stakes Testing on Achievement: Preliminary Findings About Generalization Across Tests," paper presented at the Annual Meeting of the American Educational Research Association, Chicago, IL, April 1991.

Koretz, D. M., K. Mitchell, S. Barron, and S. Keith, *The Perceived Effects of the Maryland School Performance Assessment Program,* Los Angeles, CA: Center for Research on Evaluation, Standards, and Student Testing, CSE Technical Report 409, 1996.

Kotlikoff, Laurence, and Jagadeesh Gokhale, "Estimating a Firm's Age-Productivity Profile Using the Present Value of Workers' Earnings," *Quarterly Journal of Economics,* Vol. 107, No. 4, 1992, pp. 1215–1242.

Krueger, Alan, "Are Public Sector Workers Paid More Than Their Alternative Wage? Evidence from Longitudinal Data and Job Queues," in R. Freeman and B. Ichniowski (eds.), *When Public Sector Workers Unionize,* Chicago, IL: University of Chicago Press, 1988.

Krueger, Alan, "Experimental Estimates of Education Production Functions," *Quarterly Journal of Economics,* May 1999.

LaLonde, R., "Evaluating the Econometric Evaluations of Training Programs with Experimental Data," *American Economic Review,* Vol. 76, No. 4, 1986, pp. 604–620.

Lambert, Richard A., David F. Larcker, and Keith Weigelt, "The Structure of Organizational Incentives," *Administrative Sciences Quarterly,* Vol. 38, 1993, pp. 438–461.

Landy, Frank, and James Farr, "Performance Ratings," *Psychology Bulletin,* Vol. 87, 1980, pp. 72–107.

Langlois, Richard N., "Chandler in a Larger Frame: Markets, Transaction Costs, and Organizational Form in History," Social Science Research Network, working paper, January 2004 (available at http://ssrn.com/abstract=486184).

Larkey, P. D., and J. P. Caulkins, *All Above Average and Other Unintended Consequences of Performance Appraisal Systems,* Pittsburgh, PA: H. John Heinz II School of Public Policy and Management, Carnegie Mellon University, Working Paper 92-41, 1992.

Larrabee, F. Stephen, et al., "The Changing Global Security Environment: New Opportunities and Challenges," Santa Monica, CA: RAND Corporation, unpublished research, August 2003.

Lawther, Wendell C., "Contracting for the 21st Century: A Partnership Model," in Mark A. Abramson and Roland S. Harris III (eds.), *The Procurement Revolution*, Lanham, MD: Rowan and Littlefield, 2003, pp. 167–216.

Lazear, Edward, "Why Is There Mandatory Retirement?" *Journal of Political Economy*, Vol. 87, 1979, pp. 1261–1264.

Lazear, Edward, "Pensions as Severance Pay," in Zvi Bodie and John Shoven (eds.), *Financial Aspects of the United States Pension System*, Chicago, IL: University of Chicago Press, 1983, pp. 57–89.

Lazear, Edward, "Salaries vs. Piece Rates," *Journal of Business*, Vol. 59, 1986, pp. 405–431.

Lazear, Edward, "Pay Equity and Industrial Politics," *Journal of Political Economy*, Vol. 97, No. 3, 1989, pp. 561–580.

Lazear, Edward, *Personnel Economics*, Cambridge, MA: MIT Press, 1995.

Lazear, Edward P., "Performance Pay and Productivity," *American Economic Review*, Vol. 90, No. 5, 2000, pp. 1346–1361.

Lazear, Edward, "The Future of Personnel Economics," *Economic Journal*, Vol. 110, 2000, pp. F610–F639.

Lazear, Edward P., "Paying Teachers for Performance: Incentives and Selection," Stanford, CA: Stanford University, mimeo, 2001.

Lazear, Edward, and Robert Moore, "Incentives, Productivity, and Labor Contracts," *Quarterly Journal of Economics*, Vol. 99, No. 2, 1984, pp. 275–296.

Lazear, Edward, and Sherwin Rosen, "Rank-Order Tournaments as Optimal Labor Contracts," *Journal of Political Economy*, Vol. 8, Pt. 2, 1981, pp. S106–S123.

Lempert, Robert J., Steven W. Popper, and Steven C. Bankes, "Confronting Surprise," *Social Science Computing Review*, Vol. 20, No. 4, 2002, pp. 420–440.

Lempert, Robert J., Steven W. Popper, and Steven C. Bankes, *Shaping the Next One Hundred Years: New Methods for Quantitative, Long-Term Policy Analysis*, Santa Monica, CA: RAND Corporation, 2003.

Lerner, J., and R. P. Merges, "The Control of Technological Alliances: An Empirical Analysis of the Biotechnology Industry," *Journal of Industrial Economics*, Vol. 46, 1998, pp. 125–156.

Leventis, Andrew, "Cardiac Surgeons Under the Knife," mimeo, Princeton University, 1997.

Levy, D., J. S. Moini, T. Kaganoff, E. G. Keating, C. H. Augustine, T. K. Bikson, K. Leuschner, and S. M. Gates, *Base Realignment and Closure (BRAC) and Organizational Restructuring in the DoD: Implications for Education and Training Infrastructure*, Santa Monica, CA: RAND Corporation, MG-153-OSD (forthcoming).

Lewis, Bernard, "Why Do They Hate Us?" *The Atlantic*, September 1990.

Light, P. C., *The Tides of Reform: Making Government Work 1945–1995*, New Haven, CT: Yale University Press, 1997.

Light, Paul C., *The True Size of Government*, Washington, DC: Brookings Institution, 1999.

Light, Paul, "To Restore and Renew: Now Is the Time to Rebuild the Federal Public Service," *Government Executive*, November 2001.

Light, Paul C., and Virginia L. Thomas, *The Merit and Reputation of an Administration: Presidential Appointees on the Appointment Process, A Report on a Survey Conducted by Princeton Survey Research Associates on Behalf of the Presidential Appointee Initiative*, April 28, 2000 (available at http://www.appointee.brookings.org/events/report.pdf, accessed September 21, 2004).

Lindstrom, Gustav, Tora K. Bikson, and Gregory F. Treverton, *Developing America's Leaders for a Globalized Environment: Lessons from Literature Across Public and Private Sectors*, Santa Monica, CA: RAND Corporation, DRU-2823-IP, 2002.

Linn, R. L., M. E. Graue, and N. M. Sanders, "Comparing State and District Test Results to National Norms: The Validity of Claims That 'Everyone Is Above Average,'" *Educational Measurement: Issues and Practice*, Vol. 9, 1990, pp. 5–14.

Lipton, D., and J. Sachs, "Creating a Market Economy in Eastern Europe: The Case of Poland," *Brookings Papers on Economic Activity*, No. 1, 1990, pp. 75–133.

Mackenzie, G. Calvin, *Starting Over: The Presidential Appointment Process in 1997,* The Century Foundation [formerly The Twentieth Century Fund], 1998 (available at http://web.archive.org/web/20030906005238/www.tcf.org/task_forces/nominations/mackenzie/Starting_Over.html, accessed September 21, 2004).

Mackenzie, G. Calvin, *Scandal Proof,* Washington, DC: Brookings Institution, 2002.

Mackenzie, G. Calvin, and Robert Shogan, *Obstacle Course: The Report of the Twentieth Century Fund Task Force on the Presidential Appointments Process,* New York: Twentieth Century Fund Press, 1996.

Malcomson, James, "Individual Employment Contracts," in Orley Ashenfelter and David Card (eds.), *Handbook of Labor Economics,* Amsterdam: Elsevier, 1999, pp. 2291–2365.

March, James, and Herbert Simon, *Organizations,* John Wiley, 1958.

Masten, Scott E., "Contractual Choice," Topic 4100 in B. Boukaert and G. De Geest (eds.), *Encyclopedia of Law and Economics,* Cheltenham, UK: Edward Elgar Publishing, 1999.

Mathews, Jessica T., "Power Shift," *Foreign Affairs,* Vol. 76, No. 1, January/February 1997.

May, Ernest R., "The U.S. Government, a Legacy of the Cold War," *Diplomatic History,* Vol. 16, No. 2, Spring 1992.

Mazmanian, Daniel A., and Paul A. Sabatier, *Implementation and Public Policy,* Lanham, MD: University Press of America, 1989.

McCaffrey, Daniel F., Daniel M. Koretz, J. R. Lockwood, and Laura S. Hamilton, *Evaluating Value-Added Models for Teacher Accountability,* Santa Monica, CA: RAND Corporation, MG-158-EDU, 2004a.

McCaffrey, D., J. R. Lockwood, D. Koretz, T. Louis, L. Hamilton, et al., "Models for Value-Added Modeling of Teacher Effects," *Journal of Educational and Behavioral Statistics,* Vol. 29, No. 1, Spring 2004b, pp. 67–101.

McCall, Morgan W., Jr., *High Flyers: Developing the Next Generation of Leaders,* Boston, MA: Harvard Business School Press, 1998.

McCall, Morgan W., Jr., Michael M. Lombardo (contributor), and Ann M. Morrison (contributor), *The Lessons of Experience: How Successful Executives Develop on the Job,* New York: The Free Press, 1989.

McGlynn, E. A., S. Asch, J. Adams, J. Keesey, J. Hicks, A. DeCristofaro, and E. Kerr, "The Quality of Health Care Delivered to Adults in the United States," *New England Journal of Medicine*, Vol. 348, No. 26, June 26, 2003, pp. 2635–2645.

McLaughlin, M. W., and J. E. Talbert, *Contexts That Matter for Teaching and Learning: Strategic Opportunities for Meeting the Nation's Education Goals,* Stanford, CA: Center for Research on the Context of Secondary School Teaching, Stanford University, 1993.

Mecham, Leonidas Ralph, Secretary, Judicial Conference of the United States, letter submitted to the commission, June 14, 2002.

Medoff, James, and Katherine Abraham, "Experience, Performance, and Earnings," *Quarterly Journal of Economics*, Vol. 95, 1980, pp. 703–736.

Megginson, William L., and Jeffrey N. Netter, "From State to Market: A Survey of Studies of Privatization," *Journal of Economic Literature*, Vol. 39, No. 2, 2001, pp. 321–389.

Meyer, Bruce, "Natural and Quasi-Experiments in Economics," *Journal of Business and Economic Statistics*, Vol. 13, April 1995, pp. 151–162.

Milgrom, Paul, "Employment Contracts, Influence Activity and Efficient Organization," *Journal of Political Economy*, Vol. 96, 1988, pp. 42–60.

Milgrom, Paul, and John Roberts, "An Economic Approach to Influence in Organizations," *American Journal of Sociology*, Vol. 94, 1988, pp. S154–S179.

Milgrom, Paul, and John Roberts, *Economics, Organization, and Management*, Englewood Cliffs, NJ: Prentice Hall, 1992.

Mintzberg, Henry, *The Nature of Managerial Work*, New York: Harper and Row, 1973.

Mintzberg, H., *The Rise and Fall of Strategic Planning*, New York: The Free Press, 1994.

Mintzberg, H., B. Ashland, and J. Lampel, *The Strategy Safari: A Guided Tour Through the Wilds of Strategic Management*, New York: The Free Press, 1998.

Moe, R., "The Reinventing Government Exercise," Public Administration Review, Vol. 54, March/April 1994, pp. 111–122.

Moe, T., "The Politics of Bureaucratic Structure," in J. Chubb and P. Peterson (eds.), *Can the Government Govern?* Washington, DC: Brookings Institution, 1989, pp. 267–329.

Moore, Mark H., *Creating Public Value: Strategic Management in Government*, Cambridge, MA: Harvard University Press, 1997.

Moore, Nancy Y., Laura H. Baldwin, Frank A. Camm, and Cynthia R. Cook, *Implementing Best Purchasing and Supply Management Practices: Lessons from Innovative Commercial Firms*, Santa Monica, CA: RAND Corporation, DB-334-AF, 2002.

Morgan, M. Granger, and Max Henrion, *Uncertainty: A Guide to Dealing with Uncertainty in Quantitative Risk and Policy Analysis*, Cambridge, MA: Cambridge University Press, 1990.

Morrison, Robert F., and Roger R. Hock, "Career Building: Learning from Cumulative Work Experience," in Douglas T. Hall (ed.), *Career Development in Organizations*, San Francisco, CA: Jossey-Bass, 1986.

Mosher, Frederick C., *Democracy and the Public Service*, 2nd ed., New York: Oxford University Press, 1982.

Moulton, Brent, "A Reexamination of the Federal-Private Wage Differential in the United States," *Journal of Labor Economics*, Vol. 8, No. 2, 1990.

Murnane, R. J., and D. K. Cohen, "Merit Pay and the Evaluation Problem: Why Some Merit Pay Plans Fail and a Few Survive," *Harvard Educational Review*, Vol. 56, No. 1, 1986, pp. 1–17.

Murnane, Richard J., John B. Willett, and Frank Levy, "The Growing Importance of Cognitive Skills in Wage Determination," *Review of Economics and Statistics*, Vol. 77, No. 2, 1995, pp. 251–266.

National Academy of Public Administration, Report of the Panel for the National Commission on the Public Service, July 2002.

National Academy of Public Administration, Report on the Senior Executive Service prepared for the Office of Personnel Management, December 2002.

National Commission on the Public Service, *Leadership for America: Rebuilding the Public Service*, Washington, DC: Brookings Institution, 1990.

National Commission on the Public Service, *Urgent Business for America: Revitalizing the Federal Government for the 21st Century*, Washington, DC: Brookings Institution, 2003.

National Intelligence Council, *Global Trends 2015: A Dialogue About the Future with Nongovernment Experts*, 2000 (available at http://www.foia.cia.gov).

National Research Council, *Pay for Performance: Evaluation Performance Appraisal and Merit Pay*, Washington, DC: National Academy Press, 1991.

National Research Council, *Scientific Research in Education*, Committee on Scientific Principles for Education Research (R. J. Shavelson and L. Towne, eds.), Center for Education, Division of Behavioral and Social Sciences and Education, Washington, DC: National Academy Press, 2002.

Neal, Derek A., and William R. Johnson, "The Role of Premarket Factors in Black-White Wage Differences," *Journal of Political Economy*, Vol. 104, October 1996, pp. 869–885.

Nelson, Doug, "Some 'Best Practices' and 'Most Promising Models' for Welfare Reform," Baltimore, MD: Annie E. Casey Foundation, memorandum, 1997.

Nichols, Albert, and Richard Zeckhauser, "Targeting Transfers Through Restrictions on Recipients," *American Economic Review*, Vol. 72, No. 2, 1982, pp. 372–377.

Nickles, Steve, Chairman, Personnel and Organization Committee, IRS Oversight Board, letter submitted to the commission, July 3, 2002.

No Child Left Behind Act of 2001, Public Law 107-110 (January 8, 2002), *Reauthorizations to the Elementary and Secondary Act of 1965*, U.S. Code 20.

Nye, Joseph, *The Paradox of American Power: Why the World's Only Superpower Can't Go It Alone*, New York: Oxford University Press, 2002.

Odden, A., "Incentives, School Organization, and Teacher Compensation," in S. H. Fuhrman and J. A. O'Day (eds.), *Rewards and Reform: Creating Educational Incentives That Work*, San Francisco, CA: Jossey-Bass, 1996, pp. 226–256.

Oken, Carole, and Beth J. Asch, *Encouraging Recruiter Achievement: A Recent History of Military Recruiter Incentive Programs*, Santa Monica, CA: RAND Corporation, MR-845-OSD/A, 1997.

Osborne, David, and Ted Gaebler, *Reinventing Government: How the Entrepreneurial Spirit Is Transforming the Public Sector*, Reading, MA: Addison-Wesley, 1992.

Panel on Presidentially Appointed Scientists and Engineers, National Academy of Sciences, National Academy of Engineering, and Institute of Medicine, *Science and Technology Leadership in American Government: Ensuring the Best Presidential Appointments*, 1992 (available at http://books.nap.edu/books/0309047277/html/index.html, accessed September 21, 2004).

Parent, Daniel, "Methods of Pay and Earnings: A Longitudinal Analysis," *Industrial and Labor Relations Review*, Vol. 53, No. 1, 1999, pp. 71–86.

Park, George, and Robert J. Lempert, *The Class of 2014: Preserving Access to California Higher Education*, Santa Monica, CA: RAND Corporation, 1998.

Parsons Brinckerhoff Quade & Douglas, Inc., "Evaluation of Options for Forming a Public-Private Partnership for Effective Dissemination of Disaster Information, Final Report, Tasks 1 and 3," submitted to U.S. Geological Survey, Reston, VA, October 27, 1998.

Pedulla, J. J., L. M. Abrams, G. F. Madaus, M. K. Russell, M. A. Ramos, and J. Miao, *Perceived Effects of State-Mandated Testing Programs on Teaching and Learning: Findings from a National Survey of Teachers*, Boston, MA: National Board on Educational Testing and Public Policy, 2003.

Pennsylvania Department of Education, "Performance Incentives: How Performance Incentives Reward Results," 2002 (available at http://www.pde.state.pa.us/k12_initiatives/cwp/view.asp?A=173&Q=4948).

Pesaran, M. H., Y. Shin, and R. P. Smith, "Pooled Mean Group Estimation of Dynamic Heterogeneous Panels," *Journal of the American Statistical Association*, Vol. 94, 1999, pp. 621–634.

Pint, Ellen M., and Laura H. Baldwin, *Strategic Sourcing: Theory and Evidence from Economics and Business Management*, Santa Monica, CA: RAND Corporation, MR-865-AF, 1997.

Pint, Ellen M., J. Bondanella, Jonathan A.K. Cave, Rachel Hart, and Donna J. Keyser, *Public-Private Partnerships: Background Papers for the U.S.-U.K. Conference on Military Installation Assets, Operations, and Services*, Santa Monica, CA: RAND Corporation, MR-1309-A, 2001.

Polich, Michael, James Dertouzos, and James Press, *The Enlistment Bonus Experiment*, Santa Monica, CA: RAND Corporation, R-3353-FMP, 1986.

Popper, Steven W., "Technological Change and the Challenges for 21st Century Governance," *2003 Science and Technology Policy Yearbook*, American Association for the Advancement of Science, 2003.

Popper, Steven W., *The Third Ape's Problem: A Parable of Reasoning Under Deep Uncertainty*, Santa Monica, CA: RAND Corporation, P-8080, 2004.

Powell, A. G., "Motivating Students to Learn: An American Dilemma," in S. H. Fuhrman and J. A. O'Day (eds.), *Rewards and Reform: Creating Educational Incentives That Work,* San Francisco, CA: Jossey-Bass, 1996, pp. 19–59.

Prahalad, C. K., and Gary Hamel, "The Core Competence of the Corporation," *Harvard Business Review*, May–June 1990.

Prendergast, Canice, "The Provision of Incentives in Firms," *Journal of Economic Literature*, Vol. 37, No. 1, March 1999, pp. 7–63.

Prendergast, Canice, "The Limits of Bureaucratic Efficiency," *Journal of Political Economy*, Vol. 5, 2003, pp. 929–958.

Prendergast, Canice, and Robert Topel, "Favoritism in Organizations," *Journal of Political Economy*, Vol. 104, 1996, pp. 958–978.

President's Council on Integrity and Efficiency, "Compendium of Federal Environmental Programs," September 1, 2002 (available at http://www.epa.gov/oigearth/index.htm, last accessed October 15, 2002).

Price, Jeff, President, National Association of Disability Examiners, "Challenges Facing the New Commissioner of Social Security," written testimony submitted to the U.S. House of Representatives Subcommittee on Social Security and Human Resources, May 2, 2002.

Procurement Round Table, "Statement of the Procurement Round Table to the National Commission on the Public Service," paper submitted to the commission, July 12, 2002.

Public Agenda, *Where We Are Now: 12 Things You Need to Know About Public Opinion and Public Schools*, 2003 (available at http://www.publicagenda.org/pdfstore/PDFs/where_we_are_now.pdf, accessed September 16, 2003).

Radelet, Steven, "Bush and Foreign Aid," *Foreign Affairs*, September/October 2003, pp. 104–117.

Radelet, Steven, "Will the Millennium Challenge Account Be Different?" *Washington Quarterly*, Vol. 26, No. 2, 2003, pp. 171–186.

Raiffa, Howard, *Decision Analysis: Introductory Lectures on Choices Under Uncertainty*, Reading, MA: Addison-Wesley, 1968.

RAND Corporation, *Define-Measure-Improve: The Change Methodology That Has Propelled the Army's Successful Velocity Management Initiative*, Santa Monica, CA: RAND Corporation, RB-3020-A, 2000 (available at http://www.rand.org/publications/RB/RB3020/index.html, accessed September 21, 2004).

RAND Corporation, *Improved Inventory Policy Contributes to Equipment Readiness*, Santa Monica, CA: RAND Corporation, RB-3026-A, 2001 (available at http://www.rand.org/publications/RB/RB3026/, accessed September 21, 2004).

RAND Corporation, *CWT and RWT Metrics Improve Army's Supply-Chain Performance*, Santa Monica, CA: RAND Corporation, RB-3035-A, 2003 (available at http://www.rand.org/publications/RB/RB3035/index.html, accessed September 21, 2004).

Raudenbush, S. W., B. Rowan, and Y. F. Cheong, "Higher Order Instructional Goals in Secondary Schools: Class, Teacher, and School Influences," *American Educational Research Journal*, Vol. 30, 1993, pp. 523–554.

Report of the National Commission on the Public Service, *Urgent Business for America: Revitalizing the Federal Government for the 21st Century*, Washington, DC: Brookings Institution, January 2003.

Resetar, Susan A., Frank A. Camm, and Jeffrey A. Drezner, *Environmental Management in Design: Lessons from Volvo and Hewlett-Packard for the*

Department of Defense, Santa Monica, CA: RAND Corporation, MR-1009-OSD, 1998.

Resnick, L. B., and D. P. Resnick, "Assessing the Thinking Curriculum: New Tools for Educational Reform," in B. R. Gifford and M. C. O'Connor (eds.), *Changing Assessment: Alternative Views of Aptitude, Achievement, and Instruction*, Boston, MA: Kluwer, 1992, pp. 37–75.

Riccio, Daniel, Daniel Friedlander, and Stephen Freedman, *GAIN: Benefits, Costs, and Three-Year Impacts of a Welfare-to-Work Program*, New York: Manpower Research Demonstration Corporation, 1994.

Rivkin, Steven G., Eric A. Hanushek, and John F. Kain, *Teachers, Schools, and Academic Achievement*, mimeo, July 2002.

Robbins, Marc, Patricia Boren, and Kristin Leuschner, *The Strategic Distribution System in Support of Operation Enduring Freedom*, Santa Monica, CA: RAND Corporation, DB-428-USTC/DLA, 2003.

Roderick, M., B. A. Jacob, and A. S. Bryk, "The Impact of High-Stakes Testing in Chicago on Student Achievement in Promotional Gate Grades," *Educational Evaluation and Policy Analysis*, Vol. 24, 2002, pp. 333–357.

Rogosa, David, *Confusions About Consistency in Improvement*, Stanford, CA: Stanford University, June 2003.

Romberg, T. A., E. A. Zarinia, and S. R. Williams, *The Influence of Mandated Testing on Mathematics Instruction: Grade 8 Teachers' Perceptions*, Madison, WI: National Center for Research in Mathematical Science Education, University of Wisconsin-Madison, 1989.

Rosen, Bernard, letter submitted to commission, August 29, 2002.

Rosen, Sherwin, "Authority, Control, and the Distribution of Earnings," *Bell Journal of Economics*, Vol. 13, 1981, pp. 311–323.

Rosen, Sherwin, "Prizes and Incentives in Elimination Tournaments," *American Economic Review*, Vol. 45, 1982, pp. 701–715.

Rosenbaum, Dorothy, and David Super, *Understanding Food Stamp Quality Control*, Washington, DC: Center for Budget and Policy Priorities, 2001.

Rosenthal, Douglas, Margaret Barton, Douglas Reynolds, and Beverly Dugan, *Improving the Recruitment, Retention, and Utilization of Federal*

Scientists and Engineers, Washington, DC: National Academies Press, 1993.

Ross, Jim, "Introduction to Project Alliancing," paper presented at Alliance Contracting Conference, Sydney, Australia, April 30, 2003.

Rossi, Peter H., "Issues in the Evaluation of Human Services Delivery," *Evaluation Quarterly*, Vol. 2, No. 4, November 1978, pp. 573–599.

Rowan, B., "Standards as Incentives for Instructional Reform," in S. H. Fuhrman and J. A. O'Day (eds.), *Rewards and Reform: Creating Educational Incentives That Work*, San Francisco, CA: Jossey-Bass, 1996, pp. 195–225.

Ryall, M. D., and R. C. Sampson, "Do Prior Alliances Influence Contract Structure? Evidence from Technology Alliance Contracts," Social Science Research Network, working paper, 2003 (available at http://ssrn.com/abstract=396601).

Salamon, Lester (ed.), *The Tools of Government*, New York: Oxford University Press, 2002.

Salancik, G. R., and J. Pfeffer, "Organizational Context and the Characteristics and Tenure of Hospital Administrators," *Academy of Management Journal*, Vol. 20, No. 1, 1977, pp. 74–88.

Sanders, William L., and Sandra P. Horn, "Research Findings from the Tennessee Value-Added Assessment System (TVAAS) Database: Implications for Educational Evaluation and Research," *Journal of Personnel Evaluation in Education*, Vol. 12, 1998, pp. 247–256.

Savas, E. S., *Privatization and Public-Private Partnerships*, New York: Chatham House, 2000.

Savych, Bogdan, "A Review of Economic Models of Compensation and Their Relevance to the Military Compensation System," Santa Monica, CA: RAND Corporation, unpublished research, July 2004.

Schelling, Thomas C., "The Global Dimension," in Graham Allison and Gregory F. Treverton (eds.), *Rethinking America's Security: Beyond Cold War to the New World Order*, New York: Norton, 1992.

Schneider, M., P. Teske, and M. Marshall, *Choosing Schools: Consumer Choice and the Quality of American Schools*, Princeton, NJ: Princeton University Press, 2000.

Schwartz, Peter, *The Art of the Long View*, New York: Doubleday, 1996.

Seidman, H., *Politics, Position, and Power: The Dynamics of Federal Organization*, 3rd ed., New York: Oxford University Press, 1980.

Setear, John K., Carl H. Builder, Melinda D. Baccus, and E. Wayne Madewell, *The Army in a Changing World: The Role of Organizational Vision*, Santa Monica, CA: RAND Corporation, R-3882-A, 1990.

Shelanski, H. A., and P. G. Klein, "Empirical Research on Transaction Cost Economics: Review and Assessment," *Journal of Law, Economics, and Organization*, Vol. 11, No. 2, 1995, pp. 335–361.

Shenkar, Oded, *Public-Private Strategy Partnerships: The U.S. Postal Service-Federal Express Alliance*, Arlington, VA: IBM Endowment for the Business of Government, May 2003.

Shepard, L. A., and K. C. Dougherty, "Effects of High-Stakes Testing on Instruction," paper presented at the Annual Meeting of the American Educational Research Association and National Council on Measurement in Education, Chicago, IL, 1991.

Shiffert, Sarah, Senior Director of Association Services, International Personnel Management Association, "A Call to Action: A Coalition on the Future of the Federal Human Resource Management Profession," paper submitted to the commission, July 2002.

Skinner, R. A., and L. N. Staresina, "State of the States," *Education Week*, Vol. 23, No. 17, January 8, 2004, pp. 97–99.

Smith, M. L., C. Edelsky, K. Draper, C. Rottenberg, and M. Cherland, *The Role of Testing in Elementary Schools*, Los Angeles, CA: Center for Research on Evaluation, Standards, and Student Testing, CSE Technical Report 321, 1991.

Smith, Sharon, "Pay Differentials Between Federal Government and Private-Sector Workers," *Industrial and Labor Relations Review*, Vol. 29, 1976.

Smitka, Michael J., *Competitive Ties: Subcontracting in the Japanese Automotive Industry*, New York: Columbia University Press, 1991.

South African Revenue Service, "Container Scanner Public Private Partnership Project (CSPPP)," Request for Information, RFI 14/2003, Pretoria, South Africa, 2003.

Sowell, Thomas, *Affirmative Action Around the World: An Empirical Study*, New Haven, CT: Yale University Press, 2004.

Spitz, Janet, "Productivity and Wage Relations in Economic Theory and Labor Markets," doctoral dissertation, Stanford University Graduate School of Business, 1991.

Stecher, B. M., and S. I. Barron, *Quadrennial Milepost Accountability Testing in Kentucky*, Los Angeles, CA: National Center for Research on Evaluation, Standards, and Student Testing, CSE Technical Report 505, 1999.

Stecher, B. M., S. I. Barron, T. Chun, and K. Ross, *The Effects of the Washington State Education Reform on Schools and Classrooms*, Los Angeles, CA: Center for Research on Evaluation, Standards, and Student Testing, CSE Technical Report 525, 2000.

Stecher, B. M., S. I. Barron, T. Kaganoff, and J. Goodwin, *The Effects of Standards-Based Assessment on Classroom Practices: Results of the 1996–97 RAND Survey of Kentucky Teachers of Mathematics and Writing*, Los Angeles, CA: National Center for Research on Evaluation, Standards, and Student Testing, CSE Technical Report 482, 1998.

Stecher, B. M., L. S. Hamilton, and G. Gonzalez, *Working Smarter to Leave No Child Behind*, Santa Monica, CA: RAND Corporation, 2003.

Stigler, George J., "The Optimum Enforcement of Laws," *Journal of Political Economy*, Vol. 78, No. 3, May–June 1970, pp. 526–536.

Stone, Erin G., et al., "Interventions That Increase Use of Adult Immunization and Cancer Screening Services: A Meta-Analysis," *Annals of Internal Medicine*, Vol. 136, No. 9, May 2002, pp. 641–651.

Talbert, J. E., *Boundaries of Teachers' Professional Communities in High Schools*, Stanford, CA: Center for Research on the Context of Secondary School Teaching, Stanford University, Report P91-130, 1991.

Talbert, J. E., M. W. McLaughlin, and B. Rowan, "Understanding Context Effects on Secondary School Teaching," *Teachers College Record*, Vol. 95, 1993, pp. 45–68.

Texas Education Agency, "Texas TAAS Passing Rates Hit Seven-Year High; Four Out of Every Five Students Pass Exam," press release, May 17, 2000.

Thompson, Fred, Chairman, U.S. Senate Governmental Affairs Committee, *Government at the Brink, Vols. I and II: An Agency by Agency Examination of Federal Government Management Problems Facing the*

Bush Administration, Washington, DC: Government Printing Office, June 2001.

Tirole, Jean, "The Internal Organization of Government," *Oxford Economic Papers,* Vol. 46, 1994, pp. 1–29.

Toffler, Alvin, and Heidi Toffler, *The Third Wave,* New York: William Morrow and Co., 1980.

Treverton, Gregory F., *Reshaping National Intelligence for an Age of Information,* Cambridge, MA: Cambridge University Press, 2001.

Treverton, Gregory F., "The State of Federal Management," *Government Executive,* January 2004.

Treverton, Gregory F., and Tora K. Bikson, *New Challenges for International Leadership: Positioning the United States for the 21st Century,* Santa Monica, CA: RAND Corporation, IP-233-IP, 2003.

UK Ministry of Defence, Joint Doctrine and Concept Centre (JDCC), "Strategic Trends" (available at http://wwwjdcc-strategictrends.org/index.asp).

United Nations Economic Commission for Africa, "The African Peer Review Mechanism: Process and Procedures," *African Security Review,* Vol. 11, No. 2, 2002, pp. 7–13.

U.S. Agency for International Development [USAID], *Foreign Aid in the National Interest: Promoting Freedom, Security, and Opportunity,* Washington, DC: U.S. Agency for International Development, 2002 (released January 7, 2003).

U.S. Commission on National Security/21st Century, *Road Map for National Security: Imperative for Change,* March 2001 (available at http://www.nssg.gov/PhaseIIIFR.pdf).

U.S. Congressional Budget Office, *CBO Memorandum: Comparing the Pay and Benefits of Federal and Nonfederal Executives,* Washington, DC: Government Printing Office, November 1999.

U.S. Congressional Budget Office, *The Looming Budgetary Impact of Society's Aging,* Long-Range Fiscal Policy Brief, No. 2, July 3, 2002 (available at www.cbo.gov/showdoc.cfm?index=3581&sequence=0, last accessed May 18, 2004).

U.S. Department of Defense, "Factors in the Retention of DoD Civilian Professional and Administrative Employees: Follow-up on an Entering Cohort," Defense Manpower Data Center, May 1990.

U.S. Department of Education, "It's Not the Spending: The Real Root Causes of Academic Poverty in America's Schools—and the Path to Authentic Reform," presentation, Washington, DC: U.S. Department of Education, 2003.

U.S. Office of Management and Budget, *The President's Management Agenda,* Fiscal Year 2002.

U.S. Office of Personnel Management, "HRM Policies and Practices in Title-5 Exempt Organizations," Office of Merit Systems Oversight and Effectiveness, MSE-98-4, August 1998.

U.S. Office of Personnel Management, "Human Resources Flexibilities and Authorities in the Federal Government," Office of Merit Systems Effectiveness, Center for HR Innovation, July 2001.

U.S. Office of Policy and Evaluation, Merit Systems Protection Board, *The Federal Merit Promotion Program: Process vs. Outcome,* Washington, DC: Government Printing Office, December 2001.

U.S. Office of Personnel Management, *A Fresh Start for Federal Pay: The Case for Modernization,* Washington, DC: Government Printing Office, OPM white paper, April 2002 (available at www.opm.gov/strategiccomp/whtpaper.pdf, last accessed October 15, 2002).

U.S. Office of Policy and Evaluation, Merit Systems Protection Board, *Making the Public Service Work: Recommendations for Change,* Washington, DC: Government Printing Office, September 3, 2002.

U.S. Office of the Assistant Secretary of the Navy (Research Development, and Acquisition), *Naval Research Advisory Committee Report on Science and Technology Community in Crisis,* Washington, DC, 2002.

U.S. Railroad Retirement Board, *Examining the Inefficiencies of the Federal Workplace: Recommendations for Reform,* Washington, DC: Government Printing Office, July 2002.

Van Wart, Montgomery, "Public-Sector Leadership Theory: An Assessment," *Public Administration Review,* Vol. 63, No. 2, 2003, pp. 214–228.

Voinovich, George V., Chairman, Subcommittee on Oversight of Government Management, Restructuring, and the District of Columbia, Governmental Affairs Committee, *Report to the President: The Crisis in Human Capital*, Washington, DC: Government Printing Office, December 2000.

Wainer, H., et al., *Computerized Adaptive Testing: A Primer*, Hillsdale, NJ: Lawrence Erlbaum Associates, 1990.

Walker, David M., Chairman, Commercial Activities Panel, *Improving the Sourcing Decisions of the Government: Final Report*, April 30, 2002.

Walker, David M., *Performance-Based Budgeting: Opportunities and Challenges*, statement of the Comptroller General, Washington, DC: General Accounting Office, GAO 02-1106T, September 19, 2002.

Wang, Mark, *Accelerated Logistics: Streamlining the Army's Supply Chain*, Santa Monica, CA: RAND Corporation, MR-1140-A, 2000 (available at http://www.rand.org/publications/MR/MR1140/, accessed September 21, 2004).

Webster, W., and R. Mendro, "The Dallas Value-Added Accountability System," in J. Millman (ed.), *Grading Teachers, Grading Schools: Is Student Achievement a Valid Evaluation Measure?* Thousand Oaks, CA: Corwin Press, 1997, pp. 81–99.

Webster, W. J., R. L. Mendro, T. H. Orsak, and D. Weerasinghe, "An Application of Hierarchical Lineal Modeling to the Estimation of School and Teacher Effect," paper presented at the Annual Meeting of the American Educational Research Association, San Diego, CA, April 1998.

Weingast, B., and W. Marshall, "The Industrial Organization of Congress: Or, Why Legislatures, Like Firms, Are Not Organized as Markets," *Journal of Political Economy*, Vol. 96, No. 1, February 1988, pp. 132–163.

Weiss, Andrew, "Job Queues and Layoffs in Labor Markets with Flexible Wages," *Journal of Political Economy*, Vol. 88, No. 3, 1980, pp. 526–538.

Weiss, Andrew, "Incentives and Worker Behavior: Some Evidence," in Hal Nalbantian (ed.), *Incentives, Cooperation, and Risk Sharing*, New York: Rowman and Littlefield Press, 1987.

White, L. D., *The Republican Era: 1869–1901*, New York: Macmillan, 1958.

Williams, Trefor P., "Moving to Public-Private Partnerships: Learning from the Experience of Others," in Mark A. Abramson and Roland S. Harris III (eds.), *The Procurement Revolution*, Lanham, MD: Rowan and Littlefield, 2003, pp. 217–248.

Williamson, Oliver E., *The Economic Institutions of Capitalism*, New York: Free Press, 1985.

Williamson, Oliver E., "Comparative Economic Organization: The Analysis of Discrete Structural Alternatives," *Administrative Science Quarterly*, Vol. 36, No. 2, 1991, pp. 269–297.

Wilson, James Q., *Bureaucracy: What Government Agencies Do and Why They Do It*, New York: Basic Books, 1989; reprint ed., 1991.

Wilson, James Q., and George L. Kelling, "Broken Windows: The Police and Neighborhood Safety," *Atlantic Monthly*, Vol. 249, No. 3, 1982, pp. 29–38.

Wilson, Woodrow, "The Study of Administration," *Political Science Quarterly*, Vol. 2, June 1887, pp. 197–222.

Winfield, L. F., "School Competency Testing Reforms and Student Achievement: Exploring a National Perspective," *Educational Evaluation and Policy Analysis,* Vol. 12, 1990, pp. 157–173.

Wolf, Martin, "The Building Pressures That Threaten the World's Oil Well," *Financial Times*, December 4, 2002.

Woodward, Bob, *Bush at War*, Simon & Schuster, 2002.

World Economic Forum, *Global Competitiveness Report 2003–2004*, New York: Oxford University Press, 2004.

Zax, Jeffrey S., and Daniel I. Rees, *Environment, Ability, Effort, and Earnings*, Boulder, CO: University of Colorado, Center for Economic Analysis, Working Paper 98-35, 1998.

Zirimwabagabo, Irene, "NEPAD's Peer Review Mechanism—'Our Brother's Keeper,'" *Science in Africa,* August 2002 (available at http://www. scienceinafrica.co.za/2002/august/aprm.htm).

About the Editors

Robert Klitgaard is Dean and Ford Distinguished Professor of International Development and Security at the Pardee RAND Graduate School. His seven books include *Controlling Corruption* and *Choosing Elites*.

Paul C. Light is Paulette Goddard Professor of Public Service at New York University. He was the Founding Director of the Center for Public Service at the Brookings Institution and Senior Adviser to the Volcker Commission. Light is the author of several books, including *The Four Pillars of High Performance: How Robust Organizations Achieve Extraordinary Results* and *Government's Greatest Achievements: From Civil Rights to Homeland Security*.

About the Authors

Kamil Akramov is a doctoral fellow at the Pardee RAND Graduate School. He was a member of the Central Bank team responsible for monetary policy in his native country of Uzbekistan.

Beth Asch is a professor at the Pardee RAND Graduate School and a senior economist at RAND. Her publications include *Financial Incentives and Retirement: Evidence from Federal Civil Service Workers* and *Policy Options for Military Recruiting in the College Market: Results from a National Survey*.

Frank Camm is a senior economist at RAND who analyzes defense resource management policies and processes. His publications include *Recent Large Service Acquisitions in the Department of Defense: Lessons for the Office of the Secretary of Defense* and "Adapting Best Commercial Practices to Defense" in *New Challenges, New Tools for Defense Decisionmaking*.

Lynn E. Davis is a senior RAND analyst. She has served as Under Secretary of State for Arms Control and International Security Affairs and on the staffs of the Secretary of Defense, the National Security Council, and the Senate Select Committee on Intelligence. Her publications include *Coordinating the War on Terrorism* and *The U.S. Army and the New National Security Strategy.*

John Dumond was Director of the Military Logistics Program at the RAND Arroyo Center until April 2004. He is now an adjunct RAND staff member. Prior to joining RAND, he served as Head of the Department of System Acquisition Management at the Air Force Institute of Technology. He is a co-author of *Velocity Management: The Business Paradigm That Has Transformed U.S. Army Logistics.*

Rick Eden is a senior defense research analyst at RAND, where he is also Associate Director of Research Quality Assurance. He previously served on the faculty of the University of New Mexico. His publications include *Velocity Management: The Business Paradigm That Has Transformed U.S. Army Logistics* and *Indirect Costs: A Guide for Foundations and Nonprofit Organizations.*

Johannes Fedderke is a professor of economics at the University of Cape Town, South Africa. He has been a visiting scholar at the Pardee RAND Graduate School and is the immediate past president of the African Econometric Society.

Laura Hamilton is a senior behavioral scientist at RAND. Her research focuses on educational measurement and evaluation. Her recent publications include *Working Smarter to Leave No Child Behind: Practical Insights for School Leaders* and *Making Sense of Test-Based Accountability in Education.*

Robert Lempert is a professor of policy analysis at the Pardee RAND Graduate School. His research focuses on the development and application of methods for decisionmaking under conditions of deep uncertainty in a wide range of policy areas. He is a Fellow of the

America Physical Society, a member of the Council on Foreign Relations, and a co-author of *Shaping the Next One Hundred Years: New Methods for Quantitative, Longer-Term Policy Analysis*.

Susan M. Gates is a professor of economics at the Pardee RAND Graduate School and Director of the Kauffman-RAND Center for the Study of Small Business and Regulation, launched recently by the RAND Institute for Civil Justice. Her publications include *A Strategic Governance Review for Multi-Organizational Systems of Education, Training, and Professional Development* and *Who Is Leading Our Schools?: An Overview of School Administrators and Their Careers*.

Jacob Klerman is a senior economist at RAND, Director of the RAND Center for Social Welfare Policy, and a professor of economics at the Pardee RAND Graduate School. His recent research has focused on welfare policy and welfare reform at the federal, state, and local levels. He is a co-author of *Welfare Reform in California: Early Results from the Impact Analysis*.

Steven W. Popper is a professor of science and technology policy at the Pardee RAND Graduate School and a senior economist at RAND. He has served as Associate Director of the Science and Technology Policy Institute at RAND and has conducted research on behalf of the White House, the National Science Board, DARPA, and other federal agencies. His publications include *Shaping the Next One Hundred Years: New Methods for Quantitative, Longer-Term Policy Analysis* and *New Forces at Work: Industry Views Critical Technologies*.

Al Robbert is Director of the Manpower, Personnel, and Training Program at RAND Project AIR FORCE. He has led and contributed to research on competency requirements for senior leadership positions in defense and other public sector organizations, and he is a co-author of *An Operational Process for Workforce Planning*.

Gregory Treverton is a professor of policy analysis and Associate Dean for Research at the Pardee RAND Graduate School, and a senior analyst at RAND. His publications include *New Challenges, New Tools for Defense Decisionmaking* and *Reshaping National Intelligence for an Age of Information*.